TAIWAN'S SECURITY IN THE
POST-DENG XIAOPING ERA

TAIWAN'S SECURITY IN THE POST-DENG XIAOPING ERA

Martin L. Lasater
Peter Kien-hong Yu
with contributions from
Kuang-ming Hsu and Robyn Lim

FRANK CASS
LONDON • PORTLAND, OR

First published in 2000 in Great Britain by
FRANK CASS PUBLISHERS
Newbury House, 900 Eastern Avenue
London IG2 7HH

and in the United States of America by
FRANK CASS PUBLISHERS
c/o ISBS, 5804 N.E. Hassalo Street
Portland, Oregon 97213-3644

Website: www.frankcass.com

British Library Cataloguing in Publication Data

Lasater, Martin L.
  Taiwan's security in the post-Deng Xiaoping era
  1. National security – Taiwan 2. Taiwan – Strategic aspects
  3. Taiwan – Foreign relations – China – 1945– 4. China –
  Foreign relations – Taiwan – 1976– 5. Taiwan – Foreign
  relations – United States – 1945– 6. United States – Foreign
  relations – Taiwan – 1989–
  I. Title II. Yu, Peter Kien-hong III. Hsu, Kuang-ming IV. Lim,
  Robyn
  355'.031'0951249'0951

ISBN 0-7146-5083-8

Library of Congress Cataloging-in-Publication Data

Lasater, Martin L.
  Taiwan's security in the post-Deng Xiaoping era / Martin L. Lasater,
Peter Kien-hong Yu; with contributions from Kuang-ming Hsu and Robyn
Lim.
    p.   cm.
  Includes bibliographical references and index.
  ISBN 0-7146-5083-8
  1. National security–Taiwan. 2. Taiwan–Defenses. 3. Taiwan–Foreign
relations. I. Yu, Peter Kien-hong, 1953– . II. Title.

DS799.847 .L37 2000
355'.033051249–dc21
                                                              00-031562

Typeset by Vitaset, Paddock Wood, Kent
Printed in Great Britain by
MPG Books Ltd, Bodmin, Cornwall

Contents

Tables

Notes on Contributors

Kuang-ming Hsu. Dr. Hsu is the head of the Political Science Department at the Republic of China (ROC) Air Force Academy, in Taiwan, ROC. He is the author of *China Policy Toward Japan Before and After the Mukden Incident*, *The 21st Century National Strategy of the PRC* and many articles on Taiwan and China military affairs.

Martin L. Lasater. Dr. Lasater is a strategic analyst for Asia–Pacific security affairs. Currently a Non-Resident Scholar at the Atlantic Council of the United States, he is the author of *The Taiwan Conundrum in U.S. China Policy* (1999) and more than ten other books on China, Taiwan and East Asian political–security matters.

Robyn Lim. Dr. Lim is professor of international relations at Nanzan University in Nagoya, Japan. In addition to her academic work, she has served with the Australian Foreign Ministry and Office of National Assessments. A specialist in East Asian regional security affairs, her most recent publication is 'Australian Security After the Cold War', *Orbis* (Winter 1998).

Peter Kien-hong Yu. Dr. Yu is former Professor of Politics at National Sun Yat-sen University in Taiwan, ROC. He is currently teaching at Lingnan University in Tuen Mun, Hong Kong, China. In March 2000, he again received a senior research fellowship from the East Asian Institute, National University of Singapore. His latest book is *Bicoastal China: A Dialectical, Paradigmatic Analysis* (1999). He also has some 50 research papers published in the West.

Acknowledgments

The authors would like to express their appreciation to the Chiang Ching-Kuo Foundation for International Scholarly Exchange for a research grant covering the initial research and writing of this book. Appreciation is also given to the Atlantic Council of the United States, which administered the grant. All views expressed in the book are the sole responsibility of the individual authors and are not intended to represent the views of any institutions with which they may be affiliated.

Abbreviations

ABM treaty	Anti-Ballistic Missile treaty
ADB	Asian Development Bank
AIT	American Institute in Taiwan
AMRAAM	advanced medium-range air-to-air missile
APEC	Asia–Pacific Economic Cooperation
ARATS	Association for Relations Across the Taiwan Strait
ASEAN	Association of Southeast Asian Nations
ASW	anti-submarine warfare
AWACS	airborne warning and control system
CCP	Chinese Communist Party
CEP	circular error probable
CMC	Central Military Commission
CPC	Communist Party of China (see also CCP). Also Chinese Petroleum Company
CPLA	Chinese People's Liberation Army
CSC	China Shipbuilding Corporation
DIA	Defense Intelligence Agency
DOD	Department of Defense
DCS	direct commercial sales
DMS	dual mount Stinger
DPP	Democratic Progressive Party
EDA	excess defense article transfer
EMP	electro-magnetic pulse
FMS	foreign military sales
FY	fiscal year
GATT	General Agreement on Tariffs and Trade
GOP	Grand Old Party – Republican Party (US)
HMMWV	high-mobility multi-purpose wheeled vehicle
ICBM	intercontinental ballistic missile
IDF	indigenous defense fighter
IISS	International Institute for Strategic Studies
KMT	Kuomintang

LANTIRN	low-altitude navigation and targeting infrared system for night
MAC	Mainland Affairs Council
MAD	mutually assured destruction
MADS	modified air defense systems
MEADS	medium extended air defense system
MLU	mid-life upgrade
n.m.	nautical mile
PAC	Patriot Advanced Capability
PLA	People's Liberation Army
PRC	People's Republic of China
ROC	Republic of China
ROT	Republic of Taiwan
SAM	surface-to-air missile
SEF	Straits Exchange Foundation
SLOC	sea lines of communication
SLBM	submarine-launched ballistic missile
SSBN	nuclear-fueled ballistic missile submarine
TAMD	theater air and missile defense
THAAD	theater high-altitude area defense system
TMD	theater missile defense
TOW	Tube-launched Optically tracked Wire-guided missile
TRA	Taiwan Relations Act
UNSC	UN Security Council
WTO	World Trade Organization

ABBREVIATIONS OF JOURNALS, NEWSPAPERS, ETC.

ADJ	*Asian Defence Journal*
AFJI	*Armed Forces Journal International*
AWSJ	*Asian Wall Street Journal*
CD	*Commons Daily*
CDN	*Central Daily News*
CM	*Central Monthly*
CN	*China News*
ComT	*Commercial Times*
CPSR	*Chinese Political Science Review*
CS	*China Spring*
CSA	*Contemporary Southeast Asia*
CT	*China Times*
CTE	*China Times Express*
DN	*Defense News*
FCJ	*Free China Journal*

LIST OF ABBREVIATIONS

FCR	*Free China Review*
GJJ	*Guangjiaojing* (Wide-Angle Mirror)
GJJM	*Guangjiaojing Monthly*
GJRB	*Guojiribao*
IEP	*Independence Evening Post*
IMP	*Independence Morning Post*
IT	*International Times*
JDW	*Jane's Defence Weekly*
JIR	*Jane's Intelligence Review*
LHZB	*Lianhezaobao*
LT	*Liberty Times*
MCM	*Mainland China Monthly*
NPQ	*National Policy Quarterly*
NYT	*New York Times*
SHDN	*See Hua Daily News*
SR	*Straits Review*
ST	*Straits Times*
THWDN	*Taiwan Hsin Wen Daily News*
TNR	*The New Republic*
TP	*Theory and Policy*
TT	*Taiwan Times*
UDN	*United Daily News*
UM	*United Monthly*
WJ	*World Journal*
WWP	*Wen Wei Pao*
XDJS	*Xiandaijunshi*
YDN	*Youth Daily News*
ZB	*Zhongbao*

PART I
Overview

1

Critical Factors in Taiwan's Security

Martin L. Lasater

On February 19, 1997, Chinese leader Deng Xiaoping left this world with one of his most cherished goals unfulfilled: the unification of Taiwan with the motherland of China. His successor, President Jiang Zemin, also has set this goal as one of his highest priorities. But why is Taiwan so important to China? Are the Chinese serious when they warn that they would shed blood to ensure that Taiwan does not become an independent state, even if conflict in the Taiwan Strait would postpone China's modernization and could lead to war with the United States?

This chapter introduces several key factors related to Taiwan's security in the post-Deng era: first, Taiwan's value to China; second, US interests in Taiwan and its future; third, the respective strengths of the militaries of the People's Republic of China and the Republic of China; and, fourth, US arms sales to Taiwan. Since it is highly unlikely that Taiwan would attack the mainland, we start with one of the most critical determinants of Taiwan's future security: the willingness of China to go to war over Taiwan. Perhaps the best way to understand the firmness of that PRC commitment is to review why China places such great value on Taiwan.

CHINESE VIEW OF THE VALUE OF TAIWAN

As discussed in greater detail by Peter Yu in Chapters 4 and 5, the PRC has indicated that it would use force against Taiwan under several circumstances. These include: (a) if Taiwan moves toward independence; (b) if social chaos occurs on Taiwan; (c) if foreign countries intervene in Taiwan affairs; (d) if Taipei refuses over a long period of time to negotiate unification with Beijing; and (e) if Taiwan develops nuclear weapons. Two other conditions are sometimes mentioned by analysts: (f) if the military strength of the Republic of China (ROC) is significantly weaker than that of the People's Republic of China (PRC); and (g) if Taipei's strategy of seeking to overturn Chinese Communist Party (CCP) rule on the mainland through peaceful evolution seems to be working.

3

Circumstances (f) and (g) reflect the twin motivations of opportunism and self-preservation on the part of Beijing. Circumstances (a) to (e), on the other hand, have two major themes in common: first, PRC concern over Taiwan's permanent separation from the mainland; and, second, PRC concern over the possible use of Taiwan as a foreign base of operations against the PRC. These concerns can be readily seen in statements from Chinese analysts during the period of tension in the Taiwan Strait during 1995–96.

Chinese determination to fight over Taiwan

From China's point of view, a worst-case scenario would be a war in the Taiwan Strait which would bring into conflict the People's Liberation Army (PLA) and the US military. Such a war would be immensely costly to China, not only militarily but also politically and economically. Because of the great costs of a Sino-American war, many American analysts – within and outside the US government – firmly believe that Beijing would not fight Washington over Taiwan.

It is impossible to forecast with 100 percent confidence what the PRC would do in such circumstances, but there is danger in underestimating Chinese determination to preserve China's unity and to prevent American domination of Taiwan affairs. Chinese officials and scholars repeatedly have warned that China should not be underestimated in this regard. For example, Chu Shulong, director of the North American division of the state-run China Institute of Contemporary International Relations, said during the 1995–96 Taiwan Strait crisis that there was considerable support in China for the PLA to fight the United States over Taiwan to preserve China's territorial integrity and to end the humiliation of foreigners intervening in Chinese affairs.[1]

Noting the 'strong degree of support for the country's leadership to go to war with the United States over Taiwan' Chu explained that two major factors contributed to 'this national feeling and national will'. First, the 'Chinese tend to consider unification as normal and reasonable, while separation is temporary and wrong'. Second, and more importantly for people in the PRC, 'Taiwan's separation from the mainland is a living example of China's humiliation in the last 150 years … Taiwan is the last piece of land that other governments still want to take away from China … The people in the PRC just cannot let this history of humiliation perpetuate itself, they have got to stop it'.

Chu cautioned that the Chinese used a different calculus from the West to determine whether the costs of war with the United States would be worth the effort. First, the PRC has already fought the United States in the Korean War. Second, even though the PRC would be at a disadvantage in a naval and air war in the Western Pacific, China 'does have the capability to kill U.S. personnel and destroy U.S. ships, and aircraft, including aircraft carriers in the Western Pacific'.

> Third, different people have different standards in evaluating the result of a war; in other words, they have a different conception of victory. For the people of the PRC, to have the courage to fight with a superpower when that superpower tries to bully their country would itself be a victory. To destroy two capital ships of such stronger forces would be a victory, no matter whether eight or ten PRC ships were destroyed at the same time ... So it is correct ... to argue that the Chinese should not assume that the United States would not become involved [in a war in the Taiwan Strait]. However, it is equally important for Americans not to assume that, because the Chinese are afraid of U.S. involvement, they would not do what they think they have to do.

Chu argued, 'For the PRC, what the United States does about Taiwan is the clearest indication of U.S. intentions regarding the strategic goal of containing the PRC.' The Chinese saw a series of events which were not isolated but rather part of a strategic plan to divide and weaken China. Since the end of the Cold War these events included:

- Starting from 1989, the United States has undertaken sanctions against the PRC. Some of these sanctions are still in place.
- In 1992 the United States sold Taiwan 150 F-16s in clear violation of the August 17 communiqué.
- In the summer of 1993 the United States provoked the *Yinhe* incident in international waters.[2]
- Also in 1993 the United States worked hard to prevent China from hosting the year 2000 Olympic Games.
- In September 1994 the Clinton administration's Taiwan Policy Review legalized high-level official visits and contacts between the United States and Taiwan.
- In the spring of 1995 the US government allowed Lee Teng-hui to visit and even treated him as a president in some ways.
- In March 1996 the United States sent two aircraft-carrier battle groups to the Taiwan area to provoke and intimidate the PRC and encourage and protect Lee Teng-hui.

Moreover, the United States had adopted 'some strategic policies that seem to lie behind those actions'. According to Chu, these included:

- In the spring of 1992 the Bush administration adopted a grand strategy to prevent any country in the world from becoming another superpower to challenge the US position. The current challenger is seen to be the PRC.

- In the autumn of 1993 the Clinton administration adopted a strategy of enlargement, calling the PRC a backlash state, and pursuing a strategic goal of changing the PRC from a non-democratic into a democratic state.
- In early 1995 the East Asia and Pacific strategic report of the Pentagon was issued, and subsequent actions in 1996 indicated that in the post-Cold War period the chief threats to regional security were seen as North Korea and the PRC.
- In April 1996 the United States and Japan issued a joint declaration on their security alliance which both identified the PRC as a new target and enlarged the area of the alliance coverage to include the Taiwan Strait and the South China Sea.

Chu observed that 'The "Taiwan card" seems to be a strategic card that the United States can play against the PRC':

> Compared with other cards – such as human rights, trade sanctions, or non-proliferation – the Americans have found the Taiwan card is more effective in dealing with the PRC, simply because it can hurt the PRC most and serve all the purposes that the United States pursues. When you want to 'democratize' the PRC, Taiwan can be a good Chinese example in adopting the American system; when you do not want to see the PRC becoming too strong, a united China is a nightmare; when you want to keep China weak by dividing the country, as happened in the USSR, Taiwan is the best starting place – Hong Kong, Macau, Tibet and Xinjiang are more difficult to use. Playing the Taiwan card can also cause the PRC's neighbors to become concerned about the PRC, so they follow US interests more closely.

As Chu Shulong made clear, many Chinese analysts believe the United States is using the Taiwan issue both to keep China divided and weakened so as not to challenge the United States in the Western Pacific, and as an instrument to change China into a democracy. In large measure because of China's historical experience, such a strategy is both credible and deeply resented.[3] To China, Taiwan is worth fighting for and any Chinese leader who fails to defend PRC interests in this regard will face severe criticism and possibly dissent. In this sense, therefore, it would appear likely that China would fight the United States over Taiwan, despite the horrendous cost.

The probability of China going to war over Taiwan is increased still further by the strategic value of Taiwan to China both as a doorway to the open Pacific and as a defensive barrier to foreign threats and encroachment from the east.

Chinese views of Taiwan's strategic importance

Many Chinese strategists have explained the close relationship between Taiwan and the security of mainland China. According to PLA researchers Jiang Minfang and Duan Zhaoxian, Taiwan is not merely a Chinese territory to be recovered but also an extremely important geostrategic possession which China needs to control for its own security and destiny as a leading Asian power.[4] In a mirror image of the security concerns voiced by Robyn Lim in Chapter 3, Jiang and Duan argue: 'China is semi-enclosed by the first island chain. If it wants to prosper, it has to advance into the Pacific in which lies China's future. Taiwan, facing the Pacific to the east, is the only unobstructed exit for China to move into the ocean. If this gateway is opened for China, then it becomes much easier for China to manoeuvre in the Western Pacific.'

Jiang and Duan noted that the PLA also assesses the geostrategic value of Taiwan in terms of its being adjacent to critical sea lines of communication, enabling it 'conveniently to control the Balin and Bashi Straits in the south, to block Gonggu and Naguo waterways in the north, and to protect the mainland in the east. As such, it may be used to adversely affect U.S. forward deployment, Japan's economic lifeline, and Russia's freedom of manoeuvre. So if Taiwan returns to the PRC, it will not only help to resolve the South China Sea problem but also disrupt the United States' strategic chain in the Asia–Pacific region.'

A similar view was taken by Lu Junyuan, who wrote in 1996 that 'Taiwan's national security value derives mainly from its unique geographical location'.[5] Lu examined Taiwan's strategic value from several perspectives, including Spykman's view of critical marginal zones sandwiched between a continent and its neighboring waters, Taiwan's position as a communications hub in the Western Pacific, the focus it receives in the world's political arena, and the great value attached to Taiwan by the United States and Japan for their own strategic purposes. Lu concluded that Taiwan's 'pivotal role in the mainland's security' makes unification essential. According to the Chinese scholar, 'Taiwan's strategic significance for the mainland and even the entire nation is at least three-fold'.

> First, Taiwan directly impacts the mainland's security status. The island of Taiwan stands guard off China's southeastern coast, the nation's only large island in that area. Taiwan is superb as a shield for southeastern China, a 'screen for several provinces in the hinterland'. Taiwan is one of the 'two eyes', the other being Hainandao, in China's southeasterly coastal defense. *If China controls Taiwan, mainland security is assured. Conversely, if Taiwan is under the control of hostile forces, the mainland's security environment would deteriorate* ...
>
> Second, Taiwan influences the strategic links between the two major bodies of water off north and south China. Between the island of Taiwan

and Fujian is a wide waterway known as the Strait of Taiwan. The northern entrance to the strait separates the mouth of the Min Jiang from Fuguijiao at the northern tip of Taiwan. The southern entrance separates Nanaodao, which is where the two provinces of Fujian and Guangdong meet, from E'luanbi at the southern end of Taiwan ... The Strait of Taiwan is a shortcut between the East China Sea and South China Sea and a vital shipping lane in the Western Pacific. Just about all strategic links between China's eastern and northern coasts and the waters off its southern coast run through the Strait of Taiwan. If it falls under the control of hostile forces, China would have difficulty asserting total control over the strait. Not only will this threaten shipping lanes in China's coastal waters, but the strategic linkage between the two major bodies of water in the north and south would also be in danger of being severed, which would divide the theater of naval warfare off the Chinese coast and prevent joint action. *In a certain sense, therefore, China has no coastal defense without Taiwan.*

Third, Taiwan is critical to the preservation and development of China's naval power. China is both a land power and a sea power with a very long coastline and extensive maritime interests and rights. However, only a small portion of China's coastline opens directly to the Pacific Ocean. Its oceanic shipping lanes are liberally dotted with geographical barriers. The Yellow Sea and East China Sea are blocked by Japan and the Ryukyu Islands while the South China Sea is all but encircled by the various Southeast Asian nations. Taiwan, on the other hand, hubs the Philippine Sea. The waters to the east of Taiwan are the only part of the Pacific over which China has sovereignty and where it enjoys economic interests, providing China with its lone direct strategic entrance to the Pacific Ocean. And what a passageway it is, safe, wide, affording freedom of movement. All of that is immensely helpful to China as it develops naval power in the Pacific Ocean. *If Taiwan and the mainland cannot be reunified, China would lose its only direct passageway to the Pacific Ocean and its drive for naval power would be severely hampered.*

It can thus be seen that Taiwan has outstanding geostrategic value, which is precisely why powers like the United States have given it extra attention. Casting a covetous glance toward Taiwan's strategic position, they often interfere and meddle in Taiwan's affairs, which is a major external factor in the Taiwan issue. Taiwan is China's sacred territory. *Both in sovereignty and in strategic terms, it is an inseparable part of China and has extraordinary significance for China's national security. National reunification must be achieved to protect China's fundamental interests.* (emphasis added)

Thus, to the PRC, Taiwan is strategically vital for several reasons:

- Taiwan is the last major territory seized from China that must be returned in order to effect the nation's reunification.
- Taiwan is home to the last major obstacle to the Chinese Communist Party in asserting its control over all of China.
- Taiwan is well positioned as a communications and financial hub for all of Eastern Asia.
- Taiwan controls vital shipping lanes in the Western Pacific.
- In hostile hands, Taiwan would be an ideal base from which to attack China.
- Taiwan is used by the United States in its strategy to contain the PRC.
- Taiwan must be denied to the United States and Japan to prevent these nations from dividing and weakening China.
- Taiwan is the key to an effective defense of eastern China.
- Taiwan is China's gateway to the Pacific for its future blue-water navy.
- Taiwan is essential to China if Beijing is to be able to project military force into the Pacific in the future.

Because of Taiwan's strategic importance to China, there is a very high probability that the PRC would be willing to go to war over Taiwan, if necessary to prevent the island from becoming an independent nation-state or a base for foreign forces.

Policy implications

Seasoned China watchers have learned to take reports from Chinese newspapers with a grain of salt. However, in view of the above strategic perceptions, some credibility can be given to reports such as one appearing in Hong Kong's *Sing Tao Jih Pao* in January 1999.[6] According to the Chinese-language newspaper, the Political Bureau of the CCP Central Committee determined that making progress on unification with Taiwan should assume a much higher priority at the turn of the century. Within two or three years after Lee Teng-hui leaves office in 2000, the new Taiwan leaders must decided whether peaceful unification talks will go forward or whether Taiwan will resist the mainland by force. In the meantime, Beijing's strategy will emphasize cross-Strait political talks, criticizing the concept of 'new Taiwanese'[7] as the identity of Taiwan residents rather than 'Chinese', narrowing Taiwan's diplomatic space, and opposing US arms sales to Taiwan. As part of its military strategy, according to this report, the CCP will limit Taiwan's development of nuclear weapons and advanced weapons such as long-range missiles and satellites, and oppose the sale of advanced US arms to Taiwan, in particular the inclusion of Taiwan in theater missile defense (TMD) programs. The Political Bureau reportedly decided: 'When necessary, various military measures like military exercises in 1996, or even short-term military blockade will be adopted. To take into account the principled issue of defending state sovereignty and territorial integrity, China will balk at no sacrifice, even that of Sino-U.S. relations.'

Whatever the accuracy of the *Sing Tao Jih Pao* report, it should be clear from the above discussion of China's interests in Taiwan that (a) China is serious about unification with Taiwan; (b) under certain conditions Beijing probably is willing to use force to achieve that goal; (c) the patience of the mainland on the Taiwan issue will not last forever; and (d) US opposition to Chinese military pressure on Taiwan might not suffice to deter the PRC. The validity of these fundamental points – and their obvious implications for Taiwan's security – will become increasingly clear as this book progresses.

US INTERESTS IN TAIWAN

The willingness of the PRC to use force against Taiwan is one key factor in Taiwan's security in the post-Deng era. Another critical factor is the willingness of the United States to defend Taiwan should it be attacked. Although no one can predict the US response, an important indicator of the probability of US intervention is American interests in Taiwan and in the various scenarios for Taiwan's future.

Without question, China has important and probably vital interests in Taiwan. But the United States has important interests in Taiwan as well. It has been demonstrated more than once since June 1950 that the United States is willing to defend Taiwan, especially when Taipei is threatened by Beijing without major provocation. (An attack with provocation has not occurred, giving rise to considerable speculation in Washington as to an appropriate US response should Taiwan attempt to separate itself from China by becoming an independent nation-state.) But why should Americans risk their lives for Taiwan? The answer is perhaps best found by considering some of the major reasons the United States has interests in Taiwan and in its future relationship with the mainland:

- Taiwan is a critical factor in the strategically important US relationship with the PRC.
- US support for Taiwan's security is a vital factor in American credibility in Asia.
- Taiwan is a volatile political issue in American domestic politics.
- Taiwan can exert a positive influence on mainland Chinese domestic and foreign policies.
- Taiwan is a key factor in the geopolitical power of China.

- Taiwan is a critical indicator of whether China will be a cooperative partner or foe of the United States in the twenty-first century.
- Taiwan is a major US trading partner.
- Taiwan is a key source of capital investment to regions of importance to US foreign policy, such as Southeast Asia, Latin America, Africa and the Pacific island states.
- Taiwan is a highly successful model of free enterprise and capitalism in Asia.
- Taiwan is a successful model of how to develop democracy from authoritarian rule.
- Taiwan is a well-established member of the community of market democracies, a community the United States is committed to expand and defend.
- Taiwan is an approximate model of what the United States hopes one day all of China will become – a market democracy on friendly terms with the West.
- Taiwan is an historical ally and friend of the United States, often supporting US regional and global policies.

Four key interests

As suggested by the above list, four of the most important US interests related to Taiwan are (1) the maintenance of a favorable balance of power in the Western Pacific; (2) the continuation of Taiwan's positive influence on China's modernization; (3) the preservation of a domestic American political consensus on US China policy; and (4) Taiwan's role in American credibility in Asia. Each of these interests deserves some elaboration.

In the first instance, US strategy in the Asia–Pacific centers around the maintenance of a favorable balance of power, a corollary of which is American opposition to rival hegemons. In the post-Cold War period, Taiwan plays an indirect role in this strategy by providing a hedge against a potentially hostile China in the future. Simply put, no one knows whether China will be an ally, enemy, friend or rival of the United States over the next decade, or even if China will succeed in its modernization efforts. Until China's intentions and capabilities become clearer, it could be a strategic mistake for the United States to abandon its interests in Taiwan.

This lesson certainly has been learned during the Clinton administration. A policy of comprehensive engagement has managed to maintain dialogue between Washington and Beijing, and on occasion has led to incremental agreement on some bilateral issues, but engagement has not resolved the deep-seated issues of missile and nuclear proliferation, trade imbalance, unfair trading practices, human rights violations, the rapid

11

modernization of the People's Liberation Army, Chinese military action in the South China Sea, or the Taiwan issue. As China becomes stronger, areas of conflicting interests between Beijing and Washington will likely increase as each country seeks to define and maintain its sphere of influence in the Western Pacific. This assumes, of course, that the United States will not withdraw from the region and that China will not abandon its claims to leadership in Asia – both unlikely.

If the United States allows the PRC to take over Taiwan by force – particularly in the absence of a provocation such as a formal declaration of independence by Taipei – or even to intimidate Taiwan through military threat as in 1995–96, then the balance of power in East Asia will be changed in directions unfavorable to Washington. US credibility, influence and prestige will be damaged, while that of China will be strengthened. Moreover, having access to Taiwan's ports, airfields and investment capital would tremendously expand PRC national power, positioning it to project power much further into the Western Pacific and toward Japan and Southeast Asia. Also, China's success in using force or the threat of force against Taiwan might encourage Beijing to use its military instruments to help resolve some of its other regional problems. China's neighbors want the United States and China to maintain cooperative relations, but they do not want to see the PRC take Taiwan by force. For their own interests, they prefer a balance of power in the region supported by the United States.

Second, Taiwan can exert a positive influence on China's modernization. As a Chinese society, Taiwan has become an important testing ground for various approaches to China's modernization. Although still evolving, Taiwan has successfully developed institutions of democracy and capitalism in a Chinese context, experiences that can prove useful to mainland China as well. One of the long-term US goals during this century has been for China to become more democratic and market oriented. US support for Taiwan's market democracy advances this goal. It is counter-intuitive to believe that democracy and free enterprise on mainland China would gain a greater foothold if the United States ended its support of democracy and free enterprise on Taiwan. Moreover, US support for Taiwan can be viewed as part of the American global objective of strengthening and expanding the community of market democracies around the world.

Third, friendly ties with Taiwan help Washington to maintain a domestic consensus on US China policy. American policy toward China and Taiwan has frequently been a divisive issue in American politics, a divisiveness that was once again seen in 1999 in bitter debates between the administration and the Congress over issues such as security at Los Alamos, World Trade Organization (WTO) status for China, human rights violations, and the launching of American satellites aboard Chinese rockets. As illustrated in Chapter 7, every year there are numerous bills and resolutions passed by Congress criticizing China and voicing support for Taiwan, often including calls for more advanced weapons sales to Taipei. As controversial as US China policy now is, it would lose all hope for consensus if support for Taiwan were ended by an administration seeking to make a deal with Beijing.

Fourth, although not directly an American interest in Taiwan, US friends and allies in the Western Pacific view Taiwan in a favorable light. Japan sees Taiwan as a valued trading partner, a key destination of Japanese investment, a security gateway to the southern approaches to Japan, and a key factor in Sino-Japanese relations. Many in Tokyo also believe that Taiwan falls under regional security concerns in the US–Japan defense alliance. The Philippines also see Taiwan as being strategically important, primarily because of Manila's security concerns in the Luzon Strait and South China Sea. Both Japan and the Philippines play key roles in the US island chain defense, and their views of Taiwan have weight in Washington. The Philippines, as well as most other Southeast Asian countries, consider Taiwan an important trading partner and source of investment in their economies. Most countries in the Asia–Pacific view Taiwan as being an important key to China's national power and future policy direction, a potential military flashpoint in the region, and an indicator of the US commitment to maintain a military presence in the region and to sustain a balance of power – both critical to preventing Chinese regional hegemony. Hence, Taiwan is important to American credibility in the Western Pacific.

Adverse effects of war in the Taiwan Strait

Yet another way to understand the wide range of US interests in a peaceful settlement of the Taiwan issue – one in which Taiwan agrees without force or excessive pressure – is to consider how American interests would be adversely affected by a war between mainland China and Taiwan. The extent of these interests goes far in explaining why a fundamental and long-standing element of US policy is the preservation of peace in the Taiwan Strait.

First, a war between China and Taiwan might not be confined to the Taiwan Strait. Taiwan's war-fighting strategy is to expand the conflict as widely and rapidly as possible to maximize damage to the PRC. To be effective, a PRC blockade of Taiwan would have to extend into international waters. Trade to and from Kaohsiung and Keelung – Taiwan's principal, world-class ports – would be disrupted, as well as trade to Chinese ports between Shanghai and Hong Kong. Some mainland coastal facilities would be attacked by Taiwan, and PRC harbors no doubt would be mined. Taiwan's infrastructure and industrial capability would probably be heavily damaged. Thus, as a result of the conflict, the commercial interests of all countries trading with Taiwan and China would be harmed.

Second, the use of PRC submarines to impose a blockade on Taiwan would pose a danger to all merchant ships passing through the Luzon Strait and the Taiwan Strait. These are choke points through which flow vast amounts of cargo moving between Northeast Asia and ports in southern China, Southeast Asia, South Asia and the Middle East. Since identification of friend or foe on the high seas is difficult for submarines, a submarine-enforced blockade of Taiwan might result in neutral shipping being harmed. Much of the air traffic in the Western Pacific would likewise be severely disrupted.

Third, a war in the Taiwan Strait would harm the economies not only of Taiwan and China but also of many other Asian–Pacific countries. Both Chinese economies are major engines of regional economic growth; both are important trading partners of Pacific Rim countries; China is a recipient of vast amounts of Asian capital; and Taiwan provides vital investment capital to many regional nations. In the event of war in the Taiwan Strait, the Asian economic 'miracle', already shaken by the financial crisis of 1997–99, could be further derailed. Since continued economic growth is a key factor in regional political stability, a war in the Taiwan Strait could have severely negative political repercussions as well.

Fourth, a war between Taiwan and China would cause deep security concerns throughout Asia. Most countries of the region are wary of Chinese hegemony, and a conflict in the Taiwan Strait would fuel that anxiety. The purchase of advanced weapons by other countries would increase and perhaps, in some cases, extend to ballistic missiles and weapons of mass destruction. Many Asian nations possess the financial and technological capabilities of producing such weapons. US interests in non-proliferation would be greatly harmed by such a development.

Fifth, because of traditional US commitments to the defense of Taiwan, war in the Taiwan Strait would immediately focus attention on the US response. American credibility in the region is tied closely to how Washington responds to PRC military threats to Taiwan. In the post-Cold War period, Asian countries are very sensitive to American credibility; and US allies constantly assess their own security links with the United States. An ineffective US response to a crisis in the Taiwan Strait would significantly diminish the deterrent value of security ties with the United States and greatly weaken American influence in the region. If not handled correctly, a crisis over Taiwan could begin to unravel the US security architecture in Asia at a time when China is advancing alternative, multilateral-based architectures designed to weaken the preeminent American position in the Western Pacific.

Sixth, there is high probability that a war in the Taiwan Strait would involve the United States. Washington has a long history of commitment to the security of Taiwan and a proven record of military support to Taipei during times of crisis. Whatever the circumstances that might precipitate a conflict in the Taiwan Strait, there would be strong domestic pressure in the United States for military intervention on behalf of Taiwan. This might result in a military confrontation between the United States and China that neither side would want but neither side could avoid.

US policy toward Taiwan

From the above discussion, it can be seen that the United States has many direct and indirect interests in Taiwan. Although Taiwan is isolated diplomatically, the island is integrated economically with the rest of the Asia–Pacific community and is a significant contributor to regional stability and prosperity. Most Pacific Rim nations favor current US policy toward Taiwan, if only to ensure continued US engagement in Asia as a counterbalance to the rising and unpredictable power of China.

For these and other reasons, an especially close relationship exists between the United States and Taiwan. Despite the difficulty of trying to manage the Taiwan issue in the strategically important but prickly US relationship with China, the United States will probably continue to be friendly and supportive toward Taiwan. In particular, the US government will ensure that Taiwan has an adequate self-defense, that it is represented in international organizations dealing with non-political matters, that its trade ties with the United States remain strong, and that the Taiwan people have a voice in their own future.

The details of US policy toward Taiwan, particularly under President Bill Clinton, will be discussed in Chapter 7. At this point, however, it should be noted that for several decades the United States has pursued a 'dual-track' policy of engagement with China and friendship toward Taiwan in an attempt to serve US interests with both Beijing and Taipei. This policy is ambiguous and prone to contradiction, but it has proved to be pragmatic and durable. Further, the dual-track policy seems to be supported by a majority of the US foreign policy establishment, a consensus reached only after many bruising political battles. Although policy debate and controversy continue, any change in US policy toward either Taiwan or China would result in renewed domestic political fighting with uncertain outcome. Thus, if only from the viewpoint of domestic politics – always a highly determining factor in American foreign policy – the dual-track policy will probably remain in place.

Taiwan's political, economic and security policies rarely harm US interests, although they do sometimes pose a challenge due to the sensitivity of the Taiwan issue in Sino-American relations. The greatest of these challenges arises from the desire of the people on Taiwan for self-determination – a desire which translates into demands upon the ROC government to seek international respect and recognition and to avoid unification with China as long as the mainland is under a communist government. Despite the numerous difficulties arising in Sino-American relations because of Taiwan's pursuit of self-determination, it is extremely doubtful that the resolution of the Taiwan issue along lines favored by Beijing would resolve other conflicting interests between the United States and the PRC. Thus, there is no strategic imperative for a change in US policy toward Taiwan in order to improve Washington's relations with Beijing.

As a result, and if only by default, the best US policy remains the dual-track approach that maintains cooperative, official relations with the PRC and friendly, unofficial relations with the people of Taiwan. This approach serves the pragmatic interests of the United States in both China and Taiwan, while giving the two Chinese societies time to work out their differences. The principal role for the United States in this prolonged Chinese process is to ensure that their differences are worked out, or at least managed, peacefully. As reaffirmed by successive administrations since 1979, such a policy serves vital US interests in the Western Pacific and thus probably will continue for the foreseeable future.

US interests in Taiwan's alternative futures

Given the close US involvement in the Taiwan issue, American interests will be affected by the future of Taiwan. Generally speaking, the various alternative futures for Taiwan include such well-known scenarios as unification, two Chinas, one China–one Taiwan, Taiwan independence or prolongation of the status quo in the Taiwan Strait. These alternative futures can be achieved either by peaceful or non-peaceful means. For the sake of clarity, these scenarios might be described as follows:

- *Unification.* A condition under which Taiwan becomes a legally recognized part of China as a province, special administrative region, special autonomous region or some other arrangement.
- *Two Chinas.* A condition under which two legal governments of a divided China are recognized, such as the Republic of China on Taiwan and the People's Republic of China on the mainland.
- *One China–one Taiwan.* A condition under which Taiwan would be considered separate from China but not an independent country.
- *Taiwan independence.* A condition under which Taiwan would be recognized as a sovereign nation-state, entirely separate from China.
- *Status quo in the Taiwan Strait.* A condition under which two competing Chinese governments – the ROC and PRC – both claim there

16

is but one China and Taiwan is part of China, but disagree over the definition of that China and govern separate parts of China.

There is not a great deal of clarity in these definitions, and each reflects something of existing reality in the Taiwan Strait. As will become obvious in Chapter 2, the ROC and PRC freely use these terms to their own advantage. The key point to note here is that neither side is willing to accept the other's definition of what comprises China, nor is either willing to accept the other side's proposals for Taiwan's future relationship with the mainland. Essentially, Beijing is playing a zero-sum game in which it wants to finalize its political victory in the Chinese civil war; Taipei is seeking a way to survive until such time as conditions on the mainland change to its advantage. The United States and other nations are observers of this ongoing process, trying to find ways to serve their interests in both sides of the Taiwan Strait. Still, it is possible to forecast, to some extent at least, how the various scenarios for Taiwan's future might affect US interests.

Peaceful resolution
Assuming that the resolution of the Taiwan issue is peaceful, how would the various scenarios for Taiwan's future affect US interests? The key here is the nature of future Sino-American relations – which is itself controversial and yet to be determined:

- If China were democratic, market-oriented, non-hegemonic, and wanted cooperative, friendly relations with the United States, then Taiwan's unification with the mainland would not directly harm US interests. In fact, US relations with the Greater China would probably be quite friendly, although perhaps competitive.
- If China were communist, socialist-oriented, hegemonic, and considered the United States an enemy, then Taiwan's unification with the mainland could adversely affect US interests. Beijing certainly would be better positioned in the Western Pacific to project power and to oppose the United States.
- If Taiwan were independent, if there were two Chinas (one China and one Taiwan), or if the status quo in the Taiwan Strait were maintained indefinitely, US interests would not be harmed if China were democratic and friendly. And if China were hostile, US interests would not be harmed by these scenarios, since a divided China is a weakened China.

In short, assuming both sides were able to agree peacefully upon Taiwan's future relationship with the mainland, only under the circumstance of Taiwan unifying with a China hostile to the United States would American interests be seriously threatened.

Status quo or non-peaceful resolution

If it is assumed that the two sides cannot agree on Taiwan's future, either the status quo would persist indefinitely or the issue would be settled by military or other pressure exerted on Taiwan. Under these conditions:

• US interests would not be harmed by a continuation of the status quo (although some Americans would add the caveat: except insofar as it hinders better US–PRC relations).
• US interests would definitely be harmed if the PRC used force to resolve the Taiwan issue. War between the two sides would disrupt regional peace and stability, and the outcome of the struggle would not be accepted easily by the losing party, perhaps leading to a prolonged period of agitation and repression.

To summarize, Table 1 suggests the positive and negative impact on US interests likely to occur from the various scenarios for Taiwan's future.

In sum, it is clear that US interests are best served by a peaceful resolution of the Taiwan issue, that is a resolution agreed to by both sides. Such a resolution is not yet in sight. Estimates of the probability of the two sides eventually agreeing to a political settlement vary considerably. But, until such a formula can be found, US interests are best served by ensuring, first, that no war erupts in the Taiwan Strait and, second, by encouraging both sides to continue their dialogue and exchanges. If a war does occur in the Taiwan Strait, the United States would face a policy environment of sharply conflicting interests: first, avoiding a major war with China; second, protecting a fellow market democracy; third, maintaining domestic political support for the administration in office at the time; and, fourth, countering Chinese hegemony in the Western Pacific. These conflicting interests mean that the immediate US response to a conflict in the Taiwan Strait would likely be heavily influenced by the cause of the conflict; and the United States would likely seek to end the conflict as quickly as possible on the basis of *status quo ante bellum*.

At present, the United States follows a multidimensional strategy to prevent a conflict in the Taiwan Strait. On one level, Washington maintains a powerful forward-deployed military force in the Pacific, in part to deter PRC aggression against Taiwan. Second, the US policy of engagement with China is designed in part to give Beijing incentives not to use force in the Taiwan Strait. Third, Washington uses its considerable influence with Taipei to try to persuade the ROC to pursue non-provocative policies in its relationship with the mainland. Fourth, the United States encourages both sides of the Taiwan Strait to expand their dialogue and to find areas of mutual benefit and cooperation. And, fifth, the United States provides Taiwan with adequate advanced weapons and defense

Table 1
Scenarios for Taiwan's future: Impact on US interests

Scenario	In the US interest	Against the US interest
CONDITION 1: PEACEFUL AGREEMENT BETWEEN THE TWO SIDES OF THE TAIWAN STRAIT		
Unification	Yes, if China democratic, non-hegemonic, friendly to USA	Yes, if China communist, hegemonic, hostile to USA
Taiwan independence	Yes	No
Two Chinas	Yes	No
One China–one Taiwan	Yes	No
Status quo	Yes	No
CONDITION 2: DISAGREEMENT BETWEEN THE TWO SIDES OF THE TAIWAN STRAIT		
Unification	No, unless unified China democratic, non-hegemonic and friendly to USA	Yes, if achieved through military force
Taiwan independence	Maybe, if war can be prevented in Taiwan Strait, and US–China relations not undermined	Yes, if war breaks out in Taiwan Strait
Two Chinas	Maybe, if war can be prevented in Taiwan Strait, and US–China relations not undermined	Yes, if war breaks out in Taiwan Strait
One China–one Taiwan	Maybe, if war can be prevented in Taiwan Strait, and US–China relations not undermined	Yes, if war breaks out in Taiwan Strait
Status quo	Yes, if war can be prevented, and US–China relations not undermined	Yes, if war breaks out in Taiwan Strait

technology to deter most PRC temptations to resolve the Taiwan issue quickly by force. However, the United States does not provide Taiwan with advanced offensive weapons which might give Taipei incentives either to threaten the mainland or pursue provocative policies such as Taiwan independence.

For the purposes of this book, the role of American arms sales to Taiwan has special relevancy. (Note that, throughout the book, unless stated, references are to US dollars.) Before discussing US arms sales, however, a brief summary of the recent military balance in the Taiwan Strait is in order.

Table 2
Comparison of ROC and PRC armed forces

Category	People's Republic of China	Republic of China
Gross domestic product (1997)	$639 billion	$293 billion
Per capita GDP (1997)	$3,400	$13,800
GDP growth (1997)	8.8 percent	6 percent
Debt (1997)	$133 billion	$24.6 billion
Defense expenditure (1997)	$36.6 billion (estimated)	$13.6 billion
Defense budget (1998)	$11 billion (official figure)	$8.3 billion
Population	1,232,765,000	21,631,000
Total active duty personnel	2,820,000	376,000
Total reserves	1,200,000+	1,657,000
Intercontinental ballistic missiles	17	none
Intermediate-range ballistic missiles	46+	none
Nuclear-fueled ballistic missile submarines (SSBN)	1 with 12 submarine-launched ballistic missiles	none
Short-range ballistic missiles	M-9 (range 600 km) and M-11 (range 300+ km)	none
Total army personnel	2,090,000	240,000
Army units deployed in immediate Taiwan area	Nanjing Military Region: 3 group armies, 2 tank divisions, 8 infantry divisions, 1 artillery division	Quemoy: 4 infantry divisions; Matsu: 1 infantry division; remainder on Taiwan Island
Total navy personnel	260,000 (including 5,000 marines)	68,000 (including 30,000 marines)
Submarines	63 (including 1 SSBN; 5 nuclear-fueled submarines; 1 non-ballistic missile submarine; 56 patrol submarines)	4 (including 2 patrol submarines and 2 training submarines)
Destroyers	18	18
Frigates	35	18
Patrol and coastal combatant craft	747	101
Mine warfare vessels	119	12
Amphibious vessels	73	19
Naval combat aircraft	541, plus 25 armed helicopters	31, plus 21 armed helicopters
Total air force personnel	470,000	68,000

Table 2 *continued*

Category	People's Republic of China	Republic of China
Bombers	320+ medium and light	none
Fighters	2,900 (including 46 Su-27s)	462 (including 272 F-5s; 100 Ching-kuo indigenous fighters; 30 Mirage 2000-5s with 30 more to be delivered; 30 F-16A/Bs with 120 more to be delivered)
Airborne early warning	none	4 E-2Ts

MILITARY BALANCE IN THE TAIWAN STRAIT

In addition to Chinese intentions to use force against Taiwan and the extent of US interests in Taiwan, another key factor in Taiwan's security in the post-Deng era is the military balance of power in the Taiwan Strait. Table 2, summarized from *The Military Balance: 1998/99*, provides a general comparison of the military strength of the People's Republic of China and the Republic of China as of early 1998.[8]

Modernization programs

Also noted in *The Military Balance 1998–99* were several modernization programs under way in China and Taiwan. In the case of the PRC, its defense budget and arms acquisition from both domestic and foreign sources were increasing. Three strategic ballistic missiles were being developed: the 8,000 km-range Dong Feng-31 (DF-31), an intercontinental ballistic missile (ICBM) scheduled to enter service in 1999; the 12,000 km DF-41 to enter service between 2002 and 2005; and the second-generation JL-2, a submarine-launched ballistic missile scheduled for completion by 2002. The JL-2 was to be used in the first Project 094 nuclear-fueled ballistic missile submarine, entering service by 2010. Another submarine program, the Type 093 with dedicated non-ballistic missile launchers, was expected to be launched in 2000. The first Song-class submarine was undergoing sea trials, with two others under construction. A second Kilo 636-class from Russia was to be delivered in October 1998. A new Luhai-class destroyer was also under construction, scheduled for launch in June 1999. It would join the two Sovremennyy-class destroyers purchased from Russia in December 1996. In April 1998, China ordered SS-N-22 anti-ship missiles from Russia to equip the Sovremennyy destroyers and possibly the Luhai destroyers. Production under license had begun for up to 150 Russian Su-27 ground attack fighters. Development of the F-10 ground attack fighter continued with Israeli technical assistance, but operation was not expected until about 2005. Under French license, production continued of the Z-9A and Z-11 helicopters. China's Red Arrow 8E anti-tank missile was set to enter production. Air-portable armored vehicles were acquired from Russia, and production under license for the Russian RPO-A Shmel rocket launcher was begun.

In addition to data provided by IISS, additional information on China's military modernization can be noted. According to Russian sources, Moscow's arms sales to China amounted to $6 billion between 1991 and 1997. Contracts included the sale of 26 Su-27 fighters in 1992; another 48 Su-27s in 1995–96; the 1996 sale of a license to China to manufacture an additional 200 Su-27s; the delivery of four Kilo-class submarines and six S-300 air defense complexes in 1994; and two Sovremennyy-class destroyers and 'a host of other naval weapons'.[9] There were also persistent reports that China and Russia were negotiating the purchase of Su-30s, and some of these reports mentioned that the Su-27 license was for 250 rather than 200 of the fighters.[10]

According to a report from *Defense News*, China agreed in Moscow in early July 1999 to purchase at least 50 Su-30s – an all-weather, long-range strike fighter. The letter of intent signed by the PLA and AVPK Sukhoi, Moscow, stated that China would purchase two regiments of 25 Su-30MKK fighter-bombers at an estimated cost of $37 million each. Deliveries were expected in 2002. The *Defense News* report further clarified the earlier Su-27 purchase, noting that China had purchased 48 of the aircraft outright and received license rights to co-produce another 200 planes, to be called the J-11.[11]

By the fall of 1999, additional information about Russian arms sales to China had appeared in the press. According to an October 9, 1999 report from Agence France Presse, Beijing finally decided to purchase 30 Su-30 fighters at a cost of $2 billion to be used primarily in an anti-ship role. The *Hong Kong Standard* on September 1, 1999, cited PRC diplomatic sources who reported that Russia would sell Beijing two Typhoon-class nuclear-powered ballistic missile submarines at a cost of $1 billion. The SSBN sale, along with persistent rumors of a pending Russian or Ukrainian aircraft-carrier sale, while not impossible, probably should be taken with a grain of salt.

It should be noted in passing that the M-11 and M-9 short-range ballistic missiles, approximately 200 of which are deployed near Taiwan and would likely be used during a conflict with the island, have the following characteristics: the road-mobile, solid propellant M-11, or CSS-7 or DF-11, has a range of 300 km, an accuracy of 600 m CEP (circular error probable), a high-explosive warhead of 500 kg payload, and an inertial guidance system with terminal control. A longer-range version may be under development. The M-9, or CSS-6 or DF-15, has a range of 600 km, an accuracy of 300 m CEP, a high-explosive warhead of 500 kg payload, and an inertial guidance system with terminal control. The M-9 was used during the Taiwan missile crisis of 1995–96.

For further details, the reader is referred to the report of the US Secretary of Defense on the modernization of the PLA, written in November 1998 at the request of Congress, found in Appendix 1.

In the case of Taiwan, while its defense budget was contracting slightly, its acquisition of modern weapons continued at a fast pace. By August 1998 over 30 F-16s out of 150 ordered had been received from the United States, and half of the French Mirage 2000s had been delivered. At the end of 1998, all of the 120 Ching-Kuo indigenously produced fighters had been delivered. Also in 1998, the final deliveries of seven Perry-class Cheng-Kung frigates, produced domestically under license from the United States, were scheduled, as well as the final delivery of the six LaFayette-class frigates purchased from France. Taiwan also received six Patriot surface-to-air launchers from the United States in 1998.

Further details on US arms sales to Taiwan will be provided in the next section. Also, a more formal assessment of the military balance in the Taiwan Strait may be seen in Appendix 2, which contains the February 1999 US Department of Defense report on the security situation in the Taiwan Strait, again mandated by Congress.

Other factors in military balance

The above summary of the relative military strengths of the PRC and Taiwan is useful but not definitive. The summary accurately reflects the overwhelming PRC advantage over Taiwan in terms of strategic forces, army divisions, submarines and combat aircraft. However, a conflict between the PRC and ROC is unlikely to use nuclear weapons or other weapons of mass destruction, thereby limiting the utility of Chinese strategic weapons – other than as a possible deterrent to American intervention. China's armies must first be transported to Taiwan before their overwhelming numbers can be brought into play, a task deemed impossible by most Western analysts because of the limited seaborne transportation and amphibious assault craft available to Beijing. (An invasion by Chinese junks is considered a possibility by some Taiwan observers.) A submarine-enforced blockade is unlikely – in and of itself – to bring Taiwan to its knees. And the quantitative advantage of the PLA air force is counterbalanced to a great extent by the short loiter time over Taiwan, the superior training of ROC pilots, the large number of advanced fighters and air-to-air missiles possessed by Taiwan, and the formidable air defense systems in place throughout Taiwan.

In assessing the military balance, there are other factors to consider as well. For example, China needs to protect a territory of 9,596,960 sq km, with 22,143 km of land borders and 14,500 km of coastline, while Taiwan needs to protect 35,980 sq km with no land borders and 1,448 km of coastline. This is roughly a comparison of the need to defend the continental United States versus the need to defend an island the size of West Virginia. China must consider not only potential external threats to its security, but also internal threats from rebellious minorities in Tibet and Xinjiang. It is clear that Beijing cannot and will not deploy all of its military assets against Taiwan, whereas Taiwan has no higher priority than survival from PRC attack.

Another key factor is the difficulty of conquering Taiwan. Although relatively small in comparison to the mainland, the island is extremely mountainous and heavily forested. There are 200 peaks more than 3,000 m in height, with deep gorges and sharp valleys. Those who have traveled to Taiwan know that, along the coastal plains and basins on the west coast, there are innumerable pillboxes and other strongholds built to defend against a possible invasion by the Chinese army. Ironically, there are few places in the world better situated to prove the advantages of a people's war than Taiwan. And the Taiwan Strait, approximately 100 nautical miles across, is notoriously difficult to transit, especially northward during the October to March monsoons, which typically bring winds of nearly 25 m per second in the Pescadores. Most American military strategists view an amphibious invasion of Taiwan as being far more complex and difficult than the Normandy invasion. General John Shalikashvili, Chairman of the Joint Chiefs of Staff during the 1995–96 Taiwan crisis, was of that opinion, for example.[12]

At the same time, the island of Taiwan is heavily dependent upon trade for its economic prosperity, although not for its sustenance. Theoretically, this makes Taiwan highly vulnerable to a blockade, and no doubt such a strategy is a preferred PLA option. On the other hand, a blockade is easy to declare but difficult to enforce: the Taiwan Strait is dangerously shallow for submarines to operate (albeit easy to mine); the international waterways used by ships to and from Taiwan are also heavily used by other nations whose interests would be adversely affected by a blockade; and Taiwan's eastern ports are far from the mainland and difficult to seal. For these and other reasons, a blockade of Taiwan would probably be only partially successful and probably not sufficiently damaging to force Taipei's capitulation – especially within a short time frame.[13]

What all of this means is that defeating Taiwan is no easy matter, despite the seemingly overwhelming forces at the disposal of the PRC. When one factors in the strong possibility of the United States intervening on Taiwan's behalf in a confrontation with the mainland, then Beijing's military options seem very limited indeed.

Still, this is a near-term assessment and does not adequately reflect the huge influence of military modernization on the balance of power beyond ten years. ROC Defense Minister Tang Fei told Taiwan's legislature in March 1999 that, while Taiwan's armed forces can match those of China until 2005, if the PLA's military modernization continues, 'the military threat to Taiwan is highly likely to be beyond control after 2005'.[14] The US Department of Defense (DOD), in its congressionally mandated report to Congress in February 1999, 'The Security Situation in the Taiwan Strait', reached a somewhat similar conclusion, albeit clothed in more indirect language:[15]

> In order for an invasion to succeed ... Beijing would have to possess the capability to conduct a multi-faceted campaign, involving air assault, airborne insertion, special operations raids, amphibious landings, maritime area denial operations, air superiority operations and conventional missile strikes. The PLA likely would encounter great difficulty conducting such a sophisticated campaign by 2005. Nevertheless, the campaign likely would succeed – barring third party intervention – if Beijing were willing to accept the almost certain political, economic, diplomatic, and military costs that such a course of action would produce.

In its conclusion, the DOD report pointed to the importance of the acquisition of new military systems by the PRC and ROC:

> Despite anticipated improvements to Taiwan's missile and air defense systems, by 2005, the PLA will possess the capability to attack Taiwan with air and missile strikes which would degrade key military facilities and damage the island's economic infrastructure. China will continue to give priority to long-range precision-strike programs. Similarly, despite improvements in Taiwan's ability to conduct ASW operations, China will retain the capability to interdict Taiwan's SLOCs and blockade the island's principal maritime ports. Should China invade Taiwan, such an operation would require a major commitment of civilian air and maritime transport assets, would be prolonged in duration, and would not be automatically guaranteed to succeed. In the end, any of these options would prove to be costly to Beijing – politically, economically, diplomatically, and militarily ...
>
> On the other side of the Taiwan Strait, by 2005, Taipei will possess a qualitative edge over Beijing in terms of significant weapons and equipment. The TAF [Taiwan air force] will have over 300 fourth generation fighters. Six French-built LaFayette-class frigates, eight U.S. Knox-class frigates, and eight Perry-class frigates will form the nucleus of Taiwan's naval force. Taiwan will possess an advanced air defense network, comprising an AEW capability, an automated C2 system, and several modern SAM systems, which will provide Taiwan with an

enhanced defensive capability against both aircraft and missiles. The mobility and firepower of Taiwan's ground forces will have been improved with the acquisition of additional tanks, armored personnel carriers, self-propelled artillery and attack helicopters.

Since Taiwan's capacity to produce weapons domestically is very limited in comparison to that of the mainland, the DOD report's emphasis on the importance of new weapons systems indirectly reaffirmed the vital role played in Taiwan's security by US arms sales – a subject to which we now turn in some detail.

US ARMS SALES TO TAIWAN

Thus far in this chapter, we have argued that the PRC has vital incentives to use force against Taiwan under certain circumstances and that the United States also has compelling reasons – because of its extensive interests in the Taiwan issue – to intervene in a war in the Taiwan Strait under most circumstances. We have further described the military balance in the Taiwan Strait as one favoring the PRC but not sufficiently to enable Beijing to undertake operations against Taiwan with a high degree of certainty for success. However, the military balance in the Taiwan Strait is undergoing significant change due to the rapid modernization of both PRC and ROC armed forces. Of special importance in this regard is China's acquisition of modern weapons systems and technology from Russia and Taiwan's procurement of defensive arms and technology from the United States.

In the case of China, the fairly rapid acquisition of Russian weapons and technology has at least two negative effects on Taiwan's security. First, the acquisitions greatly complicate Taiwan's defense posture since Taipei must continually upgrade ROC weapons systems and take into account new Chinese capabilities to attack Taiwan. Second, the acquisitions increase the probable military costs to the United States should it wish to intervene on Taiwan's behalf – thus acting as a more viable deterrent to that intervention.

Thus, an especially important factor in Taiwan's security in the post-Deng era is the extent of US arms sales to Taiwan. Although these weapons cannot in themselves guarantee Taiwan's security, they do play a key role in helping to deter possible PRC aggression and to link Taiwan's security to the security interests of the United States.

US policy – codified in domestic law by the 1979 Taiwan Relations Act – is to provide Taiwan with military services and equipment necessary for Taipei to maintain a sufficient self-defense capability. What actually comprises self-sufficiency in such sales has always been controversial, however, if only because PLA forces are rapidly changing and US–PRC relations are notoriously unstable.

The stated reason why the United States provides such weapons to Taiwan is to protect the long-standing American interest in seeing that the Taiwan issue is settled peacefully. If fact, US arms sales to Taiwan serve several additional American interests by helping to (a) maintain a favorable balance of power in the region; (b) contribute to peace and stability in the Western Pacific; (c) reaffirm the US commitment to regional security; (d) strengthen American credibility in the region; (e) protect US commercial interests; (f) support democracy and human rights in Asia; (g) sustain a domestic consensus on US China policy; and (h) moderate PRC domestic and foreign policies. Unstated but possibly beneficial results of such arms sales include keeping a potentially hostile China divided and hence weakened and maintaining substantial American influence over Taipei's policies.

As long as China is potentially hostile toward the United States and as long as US ties with Taiwan serve American interests, there will probably be large-scale arms and defense technology exchanges between Washington and Taipei. (Assuming, of course, the two Chinese sides do not resolve their differences peacefully – a subject discussed in Chapter 2.) Given the importance of US arms sales to Taiwan's security, therefore, it might be useful to consider some of these transfers in greater detail.

History of arms sales

In terms of outright military aid, the United States provided Taiwan with about $4.2 billion in military assistance from 1950 to the mid-1970s, when the aid program was terminated. This aid provided Taiwan with an American-based military arsenal and the logistics and infrastructure that make continued US military transfers to Taiwan much easier than transfers from other countries. In 1972, for example, the United States authorized Northrop Corporation to co-produce with Taiwan nearly 250 F-5E fighters. Taiwan's navy and army were likewise equipped with American weapons through military assistance programs, outright purchases, and co-production arrangements.

Shortly after the 1979 switch in diplomatic relations and the passage of the Taiwan Relations Act a few months later, several major US military sales were concluded with Taiwan:[16]

- December 1979. 500 Maverick missiles worth $25 million (delivered in 1982)
- January 1980. Various types of missiles, including I-Hawk and Sea Chaparral, worth $280 million
- July 1980. 14 M110A howitzers worth $3.7 million

- April 1982. Aircraft spare parts worth $640,000
- June 1982. 164 armored vehicles, 72 trench mortar trucks, and 31 command vehicles worth $97 million.

In August 1982 the United States and China agreed to qualitative and quantitative restrictions on future US arms sales to Taiwan, as long as Beijing maintained its policy of peaceful reunification, which had been formally in place since late 1978. The August 17, 1982 Joint Communiqué and the Taiwan Relations Act (TRA) are somewhat contradictory. Under the communiqué, as long as Beijing pursues a peaceful policy toward Taiwan, US arms sales to Taiwan should be reduced. No provision is made for increased sales if the PLA improves its capability to attack Taiwan. Under the TRA, however, US arms sales are linked to Taiwan's defense needs – a threat assessment taking into account both PRC intentions and PLA capabilities. Using TRA guidelines, as the PLA modernizes, US arms sales to Taiwan should increase – regardless of PRC policy. There are semantics involved here, giving rise to much 'creative ambiguity' as Senator S. I. Hayakawa was fond of saying,[17] but the above interpretation of the communiqué and the TRA generally reflect Washington's interpretations.

Policy adjustments after August 1982

To avoid harming the security interests of Taiwan, the Reagan administration, after the departure of Secretary of State Alexander Haig,[18] made four important decisions relative to the August 17 communiqué. First, it assured the Congress that the TRA took legal precedence over the August 17 communiqué. State Department Legal Adviser Davis Robinson told Congress on September 27, 1982:

> [The August 17 communiqué] is not an international agreement and thus imposes no obligations on either party under international law. Its status under domestic law is that of a statement by the President of a policy which he intends to pursue ... The Taiwan Relations Act is and will remain the law of the land unless amended by Congress. Nothing in the joint communiqué obligates the President to act in a manner contrary to the Act or, conversely, disables him from fulfilling his responsibilities under it.[19]

As will be seen in a discussion of congressional involvement in the security of Taiwan in Chapter 7, there are continuing disagreements between the administration and the Congress over the precedence of the communiqué and the TRA. The administration prefers a flexible interpretation of precedence, whereas the Congress insists on the TRA's higher legal standing. Simply put, the TRA, as law of the land, cannot be subsumed by the communiqué, despite the communiqué's status as one of the foundations of Sino-American relations. On the other hand, the PRC rejects any role the TRA may have in US–China understanding over the Taiwan issue.

Second, the Reagan administration adopted an inflationary index to its interpretation of the communiqué, helping to ensure that Taiwan received adequate weapons. Thus, for example, the State Department released figures setting ceilings for arms sales to Taiwan for fiscal year (FY) 1983 at $800 million and for FY 1984 at $780 million. These figures far exceeded the actual amount of weapons sold to Taiwan in 1979 ($598 million), 1980 ($601 million) and 1981 ($295 million). The State Department explained that the $598 million in 1979 would be equivalent to $800 million in current, inflated dollars.[20]

Third, the Reagan administration established the precedent of increasing the amount of commercial export license sales to Taiwan, even while it reduced foreign military sales. For example, in FY 1985 the administration sold to Taiwan $700,537,000 in military items and $54,463,000 in commercial 'dual-use' sales. The next year, the administration announced its intention to sell Taiwan military items valued at $640 million, but also increased commercial sales to over $100 million. In 1986 the administration rejected PRC arguments that technology transfers should fall under the August 17 guidelines. The Reagan, Bush and Clinton administrations all used commercial sales and technology transfers to help Taipei develop its defense capabilities. Taiwan's indigenous defense fighter and the FFG-7 frigate programs are examples of this kind of cooperation. More recently, *Defense News* reported that Taipei and Washington had decided to pursue a program of 'Software Initiatives', a multibillion dollar, multiyear program designed to integrate Taiwan's varied military systems into a much more effective defense.[21] And in December 1998, the same journal reported that Taiwan and the United States were considering a greatly increased program of bilateral military training programs, with emphasis on C4I and combined arms and joint warfare operations.[22]

And, fourth, the Reagan administration decided that it would sell Taiwan more advanced models of military equipment when stocks of spare parts were depleted or when the units themselves became obsolete. An early example of this precedent included 12 C-130 transport aircraft sold to Taiwan in 1984. Several new advanced weapons systems – for example F-16s, Harpoon anti-ship missiles, and Patriot air defense missiles – have been sold to Taiwan since then.

Thus, even after the signing of the August 17 communiqué, the United States continued to make significant arms sales to Taiwan. Under Reagan, for example, such sales included:

- August 1982. Northrop Corporation and Taiwan were allowed to co-produce an additional 30 F-5Es and 30 F-5Fs, a package worth $622 million
- February 1983. 66 F-105G fighters, previously owned by West Germany: $31 million
- July 1983. Chaparral missiles, SM-1 Standard missiles, AIM-7F Sparrow missiles, conversion kits for M-4 tanks, tank-recovery vehicles, and aircraft spare parts: $530 million
- May 1984. Anti-aircraft missiles: $291 million
- September 1984. 12 C-130 transport aircraft: $325 million
- February 1985. Radar and spare parts for the F-5, F-100, T-33 and T-28: $86 million
- April 1985. Tank hulls: $60 million
- June 1985. 262 Chaparral missiles: $94 million
- Early 1986. 200 MGM-71 TOW anti-tank missiles: $15.6 million
- August 1986. S-2T anti-submarine airplane engines and avionics: $260 million.

As mentioned earlier, after 1982 but especially from 1986, the Reagan administration shifted its strategy of arms sales somewhat, concentrating more on technology transfers as a means of building up the ROC's defense industrial capacity. This effort has been successful to some extent, but the cost-per-unit for Taiwan has been large. Examples of well-known US technology sales and transfers to Taiwan include:

- 1983. General Dynamics, Lear Siegler and other American companies help Taiwan design and develop an indigenous defense fighter (IDF), enabling Taiwan to produce 130 Ching-kuo fighters.
- 1987. Bath Ironworks and Taiwan's China Shipbuilding Corporation agreed to build eight modified FFG-7 (redesignated PFG-2) Oliver Hazard Perry-class frigates for $1.6 billion.

The close interrelationship between Taiwan's locally produced weapons and US technology is difficult to trace in its entirety and government officials are reluctant to discuss it. However, there is ample evidence that it does exist at the multibillion dollar level. Dennis Hickey, for example, has provided interesting statistics on the number of Commodity Control List 'dual-use' licenses approved by the US Department of Defense for export to Taiwan. Of particular importance were items such as electronic assemblies and integrated circuits, computing equipment and electronic machinery. According to an October 1992 letter from the Department of Commerce to Senator John C. Danforth, 'applications approved for Taiwan during the period January 1, 1988 through December 31, 1991 totaled 11,601, representing 221 commodity control numbers and the total dollar value was \$23,439,176,150'.[23]

Given extensive technology transfers, it is not surprising to find that many of the weapons produced on Taiwan bear a strong resemblance to their American counterparts. Examples are the Tien Kung (Sky Bow) air defense system, similar to the Patriot system; the Chang Bai air defense system, similar to the Aegis system; the Tien Chien (Sky Sword) air-to-air missile, similar to the AIM-9; and the Hsiung Feng (Male Bee) anti-ship missile, the latest version of which is similar to the Harpoon.

Arms sales list

Despite the new emphasis on technology transfers, sale of dual-use items, and production cooperation, the level of US arms sales to Taiwan continued to remain high. Examples of sales during the Bush and first-year Clinton administrations include:

- May 1989. Spare parts, including radar, for F-5s, F-100s, F-104s, T-33s, T-28s and C-130s: \$108 million
- 1989. 88 Standard missiles: \$44 million
- September 1991. 110 M60A3 tanks: \$119 million
- 1992. 8 C-130 transport planes: approximately \$25 million
- 1992. 42 AH-1W Super Cobra attack gunships: \$828 million
- 1992. 26 OH-58D Kiowa Warrior scout helicopters: \$367 million
- July 1992. Three leased Knox-class frigates worth \$230 million; six more to be acquired in 1994 and 1995
- August 1992. 207 SM-1 Standard missiles: \$126 million
- September 1992. President George Bush announces US will sell Taiwan 150 F-16 Mid-Life Upgrade fighters valued at \$6 billion
- October 1992. 12 Kaman SH-2F light airborne multi-purpose system ASW helicopters and 12 spare engines: \$161 million
- November 1992. 180 engines and spare parts for F-16s: \$1 billion
- March 1993. 4 E-2T Hawkeye early-warning command and control aircraft: \$900 million (other sources say \$760 million)[24]
- March 1993. Taiwan and Raytheon Company, manufacturer of the Patriot missile system, negotiate the co-production of the hardware and software for a Patriot derivative known as the modified air defense systems (MADS). MADS would replace Taiwan's existing air defense system, based on the Nike: \$1.3 billion
- September 1993. 41 Harpoon anti-ship missiles: \$68 million
- October 1993. Reported that the United States would sell Taiwan the Stinger ground-to-air missile installed on military vehicles[25]

- April 1994. ROC army announces it would purchase 200 Patriot missiles at a cost of about $377 million[26]
- August 1994. ROC army announces it had purchased 160 M-60A3 tanks, equipped with thermal sights, from the United States at a cost of $91 million.[27]

According to information compiled by the Federation of American Scientists from the Federal Register, the following notifications of proposed sales to Taiwan were sent to Congress by the Clinton administration from December 1993 to October 1998. These sales, leases and transfers include government-negotiated foreign military sales (FMS), reduced price or free excess defense article transfers (EDA), and industry-negotiated direct commercial sales (DCS). None of these proposed transfers to Taiwan – listed below by date, item, and transfer type and cost where available – was challenged by the Congress.[28]

- December 1, 1993. 1 Mk41 vertical launch system, equipment and support: DCS, $103 million
- December 10, 1993. 65 20 mm M61AE2 cannon for indigenous defense fighter: DCS, $14 million
- May 18, 1994. 3 Newport-class tank landing ships: 2-year lease, $4.7 million
- June 9, 1994. 20 AT-38 and 40 T-38 trainer aircraft, 18 spare engines, spares and support: lease, free
- June 29, 1994. License to manufacture SINCGARS radios: DCS, $50 million
- August 1, 1994. 80 Raytheon AN/ALQ-184 ECM pods, spares and support: FMS, $150 million
- September 13, 1994. 1 FMC Mk-45 5-inch gun, spares and support: FMS, $21 million
- March 24, 1995. 6 OTO Melara Mk-75 guns, 5 Hughes PHALANX 20 mm guns, ammunition, spares and support: FMS, $75 million
- April 6, 1995. Manufacturing lease for mortar and artillery shells: DCS, $50 million
- June 8, 1995. Cooperative Logistics Supply Support Agreement to support aircraft, radars, and avionics: FMS, $192 million
- July 13, 1995. 21 Northrop Grumman AT-38B trainer aircraft: 2-year lease, free
- February 9, 1996. 3 Knox-class frigates: EDA, $8.3 million
- March 5, 1996. 8 M-48A2 Chaparral anti-aircraft missile launchers, 148 Chaparral anti-aircraft missiles: EDA, $2.5 million
- May 10, 1996. GTE tactical communications system: FMS, $188 million

- May 10, 1996. 30 Bell Textron TH-67 training helicopters, 30 sets of AN/AVS-6 night-vision goggles, support: FMS, $53 million
- May 17, 1996. Tank landing ship: lease, free
- May 23, 1996. 465 Hughes Stinger-RMP missiles, 55 dual-mounted Stinger missile launch systems, 55 trainer missiles, spares: FMS, $84 million
- June 24, 1996. 300 M60A3 main battle tanks with thermal sights and 105 mm gun, 30 spare tank engines, 315 PVS-7B night-vision goggles, 330 M240 machine guns, smoke-grenade launchers, support and training: EDA/FMS, $223 million
- August 23, 1996. 1,299 Stinger-RMP missiles, 74 standard vehicle-mounted launchers, 96 high-mobility multi-purpose wheeled vehicles (HMMWV), 74 trainer missiles, 500 rounds .50 caliber ammunition: FMS, $420 million
- September 5, 1996. 110 Alliant Techsystems MK-46 MOD 5 torpedoes: FMS, $66 million
- December 9, 1996. Tank-landing ship *Sumter* and equipment: lease, $11.2 million, rental charge of $5.1 million
- February 1, 1997. 114 SM-1 Block VIB Standard missiles in lieu of 114 SM-1 Block VIA Standard missiles sold August 4, 1992: FMS, unknown cost
- February 14, 1997. 54 McDonnell Douglas Harpoon ship-to-ship missiles and equipment: FMS, $95 million
- February 25, 1997. Improved radar warning receiver (IRWR) production system, associated support equipment, test equipment and spares: DCS, $14 million
- April 10, 1997. Tank landing ship *Newport* (LST 1179) and associated equipment: 2-year lease, $3.05 million
- April 10, 1997. Rocsat I scientific satellite along with associated hardware and ground support equipment: DCS, unknown cost
- April 21, 1997. 2 Knox-class frigates, to be sold as logistics assets: EDA, $4.5 million
- May 7, 1997. Gun mount, barrel and power panel for the 5-inch 54 naval gun: EDA, $89,000
- May 23, 1997. 1,786 TOW 2A anti-armor guided missiles and 114 TOW launchers, made by Hughes Aircraft Co., 100 M1045A2 HMMWV trucks, spare parts, program support: FMS, $80 million
- June 18, 1997. Excess Knox-class training devices: EDA, $27,400
- July 24, 1997. 21 Bell Textron AH-1W Super Cobra attack helicopters, spares, training and support: FMS, $479 million
- September 3, 1997. 13 Bell OH-58D Kiowa Warrior armed scout

helicopters, 13 engines, 13 Hellfire rocket launchers, rockets, ammunition: FMS, $172 million

- November 10, 1997. Continuation of pilot training program and logistical support for F-16 aircraft, including parts, fuels and support: FMS, $280 million
- November 10, 1997. Spare parts for F-5B/E/F, F-104, C-130, C-119, C-47 and T-38 aircraft and for US systems and subsystems in the IDF aircraft: FMS, $140 million
- November 24, 1997. 3 Knox-class frigates and associated equipment: lease, unknown cost
- January 28, 1998. 3 Knox-class frigates, 15 Phalanx close-in weapons systems and 30,000 rounds of 22 mm ammunition, AN/SWG-1A Harpoon launcher: FMS, $300 million
- February 18, 1998. 4 S-70A helicopters: DCS, $14 million
- February 24, 1998. Licensed production of 40 mm ammunition: DCS, unknown cost
- March 5, 1998. Chaparral system equipment and support: EDA, unknown cost
- March 5, 1998. 2 harbor tugs: EDA, unknown cost
- March 5, 1998. 100 Hughes SM-1 Standard medium-range missiles: EDA, unknown cost
- March 17, 1998. 2 ambient noise buoys: lease, unknown cost
- April 13, 1998. Knox-class frigate: lease, unknown cost
- June 1, 1998. 28 sets of Pathfinder/Sharpshooter navigation and targeting pods, integration of the pods with the F-16A/B aircraft, flight testing, personnel training and training equipment, publications and technical data, US government and contractor engineering and logistics personnel services, spare and repair parts, support: FMS, $160 million
- July 20, 1998. Licensed production, involving the transfer of 77 F124 aircraft engines to the Czech Republic for use on L-159 aircraft: DCS, unknown cost
- August 27, 1998. 61 dual-mount Stinger missile systems consisting of 61 dual-mount Stinger (DMS) launchers, 61 Stinger RMP captive flight trainers, 728 complete Stinger RMP missile rounds, 132 AN/VRC-91 export version SINCGAR radios, spare and repair parts, support equipment, Interrogator Friend or Foe sets, interrogator programmers, utility carrier trucks, aerial flight handling and launcher trainers, and various other elements of logistics support: FMS, $180 million
- August 27, 1998. 131 MK-46 MOD 5 (A)S torpedoes, containers, support and test equipment, publications and technical documentation, engineering and technical assistance, supply support and other

related elements of logistics support: FMS, $69 million

- September 15, 1998. 58 Harpoon missiles, 8 Harpoon training missiles, containers, Harpoon interface adapter kits, parts, equipment, training, and other support: FMS, $101 million
- September 22, 1998. Knox-class frigate (USS *Kirk* – FF1087) and associated equipment: lease, $8.2 million
- October 9, 1998. 9 CH-47SD Chinook helicopters, chaff, radar warning receiver, 3 T-55-L-714A spare turbine engines, spare and repair parts, support equipment, publications and technical data, communications equipment, maintenance, personnel training, and other related elements of support: FMS, $486 million.

Not reported by the FAS was the approval in March 1998 for an unspecified number of AGM-65 Maverick missiles to be used in F-16 air-to-ground missions, along with air-launched Harpoon missiles.[29]

According to *The Military Balance: 1998/99*, Taiwan had the following arms orders and deliveries in the pipeline during the period 1996–98:[30]

- Patriot surface-to-air missile (SAM). 6 units ordered from the United States in 1993 and delivered in 1997; to be deployed in 1998
- Sky Halberd surface-to-surface missile. Unknown number of units to be produced domestically with order placed in 1984 and delivered in 1997
- Indigenous defense fighter with ground attack capabilities (FGA). 130 units first delivered in 1994 and scheduled to be completed in 1998
- Mirage 2000-5 fighter (FGA). 60 units ordered from France in 1992 with delivery to begin in 1997 (the last of the Mirages arrived in Taiwan in October 1998)
- F-16A/B fighter (FGA). 150 units ordered from the United States in 1992 with delivery to begin in 1997 (more than 100 had been received as of December 1998)
- AT-3 trainer aircraft. 40 units to be produced domestically with orders placed in 1997
- S-70C search-and-rescue helicopter. 4 units ordered from the United States in 1994 with 1998 delivery date
- LaFayette-class frigate. 6 units ordered from France in 1992 with final deliveries through 1998
- Perry-class frigate. 7 units ordered from the United States in 1979 with last commissioned in 1998
- Knox-class frigate. 5 units ordered from the United States in 1997 with deliveries to begin in 1998 (later reported to be 6 frigates to be purchased by Taiwan)[31]

- Newport-class tank landing ship. 2 leased from the United States in 1994 with deliveries in 1997 (later to be purchased by Taiwan)
- Kuang Hua IV-class missile-armed fast patrol craft. 50 units to be produced domestically, with orders placed in 1998 and deliveries to begin in 2001
- M-60A3 main battle tank. 340 units ordered from the United States in 1995 with deliveries to begin in 1997
- M 109A5 artillery. 28 units ordered from the United States in 1995 with delivery scheduled for 1998
- AH-1W attack helicopter. 21 units ordered from the United States in 1997 and scheduled for delivery in 2000
- OH-58D armed scout helicopter. 13 ordered from the United States in 1998, with deliveries scheduled for 2001
- TH-67 helicopter. 30 ordered from the United States in 1996 with deliveries in 1998
- Stinger SAM. 465 ordered from the United States in 1996 and scheduled for 1998 delivery
- Mistral SAM. 550 ordered from France in 1995 and scheduled for delivery in 1997
- Avenger SAM. 74 ordered from the United States in 1996 and scheduled for delivery in 1998.

A quick review of articles and newspapers from 1998 up to spring 1999 revealed a further wide range of additional weapons then being sought by Taiwan and under consideration by the United States:

- According to *Jane's Defence Weekly*, analysts believed that Taiwan needed a range of new equipment such as Aegis-type vessels, the Lockheed Martin P-3 Orion maritime patrol aircraft, and the AIM-120A advanced medium-range air-to-air missile.[32]
- According to *Defense News*, Taiwan wanted the United States to lift restrictions on the range, endurance and payload capabilities of unmanned aerial vehicles sold to the ROC so it may better monitor PLA deployments across the Taiwan Strait. Medium-altitude systems such as the USAF's Predator and discontinued US army's Hunter system were attracting interest in Taipei.[33]
- According to a Taipei newspaper, the ROC army formed a special 'Cheetah' panel to determine which second-generation main battle tank should replace its existing inventory. Some 700 to 1,000 tanks of the M1A1/A2-class were being considered, at an estimated cost of $5–8 billion.[34]
- According to reports from AFP in Hong Kong, Taiwan wanted to

purchase at least four Aegis-class destroyers at a cost of $1.2 billion each.[35]

- According to a Taiwan newspaper, the ROC military would once again request during its April 1999 US–Taiwan arms sales meeting that the United States sell to the ROC several 209-model conventionally powered submarines. The 209 was designed by Germany and manufactured in the United States.[36] Earlier, another Taiwan source said Taiwan would build between six and ten of the submarines under a program 'domestically manufactured using foreign technology'.[37]

- According to reports from Taiwan, the United States had agreed to sell the ROC military man-portable Stinger missiles, in addition to those vehicle-mounted in the Avenger system.[38]

Taiwan's interest and possible participation in theater missile defense (TMD), including the purchase of advanced radars and Patriot-3 missiles, will be discussed in Chapter 8.

Additional considerations

It should be noted in passing at this point that Congress pushes the envelope of US arms sales to Taiwan. One example was the 1993–94 Murkowski amendment to the TRA, which eventually was written as a section in the FY 1994–95 State Department Authorization Bill signed into law by President Clinton as Public Law 103-236. As discussed in Chapter 7, this congressional initiative prodded the administration to sell Taiwan radar, electronic countermeasures, and an entire electronic combat suite for the six LaFayette frigates Taipei had earlier purchased from France. Although its impact has yet to be determined, S. 693 (the Taiwan Security Enhancement Act), introduced by Senators Helms and Torricelli in March 1999, specifically instructed the Department of Defense to sell Taiwan AIM-120 AMRAAM air-to-air missiles, additional advanced fighters, advanced AWACS systems, diesel-powered submarines and Aegis destroyers. It should come as no surprise if these and other advanced sales are made over the next few years.

Most weapons sold to Taiwan have come from the United States. Arms sales from third countries have been effectively deterred by PRC threats of retaliation. An example is the case of the sale of two Dutch Zwaardvis-class submarines to Taiwan in 1980–81. Built by the Dutch Rotterdamse Droogdok Mij (RDM) shipyard and delivered to Taiwan in the late 1980s, the sale prompted the PRC to downgrade relations with the Dutch government to the level of chargé d'affaires in January 1981. The strong PRC reaction to the Dutch sale is credited with having helped to persuade the Reagan administration not to proceed with the FX fighter sale to Taiwan in January 1982.[39]

In 1991 France sold Taiwan six LaFayette-class frigates for $4.8 billion. In 1993 Taipei consummated the purchase of 60 Mirage 2000-5 fighters and some 1,500 Mica air-to-air missiles from France for $6 billion. In retaliation to these arms sales, Beijing closed the French consulate in Guangzhou and banned French companies from participating in several major infrastructure projects. Finally bowing to PRC pressure, Paris agreed in January 1994 to sign a communiqué in which 'the French Government pledges not to authorize French enterprises to participate in arming Taiwan in the future'.[40]

The level of these arms sales – mostly from the United States but with significant French additions in the areas of air defense fighters and frigates – strongly suggests, first, that Taiwan has a substantial military force for its self-defense and, second, that Washington, at least, has a vested interest in ensuring that Taiwan is not defeated by the PLA. Still, the United States does not give Taiwan carte blanche in its arms sale requests. Indeed, there are many restrictions imposed on US arms sales.

Restrictions on US arms sales to Taiwan
In addition to the well-known limitation that only defensive systems are to be sold to Taiwan, the US government since 1979 has self-imposed many other restrictions on the weapons sold to the ROC. A few examples will suffice.

For many years Taiwan tried without success to acquire navigation and targeting pods for the F-16s it purchased from the United States. Finally, in June 1998, the United States agreed to sell Taiwan 28 sets of Pathfinder and Sharpshooter pods for $160 million. According to US government sources quoted by *Defense News*, the decision to release the export version of LANTIRN (low-altitude navigation and targeting infrared system for night) had been made two years previously, but no notification was sent to Congress to avoid a harsh PRC reaction. When the announcement was made in mid-1998, the United States decided to strip the pods of their laser designators and special sights required for precision strike missions, thereby limiting considerably the effectiveness of the F-16, in order to deflate PRC protests.[41]

In a February 1999 essay written for the Taiwan Research Institute, former US defense official Carl Ford cited several other 'silly rules and regulations that not only harm the island's ability to defend itself, but in the future could also put American military personnel in jeopardy'.[42] Examples cited by Ford included:

- The E-2Ts (T = Taiwan version) sold to Taiwan were required to contain parts salvaged from aircraft no longer in service.
- US assistance to the IDF was highly restricted, not allowing existing

US military engines because they were 'too capable' and seriously limiting the aircraft's armaments and avionics.

- The F-16s sold to Taiwan had severely limited armaments and avionics.
- The United States keeps working-level contacts between the US and Taiwan militaries 'to a bare minimum', eliminating 'almost entirely operational interactions'.
- The US military cannot communicate directly with Taiwan, 'even for safety precautions involved with air and naval transits through the region'.

Thus, while very significant US arms transfers to Taiwan have taken place, there are also severe restrictions on what the United States sells to Taiwan. These restrictive guidelines reflect American ambiguity toward the Taiwan issue in general: simply put, Washington wants the best of all worlds, maintaining a cooperative strategic partnership with the PRC and continued close ties to the people of Taiwan. These arms sales guidelines also are designed to serve US interests in preserving peace in the Taiwan Strait and in sustaining a favorable balance of power in the region. Since there is no indication that these fundamental American interests will change, US arms sales policy will likely remain unaltered in the foreseeable future – that is, the United States will try to ensure that Taiwan is able, with American backing, to deter PRC aggression, yet also to ensure that Taipei is not strong enough to declare the island an independent nation-state, or otherwise unduly provoke Beijing.

CONCLUSION

The objective of this chapter has been to introduce several key factors contributing to Taiwan's security equation in the post-Deng era. First, the chapter explained why the recovery of control over Taiwan is so impor-tant to mainland China, not merely for reasons of national sovereignty but also because Taiwan can play a key role in the future great power status of China, especially if Beijing pursues maritime ambitions. Second, the chapter outlined the many US interests in Taiwan and explained American concern over the future of the island and its relationship with mainland China. Third, the chapter examined the relative military balance of power across the Taiwan Strait, noting especially the impor-tance of each side's military modernization. And fourth, the chapter detailed the extent of US arms sales to Taiwan, without which ROC armed forces would be highly vulnerable to PRC military pressure.

In addition to these factors, Taiwan's security is heavily dependent upon whether a peaceful resolution of the differences between Beijing and Taipei is likely or even possible. The next chapter, therefore, will consider the probability of China's unification by reviewing PRC and ROC proposals for reconciliation and by reviewing domestic political opposition to the official policies of Taipei and Beijing.

NOTES

1. Chu Shulong, 'The Second PRC–US War: International Involvement in China's Unification', in Greg Austin, ed., *Missile Diplomacy and Taiwan's Future: Innovations in Politics and Military Power* (Canberra: Strategic and Defence Studies Centre, Australian National University, 1997), pp. 227–39.
2. In this 1993 incident, the United States accused China of shipping chemicals for mustard gas and nerve gas on the Chinese cargo ship *Yinhe*, destined for Iran, in violation of the newly negotiated Chemical Weapons Convention. After heated diplomatic exchanges, the ship was inspected by American officials in the Saudi port of Damman in September. No trace of the banned chemicals was found, and the PRC Foreign Ministry made much of this example of 'a show of hegemony and power politics, pure and simple'. See *Beijing Review*, September 13–19, 1993, p. 4.
3. For a brief history of (mostly) well-meaning Western attempts to change China into something more acceptable to Western standards, see Jonathan Spence, *To Change China: Western Advisers in China, 1620–1960* (New York: Penguin Books, 1980).
4. Jiang Minfang and Duan Zhaoxian, 'Taiwan zhanlue diwei danxi' (The Analysis of Taiwan's Strategic Position), *The Navy* 8 (1995), p. 9. Cited in You Ji, 'Missile Diplomacy and PRC Domestic Politics', in Austin, *Missile Diplomacy and Taiwan's Future*, pp. 46–7.
5. Lu Junyuan, 'Taiwan's Geostrategic Value Makes Reunification Essential', *Taiwan Studies* (Beijing), March 20, 1996, as translated in Foreign Broadcast Information Service, *Daily Report: China* (henceforth, *FBIS-China*), March 20, 1996.
6. Hsiao Peng, 'The Mainland Defines Phased Targets of Cross-Strait Reunification', Hong Kong *Sing Tao Jih Pao*, January 19, 1999, in *FBIS-China*, January 19, 1999.
7. The term 'New Taiwanese' has become prominent on Taiwan in recent years. It symbolizes an identification of Taiwan as being 'home' to all residents of the island, whether 'Taiwanese' or 'mainlander'.
8. International Institute for Strategic Studies, *The Military Balance: 1998/99* (London: Oxford University Press, 1998).
9. Jamestown Foundation *Monitor* 4, 196 (October 23, 1998), citing *Russky Telegraf*, January 29, 1998; and *Itar-Tass*, October 20, 1998.
10. See, for example, Fong Tak-ho and Michelle Lee, 'Beijing Expected to Strengthen Military Against Taiwan', *Hong Kong Standard*, March 2, 1999, in *FBIS-China*, March 2, 1999.
11. Barbara Opall-Rome, 'China Sets Sights on 50 Su-30s', *Defense News This Week*, July 5, 1999. See also Richard D. Fisher, Jr., 'China's New Jets Will Increase Taiwan's Vulnerability', *Taipei Times*, June 30, 1999, p. 9.
12. General Shalikashvili said on February 15, 1996: 'We do not believe that [the Chinese] have the capability to conduct amphibious operations of the nature that would be necessary to invade Taiwan.' Reuters report from Washington DC, February 15, 1996; also Associated Press report from Washington DC, February

15, 1996.

13. An older but still useful discussion of PRC advantages and risks in a blockade of Taiwan can be found in Martin L. Lasater, ed., *Beijing's Blockade Threat to Taiwan* (Washington DC: Heritage Foundation, 1985).

14. 'Tang Fei: Taiwan Can Match PRC's Armed Forces Until 2005', Taiwan Central News Agency, March 24, 1999, in *FBIS-China*, March 24, 1999.

15. Department of Defense, 'The Security Situation in the Taiwan Strait' (Washington DC: Department of Defense, February 1999). See Appendix 2.

16. See Luo Kwang-zen and Ben Wu, 'Military Procurement Under TRA Outlined', Taiwan Central News Agency, March 16, 1999, in *FBIS-China*, March 16, 1999. For more detail, see Martin L. Lasater, *The Security of Taiwan: Unraveling the Dilemma* (Georgetown University Press, 1982), *Taiwan: Facing Mounting Threats* (Heritage Foundation, 1987), *U.S. Interests in the New Taiwan* (Westview, 1993) and *The Changing of the Guard: President Clinton and the Security of Taiwan* (Westview, 1995).

17. S. I. Hayakawa, 'Ambiguity: The China Syndrome', *New York Times*, August 30, 1982, p. A17.

18. Alexander Haig was asked to resign by President Reagan because the Secretary of State and others in the State Department misled the president, vice-president, national security adviser, and the Congress over secret drafts of the August 17 communiqué. Senator Barry Goldwater commented: 'It was clear to me and to the White House that President Reagan, Vice President Bush, and National Security Adviser William Clark had been lied to by the State Department about what they were planning.' See *Washington Times*, July 2, 1982, p. 1; *Washington Post*, July 2, 1982, p. A26.

19. Prepared statement of Davis R. Robinson, Legal Adviser, Department of State, given before US Congress, Senate, Committee on the Judiciary, Subcommittee on Separation of Powers, September 27, 1982, ms.

20. *Washington Post*, March 22, 1983, p. A12.

21. Barbara Opall-Rome, 'Will Boost C4i Focus, Slow Arms Purchases', *Defense News*, November 30, 1998, p. 4.

22. Barbara Opall-Rome, 'U.S., Taiwan Mull Expanded Training', *Defense News*, December 7, 1998, p. 32.

23. Letter from Jim LeMunyon, Acting Assistant Secretary, US Department of Commerce, to Senator John C. Danforth, October 29, 1992. See n. 7 in Chapter 4, in Dennis Van Vranken Hickey, *United States–Taiwan Security Ties* (Westport CT: Praeger, 1994), p. 47. The Hickey book discusses this aspect of US–Taiwan military cooperation in considerable detail.

24. *Free China Journal*, March 25, 1994, p. 1.

25. *Far Eastern Economic Review*, November 4, 1993, p. 15.

26. *Free China Journal*, April 22, 1994, p. 1.

27. *Free China Journal*, September 2, 1994, p. 1.

28. Information compiled by the Federation of American Scientists, Arms Sales Monitoring Project, as available from the FAS internet homepage, January 1999.

29. Barbara Opall-Rome, 'China Hits Lantirn Sale To Taiwan/US Removes Pod's Laser Designator; Beijing Urges Arms Ban', *Defense News*, June 8, 1998, p. 3.

30. International Institute for Strategic Studies, *The Military Balance: 1998/99*, Table 23, pp. 171–2.

31. 'Taiwan to Upgrade Knox Class Frigates', Taipei *Lien-Ho Pao*, July 20, 1998, in *FBIS-China*, July 22, 1998.

32. *Jane's Defence Weekly*, Interview with ROC General Tang Fei, Vol. 30, No. 1 (July 8, 1998).

33. Barbara Opall-Rome, 'Taiwan, US Wrangle Over Uav Sale Restrictions', *Defense News*, December 14, 1998, p. 8.
34. Lu Te-yun, 'Army to Purchase 700–1,000 Tanks for Replacement', Taipei *Lien-Ho Pao*, March 1, 1999, in *FBIS-China*, March 1, 1999.
35. 'Taiwan Plans to Buy 4 Advanced U.S.-Built Destroyers', Hong Kong AFP, February 28, 1999, in *FBIS-China*, February 28, 1999.
36. 'Military to Persuade U.S. To Sell It Submarines', Taipei *Tzu-Li Wan-Pao*, February 22, 1999, in *FBIS-China*, February 22, 1999.
37. 'Taiwan To Acquire Diesel Submarines from U.S.', *Lien-Ho Pao*, January 18, 1999, in *FBIS-China*, January 18, 1999.
38. Lin Chien-hua, 'Military Impact of U.S. Sale of Stingers Assessed', *Tzu-Li Wan-Pao*, August 28, 1998, in *FBIS-China*, September 3, 1998.
39. For the connection between the Dutch submarine sale and the FX, see Martin L. Lasater, *Policy in Evolution: The U.S. Role in China's Reunification* (Boulder CO: Westview, 1989), pp. 43–6.
40. *New York Times*, January 13, 1994, p. A11; *Far Eastern Economic Review*, January 27, 1994, pp. 12–14.
41. Barbara Opall-Rome, 'China Hits Lantirn Sale to Taiwan/U.S. Removes Pod's Laser Designator; Beijing Urges Arms Ban', *Defense News*, June 8, 1998, p. 3.
42. Carl Ford, 'America's Illogical Rules Make for Dangerous Policy in the Taiwan Strait', essay prepared for Taiwan Research Institute (Taipei), February 24, 1999, made available on the Taiwan Security Research website.

2

Chinese Unification Policies

Martin L. Lasater

With the return of Hong Kong to Chinese sovereignty in 1997 and the return of Macau in 1999, the reunification of Taiwan with the mainland has become one of the most important goals of the PRC government. No exact timetable for unification has been set – at least publicly – but several dates such as 2005, 2010 and even 2020 have been tossed around as deadlines to achieve unification or to have in place the mechanisms for unification. Regardless of the exact timetable, Beijing has been clear that unification cannot be postponed indefinitely. Vice Premier Qian Qichen, for example, said in late January 1999: 'As Hong Kong has returned to the motherland and Macao will hand over its government on 20 December 1999, the resolution of the Taiwan issue can no longer be delayed indefinitely.'[1] Hong Kong's *Sing Tao Jih Pao* reported in mid-January 1999:

> It has been learned that the highest CPC echelons maintain that within two to three years after the reversion of Macao this year, Taiwan must clearly indicate whether it will take the road of peace talks and peaceful reunification or resist the mainland, namely, reunifying the country through force. In this connection, new Taiwan leaders after Li Teng-hui will be given time to make their own choice. At present, they will not be forced to make their decision. The Taiwan authorities are not allowed to stall for time indefinitely, however.[2]

It would appear from these and similar statements that Beijing does not expect much progress toward unification as long as President Lee Teng-hui is in office. Further, it may be inferred that Beijing does not intend to resolve the issue through forceful means for several more years – although this does not exclude military pressure being exerted on Taiwan, such as was seen in 1995 and 1996. Since ROC presidential elections are slated for March 2000, and Lee has said he will not run for re-election – although some observers insist he would do so if the Kuomintang (KMT) looked as if it might be defeated by the opposition Democratic Progressive Party (DPP) – the time frame the PRC may be using for positive signs of Taipei's willingness to enter into serious political talks about the future of China could be 2003–5. If no such sign is forthcoming, then China may decide to ratchet upward its pressure on Taiwan and begin preparations in earnest for a possible use of force. It will be recalled from the previous chapter that the period beyond 2005 is also one of projected Taiwan vulnerability, if current trends of military modernization continue on both sides of the Taiwan Strait.

In terms of Taiwan's security, therefore, an essential question is whether Taipei and Beijing will be able to resolve their differences through peaceful means. The purpose of this chapter is to explore the possibility of a peaceful resolution of the Taiwan issue. Several factors will be considered: first, the major PRC and ROC proposals for a resolution of differences across the Taiwan Strait; second, each side's response to the other's proposals; third, the nature and extent of cross-Strait exchanges; and, fourth, the views and strength of domestic PRC and ROC opposition to the cross-Strait policies of Beijing and Taipei. Since these factors are highly interrelated and tend to evolve in tandem, they will be discussed in a more-or-less historical fashion. A concluding section in the chapter will assess the overall probability of continued peaceful interaction between the two sides and the implications for Taiwan's security.

BACKGROUND

Beijing now warns that its patience on the Taiwan issue is nearing an end, but that has not always been the case. Prior to the Nationalist takeover of Taiwan from Japan at the close of the Second World War, the Chinese Communist Party held little interest in Taiwan. Mao Zedong, for example, told Edgar Snow in 1936 that both Korea and Taiwan should be independent countries, vowing communist support to that end.[3] And Taiwan's Democratic Progressive Party (DPP) – pro-independence and a serious contender to one day become the ruling party on Taiwan – delights in pointing out statements from earlier Chinese leaders suggesting that Taiwan is not part of China:

> Taiwan has never been part of China. (Manchu Emperor Yung-Cheng, 1684)
> We advocate the independence of the Taiwanese nationality. (Dr. Sun Yat-sen, 1925)
> We must restore the independence and freedom of the brethren in Korea and Taiwan. (General Chiang Kai-shek, 1938).[4]

Once Taiwan became refuge for Chiang Kai-shek and the remnants of the ROC government in 1949, the Chinese communists became adamant in their determination to capture the island and bring the long Chinese civil war to a close. At first, the administration of Harry Truman did not intend to prevent the communist takeover of Taiwan – nominally because of lack of available resources. The newly formed National Security Council noted that, 'while Formosa is strategically important to the United States, the strategic importance of Formosa does not justify overt military action ... so long as the present disparity between our military strength and our global obligations exist'.[5] Secretary of State Dean Acheson in January 1950 specifically excluded Taiwan (along with Korea) in the island chain 'defensive perimeter' which the United States intended to defend in the Far East.[6] Nonetheless, when the Korean War broke out in June 1950, Taiwan's strategic importance in the island chain immediately became apparent. Truman quickly interposed the Seventh Fleet into the Taiwan Strait as part of his efforts to ensure that communist aggression did not occur elsewhere in the Pacific. The president instructed the Seventh Fleet to prevent a PRC attack against Taiwan and to prevent an ROC attack against the mainland.[7]

Truman's actions foreclosed the possibility of Taiwan's capture by the communists and initiated the current period of de facto separation of China into two parts, each administered by a sovereign Chinese government: the People's Republic of China on the mainland and the Republic of China on Taiwan. Until the present day, the heart of the Taiwan issue has been the political competition between two rival Chinese governments and US interests in containing a potentially hostile PRC.

Although there were brief periods of military confrontation in the Taiwan Strait – primarily focused on the offshore islands of Quemoy (Kinmen) and Matsu during 1954–55, 1958 and 1962 – the PRC was unable either to conquer Taiwan or persuade the ROC under Chiang Kai-shek and his successor son Chiang Ching-kuo to rejoin the motherland. PRC policy toward Taiwan was described in terms of 'liberation', often by military means. In March 1978, for instance, Premier Hua Guofeng told the Fifth National Party Congress: 'The Chinese People's Liberation Army must make all the preparations necessary for the liberation of Taiwan.'[8] And in September of that year, Vice Premier Li Xiannian said to Japanese visitors, 'Whether by peaceable means or by force, we must consider the liberation of Taiwan from an overall strategic standpoint.'[9]

In late 1978, however, a significant change in strategy toward Taiwan was approved at the Third Plenary Session of the Eleventh Party Central Committee. It was decided to reject 'armed liberation' and 'peaceful liberation' and to adopt instead a strategy of 'peaceful reunification'.[10] It is important to note that this new approach to Taiwan was made possible by (a) the consolidation of Deng Xiaoping's power; (b) the adoption of the 'four modernizations' as the pragmatic basis for China's economic development; (c) the normalization of relations with the United States and greater opening to the outside world; and (d) Chinese concerns about aggressive Soviet behavior in Afghanistan and elsewhere around China's periphery, including the Soviet-backed Vietnamese invasion of Cambodia. As part of its new policy package, the CCP leadership also decided to teach a military lesson to Hanoi – a move some have interpreted as Deng's strategy to win the support of military conservatives who hesitated to embrace his open-door policies and pragmatism in economic affairs.

Although the Moscow and Hanoi factors have largely faded, the linkage between Deng's policy of peaceful reunification – carried forward by his successor Jiang Zemin – and normal relations with the United States, openness to the outside world, and pragmatic (that is, some market-oriented) approaches to China's modernization remain very much in place. In other words, PRC policies toward Taiwan can be viewed as part of a policy package supported by moderate elements within the CCP leadership. If the moderate leadership is one day replaced by more ideologically oriented leaders or ultra-nationalists or isolationists, then policies toward Taiwan – as well as policies toward the United States, the outside world in general, and methods of modernizing China – may change.

This linkage has important implications for Taiwan's security:

- PRC policy toward Taiwan can be highly controversial in Beijing; Taiwan policy can be used by various factions to further their larger political agenda.
- PRC policy toward Taiwan is tied closely to Sino-American relations, making the Taiwan issue a 'card' to be played by the United States and China, while at the same time giving Taipei considerable leverage over both Washington and Beijing.
- PRC policy toward Taiwan can change fairly rapidly and radically from peaceful reunification to forceful liberation, depending upon the relative balance of political power between moderates and conservatives in the CCP leadership.
- Unless movement toward a peaceful solution is seen over the next few years, it would appear likely that political pressure on Taipei will increase. Without such movement, the potential for an attempted military resolution of the issue might increase dramatically as well.

What follows, then, is a brief summary of the various proposals from both Beijing and Taipei to devise an acceptable formula for unification. What should be kept in mind throughout the discussion is that neither side is willing to sacrifice its interests for the sake of unification. What we see is a 20-year period of tactical bargaining, often searching for the right 'spin' to sound good to foreign – particularly American – audiences. At the end of the century, the two governments had still not yet formally sat down to enter into political talks. This is something Beijing would like to do as soon as possible, but Taipei sees no advantages in doing so. At the same time, however, the two sides have drawn closer together since the mid-1980s through increasingly interdependent commercial and financial ties, as well as the natural attraction of a similar culture.

Given the lack of contact at the government-to-government level and concerned that time may be running out for a peaceful resolution of the Taiwan issue, many Americans, such as former Secretary of Defense William Perry, have offered their good offices in informal 'track-II' approaches to get the two Chinese sides together. The PRC generally welcomes such efforts – because they further the CCP objective of getting Taipei to the negotiating table – but the ROC government, while careful to be polite to American interlocutors, rejects the proffered help.[11] Taipei wants – and needs – to postpone political talks until such time as its negotiating position is much stronger. In essence, the cross-Strait stalemate in existence since 1950 remains alive and well, although some person-to-person, business-to-business and institution-to-institution links have been established and appear to be thriving.

CHINA'S POLICY OF PEACEFUL REUNIFICATION

The 1979 New Year's Day Letter to Taiwan Compatriots from the PRC's National People's Congress Standing Committee ushered in the new period of peaceful reunification. The letter, or 'message', called for Taiwan and the mainland to arrange for mutual visits and tours, establish postal and transportation services, set up various academic and cultural exchanges, and open up trade. Over the years, most of these links and exchanges have been established either formally or informally.

From the outset, the PRC placed conditions on the continuation of its peaceful approach to reunification. Deng Xiaoping, for example, told Senator Sam Nunn in January 1979 that Beijing would still consider the use of force against Taiwan if its authorities refused over a long period of time to enter into negotiations or if there were an attempt by an outside power to interfere in Taiwan affairs. Later that month, Deng told Hedley Donovan of *Time* magazine, 'ten years is too long a time' to wait for reunification.[12] Liao Chengzhi, head of the PRC Office of Overseas Chinese, added a further caveat in May 1979: 'if some countries arm Taiwan in their own interests, and make the Taiwan authorities become self-conceited and disregard the common wish of the entire Chinese people, then we cannot assure definitely not to use means other than peaceful ones'.[13] Earlier, in February 1979, Liao told the National Association of Overseas Chinese: 'After China has achieved peaceful unification the long-term road for Taiwan will be the socialist road. Under the leadership of a single, proletarian political party, there is no reason why one segment should have a socialist system while the other follows the capitalist road.'[14] In January 1981, an editorial in the *Beijing Review* said: 'If we are driven by the Taiwan authorities' adamant refusal to resort to non-peaceful means to solve the issue, that is entirely China's internal affair which the United States has no right to meddle in.'[15]

What should be understood, therefore, is that China's policy of peaceful reunification represented a change in strategy on the part of Beijing; it did not signal a change in the goal of gaining control over Taiwan. Further, there were strict limitations placed on the continuation of a peaceful approach to the Taiwan issue.

Ye Jianying's nine points

The first major PRC proposal for peaceful unification came in Chairman Ye Jianying's 'nine points' of September 30, 1981.[16] The nine points contain the essence of the present PRC approach to resolving the Taiwan issue:

1. Talks between the KMT and the CCP should be held 'on a reciprocal basis' so that national reunification can be achieved.
2. The two sides can 'make arrangements to facilitate the exchange of mails, trade, air and shipping services, and visits by relatives and tourists as well as academic, cultural and sports exchanges'.
3. After reunification, 'Taiwan can enjoy a high degree of autonomy as a special administrative region and it can retain its armed forces'. Also, the PRC 'Central Government will not interfere with local affairs on Taiwan'.
4. After reunification, 'Taiwan's current socio-economic system will remain unchanged, so will its way of life and its economic and cultural relations with foreign countries'. The PRC promised that 'there will be no encroachment on the proprietary rights and lawful right of inheritance over private property, houses, land and enterprises, or on foreign investments'.
5. Various leaders in Taiwan can 'take up posts of leadership in national political bodies and participate in running the state'.
6. The PRC will assist Taiwan economically 'when Taiwan's local finance is in difficulty'.
7. People on Taiwan can have 'freedom of entry and exit' on the mainland, will not be discriminated against, and may live on the mainland if they choose.
8. Taiwan's industrialists and businessmen 'are welcome to invest and engage in various economic undertakings on the mainland, and their legal rights, interests and profits are guaranteed'.

9. All residents of Taiwan were called upon to stick to the 'one-China' principle, oppose the creation of 'two Chinas', and work with the Chinese on the mainland to achieve 'the reunification of the motherland'.

The ROC rejected Ye's proposals in a point-by-point rebuttal published in May 1982.[17] Taipei's reaction to the nine points is worth noting, since it too largely reflects Taiwan's current policy:

1. 'The problem is not talks but two different ways of life.' China should be united but under a system that is free, democratic, and in the interests of the people. Unification under a communist system is not acceptable.
2. The free exchange of mail, trade, visits and services are not available to the people on the mainland, so how can Beijing offer them to the people of Taiwan, who already enjoy those freedoms in any case?
3. Since the ROC already enjoys freedom and has its own armed forces, there is no reason why it should accept Beijing's offer to become a special administrative region.
4. It is naive to think that the communists will allow the capitalist system on Taiwan to remain indefinitely in place.
5. The participation by democratically elected Taiwan leaders in the communist government of the mainland makes little sense.
6. Taiwan does not need the economic assistance of the PRC; indeed, the mainland needs investment and technology from Taiwan.
7. The people of Taiwan already have freedom of movement, and it is unrealistic to expect that the mainland will allow such freedom to Taiwan residents while denying that freedom to its own residents.
8. Taiwan businessmen operating on the mainland have not found their enterprises to be especially profitable.
9. It is hard to imagine that the communist authorities will take policy suggestions from Taiwan seriously, since criticism of CCP policy on the mainland is punishable.

Despite the ROC rejection of Ye's proposal, Beijing amended its constitution in December 1982, with Article 31 providing for 'special administrative regions' within China. The article was specifically designed for Taiwan, Hong Kong and Macau. Peng Zhen, who explained the amendment to the National People's Congress, said that China was unequivocal on the principle of sovereignty, unity and territorial integrity, but that it was highly flexible in terms of specific policies and measures to bring about reunification.[18]

One country, two systems

Deng Xiaoping's concept of peaceful reunification crystallized into the 'one country, two systems' formula during negotiations with the United Kingdom over returning Hong Kong to Chinese sovereignty. Deng explained to a group of Hong Kong businessmen in May 1984 that China had discussed the policy of two systems in one country for several years and that now it had been approved by the National People's Congress. In regards to Taiwan, Deng said:

> What is the solution to this problem? Is it for socialism to swallow up Taiwan, or for the 'Three Principles of the People' preached by Taiwan to swallow up the mainland? The answer is that neither can swallow up the other. If the problem cannot be solved peacefully then it must be solved by force. This would do neither side any good. Reunification of the country is the aspiration of the whole nation. If it cannot be reunified in one hundred years, then it will be reunified in one thousand years. In my opinion, the only solution to this problem is to practice two systems in one country.[19]

Since China promised that Taiwan could enjoy more autonomy than Hong Kong under the 'one country, two systems' formula, it might be useful to summarize a few of the main points set forth in the December 1984 Sino-British agreement on the return of Hong Kong to Chinese sovereignty in July 1997.[20] At minimum, it could be expected that an agreement for unification with Taiwan would include statements similar to the following:

* The principles of 'one country, two systems' shall be enshrined in a 'Basic Law of the Hong Kong Special Administrative Region of the People's Republic of China'.
* The Basic Law will stipulate that after 1997 'the socialist system and socialist policies shall not be practiced in the Hong Kong Special Administrative Region and that Hong Kong's previous capitalist system and life-style shall remain unchanged for fifty years'.
* A high degree of autonomy shall exist, except in foreign and defense affairs, which will be the responsibility of Beijing.
* An executive, legislative and independent judicial power shall be established with the current laws remaining basically unchanged.
* An executive shall be appointed by Beijing on the basis of local elections or consultations, and be held 'accountable to the legislature'.
* A legislature shall be constituted by elections, which 'may on its own authority enact laws in accordance with the provisions of the Basic Law and legal procedures, and report them to the Standing Committee of the National People's Congress for the record'.

- 'The Hong Kong Special Administrative Region shall maintain the capitalist economic and trade systems previously practiced in Hong Kong.'
- 'The current social and economic systems in Hong Kong will remain unchanged, and so will the life-style. Rights and freedoms, including those of the person, of speech, of the press, of assembly, of association, of travel, of movement, of correspondence, of strike, of choice of occupation, of academic research and of religious belief will be ensured by law ... Private property, ownership of enterprises, legitimate right of inheritance and foreign investment will be protected by law.'
- Hong Kong will remain a separate customs territory. It will remain an international financial center, and its markets for foreign exchange, gold, securities and futures will continue. There will be free flow of capital.
- The Hong Kong dollar will continue to circulate and remain freely convertible. Hong Kong will have independent finances and Beijing will not levy taxes on Hong Kong.
- Under the name 'Hong Kong, China', the Special Administrative Region 'may on its own maintain and develop economic and cultural relations and conclude relevant agreements with states, regions and relevant international organizations'.
- Hong Kong may issue its own travel documents and maintain its own public security forces.
- 'Apart from displaying the national flag and national emblem of the People's Republic of China', Hong Kong 'may use a regional flag and emblem of its own'.

Since the introduction of the 'one country, two systems' formula in 1984, there has been little substantive change in PRC proposals, although there have been a few more incentives added by President Jiang Zemin and others. Despite promises of freedom for a period greater than 50 years and greater autonomy than that enjoyed by Hong Kong, the PRC in essence wants Taipei to accept Beijing as the central government of China and to accept the condition that the ruling authorities on Taiwan are a local government, not a national government. If Taiwan can accept these preconditions, then almost everything else is negotiable.

For its part, the ROC government has steadfastly refused to accept any comparison between itself and Hong Kong. As stated in September 1997 by Mainland Affairs Council Vice Chairman Lin Chong-Pin:

> We wish to reiterate that the 'one country, two systems' formula is by no means applicable to cross-strait relations. The ROC has been a sovereign state since 1912. Hong Kong was and Macao still is a colony.

We have had an independent foreign policy and a self defense capability, which Hong Kong and Macao never had. The timing of sovereignty transfer of Hong Kong and Macao were stipulated under international treaties; we do not have such time limit. The Sino-British agreement reached in 1984 on Hong Kong's sovereignty transfer was made without consulting the Hong Kong people, a practice categorically impossible for us, now a full-fledged democracy.[21]

In truth, there is very little support on Taiwan for the 'one country, two systems' formula because the government of the ROC and the people of Taiwan simply do not want to accept the notion that Taiwan has to become a local government under a central government controlled by the Chinese Communist Party. Since Taipei refuses to accept local status, and the PRC refuses to accept the ROC as an equal, there is very little to negotiate on the issue of national unification.

ROC national unification guidelines

In 1991 the ROC released its most important cross-Strait document, the 'Guidelines for National Unification', containing the basic principles and timetables governing Taipei's policy of reunification with the mainland.[22] In terms of principles, the document said:

1. Both the mainland and Taiwan areas are parts of Chinese territory. Helping to bring about national unification should be the common responsibility of all Chinese people.
2. The unification of China should be for the welfare of all of its people and not be subject to partisan conflict.
3. China's unification should aim at promoting Chinese culture, safeguarding human dignity, guaranteeing fundamental human rights and practicing democracy and the rule of law.
4. The timing and manner of China's unification should first respect the rights and interests of the people in the Taiwan area, and protect their security and welfare. It should be achieved in gradual phases under the principles of reason, peace, equity and reciprocity.

No specific timetable was set for unification, but rather a three-stage process was proposed. The immediate first phase was one of building 'exchanges and reciprocity'. During this period, exchanges across the Taiwan Strait would increase, while at the same time 'not endangering each other's safety and stability ... and not denying the other's existence as a political entity'. In this stage, the PRC would begin to implement democratic reform, and Taiwan would accelerate its constitutional reform. This stage was intended to address Taiwan's immediate needs: to end the

PRC threat to use force against Taiwan and to allow the ROC to play a normal role in international affairs without interference from Beijing. During this phase, the mainland was asked to phase out communism. All exchanges between the two sides would be through intermediary organizations such as the Straits Exchange Foundation and its PRC counterpart, the Association for Relations Across the Taiwan Straits. As explained below, the organizations had been set up in 1991 to handle day-to-day interaction between the two Chinese sides.

The mid-term phase of Taiwan's unification plan focused on building 'mutual trust and cooperation'. During this stage, 'Direct postal, transport and commerce links should be allowed.' Also, Taipei and Beijing would cooperate economically to develop the coastal areas to narrow the gap between the two sides' standards of living. 'Official communication channels on equal footing' would be established; both sides would assist each other 'in international organizations and activities', and 'high-ranking officials on both sides' would exchange visits.

The final stage would be one of 'consultation and unification'. During this phase, a consultative organization for unification would be established to 'jointly discuss the grand task of unification and map out a constitutional system to establish a democratic, free, and equitably prosperous China'.

In contrast to the PRC proposal of 'one country, two systems', which set forth fairly generous conditions under which Taiwan could become part of the People's Republic of China as a special administrative region with a high degree of autonomy, the ROC guidelines asked the PRC to give up communism and work toward the unification of China under a democratic system. Stripped of all niceties, the PRC called for the ROC to give up its claims of Chinese sovereignty, while the ROC called for the PRC to become a democratic nation. In essence, both sides had in mind the unconditional surrender of the other and the establishment of control of a unified China under its own terms.

Cross-Strait exchanges

Despite the zero-sum game being played at the government-to-government level, pragmatic, unofficial exchanges between the two sides have increased dramatically since the late 1980s. For example, between 1987 and 1992, Taiwan residents made more than four million trips to the PRC, and about 40,000 mainlanders visited Taiwan. In 1992 alone, more than 18 million items of mail were exchanged and nearly 27 million phone calls were placed. By 1995, some 30,000 Taiwan firms had invested an estimated $30 billion in the mainland. An October 1997 report from the ROC Mainland Affairs Council stated that the total number of visits from Taiwan to the mainland exceeded 10 million, while people from the mainland visited Taiwan over 220,000 times. Total cross-Strait trade approached $120 billion by 1997, and mainland China was Taiwan's third largest trading partner after the United States and Japan. By 1991 there had been over 140 million items of mail exchanged and over 360 million phone calls placed between the two sides of the Taiwan Strait.[23]

To manage the growing interaction across the Taiwan Strait, Taipei and Beijing established institutions with quasi-official status to represent their interests. In February 1991 the ROC created the Foundation for Exchanges Across the Taiwan Strait, or Straits Exchange Foundation (SEF), with the major responsibilities of accepting, ratifying and forwarding entry and exit documents from the two Chinese sides; verifying and delivering documents issued on the mainland; deporting fugitives on both sides of the Taiwan Strait; arbitrating trade disputes; promoting cultural and academic exchanges; providing consultation on general affairs; and helping to protect the legal rights of ROC citizens during their visits to the mainland. Beijing created a counterpart organization in December 1991, the Association for Relations Across the Taiwan Strait (ARATS), which is closely tied to the Taiwan Affairs Office of the PRC State Council. The ROC and PRC representative offices act in accordance with their governments' instructions, but they serve as a convenient unofficial link between the two governments to avoid the appearance of state-to-state relations.

The first Koo–Wang talks

In an historic meeting, the chairmen of Beijing's ARATS and Taipei's SEF (Wang Daohan and Koo Chen-fu, respectively) met in Singapore in April 1993 to discuss a variety of non-political bilateral issues. The meeting produced four documents. Three dealt with the delivery of registered letters, document verification, and the schedule of future contacts between the two organizations. The other accord set forth the areas in which both sides wanted greater cooperation: fishing disputes, repatriation from Taiwan of illegal immigrants from the mainland, joint efforts to fight crime, protection of intellectual property rights, and efforts to reconcile differences in the two sides' legal systems. The joint exploitation of natural resources was also discussed, along with cooperation in science, culture and education. The two sides were unable to agree on the protection of Taiwan investments on the mainland, partly because Taipei wanted Beijing to sign a bilateral investment accord giving Taiwan a claim to be an equal political entity in relations with the mainland. The PRC side refused to do this, proposing instead that it provide investment guarantees directly with individual investors.[24]

Subsequent meetings over the next few months between the SEF and the ARATS were less productive. Differences over definitions of sovereignty effectively blocked agreements on trade and cultural links, and problems such as airline hijacking, fishing disputes, immigration and extradition could not be resolved due to their political implications. Essentially, Beijing refused to acknowledge Taipei as a political equal, while the ROC refused to compromise on key issues as long as the PRC did not rule out the use of force in resolving the Taiwan issue and placed obstacles in the way of Taiwan's participation in international affairs.

Relatively independent of both governments was a rising surge of personal, business and institutional contact across the Taiwan Strait. The pressure for increased contact and relaxation of limits on business and other transactions with the mainland created some difficulties for the 'no haste' approach of Taipei – an advantage accruing to the PRC side – but contact with the mainland also hardened the determination of Taiwan residents to avoid prematurely joining the economically and socially backward PRC – an advantage accruing to the ROC side.

PRC *white paper on Taiwan*

One of the most complete statements of PRC policy toward Taiwan came in the form of an August 1993 white paper, 'The Taiwan Question and the Reunification of China'.[25] The white paper noted that the Taiwan issue was a remnant of China's dismemberment in the past, with most of the blame for the continued division of China being placed on the United States: 'the U.S. Government is responsible for holding up the settlement of the Taiwan question'.

According to the white paper, the PRC's basic position on Taiwan's unification with the mainland is 'peaceful reunification; one country, two systems'. The main elements of this policy are:

1. *Only one China.* There is only one China in the world, Taiwan is an inalienable part of China and the seat of China's central government is in Beijing. This is a universally recognized fact as well as the premise for a peaceful settlement of the Taiwan question. The Chinese government is firmly against any words or deeds designed to split China's sovereignty and territorial integrity. It opposes 'two Chinas', 'one China–one Taiwan', 'one country, two governments' or any attempt or act that could lead to 'independence of Taiwan'. The Chinese people on both sides of the Straits all believe that there is only one China and espouse national reunification. Taiwan's status as an inalienable part of China has been determined and cannot be changed. 'Self-determination' for Taiwan is out of the question.

2. *Coexistence of two systems.* On the premise of one China, socialism on the mainland and capitalism on Taiwan can coexist and develop side by side for a long time without one swallowing up the other. This concept takes account of the actual situation in Taiwan and the

practical interests of compatriots there. It will be a unique feature and important innovation in the state system of a reunified China. After reunification, Taiwan's current socioeconomic system, its way of life as well as economic and cultural ties with foreign countries can remain unchanged. Private property, including houses and land, as well as business ownership, legal inheritance and overseas Chinese and foreign investments on the island will all be protected by law.

3. *A high degree of autonomy.* After reunification, Taiwan will become a special administrative region. It will be distinguished from the other provinces or regions of China by its high degree of autonomy. It will have its own administrative and legislative powers, an independent judiciary and the right of adjudication on the island. It will run its own party, political, military, economic and financial affairs. It may conclude commercial and cultural agreements with foreign countries and enjoy certain rights in foreign affairs. It may keep its military forces and the mainland will not dispatch troops or administrative personnel to the island. On the other hand, representatives of the government of the special administrative region and those from different circles of Taiwan may be appointed to senior posts in the central government and participate in the running of national affairs.

4. *Peace negotiations.* It is the common aspiration of the entire Chinese people to achieve reunification of the country by peaceful means through contacts and negotiations. People on both sides of the Strait are all Chinese. It would be a great tragedy for all if China's territorial integrity and sovereignty were to be split and its people were to be drawn into a fratricide. Peaceful reunification will greatly enhance the cohesion of the Chinese nation. It will facilitate Taiwan's socio-economic stability and development and promote the resurgence and prosperity of China as a whole. In order to put an end to hostility and achieve peaceful reunification, the two sides should enter into contacts and negotiations at the earliest possible date. On the premise of one China, both sides can discuss any subject, including the modality of negotiations, the question of what parties, groups and personalities may participate as well as any other matters of concern to the Taiwan side. So long as the two sides sit down and talk, they will always be able to find a mutually acceptable solution. Taking into account the prevailing situation on both sides of the Strait, the Chinese government has proposed that pending reunification the two sides should, according to the principle of mutual respect, complementarity and mutual benefit, actively promote economic cooperation and other exchanges. Direct trade, postal, air and shipping services and two-way visits should be started in order to pave the way for the peaceful reunification of the country.

The white paper warned that the use of force cannot be ruled out to achieve unification: 'Peaceful reunification is a set policy of the Chinese Government. However, any sovereign state is entitled to use any means it deems necessary, including military ones, to uphold its sovereignty and territorial integrity. The Chinese Government is under no obligation to undertake any commitment to any foreign power or people intending to split China as to what means it might use to handle its own domestic affairs.'

The report dismissed the idea that the Taiwan issue is analogous to the cases of Germany and Korea which were brought about as a result of international accords at the end of the Second World War. 'The Taiwan question should and entirely can be resolved judiciously through bilateral consultations and within the framework of one China.' Positive steps had been taken in recent years to improve cross-Strait relations; however, several obstacles to reunification were of grave concern to the PRC.

First, there was resistance to unification from the government of Taiwan: 'notwithstanding a certain measure of easing up by the Taiwan authorities, their current policy vis-a-vis the mainland still seriously impedes the development of relations across the Straits as well as the reunification of the country. They talk about the necessity of a reunified China, but their deeds are always a far cry from the principle of one China. They try to prolong Taiwan's separation from the mainland and refuse to hold talks on peaceful reunification.'

Second and more worrisome were increased calls for Taiwan independence and the ROC government's use of that sentiment to delay unification talks:

> In recent years the clamors for 'Taiwan independence' on the island have become shriller, casting a shadow over the course of relations across the Straits and the prospect of peaceful reunification of the country. The 'Taiwan independence' fallacy has a complex socio-historical root and international background. But the Taiwan authorities have, in effect, abetted this fallacy by its own policy of rejecting peace negotiations, restricting interchanges across the Straits and lobbying for 'dual recognition' or 'two Chinas' in the international arena. It should be reaffirmed that the desire of Taiwan compatriots to run the affairs of the island as masters of their own house is reasonable and justified. This should by no means be construed as advocating 'Taiwan independence'. They are radically distinct from those handful of Taiwan independence protagonists who trumpet 'independence' but vilely rely on foreign patronage in a vain attempt to detach Taiwan from China, which runs against the fundamental interests of the entire Chinese people including Taiwan compatriots. The Chinese Government is closely following the course of events and will never condone any maneuver for 'Taiwan independence'.

A third obstacle to unification was 'certain foreign forces who do not want to see a reunified China'. These forces 'have gone out of their way to meddle in China's internal affairs. They support the anti-communist stance of the Taiwan authorities of rejecting peace talks and abet the secessionists on the island, thereby erecting barriers to China's peaceful reunification and seriously wounding the national feelings of the Chinese people.'

In an especially hardline approach, the white paper placed severe restrictions on Taiwan's role in international affairs:

- 'As part of China, Taiwan has no right to represent China in the international community, nor can it establish diplomatic ties or enter into relations of an official nature with foreign countries.'
- 'The Chinese government has not objected to non-governmental economic or cultural exchanges between Taiwan and foreign countries.'
- The Chinese government is firmly against Taiwan's 'campaign of "pragmatic diplomacy" to cultivate official ties with countries having diplomatic relations with China in an attempt to push "dual recognition" and achieve the objective of creating a situation of "two Chinas" or "one China–one Taiwan"'.
- 'The Government of the People's Republic of China, as the sole legal government of China, has the right and obligation to exercise state sovereignty and represent the whole of China in international organizations. The Taiwan authorities' lobbying for a formula of "one country, two seats" in international organizations whose membership is confined to sovereign states is a maneuver to create "two Chinas". The Chinese Government is firmly opposed to such an attempt.'
- 'Only on the premise of adhering to the principle of one China and in the light of the nature and statutes of the international organizations concerned as well as the specific circumstances, can the Chinese Government consider the question of Taiwan's participation in the activities of such organizations and in a manner agreeable and acceptable to the Chinese Government.'
- Taiwan's re-entry into the UN system 'is out of the question'.
- 'As to regional economic organizations such as the Asian Development Bank (ADB) and the Asia–Pacific Economic Cooperation (APEC), Taiwan's participation is subject to the terms of agreement or understanding reached between the Chinese Government and the parties concerned which explicitly prescribe that the People's Republic of China is a full member as a sovereign state whereas Taiwan may participate in the activities of those organizations only as a region of China under the designation of Taipei, China (in ADB) or Chinese Taipei (in APEC). This is only an ad hoc arrangement and cannot constitute a

"model" applicable to other inter-governmental organizations or inter-national gatherings.'

- Taiwan's future participation in non-governmental international organizations has to be approved by the PRC. An understanding would have to be reached whereby 'China's national organizations would use the designation of China, while Taiwan's organizations may participate under the designation of Taipei, China or Taiwan, China'.

- 'State-run airlines of countries having diplomatic relations with China certainly must not operate air services to Taiwan. Privately-operated airlines must seek China's consent through consultations between their government and the Chinese Government before they can start reciprocal air services with privately-operated airlines of Taiwan.'

The document also said China 'firmly opposed any country selling any type of arms or transferring production technology of the same to Taiwan'. The sale of arms increases 'tension between the two sides of the Straits' and constitutes not only 'a serious threat to China's security and an obstacle to China's peaceful reunification, but also undermines peace and stability in Asia and the world at large'.

More so than most official statements on Taiwan, this PRC document makes clear that Beijing has no intention whatsoever of recognizing Taipei as an equal or even competing government of China. The PRC holds that this issue was decided on the battlefield in 1949 and in most capitals of the world since 1971. At most, the PRC is willing to allow the people of Taiwan to continue their lifestyle for an undisclosed period of time and to permit the government of Taiwan to function as a local government and to participate in international non-governmental organizations as part of China. Beijing is extremely inflexible in terms of Taiwan's participation in inter-governmental organizations.

ROC response to white paper

In September 1993 the ROC Mainland Affairs Council (MAC) responded to the PRC white paper on Taiwan in a document titled 'There Is No "Taiwan Question"; There Is Only a "China Question"'.[26] The MAC document made several important points:

1. 'There is no Taiwan question, only a question of the future of China and how to make the country democratic and free.'
2. The PRC cannot be equated with China. 'The term "China" connotes multifaceted geographical, political, historical and cultural meanings. We have always asserted that both the mainland and Taiwan are Chinese territories. [But it is also] an undeniable fact that the two have been divided and ruled separately since 1949. Although the Chinese

communists have enjoyed jurisdiction over the mainland area, they cannot be equated with China. They can in no way represent China as a whole, much less serve as the "sole legal government of all Chinese people".'

3. The ROC is a member of the international community, and the PRC never has represented, nor can it ever represent, the people of Taiwan. 'The Chinese communists have never extended their governing power to the Taiwan area, so they are not entitled to represent Taiwan in the international community, nor have they advocated the rights or fulfilled the obligations of the people in the Taiwan area in any international organizations.'

4. The main obstacle to China's reunification is the PRC's one country, two systems proposal. 'It is clear that the "one country, two systems" premise is nothing but a demand for the Taiwan area to surrender to the Chinese communists. Thus, objectively, "one country, two systems" is infeasible, and, subjectively, it is unacceptable to the people in the ROC.'

5. 'The ROC government pursues China's unification not only to unify the territories of China through peaceful and reasonable means ... The loftier goal is to allow the 1.2 billion people on the Chinese mainland to enjoy the same democratic, free and equitably prosperous lifestyle and the basic human rights and freedom that the people in the Taiwan area do.'

6. Whereas 'the two sides of the Taiwan Straits should resolve the unification question peacefully', Taiwan believes 'that so long as the Chinese communists do not implement democracy and the rule of law, and do not renounce the use of force to resolve problems, the threat they pose to the stability and prosperity of Asia, and even the world, will continue'.

7. 'We believe that the value of national unification lies not in a single jurisdiction over China's territories but in enabling the people on the Chinese mainland to enjoy the same democratic, free and equitably prosperous lifestyle as is enjoyed by the people in the Taiwan area ... We sincerely call upon the Chinese communist authorities to quickly relinquish the anachronistic communist system; commit themselves to political, economic and social reforms on the Chinese mainland; and place the fundamental rights and welfare of the 1.2 billion Chinese people above the narrow interests of the Chinese Communist Party.'

As can be seen, the position of the ROC government allows very little room for compromise on the key issues of sovereignty, political legitimacy and territorial integrity. Taipei insists that unification can proceed only after the PRC gives up the communist system.

Jiang Zemin's eight points

President Jiang Zemin put his own imprint on PRC policy toward Taiwan in his 'eight points' speech of January 30, 1995.[27] Jiang reaffirmed the basic principles of existing policy:

> We will never allow there to be 'two Chinas' or 'one China, one Taiwan'. We firmly oppose the 'independence of Taiwan'. There are only two ways to settle the Taiwan question: One is by peaceful means and the other is by non-peaceful means. The way the Taiwan question is to be settled is China's internal affairs, and brooks no foreign interference. We consistently stand for achieving reunification by peaceful means and through negotiations. But we shall not undertake not to use force.

He also restated China's intentions under the one country, two systems formula, including Taiwan's right to 'retain its armed forces and administer its party, governmental and military system by itself'.

Noting favorably the exchanges that had taken place between the two sides over the past decade, Jiang set forth eight points as 'views and propositions on a number of important questions that have a bearing on the development of relations between the two sides and the promotion of the peaceful reunification of the motherland'.

First, 'adherence to the principle of one China is the basis and premise for peaceful reunification. China's sovereignty and territory must never be allowed to suffer split. We must firmly oppose any words or actions aimed at creating an "independent Taiwan" and the propositions "split the country and rule under separate regimes", "two Chinas over a certain period of time", etc., which are in contravention of the principle of one China.'

Second, 'we do not challenge the development of non-governmental economic and cultural ties by Taiwan with other countries ... However, we oppose Taiwan's activities in "expanding its living space internationally" which are aimed at creating "two Chinas" or "one China, one Taiwan".'

Third, 'it has been our consistent stand to hold negotiations with the Taiwan authorities on the peaceful reunification of the motherland. Representatives from the various political parties and mass organizations on both sides of the Taiwan Straits can be invited to participate in such talks.' Jiang went on, 'I suggest that, as the first step, negotiations should be held and an agreement reached on officially ending the state of hostility between the two sides in accordance with the principle that there is only one China ... As regards the name, place and form of these political talks, a solution acceptable to both sides can certainly be found so long as consultations on an equal footing can be held at an early date.'

Fourth, 'we should strive for the peaceful reunification of the mother-land since Chinese should not fight fellow Chinese'. Explaining China's refusal to rule out the use of force, Jiang said: 'Our not undertaking to give up the use of force is not directed against our compatriots in Taiwan but against the schemes of foreign forces to interfere with China's reunification and to bring about the "independence of Taiwan".'

Fifth, 'in face of the development of the world economy in the twenty-first century, great efforts should be made to expand the economic exchanges and cooperation between the two sides of the Taiwan Straits so as to achieve prosperity on both sides to the benefit of the entire Chinese nation. We hold that political differences should not affect or interfere with the economic cooperation between the two sides.' Continuing, 'since the direct links for postal, air and shipping services and trade between the two sides are the objective requirements for their economic development and contacts in various fields, and since they are in the interests of the people on both sides, it is absolutely necessary to adopt practical measures to speed up the establishment of such direct links. Efforts should be made to promote negotiations on certain specific issues between the two sides. We are in favor of conducting this kind of negotiations on the basis of reciprocity and mutual benefit.'

Sixth, 5,000 years of Chinese culture is 'the tie keeping the entire Chinese people close at heart and constitutes an important basis for the peaceful reunification of the motherland. People on both sides of the Taiwan Straits should inherit and carry forward the fine traditions of the Chinese culture'.

Seventh, 'the 21 million compatriots in Taiwan, whether born there or in other provinces, are all Chinese and our own flesh and blood. We should fully respect their life style and their wish to be the masters of our country and protect all their legitimate rights and interest.' Accordingly, 'all parties and personages of all circles in Taiwan are welcome to exchange views with us on relations between the two sides and on peaceful reunification'.

Eighth, 'leaders of the Taiwan authorities are welcome to pay visits in appropriate capacities. We are also ready to accept invitations from the Taiwan side to visit Taiwan.'

Lee Teng-hui's six principles

In response to President Jiang Zemin's eight points, which many observers on Taiwan felt contained signs of increased PRC flexibility, President Lee Teng-hui set forth six principles for China's reunification in a speech to the ROC National Unification Council on April 8, 1995.[28]

The first principle, Lee said, is to 'seek China's unification on the reality of separate rules across the Strait'. This principle was based on the fact that the two sides of the Taiwan Strait have been governed since 1949 by the PRC and ROC respectively, with neither political entity subordinated to the other. 'To solve the unification problem, we must be pragmatic and respect history, and we should seek a feasible way for national unification based on the fact that the two shores are separately governed.'

A second principle was to 'step up cross-Strait exchange on the basis of the Chinese culture'. Exchanges based on traditional Chinese culture could help 'elevate the national sentiment of common existence and common prosperity' and 'further increase exchange and cooperation in the information, academic, science and technology, sports, and other fields'.

A third principle was to 'increase cross-Strait economic and trade exchanges and develop mutually beneficiary and supplementary relations'. Lee suggested that 'Taiwan should make mainland China its hinterland in developing its economy, whereas mainland China should draw lessons from Taiwan in developing its economy'. Taiwan was willing to help the mainland improve its agriculture through technology and to help develop the mainland's economy through investment and trade. The ROC president noted that cross-Strait business and shipping exchanges were complicated and required communications between the two sides 'to thoroughly understand the problems and exchange views'.

A fourth principle was that the two sides should 'join international organizations on equal footing and leaders of the two sides will naturally meet each other on such occasions'. Lee said the most natural setting for leaders from the two sides to meet would be in international organizations to which their respective governments belonged. Such meetings 'will be conducive to developing bilateral relations and to promoting the process of peaceful reunification'. The status of the two sides in such organizations, however, should be equal.

As a fifth principle, the two sides 'should persist in using peaceful means to resolve disputes'. Lee noted that in 1991 the ROC announced that it would no longer use force against the mainland. He said 'the mainland authorities should show their goodwill by renouncing the use of force against Taiwan, Penghu, and Kinmen and Matsu'. Should this occur, 'a preliminary consultation on how to end the state of hostile confrontation between the two sides will be held at a most appropriate time and opportunity'.

Sixth, 'the two sides should jointly maintain the prosperity of and promote democracy in Hong Kong and Macao'.

Like the eight points of Jiang Zemin, the six principles of Lee Teng-hui were not noteworthy in terms of new ideas; in fact, the positions of the two Chinese governments remain pretty much unchanged since they were outlined by Lee and Jiang in early 1995. However, the moderate-sounding tones of Jiang and Lee were taken as important indicators that both Beijing and Taipei were inclined to increase the level of cross-Strait dialogue and to explore wider areas of possible cooperation. Neither side was willing to compromise its basic principles: Beijing continued to view Taiwan as a province of the PRC and the ROC government as a local Chinese entity; Taipei continued to insist that unification could be achieved only when the PRC stopped threatening Taiwan with force, accepted the reality of a divided China ruled by two equal governments, and agreed to unite China under a democratic government.

In May 1995 the SEF and the ARATS successfully concluded preliminary consultations for a second round of Koo–Wang talks scheduled for July in Beijing. According to the ROC, the basis of those talks was that 'the meaning of one China is subject to the interpretations of the two sides'.[29] These signs of optimism that light had been sighted at the end of the tunnel for a peaceful, equitable resolution of the Taiwan issue quickly faded later in May, when it became known that Lee Teng-hui would visit the United States the following month. The ARATS immediately notified the SEF by letter that the Koo–Wang talks would have to be postponed and that Taipei would be contacted at an appropriate time in the future. High-level discussions between the ARATS and SEF did not resume again until 1998.

REPERCUSSIONS OF LEE'S VISIT TO THE UNITED STATES

The optimism of early 1995 that significant progress was at last being accomplished in cross-Strait relations deteriorated rapidly after May 22, when the US government announced that it would give permission to Lee Teng-hui to pay a private, unofficial visit to the United States. Relations between Taipei and Beijing have never fully recovered.

President Clinton, under intense pressure from Congress and the American public, personally made the decision to issue a visa to Lee. The unexpected decision surprised the PRC. Clinton had told Jiang Zemin in the 1994 Asia–Pacific summit in Indonesia that Lee Teng-hui would not be allowed to visit the United States, and this promise had been reiterated by Secretary of State Warren Christopher to Foreign Minister Qian Qichen.[30]

In his six-point proposal in April 1995, President Lee had indicated a willingness to move cross-Strait relations forward. At the same time, however, the Lee government was expanding Taiwan's international presence through pragmatic diplomacy – in essence, expanding political contacts through all available means. Part of this strategy involved quasi-official trips abroad by high-ranking Taiwan authorities. Lee himself, for example, made high-profile visits to Singapore in 1989, to Indonesia,

Thailand, the Philippines, three Central American countries, South Africa and Singapore in 1994, to Jordan, the United Arab Emirates and the United States in 1995, and to several Latin American countries in 1996.

Lee's attempt to secure permission to visit the United States should be viewed as part of pragmatic diplomacy, not a simple request for a tourist visa or to give a lecture at Cornell University. Nonetheless, his efforts were supported by many in the United States. In May 1995, for example, the Senate voted 97–1 in favor of H. Con. Res. 53, expressing the sense of Congress that President Lee should be permitted to make a private visit to his alma mater at Cornell.

China interpreted Taiwan's efforts to expand its international presence, especially through a trip by Lee Teng-hui to the United States, as a threat to PRC plans for national unification. Already suspecting that Lee favored Taiwan independence and was working toward that end, the PRC was convinced it had to take firm measures to stop all efforts to upgrade Taiwan–US ties. Beijing believed that if Taipei succeeded in its pragmatic diplomacy with the United States, the ROC government might draw out indefinitely political talks over reunification, perhaps leading to growing international recognition of two Chinas or increasing international support for one China, one Taiwan – or even an independent Taiwan. There also was suspicion on the part of some in Beijing that the United States was using Taiwan's efforts to expand its international presence as part of a secret American strategy to contain China before it became a powerful rival in the twenty-first century. Because of the wide implications of the Lee visit to the United States, Beijing determined that it had to react strongly toward both Taipei and Washington. The intensity of the PRC reaction also reflected a shift in power toward the hardliners in policy toward Taiwan and the United States.

According to May and June reports in Hong Kong's *Lien-Ho Pao*, hardliners within the Chinese Communist Party seized upon Lee's invitation as an opportunity to criticize those departments responsible for relations with Taiwan and the United States as being too weak. In the wake of Lee's visit, the influence of the hardliners rose in policy-making circles, while the influence of the moderates declined. The hardliners insisted that cooperation with the United States in all areas be curtailed and that the Chinese ambassador to the United States be recalled in protest. The hardliners further insisted that Lee Teng-hui and his government were pursuing an independent Taiwan, a movement the mainland should no longer tolerate. This group lobbied hard against any further concessions to Taiwan and insisted that Taiwan's international activities be vigorously opposed.[31]

Reflecting the harder line, PRC media warned the United States about 'playing with fire'. On June 10, 1995, *Renminribao* editorialized:

The Taiwan issue is a powder keg. It is extremely dangerous to keep warming it up, no matter whether this is done by the United States or by Li Denghui. If their activities lead to its explosion, the consequences will be unimaginable.

People who play with fire always think they know what they are doing and think it is fun. But elements such as fire and water are cruel and indifferent and have their own principles, after crossing a certain threshold, running independent of human will and ultimately burning the players, much to their surprise.

We advise the U.S. Government, people like Li Denghui, and those who seek the 'independence of Taiwan' in service of their immediate interests by warming up the powder keg: Be cautious, be cautious![32]

A common theme expressed by the PRC media in this hardened atmosphere was that the US invitation to Lee was part of an American strategy to contain China. Beijing Central People's Radio editorialized on June 12, 1995: 'The United States considers China the greatest obstacle standing in its way to achieving hegemony ... Guided by its hegemonic mentality, the United States does not want to see a unified China and, by hindering China through Taiwan, tries to maintain the status quo of a divided China and obstruct China from being an affluent and strong country.'[33] A *Xinhua* commentary of June 17 echoed the same theme: 'In the final analysis, the United States has never discarded the policy of regarding Taiwan as its "unsinkable aircraft carrier"; and its attempts to play the "Taiwan card", and to curb China's development, growth, and reunification of China.'[34]

Special scorn was reserved for Lee Teng-hui, who was condemned for betraying China by linking Taiwan to the United States. Lee was castigated for 'embracing foreigners to earn himself dignity and for being willing to become a person condemned by history'.[35] In June 1995 *Liaowang* detailed the steps Lee had taken in redefining Taiwan's status since coming to power in January 1988. The article said the Lee government had made a concerted effort to drop the one-China commitment of his predecessors and to adopt a de facto two-Chinas position through such schemes as 'one China, two reciprocal governments', 'one country, two governments', 'one country, two regions', 'two reciprocal political entities', 'mutual governmental recognition', 'divided country under separate rule', 'two Chinas as a phase in a long process leading toward one China', 'the ROC in Taiwan', 'Taiwan and the mainland are governed by two political entities', 'the two sides of the Strait are divided under separate rule' and so on. According to the article, this evolution of a new Taiwan identity was made possible because of three developments: democratization on the island which consolidated Lee Teng-hui's position; the rapid growth of the DPP which threatened KMT rule, necessitating compromise between the two parties; and the pursuance by some Western countries (that is, the United States) of 'a double-track policy toward China in a bid to "use Chinese to control Chinese"' by maintaining diplomatic relations with the PRC but 'substantive relations' with Taiwan.[36]

Thus, almost overnight, Lee's visit to the United States changed the atmosphere in both cross-Strait relations and Sino-American relations from one of cautious optimism and growing cooperation to one of heated recrimination from Beijing toward suspected plots to divide China on the part of Taipei and Washington. These recriminations were followed by several changes in PRC policy, leading to a significant military crisis in the Taiwan Strait lasting until March 1996.

PRC policy adjustments

Lee's visit and the subsequent PRC reaction had several effects: high-level cross-Strait talks were curtailed until 1998; the PRC military threat to Taiwan increased; the United States and China moved closer to an adversarial relationship; the stakes in the resolution of the Taiwan issue became much higher; and perceptions of China in the United States became even more polarized between those who saw Taiwan as an obstacle in Sino-American relations that should be removed and those who saw the Taiwan crisis as evidence of PRC intent to become more aggressive in Asia in the future.

Influenced by perceptions of connivance between Washington and Taipei and pressured by powerful hardliners within the CCP leadership who demanded a tougher policy line, the government of Jiang Zemin modified PRC relations with both the United States and Taiwan in the wake of Lee's visit. In the case of Taiwan, the PRC banned some business and cultural exchanges and postponed indefinitely the scheduled July meeting between Wang Daohan and Koo Chen-fu. The PRC Foreign Ministry said that Lee had 'poisoned' the climate of cross-Strait relations. This ban on high-level contacts between the SEF and ARATS continued until the end of 1997, despite efforts by Taipei to jump-start the dialogue in June 1995, April 1996, July 1996 and November 1997.[37]

In the case of the United States, Beijing on the one hand recognized that Washington wanted to maintain cooperative relations with China and that it would continue to adhere to the US 'one China' policy. On the other hand, the United States had shown greater support for Taiwan. According to Chinese Academy of Social Sciences fellow Zhang Yebai, the United States had made three 'major retrogressions' on the Taiwan issue in recent years: President George Bush's decision to sell F-16 fighters to Taiwan; the September 1994 readjustment of US Taiwan policy by President Clinton (discussed in Chapter 7); and Clinton's decision to extend a visa to Lee Teng-hui. As a result of these challenges to Chinese sovereignty,

'China has lost its trust in the United States' and was considering 'whether or not it will take a cooperative attitude toward the United States on certain specific issues' such as security in the Asia–Pacific region and economic issues.[38]

CCP leaders concluded that the United States was following a dual policy of cooperation and confrontation with China, with the ultimate US strategic objective being to westernize and split China. According to commentaries, this Chinese perception of US strategy and policy led the PRC to adopt the following line: 'strategically, the CPC will not make any concession on problems concerning its sovereignty and territorial integrity, while tactically, it will strike only after it has been struck'. On the Taiwan issue, the PRC leadership believed that greater importance should be attached to the unification of the country than to Sino-US relations. As a result, no further concessions on the Taiwan issue should be made by Beijing. Moreover, if the United States did not return to the principles of the three joint communiqués, then Sino-American friendly relations would be difficult to maintain.[39]

Other Chinese analysts reported that CCP leaders believed the United States was playing a 'Taiwan card' to cause political instability on the mainland during the post-Deng Xiaoping leadership transition. By being a willing participant in this maneuver, Lee Teng-hui had 'broken the rules of the game, plunging cross-Strait relations into a dangerous state'. Since the United States had not responded positively to the moderate 16-character Sino-American policy of Jiang Zemin ('enhancing confidence, reducing trouble, avoiding confrontation, and expanding cooperation') and since the ROC had not responded in a positive manner to Jiang's eight-point proposal, hardliners within the CCP gained much greater influence over policy toward the United States and Taiwan. These hardliners advocated a tough diplomatic stand against the United States, in particular demanding that Washington make a clear statement preventing Lee and Taiwan from pursuing pragmatic diplomacy further.[40]

According to this analysis, China's relations with the United States were more important than relations with Taiwan. Until China's relations with the United States became more stabilized, PRC relations with Taiwan had to be put on hold. China's handling of the Taiwan issue with the United States was critical, because international attention was focused on the issue and how the United States acted toward Taiwan would affect other countries' policies toward Taiwan.

It was during these heated policy debates that the PLA began to exert a greater influence over policy toward Taiwan and the United States. The PLA was deeply concerned about Lee's visit, viewing this as convincing evidence that Washington and Taipei were together pursuing policies harmful to China's sovereignty and territorial integrity. Jiang Zemin, eager to increase his stature among the military in the post-Deng leadership transition, told PLA leaders: 'The Taiwan independence movement is getting out of hand and we cannot let this go on ... We must heighten our guard and strengthen our resources and combat-readiness to curb' this movement. Jiang did not specify what action the military should take, but within the PLA there was considerable pressure from hawks to teach Taiwan a lesson. There was some concern that Jiang might use the military's worries over Taiwan to enhance his leadership credentials, just as Deng Xiaoping had used the invasion of Vietnam to establish his credentials as a worthy successor to Mao Zedong.[41]

Accordingly, the CCP reached two conclusions. First, the basic PRC policy toward Taiwan would remain unchanged: that is, 'the mainland will continue to attach primary importance to economic construction, and secondary importance to reunification of the country, while resolutely preventing Taiwan independence'. Second, preparation for possible military action against Taiwan had to be taken, since greater priority had to be given to sovereignty than to economic development.[42]

On July 18, 1995, Beijing announced that it would conduct an eight-day missile-launching drill from July 21 to July 28, with a target area some 150 km off Keelung in northern Taiwan. A second round of guided missile exercises was held between August 15 and 25. A third series of missile firings was held between March 8 and 15, 1996. Relevant aspects of the crisis will be discussed throughout the book, in particular Chapter 7.[43]

According to PRC officials, the missile tests were designed to reflect Beijing's determination to resolve the Taiwan issue either by peaceful reunification or by armed liberation. The missile drills were intended to demonstrate China's military strength and to pressure Taipei to hold early peace talks with the mainland. If Taiwan refused to hold such talks, then the mainland could resort to the use of arms. A common view in Beijing was that Lee Teng-hui had become too arrogant because of backing by the United States. Therefore, to solve the Taiwan issue China must first end the interference of the United States. Because of the dual nature of US policy, China had decided to adopt a dual policy of its own toward the United States, namely, a desire for cooperation as the best policy but a willingness to confront the United States if necessary.[44]

Having concluded that the principal obstacle to unification was US support for Taiwan – because it emboldened the government of Lee Teng-hui to pursue pragmatic diplomacy and to say 'arrogant' things – China focused on relations with the United States and largely ignored cross-Strait relations from mid-1995 until the first half of 1997. By the fall of 1997, however, there were signs that Beijing was willing to re-engage Taipei, continuing the relationship as it had been before Lee's US visit but with much greater emphasis on political talks.

RELAXATION OF CROSS-STRAIT TENSIONS

In September 1997, Foreign Minister Qian Qichen said the mainland was willing to discuss suggestions for the unification of China from almost any source. He emphasized that the PRC was directing its anger not at Taiwan itself, but at a handful of people advocating Taiwan's independence. He said: 'The Taiwan compatriots are our blood brothers, and we will continue to protect all their legitimate rights and interests ... We are willing to increase contacts with various parties and people from all walks of life in Taiwan, except for the small number of people who stubbornly stick to the stand of "Taiwan Independence", and we are willing to hear and discuss any views and suggestions that would benefit the reunification of the motherland.' Qian reiterated China's opposition to Taiwan independence, two Chinas, one China and one Taiwan, and said that the Chinese 'resolutely oppose the plot to change Taiwan's status as an inseparable part of China through conducting a referendum'. Qian emphasized the importance of establishing the three links – direct mail, shipping and trade services across the Taiwan Strait – and urged the Taiwan authorities 'to hold consultations with us in a timely fashion on the procedural arrangements for cross-Strait political talks. The purpose of conducting political talks between the two sides of the Strait is to improve and develop cross-Strait relations and gradually advance the great cause of peaceful reunification.'[45]

The Taiwan side was quick to respond, as it had been seeking a resumption of cross-Strait dialogue for some time. The ROC Mainland Affairs Council said it welcomed Qian's remarks and suggested that the two sides resume their talks through the established framework of the Straits Exchange Foundation and the Association for Relations Across the Taiwan Strait. A day later, Premier Vincent Siew (Hsiao Wan-chang) said: 'It is our unswerving stance that the two sides resume institutionalized dialogue without any premises.' Specifically, he called upon China to shelve the controversial sovereignty issue in order to facilitate the resumption of cross-Strait dialogue.[46] It was clear that by the fall of 1997, Taipei – like Beijing – wanted to resume cross-Strait contact. The main (and crucial) difference between their desire for talks in mid-1995 and fall 1997 was that the PRC was now much more adamant about starting political talks while the ROC continued to insist that talks center on substantive non-political issues within the SEF–ARATS context.

ROC explains its policy

One result of the 1995–96 crisis in the Taiwan Strait was that many began to question Taiwan's real policies toward the mainland: was the Lee Teng-hui government seeking China's eventual unification or was it secretly pursuing *de jure* independence? The answers Taiwan gave were consistent but flexible in interpretation. For example, MAC Vice Chairman Kao Koong-lian stated in December 1996: 'The most pragmatic description of the current cross-Straits situation is that Taiwan and the mainland are two parallel political entities in one country.'[47] Other government officials carefully explained that, to Taipei, 'one China' meant the Republic of China, not the People's Republic of China.[48]

Chang King-yuh, Chairman of the Mainland Affairs Council, explained the ROC and KMT position in August 1997: 'From a legal point of view, the Republic of China's sovereignty and territories cover both sides of the Taiwan Straits. But in terms of the ROC's jurisdiction, since 1949, ours only covers Taiwan, the Pescadores, Quemoy, Matzu and some neighboring islets. So, we treat cross-Strait relations from the viewpoint of "one country, two equal political entities" in a pragmatic way to deal with the separate jurisdiction.'[49]

President Lee Teng-hui personally explained his views on ROC sovereignty and China's eventual reunification in a speech to Panama's Legislative Assembly in September 1997: 'I am deeply convinced that China will eventually be reunified. As long as the Chinese communist authorities can pragmatically face the fact that the two sides of the Taiwan Strait are under separate rules and are equal international legal entities, and respect the Republic of China's legitimate right to take part in international activities, then the two sides, through interacting with good will, will gradually head for reunification.'[50]

In October 1997, Chang King-yuh further elaborated on Taiwan's position in an interview with the *Hong Kong Economic Journal*.[51] Chang said the basic condition for talks between the two sides was recognition of 'the fact that China is still a divided country at the moment'. Furthermore, 'If the mainland can see things in this way, open the door to cross-Strait consultations, and speed up cross-Strait exchanges, I believe that Taiwan will respond at any time.' He argued that 'as China is still a divided country ruled by two different governments and has not yet been reunified, the two shores should treat each other with respect, equality, and with goodwill and try to develop good and constructive relations with each other in order to lay a solid foundation for China's peaceful and democratic reunification in the future'.

The problem, he said, was that the PRC's 'one China principle is nothing but one aimed at negating the ROC's existence. This is why there has not been much space for furthering cross-Strait relations development. The fact is that we often see the mainland trying to suppress the ROC's international status on the pretext of this principle, [and this is] harmful to cross-Strait relations development. We hope that the future CPC collective leadership will see things in a pragmatic way. We will continue to work hard to this end.' In comments suggesting that the ROC saw the process of unifying China to be long and difficult, Chang speculated on what type of arrangement might be feasible for a future unified China comprising the mainland, Hong Kong, Macau and Taiwan:

> A country can choose to institute a variety of different political structures, such as a unitary structure, a federal structure, a union structure, and a commonwealth structure ... What is important is that all entities concerned should treat each other with equality, goodwill, and mutual respect ... No matter how different their respective internal mechanisms are, they should coexist with one another; operate in a basically identical spirit; and be free from intimidation, suppression, or sabotage ... It is hard to imagine that a dictatorial mechanism without any democratic experiences in tolerating different views or political parties with different views will suddenly sign a democratic consti-tution, saying that all people will live together in happiness. Will this work? I don't think that things will be so easy.

In essence, Taipei held that China was in a state of split jurisdiction and that the ROC government would not unify Taiwan with the mainland until China becomes a democratic state – or at least moves convincingly in that direction. These conditions for unification run counter to the four cardinal principles enunciated by Deng Xiaoping: adherence to the leadership of the Chinese Communist Party, to Marxism–Leninism and Mao Zedong thought, to the people's democratic dictatorship, and to the socialist road. It is extremely doubtful that Beijing will accept Taipei's terms for unification – a stalemate that perhaps serves Taipei's interest in waiting for more opportune conditions but that also increases the probability of eventual war in the Taiwan Strait.

Second Koo–Wang meeting

The first meeting between Koo Chen-fu and Wang Daohan occurred in Singapore in April 1993. A second meeting was scheduled to take place in July 1995, but it was postponed indefinitely by the PRC because of Lee Teng-hui's visit to the United States. After that postponement, ROC high-ranking officials made 114 public appeals for an early resumption of negotiations and at least four SEF letters were sent to the ARATS calling for a resumption of normal exchanges between the two sides.[52] The PRC decision to resume high-level consultations with Taiwan finally came in February 1998, although some thawing of the ice began to occur in late 1997.

The second meeting between Koo and Wang was held October 14–19, 1998, when SEF Chairman Koo visited the mainland at the invitation of his counterpart, ARATS Chairman Wang. The new Koo–Wang talks did not result in any major breakthroughs, but the 'ice-thawing' meetings did achieve an agreement to strengthen cross-Strait dialogue, to reactivate SEF–ARATS consultations, to promote cross-Strait exchange visits at various levels, and to arrange for an exchange visit to Taiwan by Wang Daohan at some time in the future. Koo's itinerary was impressive, and he held discussions with Wang in Shanghai before meeting Jiang Zemin and other top PRC officials in Beijing. Koo told Chinese leaders that Taiwan's democratic model was useful to the mainland's modernization and that unification could occur only when both sides of the Taiwan Strait were on the path to democracy. The two sides continued to disagree on their interpretations of 'one China' and whether Taiwan should have wider international representation. Nonetheless, the atmosphere of the various discussions was open and friendly, and Koo's meeting with Jiang was described as 'exchanging views in a frank yet respectful manner'.[53]

The conversations Koo Chen-fu had with Wang Daohan and other Chinese officials highlighted two points: first, fundamental differences remained between the two sides of the Taiwan Strait and that no break-through toward unification would be possible in the foreseeable future; second, both sides wanted to reduce tensions, with Taiwan becoming more circumspect in its efforts to gain international recognition and the PRC willing to give its policies of peaceful reunification additional time to bear fruit.

This overall situation continued until mid-1999. In February 1999, President Lee Teng-hui commented that 'Taiwan is a country with independent sovereignty, which is something very clear and definite'.[54] PRC Premier Zhu Rongji in his March 5 government work report to the Second Session of the Ninth National People's Congress said:

> It is in the fundamental interests of all the Chinese people to achieve the complete reunification of the motherland. Our state sovereignty and territorial integrity cannot tolerate being carved into pieces. We firmly oppose the 'independence of Taiwan' and the attempt to create 'two Chinas' or 'one China, one Taiwan' in whatever form' ...
>
> We call on the Taiwan authorities to see the current situation clearly, enter into political negotiations with us at an early date and make practical efforts to officially end the state of hostility between the two sides in accordance with the principle that there is only one China in order to further improve cross-Straits relations ...
>
> In the new year, we will continue to adhere to the basic principles of 'peaceful reunification' and 'one country, two systems' and to the eight-point proposal put forward by President Jiang Zemin and will work conscientiously in handling all work related to Taiwan. More importantly, we will be placing our hopes on the people of Taiwan, uniting with them, listening to their voices and supporting their

reasonable propositions which are in the interests of the reunification of the motherland.[55]

Zhu's words were moderate indeed when compared with those used during the Taiwan crisis three years earlier. However, disagreements between the two sides continued, as demonstrated by the difficulty in getting Taipei and Beijing to agree on a date for Wang Daohan's exchange visit to Taiwan. In June 1999, SEF Deputy Secretary-General Jan Jyh-horng and his ARATS counterpart Li Yafei were able to agree that Wang would visit either on September 12–19 or October 12–19, 1999. Numerous details still divided the two sides, however, such as the kind of dialogue the chairmen would engage in while meeting.[56]

By mid-July, however, Wang's visit appeared to be in jeopardy and PRC rhetoric had again become heated, when the Lee government unexpectedly announced that it would no longer adhere to a one-China policy.

Lee abandons one-China policy

Until mid-1999, the ROC government and the ruling KMT party held the following principles in regards to relations with the mainland:

1. The ROC is a sovereign state, equal to the PRC and legally entitled to take part as a nation-state in the international community.
2. Taiwan is not part of the PRC, and the government of the PRC is not the sole legal government of China.
3. China at present is a divided nation with two separate governments exercising jurisdiction over two separate territories.
4. The unification of China is a long-term goal which can only be achieved when the PRC recognizes the equal status of the ROC and ceases its hostile behavior in terms of military threats and diplomatic isolation.
5. Unification can be achieved gradually as the two sides narrow their differences politically, economically and socially.
6. The unification of China can only occur under the principles of democracy in which the free-will choices of residents on the mainland and Taiwan are respected.
7. When speaking of 'one China', Taipei is referring to the Republic of China, not the PRC.

The principle of 'one China' provided a common reference point around which Taipei, Beijing and Washington could build their triangular relationship. The acknowledgment that Taiwan was part of China – however it might be defined – enabled most governments of the world to

74

serve their interests in establishing diplomatic relations with the larger and more powerful PRC, while maintaining friendly and profitable unofficial relations with Taiwan. For its part, Taipei insisted that the ROC had never denied the 'one-China' principle, but rather it had maintained that the current political status of China was 'shared sovereignty with separate jurisdiction'. Taipei insisted that recognizing the fact that China was ruled by two political entities did not conflict with 'one China'.[57]

This convenient understanding began to unravel in mid-July 1999, however, when President Lee announced in a German radio interview that Taiwan's relations with mainland China had been redefined as state-to-state or special state-to-state relations. He said: 'Since we made our constitutional reforms in 1991, we have redefined cross-Strait relations as nation-to-nation, or at least as special nation-to-nation relations.' He continued: 'Under such special nation-to-nation relations, there is no longer any need to declare Taiwanese independence.'[58] His statements caused shockwaves around the world, since Taipei had previously claimed both sides of the Taiwan Strait to be equal political entities that should recognize each other's jurisdictions over the parts of China they controlled.

A few days after Lee's comment, Mainland Affairs Council Chairman Su Chi declared that Taiwan's ties with mainland China constitute 'special relations' between two Chinese states and that 'one China' would no longer describe the ROC's policy. He explained that such a decision was necessary because Beijing had used the 'one-China' principle to isolate Taiwan internationally: 'We have shown our goodwill by calling ourselves a political entity under a one-China policy, but the Chinese communists have used this policy to squeeze us internationally. We feel there is no need to continue using the one-China term.'[59] A few days later, the ROC government said the official wording of its relations with mainland China was now 'one nation, two states', rather than 'one China, two political entities' which had been in use since 1991.[60]

Upon hearing Lee's pronouncement, the PRC immediately began to issue threats against Taiwan. The PRC State Council and CCP Central Committee issued a joint statement saying 'Lee Teng-hui's remarks referring to state-to-state relations reveal the true political nature of his consistent efforts to split Chinese sovereign territory and separate Taiwan.'[61] The *People's Daily* said the 'traitorous' Lee and his cronies 'will be cast aside by history and be reviled as national criminals', and Defense Minister Chi Haotian told a visiting North Korean delegation that his military was ready to 'smash any attempts to separate the country'.[62] Taken by surprise by Lee's remarks, both Japan and the United States quickly reaffirmed their one-China policies, urging the two sides of the Taiwan Strait to resolve their differences peacefully through substantive dialogue.[63]

Major US newspapers, on the other hand, were quick to support Taiwan's new definition of its policy, saying that 'two Chinas' described a reality in the Taiwan Strait that the United States should recognize and respect.[64] The *Washington Post*, for example, editorialized on July 14, 1999: 'instead of leading China's leaders to believe that the United States will help them force Taiwan into the fold, Mr. Clinton should help those leaders understand that the United States must support the Taiwanese people's right to determine their own future'.[65] The *Wall Street Journal* blamed the 'weak and corrupt administration' of President Clinton for pushing Taiwan into a box from which it had no other choice than to assert its autonomy.[66]

In reality, Lee's remarks did not signify a major shift in policy, as the ROC president himself explained to Daryl Johnson, head of the Taipei office of the American Institute in Taiwan and the de facto US ambassador to Taiwan. Lee said he was only trying to 'clarify and specify' Taiwan's relationship with the mainland: 'our mainland policy has not changed'.[67] And this is true, if one considers that Taipei for years had been attempting to deal with the mainland on a reciprocal and equal basis. On the other hand, the dropping of the ROC's 'one-China' policy was a semantic change of great symbolic importance, since it removed the existing foundation of cross-Strait relations. As Wang Daohan said, 'This formulation means there is no basis for contact, exchange and communication' between Taiwan and the mainland.[68]

Whether Wang Daohan will eventually go to Taiwan, as agreed upon in late June 1999, was uncertain at the time of writing, as were the long-term consequences of Lee's comments. What deserves some speculation, however, is why the ROC president would make such a statement, sensitive as he must have been to its implications.

On one level, Lee Teng-hui must have been seeking to place an indelible mark on history by ensuring that Taiwan's mainland policy would be locked in a direction he approved before his expected retirement from the presidency in 2000. In this, he would be following the example of his predecessor, Chiang Ching-kuo, who during his last years in office set into motion several fundamental changes in the Republic of China. These included relaxing contact across the Taiwan Strait and implementing democratic reform through such actions as the lifting of martial law and beginning the Taiwanization of the political system.[69] Lee's vision of the ideal Taiwan-mainland relationship is perhaps captured in his 1999 book, *Taiwan's Viewpoint*, in which he proposed that China should be divided into seven autonomous regions, one of which was Taiwan, and that the concept of 'Greater China' should be scrapped.[70]

On another level, the ROC leader may have been trying to set a mark for future negotiations with the mainland. As explained by presidential adviser Lin Bih-jaw, if China would accept the new formulation of state-to-state relations, then Taipei would be willing for the first time to engage in 'political dialogue' with the mainland.[71]

Whatever Lee's long-term ambitions or negotiating ideas, most observers focused on more immediate motivations to explain Lee's rejection of the traditional one-China policy of the Republic of China: the need to ensure the KMT's victory in the March 2000 presidential elections. With Lee retiring from office, the KMT's assumed candidate would be the heir apparent, Vice President Lien Chan. Lien was facing strong opposition from within the KMT itself – popular former Taiwan provincial governor James Soong, who advocated more rapid unification with the mainland and who decided to run for president as an independent after Lee's rejection of the one-China policy (Soong commented: 'Taiwan needs a courageous but not reckless leader'[72]) – and from outside the KMT in the person of charismatic former Taipei mayor Chen Shui-bian, who would represent the opposition Democratic Progressive Party (DPP), and former DPP head Hsu Hsin-liang, an influential opposition politician who quit the DPP (because of its favoring Chen's nomination) to run as an independent. The various factions and political trade-offs are beyond the scope of this book, but suffice it to say that Lee apparently hoped that his policy change would (a) steal the thunder from Chen Shui-bian, who earlier had been advocating an independent 'Republic of Taiwan', and (b) force James Soong into either siding with the president and thus alienating his mainlander base of support on Taiwan or disagreeing with the president, thereby angering a large portion of the Taiwanese electorate.[73]

(The outcome of the March 2000 elections came as a surprise: Chen Shui-bian won with 39 percent of the vote, James Soong received 37 percent, and Lien Chan 23 percent. The security implications of Chen assuming the ROC presidency in May 2000 are enormous, but that analysis will have to await future volumes.)

WILD CARDS OF REUNIFICATION

Taiwan politics

Politics on Taiwan, as well as on the mainland and in the United States, play a highly important role in the security of Taiwan. President Lee Teng-hui's renunciation of Taiwan's 'one-China' policy is an excellent example, since the policy change, apparently done largely for domestic political reasons, had the immediate effect of causing China to issue threatening statements, to consider canceling Wang Daohan's long-awaited visit to Taiwan, and to ponder anew whether the only way to prevent Taiwan from drifting toward independence was through the use of force. Also, there were signs of alarm in Washington, not yet in the mood for another round of tension with Beijing over Taiwan.

But Taipei did have a point. The 'one-China' policy dates from the depths of the Cold War, when the United States and China were trying to find a formula to justify strategic cooperation against the common Soviet threat even while disagreeing over Taiwan. The 'one-China' policy so often referred to by China, the United States and the Republic of China did not take into account the wishes of the majority of Taiwan's residents. That omission for the sake of *Realpolitik* has come back to haunt all three governments since the mid-1980s, when democratization began to take hold in Taiwan politics.

Prior to that time, the ROC government institutions on Taiwan were dominated by mainlanders loyal to the Nationalist Chinese goal of one day recovering the mainland from the communists and unifying Taiwan with the mainland under the banner of Dr. Sun Yat-sen's vision of a democratic Chinese state. Today, largely through ten years of effort by Lee Teng-hui, Taiwan's political institutions are mostly – but not completely – controlled by Taiwanese. The so-called native sons and daughters of Taiwan view the ROC goal of recovery of the mainland as foolish and illusionary. They consider Taiwan to be their homeland, not China. This view was reflected in the comments of Professor C. L. Chiou, who said in a DPP-sponsored conference on Taiwan's role in international affairs in 1993: 'To put pressure on the Taiwanese people to feel some sort of Han chauvinistic, nationalistic duty and moral responsibility to help China modernize and democratize is unrealistic and unfair.'[74]

Lee Teng-hui

Lee himself is Taiwanese, and under his administration the parallel processes of democratization and Taiwanization of ROC politics have proceeded at an accelerated pace. Under Lee, ROC policy toward the mainland has evolved from one of claiming to be the legal government of 'one China' to one of claiming the ROC on Taiwan to be an independent state with no jurisdiction over the mainland. At minimum, this is a 'two-Chinas' policy; and under Lee this policy has leaned increasingly in the direction of Taiwan independence – without, however, issuing a formal declaration of independence that would likely precipitate a PRC military response. To the Lee government, unification, if it occurs at all, is a distant goal for the future, possible only after the CCP relinquishes its monopoly of political power and democratic institutions are in place on the mainland.

This formulation of an 'independent Republic of China' combines the traditional KMT–ROC idea of Taiwan being part of China with the popular Taiwanese notion that Taiwan ought to be an independent state, separate from China. It is similar to the concept of 'new Taiwanese', another brainchild of Lee Teng-hui born during the close Taipei mayoral race in December 1998 between second-generation mainlander Ma Ying-jeou, the KMT candidate, and Taiwanese Chen Shui-bian, the incumbent DPP mayor. Ma won, in part because of Lee's backing and the public's embrace of the 'new Taiwanese' concept: the idea that all residents of the island, whatever their home province, should now consider Taiwan to be their home.[75] Chen lost, in part because of his efforts to frame the election as an ethnicity contest between Taiwanese and mainlanders. Chen's defeat and the fall in the DPP's overall percentage of the votes convinced many that the opposition party had overemphasized its pro-Taiwanese and pro-independence platform.

What should be recognized about Taiwan politics is that extreme views – that is advocacy of early unification or early independence – are supported by vocal minorities of mainlanders and Taiwanese respectively, but that the majority of Taiwan residents, whether mainlander or Taiwanese, prefer the broad middle road of the status quo, neither moving too fast toward political union with the mainland nor moving too far in the direction of Taiwan independence. Lee and his mainstream KMT faction have drawn their political support from this majority, although in recent years he personally has leaned increasingly in the direction of greater political autonomy for Taiwan – 'doing business as' the Republic of China.

In making this personal transition, Lee has antagonized an ever larger number of mainlanders who originally supported his consolidation of power. James Soong, now a rival to Lee's chosen successor Lien Chan for the next president, is an excellent example. Earlier in 1993, several other KMT politicians dissatisfied with the direction Lee was taking the party resigned from the KMT to form the New Party, a pro-unification party that has fallen on bad times because of infighting.

What Lee may have lost in terms of mainlander political support was more than made up by growing Taiwanese support, attracted by his Taiwanese roots and pro-Taiwan policies. As Lee consolidated his power and gradually evolved his policy, he and his mainstream KMT faction brought the ruling party and ROC policy into closer and closer alignment with the moderate elements of the DPP. For example, in commenting on Lee's abandonment of the 'one-China' principle, DPP presidential candidate Chen Shui-bian said: 'What Lee Teng-hui just said, I said four years ago. I haven't changed – he has.'[76] In fact, a very common view on Taiwan is that Lee is a closet member of the DPP, a *taidu* (one favoring Taiwan independence) at heart.

Since there is a possibility – some say a strong possibility – that the DPP will one day become the dominant ruling party of Taiwan (Chen's victory in the March 2000 presidential elections may be a precursor), a few words need to be said about the DPP and its political platform, especially as they relate to Taiwan's security equation.

Democratic Progressive Party

The DPP is an important factor in cross-Strait security for several reasons: (a) the DPP, comprising mainly Taiwanese, is openly in favor of an independent Taiwan, and it might one day control policy on the island; (b) the DPP has been a major force in Taiwan politics since the mid-1980s, forcing the KMT to democratize more rapidly than it otherwise would have wanted and compelling the ROC government to become more pro-Taiwan in its foreign relations and mainland China policies; and (c) neither the PRC nor the United States wants the DPP to become the ruling party on Taiwan, fearing that it might spoil an otherwise manageable trilateral relationship between Washington, Beijing and Taipei.

The DPP was formed in 1986 by anti-KMT activists, almost all of whom were Taiwanese. Under then-existing martial law provisions, the DPP was illegal; but President Chiang Ching-kuo, convinced that the ROC political system had to be liberalized, allowed the DPP to form and to participate in the December 1986 elections. In addition to promoting Taiwan independence, the DPP's platform advocated such popular themes as more democracy, anti-corruption, an extensive social welfare system, self-determination for Taiwan residents, state-to-state relations with the PRC, joining the United Nations, streamlining Taiwan's armed forces, closing nuclear power plants, improving the environment and so forth.[77]

According to the DPP platform, 'Taiwan is sovereign and independent … it does not belong to the People's Republic of China, and … the sovereignty of Taiwan does not extend to mainland China'. Accordingly, 'an independent country should be established and a new constitution drawn up in order to make the legal system conform to the social reality in Taiwan and in order to return to the international community'. Further, 'the establishment of a sovereign Taiwan Republic and the formation of a new constitution shall be determined by all citizens of Taiwan through a national referendum'. Elsewhere, 'Taiwan's future should be determined by all residents of Taiwan according to the principles of freedom, self-determination, universality, justice and equality'. The DPP platform advocates non-confrontational, state-to-state relations with the PRC based on the principles of 'humanity, equality and peace' and 'on the interests of Taiwan people'. Both sides should seek to reduce tensions, and 'the two sides of the Taiwan Straits should be allowed to compete with each other peacefully on an equal status'. The platform emphasizes: 'We oppose any talks on the solution of this [Taiwan] issue which are against the principle of "self-determination".'

From the outset, the DPP has done fairly well at the polls. For example, in the Legislative Yuan (the legislative branch of government) elections in 1986, 1989, 1992 and 1995, the DPP won 22.2 percent, 28.3 percent, 31 percent and 33.2 percent of the votes, respectively, compared with 69.2 percent, 60.2 percent, 53 percent and 46.1 percent for the KMT, and (in the 1995 election) 13 percent for the New Party.[78] In the 1996 presidential elections, the DPP won 21.1 percent of the vote, while the KMT won 54 percent, and two independent candidates won a total of 24.9 percent.[79] In the December 1998 Legislative Yuan elections, the DPP won 29.6 percent of the vote, compared with 46.4 percent for the KMT, 7 percent for the New Party, 1.4 percent for the Taiwan Independence Party (a splinter group from the DPP) and 15.5 percent for others (New Nation Alliance, Democratic Alliance, Nonpartisan Alliance, independents and candidates running without party endorsement).[80] So roughly one-fifth to one-third of Taiwan voters regularly prefer DPP candidates over those of other parties.

Cognizant that the DPP might one day become the ruling party of Taiwan, party leaders have actively courted support in the United States. While American support has been strong in encouraging democratic reform on Taiwan, a great many US China specialists have warned the DPP that their advocacy of Taiwan independence is likely to precipitate a crisis in the Taiwan Strait. This would place the United States in the awkward position of having to decide whether to support the self-determination of the Taiwan people and risk war with China, or to avoid war with China and see the free people on Taiwan threatened by PRC military force. US government officials and laymen alike have suggested strongly to the DPP that it should not place Washington in such a dilemma.

This advice has been received with mixed feelings by the DPP. On the one hand, the issue of Taiwan independence is one of the major rallying cries of opposition to the KMT. Many DPP leaders are former political prisoners of the Nationalist government, having been imprisoned for advocating Taiwan independence or having to go into exile to countries like the United States or Japan. There is an emotional attachment to the issue of Taiwan independence that binds the disparate elements of Taiwanese opposition to the KMT. To many in the opposition, abandoning Taiwan independence would be tantamount to abandoning the DPP's *raison d'être*.

On the other hand, if the DPP is to become the ruling party of Taiwan, it must moderate its policies and abide by the wishes of the majority of the people. As reflected in elections and repeated public opinion polls, the majority of Taiwan's residents prefer a continuation of the status quo in the Taiwan Strait and do not endorse either early independence or early unification. The majority's support for the status quo does not necessarily reflect a preference for Taiwan's ideal future, but it does demonstrate a pragmatic interest in avoiding a military confrontation with the PRC, continuing to enjoy American support, and living in a relatively stable and prosperous environment.

The members and leadership of the DPP have wrestled over how to approach the issue of independence. At first, two schools of thought emerged. The more radical 'New Tide' faction considered independence to be the most important issue facing Taiwan. This group wanted to press the issue through various means, including the ideological 'purification' of DPP membership. The more moderate 'Formosa' faction adhered to the goal of Taiwan independence but wanted first to promote democracy and gain power before moving toward independence. In power struggles within the DPP, the Formosa faction generally won. In 1996 the DPP leadership under moderate Hsu Hsin-liang argued that Taiwan was already independent and hence there was no need to declare its independence. Several key DPP members thereupon left the party to form the more radical Taiwan Independence Party.

Although Hsu Hsin-liang is no longer chairman of the DPP, being replaced in 1998 by a more outspoken Taiwan independence advocate, Lin Yi-hsiung, Hsu continues to be a leading opposition figure. After it became apparent that he would lose the DPP's nomination for the 2000 presidential election to another popular DPP leader, former Taipei mayor Chen Shui-bian, Hsu in May 1999 resigned from the party he helped to found. (He ran for the presidency as an independent but won only 0.6 percent of the vote.)

One of the most striking political trends on Taiwan has been the gradual narrowing of views between the mainstream faction of the KMT and the moderate factions (mostly Formosa) of the DPP. As one of the Formosa faction leaders, Hsu has argued that if the DPP really wants to become the ruling party of Taiwan it must stop dwelling on the independence issue. In October 1997 Hsu said Taiwan was already a de facto independent state and there was no need to provoke Beijing by declaring Taiwan independence. If the DPP one day assumed power on Taiwan, it would not declare formal independence as this would unnecessarily endanger the safety of the island's people.[81] Hsu also suggested that Taiwan and mainland China hold talks on the 'three links' (business, transportation and mail) and that the DPP and CCP enter a dialogue. Government-to-government political talks were premature, however.[82]

Chen Shui-bian has been more outspoken in his support of Taiwan independence, although his public views have moderated considerably since his defeat in the December 1998 Taipei mayoral elections. Ever the politician, Chen has called for a 'new middle ground way of thinking', which seems to mean avoiding extremism on issues such as independence. In December 1997 he told a Japanese audience: 'Taiwanese people have the right to decide their future and decide where Taiwan should go.' In another interview he said: 'The Democratic Progressive Party wants to establish a sovereign independent Republic of Taiwan, to form a new constitution and to let Taiwan residents make the ultimate choice about Taiwan's future.'[83]

Realizing that a consensus has to be built within the party if the DPP is to be successful in replacing the KMT as Taiwan's ruling party, the DPP has held a series of conferences on its China policy. An effort was made in February 1998 to merge the views of the Formosa and New Tide factions, resulting in the slogan 'strengthen Taiwan, march West [toward China]'. Essentially, this meant (a) support resumption of cross-Strait dialogue; (b) refuse to accept the 'one-China' premise as a precondition to talks with the mainland; (c) refuse to negotiate over Taiwan's sovereignty; (d) stress that individual political parties on Taiwan cannot negotiate with China on behalf of the Taiwan people; (e) insist that Taiwan–China talks only be based on government-to-government contacts; (f) include in the scope of Taiwan–China talks all areas, including economic, social, educational and general affairs; and (g) insist there is no specific timetable for a resumption of Taiwan–China talks.[84]

Concerned that Taiwan–mainland integration might be proceeding too rapidly, the DPP in March 1999 published a report proposing restrictions on contact with the mainland. Policy recommendations included: (a) maintaining the Lee government's 'go slow, be patient' policy on limiting bilateral economic and trade exchanges; (b) stabilizing the government's cross-Strait exchange policy; (c) repealing only gradually the restrictions on mainland Chinese visits to Taiwan; (d) restricting visits to Taiwan by mainland residents in classified areas; and (e) only gradually recognizing diplomas issued from mainland schools. The DPP report also expressed concern over the estimated 25,000 cross-Strait marriages.[85]

In early May 1999 the DPP held a party congress, after which a proclamation was issued which 'unequivocally clarifies the outlook of the DPP regarding Taiwan's future at this juncture in time'.[86] The main points of the proclamation were as follows:

1. Taiwan is a sovereign and independent country. Any change in the independent status quo must be decided by all the residents of Taiwan by means of plebiscite.

2. Taiwan is not a part of the People's Republic of China. China's unilateral advocacy of the 'One China Principle' and 'One Country Two Systems' is fundamentally inappropriate for Taiwan.

3. Taiwan should expand its role in the international community, seek international recognition, and pursue the goal of entry into the United Nations and other international organizations.

4. Taiwan should renounce the 'One China' position to avoid international confusion and to prevent the position's use by China as a pretext for annexation by force.

5. Taiwan should promptly complete the task of incorporating plebiscite into law in order to realize the people's rights. In time of need, it can

be relied on to establish consensus of purpose, and allow the people to express their will.

6. Taiwan's government and opposition forces must establish bipartisan consensus on foreign policy, integrating limited resources, to face China's aggression and ambition.

7. Taiwan and China should engage in comprehensive dialogue to seek mutual understanding and economic cooperation. Both sides should build a framework for long-term stability and peace.

One of the most interesting passages in the DPP resolution was: 'Taiwan is a sovereign and independent country. In accordance with international laws, Taiwan's jurisdiction covers Taiwan, Penghu, Kinmen, Matsu, its affiliated islands and territorial waters. Taiwan, although named the Republic of China under its current constitution, is not subject to the jurisdiction of the People's Republic of China. Any change in the independent status quo must be decided by all residents of Taiwan by means of plebiscite.' The reference to the current name of Taiwan being 'the Republic of China' caused considerable debate within the DPP, because some thought it might imply the DPP's acceptance, at least temporarily, of Taiwan being named 'the Republic of China'. The majority prevailed in keeping the clause, however, in recognition of the party's need to appear more moderate and less offensive to the PRC so as to lower the risk of Chinese attack and also to attract wider voter support in the 2000 elections.

Hence, the current differences between the KMT and the DPP on the critical issue of Taiwan's relationship with mainland China are not that great. This convergence of views between the traditional ruling party and opposition party on Taiwan is one of the greatest concerns to policy hardliners in Beijing, who believe the time has come to increase pressure on Taipei to head off Taiwan's slide into independence.

Hardliners and track-II diplomacy

Policy hardliners
Thus far in this chapter we have considered several occasions when hard-liners within the CCP leadership opposed the moderate policy package of Deng Xiaoping and Jiang Zemin. There were also strong signs of opposition to Premier Zhu Rongji's visit to the United States in April 1999,[87] and even more opposition to his reported concessions with the United States to ease China's entry into the World Trade Organization, which prompted critics to call him a 'traitor'.[88] The power struggle between moderates and hardliners in Beijing resurfaced yet again in mid-July 1999 in internal policy debates over how best to respond to Lee Teng-hui's

rejection of the ROC's traditional 'one-China' policy. According to some reports, there appeared to be a major rallying of hardliners around former premier Li Peng, with their influence already being felt in political crackdowns on dissidents, the scaling back of certain economic reforms, and suppression of religious activities such as *Falun Dafa*. With some senior military officers openly referring to the Ministry of Foreign Affairs as the 'ministry of selling out of the country', there was a concerted effort on the part of hardliners to pursue a more aggressive and less pro-Western foreign policy. Anger at Taiwan and the United States is especially prevalent among this group.[89]

Chinese who advocate a tougher policy toward Taiwan – and generally toward the United States as well – seem to do so from several motivations:

- *Nationalism*. It is argued that Taiwan is a part of China taken away by foreign imperialism in the past. It must be recovered. Since the current policy of peaceful reunification is not working, a tougher policy must be implemented.
- *Security concerns*. Taiwan is being used by the United States to divide and weaken China. In the event of conflict, Taiwan could be used as a base of military operations against the mainland. To protect China, Taiwan must be brought back under the control of Beijing. The policy of peaceful unification has not succeeded and thus must be replaced by one of greater pressure being applied to Taipei.
- *Chauvinism*. China's destiny as the leader of Asia cannot be fulfilled unless Taiwan is reunited with the mainland. Unification thus is vital, but the current policy of using peaceful means is not achieving the desired result; indeed, Taiwan seems to be drifting away. A new, more forceful policy should be adopted.
- *Ideology*. China seems to be losing its socialist character. The continued existence of a separate Republic of China on Taiwan challenges the legitimacy of the CCP and threatens China's political–economic–social order. Taiwan is being used by the Nationalists and their Western supporters to weaken communist authority on the mainland through the strategy of 'peaceful evolution'. Since signs of social disorder are increasing on the mainland and peaceful reunification is not working, more forceful means should be adopted to end the use of Taiwan as a source of Western influence.
- *Bargaining*. China is now in a stronger bargaining position than Taiwan, but Taipei has taken advantage of PRC peaceful reunification policies to strengthen its military with US assistance and to gain recognition of its 'international presence'. Before Taiwan becomes too strong and arrogant, China should increased pressure to compel the Taiwan authorities to enter serious political talks.

The common theme of these anecdotal arguments is that peaceful reunification is not working: Taiwan is moving away from unification; social stability on the mainland is threatened because of Western influences; and US support for Taiwan, particularly in the form of arms sales, is increasing. Two major security concerns for China – namely Taiwan becoming an independent country, and the United States having access to Taiwan's bases and facilities in the case of Sino-American conflict – are seen by some Chinese to be more likely today than they were in 1979. This perceived erosion of Chinese interests requires a reassessment of PRC strategy and policy toward both Taiwan and the United States. So argue the hardliners in Beijing, and their influence could cause problems for Taiwan's security.

There are, of course, hardliners in Taipei and Washington as well. Those in Taipei who oppose Lee's brand of cooperative engagement generally favor either an increased pace toward unification or a more deliberate move toward *de jure* independence. The vast majority of Taiwan residents, however, prefer some variation of the current engagement policy since the alternatives are not very appealing.

But, in Washington, hardliners can have a pronounced effect on policy, although perhaps not as radically so as in Beijing. As will be seen in Chapter 7, opposition to Clinton's brand of engagement with the PRC is very widespread, but there are relatively few Americans who advocate an extremist policy toward China: containment, overt hostility or isolation as with Cuba. Those who do – like the former senior Senate staffer who told me, 'we like to "stick it" to China when we can' – generally are motivated by a hatred of communism, racism or a commitment to isolationism. The motivations of those who oppose Clinton's specific policies of engagement are much more numerous, and their motivations vary from sincere concern over the growing national power of China to abhorrence over Beijing's gross violations of the human rights. Whereas in China, hardliners can perhaps move PRC policy from one of engagement to confrontation, in the United States, hardliners can perhaps move US policy from one of engagement with 'pro-China' characteristics to engagement with neutral characteristics. In all likelihood, it would take a policy of confrontation on the part of Beijing to cause Washington to abandon engagement entirely.

In summary, there are hardliners in Beijing who continually lobby for tougher Chinese policies toward Taiwan and the United States. Similarly, critics of the US policy of engagement abound. Under certain circumstances, hardliners in either or both countries could gain control of policy. This could lead to a rapid escalation of tensions across the Taiwan Strait or in Sino-American relations, thus increasing the security threat to Taiwan.

Track-II diplomacy

In recent years there has been a tendency for foreigners, particularly Americans, to broker their services as mediators or facilitators in cross-Strait relations. One of the most well-known of these efforts came from former Secretary of Defense William J. Perry. In January 1998 Perry led a high-level, quasi-official US delegation to both the PRC and Taiwan. The delegation warned Taipei not to move in the direction of independence but rather to begin discussions with Beijing as a step toward resolving their differences.[90] Making it clear that they were speaking with backing from the Clinton administration, the delegation included former Chairman of the Joint Chiefs of Staff General John Shalikashvili, former National Security Adviser Brent Scowcroft, and Ashton Carter, former Assistant Secretary of Defense for International Security Policy. One of the delegation's main purposes was to open an informal channel of communications between Taiwan and mainland China, a so-called 'track-II' approach used successfully in other difficult international situations.

The delegation told Taiwan that the PRC was willing to hold unconditional talks on economic, cultural and trade issues. But Perry warned Taiwan's political leaders that they should not count on US military help if they declared independence and the mainland attacked them as a result. Perry said he told DPP leaders Hsu Hsin-liang and Chen Shui-bian: 'There is a possibility that they could be in power one day. I just wanted them to understand that independence could be a catastrophe and if they thought that the US would bail them out, they were wrong.'[91] The public warnings given by the Perry delegation, apparently made with Washington's approval, went far beyond previous statements of US intentions in regards to the circumstances under which the United States would intervene militarily in the event of a PRC attack against Taiwan.

When Perry returned to Taipei in early 1999 to once again offer his good services, the ROC government responded cautiously. Some in the KMT, such as Shao Yu-ming, Deputy Secretary-General of the ruling party, generally approved of the initiative – if the intermediary could 'stick to the principles of fairness and openness'.[92] Others – including President Lee Teng-hui himself – told Perry that he should better understand what the people in Taiwan think before contacting mainland China.[93] The Presidential Office indicated that cross-Strait dialogue should be conducted between the two organizations established to hold such talks, the Straits Exchange Foundation and the Association for Relations Across the Taiwan Strait.[94] The real concern of Taiwan was probably reflected in the comments of Lin Bih-jaw, Deputy Secretary-General of the Presidential Office, who said of the US-based organizations sponsoring Perry's track-II efforts: 'These organizations tend to listen more to what Peking has to say. This is because their representatives make longer and more frequent visits to the mainland than they do to Taiwan, resulting in an unbalanced understanding.'[95] In other words, it was difficult for Taiwan to believe that its interests would be served by American mediation at this point, a lesson perhaps learned from postwar history.

Still, the possibility of some informal breakthrough in cross-Strait relations cannot be ruled out. Indeed, given the distrust and hostility that simmers close to the surface in PRC–ROC relations, such an indirect approach may be the only face-saving way to avoid a future confrontation in the Taiwan Strait.

CONCLUSION

Reviewing the unification policies of the two Chinese sides, certain conclusions relevant to Taiwan's security can be reached. First, the two sides are still fighting, in a political way, the civil war that began in the 1920s. Neither the Kuomintang nor the Communist Party of China is willing to concede defeat. Both sides officially adhere to the goal of a future united China, but each side has its own interpretation of what that China will or should be. Beijing holds that one China equates to the People's Republic of China and that Taiwan is part of the PRC. Taipei insists that China is currently divided into two separate and equal states, but that China can and should be united in the future under a system of democracy, freedom and equitable distribution of wealth.

Second, domestic factors weigh heavily on cross-Strait relations. In the PRC, the resolution of the Taiwan issue is one of the most sensitive political issues in the country, with various factions using the issue in their bids for power. PRC leaders face a major dilemma in trying to resolve the Taiwan issue: they cannot appear too accommodating lest they lose domestic political support; yet, if they do not become more accommodating to Taiwan, China's unification – under peaceful means – seems more and more illusionary. In Taipei, the introduction of democracy has given rise to strong Taiwanese voices calling for political separation from mainland China. This view is expressed politically through the DPP, which one day may become the dominant party of Taiwan. For ROC leaders, the challenge is to devise policies that adhere in principle to a unified China yet treat Taiwan as a de facto independent state. Adopting democratic reform at home and pragmatic diplomacy abroad, the KMT managed to stay in power through the year 2000; however, these same policies created much doubt in China and suspicion in the United States.

In truth, all three governments follow a strategy of ambiguity: no one knows whether Taiwan will declare its independence; no one knows whether the PRC will use force against Taiwan; and no one knows whether the United States will intervene if China attacks Taiwan. What should be recognized is that the ambiguity followed by all three governments not only reflects a choice of strategy but also political uncertainty at home. As a result, no one can rule out the possibility of war in the Taiwan Strait.

Third, international factors play a key role in cross-Strait relations, the most critical player being the United States. All sides – including the DPP – heavily lobby the United States to gain American support or, at minimum, to influence Washington's perceptions and policies. More broadly, the PRC and ROC actively compete for international recognition and prestige. In this competition, Beijing is victor by far. As of April 1999, the ROC was recognized by only 28 countries, the latest being Macedonia – an action prompting Beijing to veto in February 1999 the presence of UN peacekeeping troops patrolling Macedonia's tense border with Yugoslavia.[96] The number of countries recognizing the PRC, on the other hand, was 156 as of October 1998. The PRC hopes to isolate Taipei from the international community, to punish it for seeking wider diplomatic recognition, and to convince Taiwan that it has no alternative but to enter into political negotiations to bring about the early unification of China under terms favorable to the PRC. The ROC, however, refuses to give up its pragmatic diplomacy, viewing even quasi-political recognition by other countries as essential to Taiwan's survival as a nation-state. Taipei is willing to fight every diplomatic battle to the best of its ability and to the extent permitted by its sizeable treasury – adding to Beijing's sense of unease.

Fourth, despite the fact that Beijing and Taipei both claim to support the goal of a united China in the future, there is an enormous gulf between their respective unification proposals. At least at present, the issue is zero-sum: either the PRC or the ROC will survive. Beijing will not allow the Republic of China to continue as a rival Chinese state; and the ROC will not allow a democratic Taiwan to unify with a communist mainland. There has been no compromise on this issue for 50 years.

Fifth, on the more practical level of economic, cultural and day-to-day exchanges, there has been considerable flexibility shown by Beijing and Taipei. Trade is flourishing; people-to-people exchanges are increasing much faster than either government can easily control; and mutual interests in interaction across the Taiwan Strait are forcing both governments to find ways to deal with each other in a more pragmatic fashion. If political differences between Beijing and Taipei can be managed in such a way as to avoid major confrontation, there is every reason to expect that cross-Strait exchanges will continue to increase in the future.

Sixth, there are several important reasons why Taipei and Beijing need to maintain high-level dialogue across the Taiwan Strait. From the point of view of Taiwan, such dialogue contributes to political restraints on Beijing not to use force in the Taiwan Strait; eases qualms in the United States over Taiwan's efforts to achieve independence and thereby possibly draw Washington into a military confrontation with Beijing; and helps to maintain social stability on Taiwan by (a) easing concerns on the part of mainlanders on the island that the Taiwanese-led government may be moving in the direction of independence, (b) satisfying demands by Taiwanese businessmen that they be allowed to conduct business on the mainland, and (c) appearing to the general public that the ROC government is pursuing a moderate, reasoned policy toward the mainland. From the point of view of Beijing, continued high-level dialogue and broad exchanges across the Taiwan Strait contribute to the PRC's strategy of peaceful reunification, an essential part of China's modernization plans and its foreign policy; influence US policy in directions generally favorable to the PRC, such as (a) moderating US arms sales to Taiwan, (b) avoiding too much American intervention in Taiwan affairs, and (c) allowing Sino-American relations to move forward without too much disruption over the Taiwan issue; restrain hardliners within the PRC leadership who want to resolve the Taiwan issue more quickly, by force if necessary; strengthen the linkages between Taiwan and the mainland, gradually integrating Taiwan with China in ways that probably will be impossible to break apart; and enable the PRC to better gauge the prospects for Taiwan independence and to influence policy debates and policy decisions on Taiwan.

In short, the various factors related to China's unification contain ample evidence that either a peaceful or a non-peaceful resolution of the Taiwan issue is possible. On the one hand, peace in the Taiwan Strait has integrated the two sides to a degree thought impossible ten years ago; moreover, the status quo in the Strait has brought tangible benefits to all parties concerned. On the other hand, the PRC seems to be losing patience since its policy of peaceful reunification has not achieved the results initially expected; indeed, Taiwan seems to be moving increasingly in the direction of national autonomy from the mainland. Thus, cross-Strait relations play a critical role in Taiwan's security in the post-Deng era, but it is difficult to determine whether those relations will exert a positive or negative influence over the long term.

The next chapter, written by Dr. Robyn Lim, a former intelligence analyst of the Australian government, will consider yet another factor in Taiwan's security equation: perceptions of the island's geostrategic importance and how those perceptions influence major power policy in the post-Cold War period.

NOTES

1. 'Qian Qichen on Reunification', *Xinhua*, January 28, 1999, in *FBIS-China*, January 29, 1999.
2. Hsiao Peng, 'The Mainland Defines Phased Targets of Cross-Strait Reunification', *Sing Tao Jih Pao*, January 19, 1999, in *FBIS-China*, January 19, 1999.
3. Edgar Snow, *Red Star Over China* (New York: Modern Library, 1944), p. 96.
4. Quoted in *Taiwan Communique*, 85 (March 1999), pp. 19–20, citing Frank S.

T. Hsiao and Lawrence R. Sullivan, 'Chinese Communist Party and the Status of Taiwan, 1928–1943', *Pacific Affairs* 52, 3 (Fall 1979), pp. 446–67.

5. See NSC 48/2 ('The Position of the United States with Respect to Asia: Conclusions – A Report to the President by the National Security Council, December 30, 1949') in Stephen P. Gibert and William M. Carpenter, eds, *America and Island China: A Documentary History* (Lanham MD: University Press of America, 1989), pp. 80–5.

6. See 'U.S. Secretary of State Acheson's Statement on U.S. Defense Perimeter in Pacific Area', in Gibert and Carpenter, *America and Island China*, pp. 91–2.

7. See 'President Truman's Statement on Sending U.S. Fleet to Taiwan Straits, July 19, 1950', in Gibert and Carpenter, p. 119.

8. *Xinhua*, March 6, 1978, in *FBIS-China*, March 7, 1978, p. D31.

9. *Kyodo*, September 19, 1979, in *FBIS-China*, September 19, 1978, p. A1.

10. Li Jiaquan, 'Formula for China's Reunification', *Beijing Review*, February 3, 1986, p. 19.

11. See, for example, Sofia Wu, 'Taipei Disapproves of Perry's Proposed "Track II" Dialog', Taiwan Central News Agency, March 12, 1999, in *FBIS-China*, March 12, 1999, citing a statement from the ROC Presidential Office.

12. *Washington Star*, January 29, 1979, p. 1.

13. *Xinhua*, May 21, 1979, in *FBIS-China*, May 24, 1979, p. D8.

14. Translated in *Inside China Mainland* (Taipei), May 1982.

15. *Beijing Review*, January 12, 1981, p. 9.

16. Ye's nine-point proposal was given in an interview with *Xinhua* on September 30, 1981. See *FBIS-China*, September 30, 1981, p. U1.

17. 'China's Reunification: Is the "Nine-Point Proposal" a Yesable Solution' (Taipei: China Mainland Research Center, May 1982).

18. *New York Times*, November 27, 1982, p. 1.

19. *Xinhua*, June 30, 1984, in *FBIS-China*, July 2, 1984, pp. E1–E2.

20. See *A Draft Agreement between the Government of the United Kingdom of Great Britain and Northern Ireland and the Government of the People's Republic of China on the Future of Hong Kong* (London: HMSO, September 26, 1984).

21. Press conference held in Taipei on September 12, 1997. See *MAC News Briefing* 0041 (September 16, 1997).

22. 'Guidelines for National Unification' (Taipei: National Unification Council, 1991).

23. *MAC News Briefing*, November 3, 1997, p. 1. For details, see Ralph N. Clough, *Reaching Across the Taiwan Strait: People-to-People Diplomacy* (Boulder CO: Westview Press, 1993) and *Cooperation or Conflict in the Taiwan Strait?* (New York: Rowman & Littlefield, 1999).

24. Hungdah Chiu, *Koo–Wang Talks and the Prospect of Building Constructive and Stable Relations Across the Taiwan Straits* (Baltimore: University of Maryland School of Law, 1993).

25. 'The Taiwan Question and the Reunification of China' (Beijing: Taiwan Affairs Office and Information Office, State Council, August 1993). An English version of the document can be found in *Beijing Review*, September 6–12, 1993, pp. I–VIII.

26. For a summary of the document, see *Free China Journal*, September 24, 1993, p. 7.

27. For the text of Jiang's speech, entitled 'Continue to Promote the Reunification of the Motherland', see *Xinhua*, January 30, 1995, in *FBIS-China*, January 30, 1995.

28. The text of Lee's speech can be found in *Lien-Ho Pao*, April 9, 1995, in *FBIS-China*, April 9, 1995.

29. See comments of MAC Chairman Chang King-yuh at January 26, 1998, news conference, in *MAC News Briefing*, February 2, 1998, p. 5.
30. See Jen Hui-wen, 'Beijing Warns Li Teng-hui Through Missile Training', Hong Kong *Hsin Pao*, July 19, 1995, in *FBIS-China*, July 21, 1995.
31. 'Infuriated by Li Teng-hui's Visit, CPC Hardliners Call for Re-explanation of Jiang's Eight-Point Proposal to Curb Taiwan Independence Forces', *Lien-Ho Pao*, May 26, 1995, in *FBIS-China*, May 26, 1995. A similar article appeared a few weeks later. See 'Irritated by Li Teng-hui's Words and Deeds and Provoked by Taiwan's Military Exercises, Hardliners in China's Taiwan Affairs Departments Get the Upper Hand', *Lien-Ho Pao*, June 11, 1995, in *FBIS-China*, June 11, 1995.
32. Bu Wen, 'The United States is Playing with Fire', *Renminribao*, June 10, 1995, in *FBIS-China*, June 10, 1995.
33. Huang Huiping commentary, 'What Role is Li Denghui Playing', Beijing Central People's Radio, June 8, 1995, in *FBIS-China*, June 12, 1995.
34. 'Commentary: Where Does the United States Really Want to Lead Sino-U.S. Relations', *Xinhua*, June 17, 1995, in *FBIS-China*, June 17, 1995.
35. Duanmu Laidi, 'Commentary: It is Unpopular to Embrace Foreigners to Earn Himself Dignity and to Split the Motherland', *Xinhua*, June 13, 1995, in *FBIS-China*, June 14, 1995.
36. Yan Jing, 'Evidence of Violations of "One China" Principles by Taiwan Authorities', *Liaowang*, June 19, 1995, in *FBIS-China*, June 19, 1995.
37. For a chronology of cross-Strait exchanges, see 'Mainland Affairs Council News Release, February 26, 1998', in *MAC News Briefing*, March 2, 1998, pp. 3–5.
38. 'China is Correspondingly Readjusting Its Cooperation with the United States – Interviewing Zhang Yebai, Research Fellow of the CASS American Studies Institute', *Wen Wei Po*, June 1, 1995, in *FBIS-China*, June 1, 1995.
39. For an extension of this argument, based on interviews with authoritative communist party leaders, see Jen Hui-wen, 'Gradual Escalation of China's Strategy against United States, Taiwan', *Hsin Pao*, June 28, 1995, in *FBIS-China*, June 30, 1995.
40. See Wang Yu-yen, 'Beijing Top Level Focuses Attention on Sino-U.S. Ties', *Lien-Ho Pao*, July 2, 1995, in *FBIS-China*, July 2, 1995. See also Wang Mei-hui, 'Koo–Wang Meeting Cannot Possibly be Held This Year Unless China and the United States Resume Political Dialogue', *Lien-Ho Pao*, July 10, 1995, in *FBIS-China*, July 10, 1995.
41. *South China Morning Post*, July 7, 1995, in *FBIS-China*, July 7, 1995.
42. 'Communist China to Comprehensively Review Policy toward Taiwan, Military has No Plan for the Time Being to Conduct Large-Scale Military Exercises', *Lien-Ho Pao*, July 4, 1995, in *FBIS-China*, July 4, 1995.
43. For more details of the crisis, see, for example, Greg Austin, ed., *Missile Diplomacy and Taiwan's Future: Innovations in Politics and Military Power* (Canberra: Australian National University Press, 1997); John W. Garver, *Face off: China, the United States, and Taiwan's Democratization* (Seattle: University of Washington Press, 1997); and James R. Lilley and Chuck Downs, eds, *Crisis in the Taiwan Strait* (Washington DC: American Enterprise Institute and National Defense University Press, 1997).
44. Jen Hui-wen, 'Beijing Warns Li Teng-hui Through Missile Training', *Hsin Pao*, July 19, 1995, in *FBIS-China*, July 21, 1995.
45. Speech to the PRC State Council's Office of Overseas Chinese Affairs, Office of Hong Kong and Macao Affairs, and Taiwan Affairs Office, as reported in *Xinhua*, September 29, 1997, in *FBIS-China*, September 29, 1997. For further elaboration

of Qian's speech, see *Zongguo Xinwen She*, September 29, 1997, in *FBIS-China*, September 30, 1997.

46. Taiwan Central News Agency, September 30, 1997, in *FBIS-China*, September 30, 1997.

47. Quoted in *Free China Journal* (Taipei), December 13, 1996, p. 1. Also, see Kao's report in *MAC News Briefing* 8 (January 6, 1997).

48. Hong Kong AFP, report from Taipei, September 19, 1997, in *FBIS-China*, September 22, 1997.

49. *MAC News Briefing* 37 (August 18, 1997).

50. 'Text of President Lee Teng-hui's Speech at Panama's Legislative Assembly', Taipei *Chung-Yang Jih-Pao*, September 10, 1997, in *FBIS-China*, September 10, 1997.

51. Chang Wei-kuo, 'Look Forward to New Pattern of Cross-Strait Relations – Interviewing Chang King-yuh, Taiwan's Mainland Affairs Commission Chairman', *Hsin Pao*, October 9, 1997, in *FBIS-China*, October 9, 1997.

52. 'MAC Vice Chairman, Spokesman Sheu Ke-sheng at the October 6, 1998, News Conference', *MAC New Briefing* 96 (October 12, 1998), p. 1.

53. For a full report on the Koo visit from Taipei's point of view, see *Free China Journal*, October 23, 1998, p. 1.

54. Lu Chao-lung, 'Li Says Taiwan "Country with Independent Sovereignty"', Taipei *Chung-Kuo Shih-Pao*, February 17, 1999, in *FBIS-China*, February 17, 1999.

55. 'Zhu Rongji Calls for Early Cross-Strait Negotiations', *Xinhua*, March 5, 1999, in *FBIS-China*, March 5, 1999.

56. See Frank Chang, 'SEF Regrets Beijing's Reluctance to Pinpoint Date for Wang Trip', *Free China Journal*, July 2, 1999, p. 1.

57. SEF official in interview, Taiwan Central News Agency, September 19, 1997, in *FBIS-China*, September 22, 1997.

58. Associated Press report from Taipei, July 10, 1999.

59. *Wall Street Journal*, July 13, 1999, p. A14; *Washington Post*, July 13, 1999, p. A14.

60. Associated Press report from Taipei, July 15, 1999.

61. Reuters report from Beijing, July 11, 1999.

62. Quoted in *Wall Street Journal*, July 15, 1999, p. A10.

63. For the US reaction, see Reuters report from Washington, July 12, 1999. Japan's reaction can be found in a Reuters report from Tokyo, July 13, 1999.

64. For an argument that the true description of China today is 'one China, two states', see James Lilley and Arthur Waldron, 'Taiwan is a "State". Get Over It', *Wall Street Journal*, July 14, 1999, p. A22. For an argument that the United States must adhere to its 'one-China' policy, see David Shambaugh, 'Two Chinas, But Only One Answer', *Washington Post*, July 18, 1999, p. B1.

65. 'Chinese Threats', *Washington Post*, July 14, 1999, p. A22.

66. 'Taiwan Speaks Up', *Wall Street Journal*, July 15, 1999, p. A18.

67. *Wall Street Journal*, July 15, 1999, p. A10.

68. Quoted in *Xinhua* and reported in *Wall Street Journal*, July 13, 1999, p. A14.

69. See the many books written by John F. Copper, who has detailed Taiwan's political evolution over more than two decades of careful analysis.

70. See a review of Lee's book by Antonio Chiang, 'No Place Like Home?' *Far Eastern Economic Review*, June 17, 1999. See also Lee Teng-hui, *The Road to Democracy: Taiwan's Pursuit of Identity* (Tokyo: PHP Institute, 1999).

71. *Wall Street Journal*, July 16, 1999, p. A12.

72. Quoted in *Washington Post*, July 17, 1999, p. A15.

73. For discussion of some of these issues, see Reuters report from Taipei, July 13,

1999; and Matt Forney, 'Lee's Shift on China is Shrewd Political Move in Taiwan', *Wall Street Journal*, July 15, 1999.

74. See Maysing H. Yang, ed., *Taiwan's Expanding Role in the International Arena* (New York: M. E. Sharpe, 1997), p. 51.

75. KMT Secretary-General Chang Hsiao-yen said the term should be translated into English as 'neo-Taiwan person', referring to all people who live on the island, love the island, and acknowledge it as their homeland. See Taiwan Central News Agency, January 14, 1999, in *FBIS-China*, January 14, 1999.

76. Quoted in *Wall Street Journal*, July 15, 1999, p. A10.

77. 'Political Platform of the Democratic Progressive Party' (Taipei: DPP, March 19, 1995).

78. See John Fuh-sheng Hsieh, 'Continuity and Change in Taiwan's Party Politics', *Working Papers in Taiwan Studies* 25 (1996), published by the Conference Group on Taiwan Studies, American Political Science Association.

79. John Fuh-sheng Hsieh, Dean Lacy and Emerson M. S. Niou, 'Retrospective and Prospective Voting in a One-Party-Dominant Democracy: Taiwan's 1996 Presidential Election', *Working Papers in Taiwan Studies* 21 (1996).

80. See *Free China Journal*, December 11, 1998, p. 1.

81. Taiwan Central News Agency, October 10, 1997, in *FBIS-China*, October 10, 1997.

82. *Chung-Kuo Shih-Pao*, October 20, 1997, in *FBIS-China*, October 23, 1997.

83. Quoted in *Taiwan Communique* 79 (February 1998), pp. 4–5.

84. 'DPP China Policy Debate', *Taiwan International Review* 4, 1 (January–February 1998), pp. 2–4.

85. Victor Lai, 'DPP Proposes Taiwan Should "Consider" Joining U.S.' TMD', Taiwan Central News Agency, March 27, 1999, in *FBIS-China*, March 27, 1999.

86. 'DPP Resolution on Taiwan's Future', DPP Party Convention, Kaohsiung, May 8, 1999. From DPP internet homepage.

87. 'Military Objects to Zhu Rongji U.S. Visit', Hong Kong *Tung Hsiang*, April 15, 1999, in *FBIS-China*, April 15, 1999.

88. See numerous newspaper articles during April and early May 1999 reflecting hardliner opposition to Zhu's trip and concessions. For example, 'China is Close to Deal on WTO, Zhu Says, But Politics Interfere', *Wall Street Journal*, April 6, 1999, p. A1; 'U.S., China Hit Snags in New Trade Talks', *Washington Post*, April 24, 1999, p. E1; 'Chinese Official Offers to Resign in Sign of Anger on WTO Reform', *Wall Street Journal*, May 3, 1999, p. A16.

89. For evidence of the moderate–hardliner policy debates, see 'China on Taiwan: What Comes Next? Beijing Power Struggle Clouds the Issue', *Washington Post*, July 18, 1999, p. A23.

90. For an analysis of the Perry visit and the reasons for the mission, see *Washington Post*, February 21, 1998, p. A16.

91. *Washington Post*, February 21, 1998, p. A16.

92. Deborah Kuo, 'KMT Deputy Secretary-General Favors "Track II"', Taiwan Central News Agency, March 17, 1999, in *FBIS-China*, March 17, 1999.

93. Flor Wang, 'Perry Urged to Better Understand Taiwan "Track II" Views', Taiwan Central News Agency, March 13, 1999, in *FBIS-China*, March 13, 1999.

94. Sofia Wu, 'Taipei Disapproves of Perry's Proposed "Track II" Dialogue', Taiwan Central News Agency, March 12, 1999, in *FBIS-China*, March 12, 1999.

95. Myra Lu, 'ROC Downplays "Track Two" Idea', *Free China Journal*, March 19, 1999, p. 1.

96. See, for example, Myra Lu, 'Peking Blasted for Veto of UN Troops in Macedonia', *Free China Journal*, March 5, 1999, p. 1.

3

Taiwan and Asia–Pacific Security

Robyn Lim

Taiwan's continued de facto independence represents a security interest of the first order for the United States. That stems from the maritime basis of American security, as well as from US responsibilities for the maritime security of Japan – a matter of great convenience for both parties. Unless the United States continues to help Taiwan defend itself, China will take it by force. The precedent set could be highly dangerous to regional security, especially because of its impact on Japan. If America forgets the maritime basis of its security, it will relearn it the hard way.

The crux of the Taiwan issue is that China insists on the right to use force to reintegrate what it sees as a renegade province. Although the United States would not oppose the peaceful reintegration of Taiwan, it has never conceded that China has the right to use force to bring the island to heel.

In relation to Taiwan, the problem for China is that it lacks the capacity which the Soviets possessed to bring overwhelming force to bear on contiguous states across land frontiers. Any People's Liberation Army (PLA) plan to invade Taiwan would invite the problem which Hitler encountered with the English Channel. (Hitler's generals were such land animals that they referred to Operation Sealion as a 'large-scale river crossing'.) Unable to take Taiwan by force, China is more likely to try to take it the way Hitler took the Sudetenland in 1938 – by credible threat which others are unwilling to resist for fear of war.

TAIWAN, THE 'FIRST ISLAND CHAIN' AND AMERICAN SECURITY

Taiwan is important to the United States because of what it represents, and where it is. A former US protectorate, Taiwan is the first democracy in the long history of the Chinese people. It is also a prosperous island of more than 22 million people. In geostrategic terms, Taiwan is a key link in the 'first island chain' that runs the length of the East Asian littoral. Because of its location, Taiwan engages interests vital to America's maritime security.

America cannot afford to ignore what is happening strategically on the opposite shores of its great oceans. That is because the United States has inherited the British role of 'offshore balancer'.[1] The only alternative is isolationism, which history suggests does not work. Separated from the East Asian littoral by the vast reaches of the Pacific Ocean, the United States needs allies and bases on the first island chain in order to maintain a balance of power in East Asia.

Strategic circumstances change, but strategic interests are remarkably enduring. Maintaining a balance of power in East Asia has been an essential US interest at least since the days of President T. R. Roosevelt, who brokered the Treaty of Portsmouth after stalemate had been reached in the 1905 Russo-Japanese war. In the 1930s, Japan collided with the US interest in the balance of power in East Asia when Japan's armed forces expanded into China and threatened the Philippines. If China pursues regional hegemony, it is bound to clash with the US need for balanced power in East Asia.

East Asia is now the global focus of unresolved great-power strategic tensions, because the collapse of Soviet power restored equilibrium in Europe. Focused on the Taiwan Strait and the Korean peninsula, tensions which were subsumed during the latter stages of the Cold War have now resurfaced. Security in these two areas is connected, because both are linked with the strategic security of Japan. China's probing in the East and South China Seas is another source of tension, and engages the interests of the maritime powers and all those who depend on their protection.

De facto allies during the latter stages of the Cold War, the United States and China now represent opposite poles of strategic interest in the Western Pacific. China is a continental state which occupies the central geographical position on the East Asian mainland. When such states start showing blue-water ambition, as China now is, alarm bells ring in the capitals of the maritime powers. That was the case, for example, when the Kaiser started to build his 'risk fleet' early this century.

Germany, occupying the central geographical position in Europe and in possession of a powerful army, wanted hegemony over Eurasia and was willing to risk war in order to obtain it.[2] The Kaiser's purpose in building his risk fleet was not to contest global command of the seas with the United Kingdom. Rather, he sought to challenge the Royal Navy in the North Sea, and thus to deter Britain from playing its traditional role of maintaining the balance of power in Europe. If Britain were no longer to play the role of offshore balancer, that would have been sufficient to give German hegemony over Europe.

The PLA navy is today's risk fleet. Having learned from the demise of the Soviet Union, China does not wish to invite bankruptcy by over-spending on its military. China's strategic needs are regional and concentrated, whereas America's are global – stemming from its role as offshore balancer. The purpose of the PLA navy is to develop sufficient maritime power to deter the United States from playing its traditional role as offshore balancer in East Asia. Because China dominates the mainland, such deterrence of the United States would be sufficient to give China regional hegemony. Then Japan could be marginalized, and the United States would be permitted to operate in East Asia only on terms set by Beijing.

China is adjacent to the East Asian littoral, while the United States is an ocean away. Enjoying the advantages of proximity within the first island chain, China would not need to develop maritime power commensurate with that of the United States in order to exercise hegemony over the Western Pacific. If China could develop sufficient naval and air power to turn the South China Sea into a Chinese lake, would the United States then risk its aircraft carriers in those confined waters?

For China, the first island chain is a two-edged sword. On the one hand, the chain makes it harder for China to get out into the open ocean. On the other hand, a base on Taiwan, which lies between Japan and the Philippines, would allow China to project power outwards into the Pacific Ocean.

Possession of Taiwan would also permit China to box in the northern entrance to the South China Sea, thus making it harder for others to get in. In 1997, China acquired the deep-water harbor of Hong Kong. Further south, China's territorial claims in the South China Sea are fueled by a drive for power and resources. These claims are so extensive that they press on the vital Strait of Malacca, which connect the Indian and Pacific Oceans. China also has a strategic foothold in Burma, at the western end of the Malacca Strait, and China is tying up mainland Southeast Asia with road and rail networks.

THE 1996 CLASH OF STRATEGIC INTERESTS IN THE TAIWAN STRAIT

It is hard to say whether China or the United States was more surprised by the clash of strategic interests demonstrated in the Taiwan Strait in March 1996.[3] When China first sent nuclear-capable missiles across the Strait in July 1995, it sought to punish Taiwan for the visit to the United States by 'splittist–traitor' Lee Teng-hui, Taiwan's president, in order to attend a Cornell alumni reunion. An inadequate US response emboldened Beijing to launch further missiles near Taiwan's ports in March 1996, in order to intimidate the island during its first direct presidential election.[4]

The Clinton administration then sent two aircraft-carrier battle groups to the vicinity of the Taiwan Strait. That naval display, led by the USS *Nimitz* and *Independence,* was the largest directed at China since the

Taiwan Strait crises of the 1950s. To the United States, the outcome seemed highly satisfactory. It demonstrated yet again the flexibility and mobility of maritime power, as well as its political utility. Taiwan's voters were not intimidated by China, and they elected Lee Teng-hui in a landslide. As foreign journalists flocked to Taiwan, Lee Teng-hui's victory was widely seen as that of a brave democrat defying the bully across the water. While China railed against 'gunboat diplomacy', it knew that the carrier battle groups could wipe out the PLA navy in short order. Beijing had not anticipated such a US response. That showed how dimly the Chinese had grasped what was at stake for the United States – its credibility as an Asia–Pacific power.

But what lessons did Beijing draw from this crisis? No doubt it identified many vulnerabilities on Taiwan, including the flight of capital and the drop in the currency. In a future crisis, Beijing might seek to create panic and confusion on Taiwan, including using subversion and assassination. Then China might offer Taiwan generous terms, provided it acknowledged the sovereignty of Beijing. China could calculate that if it acted quickly, it could present the United States with a *fait accompli*.[5]

The Taiwan issue could prove especially dangerous if China were to miscalculate in a future crisis, for example, by using missiles to target a US aircraft carrier. But if China were to damage or even sink one, 'remember the *Kitty Hawk*' would spur, not deter, the United States.[6] Democracies often look weak. But once they are attacked, or their vital interests threatened, they react with greater determination than authoritarian regimes anticipate. That is the lesson that China should have learned from the 1991 Gulf war. But did it?

AMERICAN VALUES AND INTERESTS IN RELATION TO TAIWAN

Now there is a new twist to the Taiwan problem. Taiwan emerged from the Cold War as a democracy and with a growing sense of separate identity. Most Taiwanese do not want to 'return' to still-poor and authoritarian China. Increasing economic interdependence and tourism are unlikely to ameliorate these concerns.

Taiwan now has a much greater purchase on American interests than when it was run by the Chiang Kai-shek clique. The end of martial law in 1987 marked the turning point for Taiwan, but China went in the opposite direction. In 1989, the Tiananmen massacre showed the regime's determination to maintain political control. Singapore's capitalism with political control is a model for China's leaders, whereas Taiwan's raucous democracy is an affront.

On the Taiwan issue, American values line up behind American strategic interests. Many in the United States worry that if Taiwan calculated that it could count on US protection, it might provoke Beijing with a unilateral declaration of independence. But the people of Taiwan are unlikely to give China the excuse to use force. Taiwan's voters have shown that they are capable of making sensible choices. The greater risk is that China might come to calculate that the United States would turn aside while Taiwan was forcibly reintegrated. Other Asia–Pacific countries have a vital stake in Taiwan's continued de facto independence, with Japan at the top of the list.

JAPAN'S STAKE IN THE TAIWAN ISSUE

What would be the impact on Japan if the United States looked the other way while China took Taiwan by force or threat? Most likely, Japan would lose confidence in US strategic protection, and begin to think it must look after its own security. Japan is already starting to hedge. The Clinton administration failed to respond adequately to Japan's security concerns after North Korea's unannounced launch of a Taepo-dong missile in August 1998 across the Japanese islands.[7] That led to Japan's decision to operate four reconnaissance satellites of its own, at vast cost.

Unless Japan is willing to submit to Chinese hegemony – which seems unlikely – strategic independence is Japan's only alternative to alliance with the United States. At a minimum, Japan would have to develop long-range maritime capability to protect its sea routes. That would mean a much greater investment in anti-submarine warfare, and it could also mean power-projection capabilities such as aircraft carriers and long-range strike aircraft. Japan might even opt for nuclear weapons, the 'isolation-ists' dream', as a right-wing isolationist tattoo has long urged. That is not unique to Japan. In Australia, for example, an isolationist fringe has long seen utility in nuclear weapons, and for the same reason – unwillingness to entrust one's strategic security to allies, who might prove unreliable.

If Japan chose to go it alone, that could destabilize the entire Western Pacific. The US–Japan alliance, which both protects Japan and cocoons Japanese power, has long provided stability for the region. Many countries, with an eye to the technological adeptness and determination of the Japanese, would worry if Japan cut itself loose from the US deck. China is ambivalent about the US–Japan alliance. Although Beijing wants to marginalize Japan, it does not want a strategically independent Japan either. Yet the Chinese cannot see the connections between the Taiwan issue, their own belligerence, and Japan's worries about its security. Blind-ness to the concerns of others is typical of such regimes, and no amount of US missionary education is likely to make much difference.[8]

China has long sought to deter Japan from 'interfering' in the Taiwan issue. In 1894, China lost Taiwan when Japan took it from a decaying Ching empire as a spoil of the naval war. The memory of that defeat fuels China's sense of historical grievance. And by using the war guilt issues of a later era – 'remember Nanjing' – China has long been able to push Japan in an effort to influence her policies.

What especially riles China's leaders is the background of Taiwan's President Lee Teng-hui. Lee, the first 'native' Taiwanese president, was educated in Japan (as well as the United States) and likes Japanese culture.[9] That is beyond the ken of any Chinese chauvinist. Nor do China's leaders seem to understand that for most Taiwanese, the memory of KMT atrocities in 1947 overshadows any lingering resentment at Japan's occupation of the island. Taiwan is quite different from South Korea, where hostility to Japan remains an integral part of nationalism.

Lee Teng-hui has made no secret of his wish to visit his Japanese alma mater, Kyoto University. To China's fury, as soon as the Nationalist Shintaro Ishihara was elected governor of Tokyo in April 1999, he started to talk about inviting Lee to Japan.[10] Ishihara argued that if the elected governor of Tokyo wished to invite his good friend, the elected president of Taiwan, why should the unelected leaders of a foreign state be allowed to stand in his way? A good point, but Japan's foreign ministry is most unlikely to issue Lee Teng-hui a visa. Yet China's own actions in 1995–96 brought home to the Japanese what is at stake for them in the Taiwan issue.

One of those equities is sheer proximity. Yonaguni, Japan's outlying island in the long island chain off Okinawa, is only 60 km from Taiwan. In March 1996, China's missile barrages landed close to Japan's sea and air routes, and Yonaguni was within range of a stray missile. Pointing this out to the Chinese, Japan's foreign ministry also noted the importance of maintaining democracy on Taiwan.[11]

If China succeeded in taking Taiwan by force or threat, the consequences further south would also endanger Japan's security. The great maritime highway essential to Japan's resource security, especially oil imports from the Gulf, must pass through the first island chain, whose choke points include the Malacca Strait. Many of the Southeast Asians, already wobbly, would preemptively acquiesce in Chinese hegemony. It is always the instinct of the weak to be eaten last, even though the threat to these countries is to their independence rather than to their sovereignty.

A China in possession of Taiwan and astride the Malacca Strait would be ideally placed to throttle Japan.[12] Because Japan is a resource-poor archipelago, it could be controlled without need for invasion. Japan's need for maritime protection is one of the many reasons the United States must deter China from pursuing the 'Sudetenland solution' for Taiwan.

THE MARITIME BASIS OF ASIA–PACIFIC SECURITY

The US–Japan alliance is based on a congruence of maritime strategic interests which has not changed greatly since 1945. Because forward deployment best suits America's strategic needs, the United States needs bases and allies off the East Asian littoral. For Japan, alliance with the global maritime power represents optimal security, with solitary self-defense a much less attractive option.

Defeat in 1945 taught Japan the costs of war, and forced it to abandon territorial ambition on the mainland. In any case, the Japanese themselves had long realized – at least in the case of China – that the mainland was an endless bog. By fiat of the American occupation, Japan was wrenched into the maritime orientation best suited to its strategic geography, thus ending a long struggle for supremacy between its army and navy. Japan's maritime orientation also helps reassure its neighbors. When Japan had both a blue-water navy *and* a huge army which the navy could propel to distant shores, even remote countries had cause for concern.

With the US–Japan alliance as its strategic underpinning, East Asia's future ought to lie in a growing community of market-oriented democracies linked with the United States. That network of fraternal democracies should incorporate Taiwan and a future reunified Korean peninsula. It should also include China, if China gets a government which is willing to consider the rights and interests of others.

Between them, the United States and Japan hold most of the high cards. These maritime democracies, which are the world's largest economy and its second largest, are providing security for the entire Western Pacific, while spending only 3 and 1 percent of GNP, respectively, on defense. But they often play their cards poorly, while China is expert at playing skillfully from a weak hand.

CLEVER CHINA?

In relation to regional security, the essential difference between China and Japan is that China has strategic ambition, while Japan has strategic anxieties. Those in the United States who think that it is 'all economics' fail to appreciate the distinction. During East Asia's economic crisis, China presented itself as America's 'reliable Asian ally' because it did not devalue its currency – a move which would have been against its own interests. In addition, Japan's economic paralysis gave China great leverage because it led to China and the United States jointly criticizing Japan. Only a strategically inept US administration could allow itself to be so manipulated by Beijing.

China also exploited President Clinton's domestic embarrassments resulting from a sex scandal. In June 1998, the Chinese insisted on an unprecedented nine days for Clinton's visit to China, with no stopovers in Japan or South Korea. Clinton also puffed up the Chinese by offering them 'strategic partnership'. While on Chinese soil, he omitted to mention the US–Japan alliance. Apparently self-deterred by the Taiwan Strait crisis of two years previously, the president also delivered the 'three no's' on Taiwan: that the United States does not support independence for Taiwan; or two Chinas, or one China–one Taiwan; or Taiwan's membership in any international body for which statehood is a requirement. Predictably, that statement was promptly repudiated by Congress.

The misguided notion of 'strategic partnership' did much to feed China's growing sense of self-regard. Early in 1999, for example, China used its veto in the UN Security Council (UNSC) to prevent the extension of the mandate of UN peacekeepers in Macedonia. The veto was to punish Macedonia for establishing diplomatic relations with Taiwan. Like the unlamented Soviet Union, China now claims that no world problem can be solved without its participation.

President Clinton's faith in personal diplomacy also recalls Franklin Roosevelt's naiveté about Stalin, whom he saw as another ward boss whom he could charm. No doubt, Chinese Premier Zhu Rongji and President Clinton got on well during Zhu's April 1999 visit to Washington. Zhu is no Stalin, and his advocacy of market reform represents the direction in which the United States wants China to go.

But Zhu's visit was soured by revelations that China had exploited US sloppiness in guarding its nuclear secrets. That may have helped China to develop multiple-warhead missiles which could be aimed at the United States. Yet China was arguing that the United States should not employ any form of missile defense.

In February 1999, China deployed additional short-range missiles along its coastline opposite Taiwan, bringing their number to more than 100. Zhu claimed disingenuously that these were not meant to threaten the 'brothers and sisters' on Taiwan. Most likely, Zhu knows that such attempted intimidation will backfire, because it will make the United States more inclined to support TMD for Taiwan and to sell it other kinds of sophisticated defensive weapons. Yet Zhu cannot ignore the interests of the PLA. In China, the military is much more the equal of the party than was the case in the USSR. That is another reason that US efforts at missionary education are unlikely to have much effect in Beijing.

TAIWAN: RESIDUE OF UNRESOLVED COLD-WAR STRATEGIC TENSION

Taiwan is not a problem that has suddenly emerged with the end of the Cold War. Major strategic tensions do not come as a bolt from the blue, or arise as a result of *deus ex machina*. Rather, the Taiwan issue represents a residue of strategic tension between the United States and China which remained unresolved at the end of the Cold War. It has reappeared with a vengeance because of China's enhanced post-Cold War strategic latitude.

The Taiwan problem is not amenable to resolution by diplomatic process or other panaceas. In fact, it cannot be resolved until a better government exists in Beijing. Then China might be willing to consider the legitimate rights and interests of the people of Taiwan. In the interim, it is critical that Taiwan's de facto independence be preserved. Those in Taiwan who want to proclaim *de jure* independence must also be dissuaded.

The United States and China are natural geostrategic adversaries, whose common opposition to the Soviet threat made allies of convenience during the latter stages of the Cold War. Their de facto alliance having dissolved with the collapse of the USSR, they were soon at odds again over Taiwan.

Throughout the Cold War, the strategic balance in the Taiwan Strait remained linked with security on the Korean peninsula, because both were connected with the security of Japan. Those connections date from June 1950, when Stalin gave North Korea a green light to attack the South. In the previous year, Mao Zedong's Communist Party had defeated the Nationalist forces of the Kuomintang (KMT), whose remnants fled to Taiwan. The United States entered the Korean War mainly to protect Japan. But the exercise of American maritime power around Japan, including in the Taiwan Strait, meant that China could not take Taiwan by force.

Initially, the Korean War seemed a masterstroke for Stalin, not least because it diverted US attention and resources away from Europe, at low cost to Moscow. By bringing the United States and China into collision, the war served other purposes for Stalin: keeping China subordinate to Moscow, and preserving Taiwan as a focus of Sino-US hostility.

Stalin was ambivalent toward the Chinese communists, even up to the KMT collapse and flight to Taiwan. A friendly but subordinate China was a Soviet objective that long predated the Cold War.[13] A weak China, run by a KMT dependent on Moscow, might well have suited Moscow best.

But as soon as Mao had defeated the KMT, he wanted Soviet backing for the invasion of Taiwan. Stalin had other priorities. Focused on his global strategic contest with Washington, he saw that a Soviet alliance with China would greatly complicate US strategic planning. Mao's continued hostility to the United States would confront Washington with the prospect of a two-front war, as well as with Chinese-backed revolution in Southeast Asia. As long as Mao could not take Taiwan, it would serve as an irritant between China and the United States. That would head off any US–China *rapprochement* that might increase China's power relative to that of the Soviet Union.

Others sensed opportunities in the Taiwan issue. In January 1950, US Secretary of State Dean Acheson suggested that US strategic interests in Asia were confined to an offshore perimeter. Acheson's purpose may have been to drive a wedge between Moscow and Beijing, whose mutual suspicion was no secret. Nor was it a secret that the United States was fed up with the KMT. Alluding to Soviet designs on Chinese territory in Mongolia and in Manchuria – where Stalin was pursuing Czarist ambition for warm-water ports and strategic railways – Acheson seemed to hint that the United States might tolerate Beijing's seizure of Taiwan, in the wider interests of US *rapprochement* with China.[14] Any such possibility was ruled out by North Korea's attack on the South, as Stalin no doubt intended.

Stalin succeeded in bringing China and the United States into collision at no cost to himself, and in preserving Taiwan as a source of friction between them. Soon after the outbreak of war, the US Seventh Fleet deployed into the Taiwan Strait, thus preventing Mao from invading Taiwan. In any case, the PLA was soon forced to move northwards, since the North Koreans' initial successes could not be sustained. When they were chased back up the peninsula by US-led United Nations forces, the PLA came into the war. The American presence off Taiwan and in North Korea had presented China with an unacceptable threat of two-front war.[15]

Initially, the Korean War seemed a brilliant success for Stalin, but unintended consequences soon surfaced. These included the rebirth of the Japanese economy; the American creation of a structure of bilateral alliances with Japan as its linchpin; and China's resentment at Moscow for having encouraged a war that threatened China's interests. We now know how bad Sino-Soviet relations were after the honeymoon.

Stalin had also succeeded too well in maintaining the Taiwan issue as a source of tension between Washington and Beijing. During the crises in the Taiwan Strait in 1954 and 1958, Moscow saw no interest at stake worth the risk of nuclear war with America. The Soviets did not fear conventional war. But they did fear nuclear war, because it would have destroyed their political system.

TAIWAN AND KOREA ON THE BACKBURNER: THE LATTER STAGES OF THE COLD WAR

Moscow's refusal to risk nuclear war over Taiwan contributed greatly to China's decision to reject the dubious benefits of alliance with the USSR. Beijing chose instead to build enough nuclear weapons to ward off the threat of nuclear blackmail. After the Sino-Soviet split, relations went downhill to the brink of war in 1969. That was madness from the Chinese point of view because they were bound to have come off worse. Mao's foreign policy proved as disastrous as his domestic policies.

Common resistance to a renewed Soviet bid for global hegemony then drew the United States and China into a de facto alliance, whose consequences included a desire on both sides to quarantine the Taiwan problem. The unlikely Sino-US strategic accommodation was prompted by policy failure on both sides: for the United States, the Vietnam War; for China, the humiliation of having been forced to back down in its confrontation with Moscow.

The sidelining of the Taiwan problem was symbolized by the PRC's replacing Taiwan in the United Nations in 1971, and by President Nixon's opening to China in 1972. At China's insistence, the United States abrogated its security treaty with Taiwan when it restored diplomatic relations with the PRC in 1979. Both the United States and China expected the Taiwan issue eventually to fade away. Indeed, the political systems on Taiwan and the mainland seemed to be converging towards the kind of 'developmental authoritarianism' to be found in South Korea and Singapore. This convergence, it was thought, would facilitate eventual reunification.

China tolerated continued US support for Taiwan, calculating that if it could arrest Taiwan's drift towards independence and keep it isolated, over time Beijing would gain greater leverage. Then it could quietly absorb Taiwan. Resort to force would put at risk China's wider interests in a peaceful international environment conducive to economic development and military modernization.

In contrast, no one expected great-power rivalries on the Korean peninsula to fade away. Even during the Cold War, the strategic quadrilateral (China, Russia, United States, Japan) continued to operate. Tensions flared at times, but neither of the communist great powers had anything to gain from renewed conflict on the peninsula. Their rivalry also allowed North Korea to play them off against each other, to Pyongyang's benefit. The other side of that coin was that both Russia and China had the motive and ability to restrain North Korea. Deterrence of North Korea was also maintained by US forward deployments in South Korea and Japan, as well as by American maritime power and nuclear weapons.

But although tensions in the Taiwan Strait and on the Korean peninsula were much reduced in the latter stages of the Cold War, the linkage between security in these two areas did not disappear. When the United States agreed to return Okinawa to Japan in 1969, Japan undertook not to hinder the use of US bases there in operations in defense of South Korea or Taiwan.[16] Ten years later, the United States had abrogated its defense commitment to Taiwan. But mostly at the behest of Congress via the 1979

Taiwan Relations Act (TRA), the United States continued to insist on its right to help Taiwan to defend itself. For that purpose, US access to bases in Japan would remain essential.

The Sino-US alliance of convenience did much to help win the Cold War. China's enmity posed an immense strategic complication for Moscow. It dispersed Soviet forces and made credible the threat of war on two fronts which President Reagan registered with the Maritime Strategy, to which the Japanese navy made an important contribution. In the end, growing ambition, and the resources needed to sustain it, brought down the Soviet Union. But that did not mean the end of great-power rivalry in East Asia. To the contrary, unresolved strategic tensions soon resurfaced, with potentially dangerous mutations.

CHINA'S POST-COLD WAR STRATEGIC LATITUDE

Since the end of the Cold War, China has been pointing east and south strategically toward Taiwan and the South China Sea. It is not that China has suddenly become powerful. Rather, China is enjoying a strategic latitude unprecedented in modern times, as a consequence of the way the Cold War ended.

To China's north, Russian armor no longer threatens Beijing from Mongolia. Now it is Russia that must fear China, because geography utterly exposes Russia in the Far East. One day China will present Russia with the account for 3 million square miles of territory taken by the Czars. During the Cold War, Russia occasionally sailed its naval vessels through the Taiwan Strait to underline China's lack of maritime capability. Moscow rubbed in the point after 1979, when it backed Vietnam's invasion of Cambodia, China's ally. As a reward, the Soviet navy gained access to Cam Ranh Bay, outflanking China. Now, with its Pacific Fleet rusting off Vladivostok, Russia has little choice but to appease China. It openly sides with the PRC on the Taiwan issue.

To China's south, once Vietnam had been stripped of its Soviet alliance, Hanoi was rapidly brought to heel. China had clashed with Vietnam in 1988 in the Spratly Islands in the South China Sea, when Vietnam sought in vain to stop the establishment of China's first base there. In 1992, China's rubber-stamp parliament reasserted China's claims over vast maritime areas in the East China and South China Seas. China also asserted its right to use force – including, by implication, against Japan – to recover the Senkaku/Diaoyu Islands in the East China Sea. This assertion of China's right to use force against US allies (Japan and the Philippines) seems to have been overlooked in the United States, which has persisted in seeing these territorial disputes as legal issues. Rather, these are strategic issues with legal faces.

LINKAGES AGAIN: THE KOREAN PENINSULA
AND THE TAIWAN STRAIT

Security in Korea remains linked with security in the Taiwan Strait. The resumption of great-power tensions focused on the Korean peninsula is another consequence of the way the Cold War ended. And because of the growing threat from North Korea, Japan's security policy is changing in ways that China fears might embolden independence advocates on Taiwan. Since the end of the Cold War, the Stalinist regime in North Korea has sought security, power and income in the development of missile technology and weapons of mass destruction. The regime is an orphan of the Cold War, no longer able to play off Russia against China. By 1992, both had recognized South Korea, because it had much more to offer economically than the North. (For China, there was a bonus because South Korea withdrew its recognition of Taiwan.) The loss of Russian security guarantees underlined North Korea's isolation.

On the Korean peninsula, Russia is now little more than an interested onlooker. But the three other members of the former strategic quadrilateral remain closely engaged. So far, China has managed to keep Japan out of the four-party talks on Korea (USA, China and the two Koreas). Because of Japan's guilty past, the Chinese insist, Japan is not entitled to assert any strategic interests now, either on the Korean peninsula or in relation to Taiwan. Japan is increasingly loath to tolerate these strictures.

China does not fear Japan, although that might be starting to change. For now, North Korea is the only country that China need fear. Pyongyang continues to act in ways that undermine China's interests, above all in relation to Taiwan. As a byproduct of Pyongyang's Taepodong missile launch in 1998, China faces the prospect that Taiwan will slip even further from its grasp. Japan, alarmed at the threat from North Korea, agreed to participate in US research into sea-based theater missile defense (TMD) whose 'footprint' might cover Taiwan. Once developed, this technology could undermine the political and military utility of China's missiles, which the PRC sees as its long suit against Taiwan. China has complained that Taiwan might acquire Aegis destroyers in order to facilitate co-operation with Japan and the United States in TMD.

Cooperation in TMD will also help strengthen the US–Japan alliance in ways that China thinks might further embolden Taiwan. The enhancement of the US–Japan alliance was a consequence of the changes in the global and regional balances at the end of the Cold War. In 1991, the Gulf War represented a threat to Japan's security which few in Japan seemed to appreciate. Despite Japan's dependence on imported oil, most Japanese seemed to think that they had no interest at stake when Iraq invaded Kuwait and threatened Saudi Arabia. After much dithering, which raised hackles in Congress, the government sent four minesweepers (but only after the war was over). Japan did send $13 billion, but got little thanks, including from Kuwait. Had the war gone on longer, or had American casualties been higher, the US–Japan alliance could have been ruptured. In the United States, the 'revisionists' saw this as evidence that Japan was nothing more than a mercantilist free rider, intent only on manipulating the US alliance while it grew rich by penetrating US markets.

Initially, President Clinton, much influenced by the revisionists, seemed to see little value in alliance with Japan. He seemed more inclined to retreat behind isolationist ramparts in order to fight trade wars. But his neglect of security policy worried many in his administration, especially when Japan seemed to be moving towards some kind of soft multi-lateralism and losing confidence in the US alliance. Then China's belligerence in the South China Sea and the Taiwan Strait convinced the administration that its interests demanded concerted opposition to Chinese unilateralism. Mending fences with Japan was critical, including by undertakings given during Clinton's April 1996 visit to Japan. The continued deployment of large US forces in Japan encouraged Japan to adopt a more outward-looking security policy, and to develop the forces needed to sustain it.

Speaking aboard the USS *Independence* in Tokyo Bay during his April 1996 visit, Clinton referred to the aircraft carrier's recent duty off Taiwan, which he said had 'helped calm a rising storm'. Behind the president, the television pictures showed a Japanese warship flying the naval ensign. Those pictures illustrated how China's belligerence was undermining one of its own key objectives: keeping Japan out of the Taiwan issue.[17]

As a byproduct of Clinton's visit, new US–Japan defense guidelines were drawn up. These will permit Japanese rear-area support contingent in areas surrounding Japan, with a Korean conflict particularly in mind. Both the United States and Japan know that if Americans start going home in body bags from Korea, while Japan merely waves its peace constitution, the US–Japan alliance will collapse. The new defense guidelines are only a start. As long as Japan remains willing to do no more than hold America's coat while Japan's own vital interests are at risk, the alliance will remain dangerously lopsided.

Mostly for fear of China, legislation to effect even these modest changes had been languishing in Japan's parliament. China complained that the definition of 'areas surrounding Japan' in the new defense guidelines might include the Taiwan Strait, and Beijing pressed to have the Strait specifically excluded. Japan responded that the definition of 'areas surrounding Japan' was situational, not geographical. Conceding China's demands would have been tantamount to declaring that Japan had no interests at stake in the Taiwan issue.

Japan's dithering on both TMD and the new defense guidelines came to an end after North Korea's missile launch in August 1998. After that,

Japan began to fear North Korean missiles more than it feared China's strictures. China's president, Jiang Zemin, pressed on the defense guidelines, TMD and the 'war guilt' issue during his disastrous visit to Japan in December 1998.[18] No doubt emboldened by China's success in having Clinton state the 'three no's' in relation to Taiwan, Jiang also insisted that Japan make a similar statement.

Jiang got nowhere, and his visit marked the end of Japan's postwar appeasement of China.[19] No doubt to Beijing's fury, North Korea helped out again in March 1999 when Japanese coastguard and navy vessels gave chase to two heavily armed spy ships which had intruded into Japanese waters, just at the time that the new defense guidelines were being debated in parliament.[20]

The guidelines cleared the lower house in time for Prime Minister Obuchi's May 1999 visit to Washington. Much had changed in Washington since Jiang Zemin's visit in 1997. President Clinton was said to be glad to spend time with a reliable Asian ally whose presence would not raise questions about missiles, human rights or nuclear espionage.[21]

Japan has continued to reject China's complaints that its acquisition of TMD would be 'destabilizing' and lead to an 'arms race' – the same terms once used by the Soviets to divert attention from their own relentless military build-up, especially in intercontinental ballistic missiles with multiple warheads. Apart from the risk that TMD's footprint might cover Taiwan, China also fears that TMD could undermine the value of China's minimal nuclear deterrent. That deterrent has been quietly increasing in relative value as the United States and Russia draw down their nuclear arsenals. But for Japan and the United States, the political advantage of TMD is its sea-based and defensive character.

SENKAKUS/DIAOYU ISLANDS

Japan's stake in the Taiwan issue is also linked to Tokyo's dispute with China over the uninhabited Senkaku/Diaoyu Islands off Taiwan, which Taiwan also claims. During the missile crisis in the Taiwan Strait in August 1995, Chinese warplanes entered the airspace over the Senkakus. That prompted Japanese fighters to scramble from Okinawa for the first time.

The end of the Cold War had consequences for the dispute between Japan and China over the ownership of these islands. In the late 1970s, China and Japan became allies of convenience when the United States and China came into strategic alignment. At that time, Chinese supreme leader Deng Xiaoping said that the Senkakus would be left to another generation to solve. But China reserved the right to use force to 'recover' them. In 1992, China reasserted its territorial claims in the East China and South China Seas, which included the Senkakus.

It is one thing for China to intimidate countries in the South China Sea, which do not enjoy the advantages of extended nuclear deterrence. China does not need to rattle its nuclear arsenal, since all know that China possesses such weapons. But China's use of force or threat against Japan in relation to the Senkakus would be an entirely different matter. The United States takes no position on the ownership of the Senkakus, but the islands were included in the Okinawa reversion documents of 1972 as territories 'administered by Japan'. China is unlikely to indulge in overt nuclear blackmail against Japan, since to do so would invite US intervention in an area where China is disproportionately weak.

Still, China continues to probe. Tensions were renewed in late 1995 when China began sending ocean surveillance ships and oil-drilling rigs into waters close to the islands. In July 1996, a right-wing Japanese student group put up a makeshift lighthouse on one of the islands. That aroused passions in China, Hong Kong and Taiwan. Initially, China seemed pleased by this demonstration of Han solidarity against Japan. One of China's purposes in stirring up the Senkakus issue may well have been to drive a wedge between Taiwan and Japan.

But then Beijing started to worry about what forces it might be unleashing at home, when student groups complained that the leadership was not defending Chinese territory with sufficient vigor. The involvement of right-wing extremists in Japan also pointed to the dangers of aroused chauvinist sentiment there. Emotional instinct is not far from the surface throughout North Asia, and could easily be a wild card that gets out of hand.

ASEAN ON THE TAIWAN ISSUE: A SMALL COUNTRY FAR AWAY

Further south, China gains immense leverage over the ASEAN (Association of Southeast Asian Nations) states because they profess to see no linkage between their own security and Taiwan's continued ability to resist enforced reintegration with the PRC. No one expects the ASEANs to stand up and shout at China about Taiwan. But they play into China's hands because they accept Beijing's claims that American policy toward Taiwan is driven by the urge to keep China weak and divided.

ASEAN's timidity will encourage China to pursue the 'Sudetenland solution' for Taiwan. If China's smaller neighbors seem willing to acquiesce in China's use of force or threat against Taiwan, that will weaken American strategic resolve. Why should the United States expend its blood and treasure, if most regional countries cannot see what is at stake for them in the Taiwan issue?

The ASEAN response to the Taiwan Strait crisis in 1995–96 was muted. Indeed, although Singapore remonstrated against China's use of force, long-serving Prime Minister Lee Kuan Yew (now a senior minister) continues to oppose American efforts to help Taiwan defend itself – as if no connection existed between Taiwan's right to resist enforced reintegration with China and the wider regional balance. In Malaysia, the visceral anti-Western instincts of Prime Minister Mahathir make him putty in China's hands. On a visit to Beijing in May 1999, Malaysia's foreign minister said that China's 'restrained attitude' in dealing with regional disputes 'reduced tensions with neighbors'.[22] Thailand is now a security ward of Beijing, to whom it looks for protection against still-distrusted Vietnam. Although the Thais by no means trust China, they openly sided with Beijing in the Taiwan Strait crisis of 1995–96.[23] On regional security issues, the Thais sing Beijing's song, questioning the continuing need for America's alliances now that the Cold War is over.

Pursuing conflicting territorial claims in the South China Sea, the ASEANs have been unable to combine in defense of their interests and actively to seek the countervailing power they would need to resist China. They also worry about the fifth-column potential of China's economically powerful diaspora. Beijing's strategy is to convince the Southeast Asians that they should accommodate China now, lest the price of future accommodation be made higher. 'Remember Saigon', the Chinese whisper. We will be here forever. Will America?

The Philippines also did much to let China into the South China Sea. By insisting that the United States leave its bases in the Philippines in 1991, the Filipinos removed the chief means by which America could protect them. They hobbled American maritime flexibility and emboldened China. Evidence came to light early in 1995 that China had seized Mischief Reef in the Spratlys. Mischief Reef is within the 200 n.m. Philippine Exclusive Economic zone, and 800 n.m. from Hainan. Had the US navy still been in Subic Bay, that seizure would have been unlikely. Early in 1999, the Chinese fortified Mischief Reef, but said that the buildings were merely fishing shacks.

A BALANCING COALITION-IN-EMBRYO?

But signs are emerging of resistance to Chinese strategic pressure, especially among the offshore countries. Australia strongly criticized China during the Taiwan Strait crisis in 1995–96, its defense minister warning that China's minatory behavior might incur consequences. In July 1996, Australia's alliance with the United States was updated by means of the 'Sydney Declaration'. That agreement saw renewal of arrangements covering the 'joint facilities' in central Australia. These could also have future utility in relation to TMD. Also announced was a much upgraded, combined military exercise program with US forces, all the more significant because the United States does not maintain combat forces in Australia. Australia also has growing strategic dialogues, which have a maritime focus, with Japan and South Korea. In addition, it has long-standing defense connections in Southeast Asia which America's other allies lack.

In December 1995, Australia and Indonesia entered into an unprecedented strategic alignment designed to resist Chinese strategic pressure in the South China Sea. Indonesia, by virtue of size, distance and visceral reaction, has been the bulwark of Southeast Asian resistance to China's southward probing. Jolted by the realization that China's extensive territorial claims might include the Natuna Islands, which guard the western approaches to Java, Indonesia was willing to seek the counter-vailing power it needed in order to resist China. But the economic crisis which led to the overthrow of President Suharto in May 1998 has brought turmoil to Indonesia. Indonesia's last experiment in democracy, 40 years ago, ended in chaos. China no longer has an instrument in Indonesia, as it had in the mid-1960s, when the communists came close to taking power. However, if Indonesia's multiethnic archipelago were to break up, China would stand to benefit even if did not have to lift a finger.

Southeast Asia's other archipelagic state, the Philippines, is now openly critical of the lack of support from ASEAN on the Mischief Reef issue. ASEAN has continued to avert its gaze while China fortifies a distant reef that it does not own. One consequence is that the Estrada government has applauded the new US–Japan defense guidelines, and welcomed the prospect of an increased security role for Japan – the last thing that China wanted to see. Some politicians have even called for the Philippines to switch diplomatic recognition from China to Taiwan, although that is unlikely to happen. But in May 1999, the Philippine senate ratified a new Visiting Forces Agreement with the United States. That will allow the United States to give the Philippine surplus equipment in order to improve its defense capability, now virtually non-existent.

The US navy will also gain useful access to bases in the Philippines and be able to resume exercises with the Philippine navy. As soon as the Philippines had the new agreement in its pocket, it showed a more robust attitude towards the Spratlys. When a Philippine naval vessel accidentally sank a Chinese fishing vessel (presumably one of China's armed vessels pretending to be interested in fish), the Filipinos resisted China's claims for compensation. Instead they said that the Chinese should pay rent for their occupation of Mischief Reef.[24]

Countries close to the first island chain are also cooperating with the maritime powers. Singapore, for example, is building a berth specifically to accommodate visiting American aircraft carriers. Singapore also has close defense links with Australia, where it trains much of its air force. After reunification, Korea is likely to be a swing state, typical of a peninsula caught between a continental and maritime orientation. Reunified Korea is fated to share a long border with China, but it will also need to protect its sea routes from the Gulf. With maritime cooperation high on the agenda, a *rapprochement* between South Korea and Japan is currently in train.[25] South Korea's president has also said that he wants American forces to stay in Korea after reunification. That US presence is likely to be mostly maritime, and closely linked with American forward deployments in Japan.

KOSOVO CONNECTIONS WITH THE TAIWAN ISSUE

How will the outcome in Kosovo affect China's calculations on Taiwan? Many aspects of the Balkans conflict worry Beijing. For the first time, the 'international community', in the guise of NATO, has used military force without a specific UN Security Council mandate. Even more troubling for China, NATO did so in the cause of humanitarian intervention, and in full acknowledgment of Serb sovereignty over Kosovo. Naturally, China sees implications for Tibet, Xinjiang and Taiwan. A glance at the map shows why the United States will not be intervening to help the Tibetans or the Uighurs, but the Chinese may not see it that way.

Beijing, knowing that in the future China might not be able to rely on its UNSC veto if China itself is seen as the aggressor, rails about the formation of an 'East Asian NATO'. China is accustomed to manipulating international law for its own benefit, for example in the South China Sea. It is alarmed to see international law evolving in a direction where the principle of the right of humanitarian intervention is starting to erode the previously inviolate concept of state sovereignty. And if Beijing sees an Asian NATO being formed, its own actions, and those of its erstwhile ally North Korea, are the cause.

The significant improvement in US military capability since the Gulf War also rattles Beijing. If Milosovich, indicted as a war criminal, ends up on trial in The Hague, the regime in Beijing will have new cause to worry. Nervous because of its own lack of legitimacy, Beijing was jolted by the 1989 assassination of the Ceauşescus in Romania, when their communist and dictatorial regime was overthrown in a popular uprising.[26]

On the other side of the ledger, China will have noted the extreme casualty aversion on the part of the United States and all of the European members of NATO, with the exception of the British and (possibly) the French. China will also note the lack of NATO will so clearly on display in the absence of 'credible compellence'. The failure of NATO to build up an adequate ground-force component before it started bombing Serbia played into the hands of the wily and ruthless Milosovich. The Chinese might calculate that if the United States is unwilling to risk casualties in defense of NATO credibility, which rapidly became the key US strategic interest at stake when Milosovich declined to be bombed to the negotiating table, America would not be prepared to risk casualties in defense of Taiwan. Hitler, after all, undermined the will of Western countries to defend their interests by suggesting that remote places did not justify the risk of war. 'Die for Danzig?'[27]

The accidental NATO bombing of the Chinese embassy in Belgrade, which killed three Chinese, allowed Beijing to claw back some of the moral high ground it had lost by supporting the pariahs in Belgrade. With a long record of willingness to squander the lives of Chinese in large numbers, the regime in Beijing shows great solicitude for its subjects when their deaths have political utility.

East Asia's greatest 'collateral damage' from the Balkans conflict could occur if China fails to get into the World Trade Organization. Congress was irritated by Beijing's manipulation of the Belgrade embassy bombing, including the rent-a-crowds, the barricading of the US ambassador in his embassy, and the burning of a US consulate. The May 1999 release of the Cox congressional report into Chinese espionage activities in the United States also fed the growing public perception in the United States that China is a military threat. Given China's $60 billion annual trade surplus with the United States, and the worsening human rights situation in China and Tibet, WTO entry for China is in doubt at the time of writing.

Failure could be destabilizing. It could undermine internationalists such as Zhu Rongji who argue that China needs to be integrated into the world economy, and play into the hands of the hardliners and ultra-nationalists. In Serbia, Milosovich substituted Serb nationalism for Marxism at a critical point, in order to maintain his power. He's still there ten years later, despite a huge decline in the Serb economy. Chinese hardliners could seek legitimacy in nationalism, which has an integral anti-Japanese element. They might seek to unsettle Japan by another probe towards the Senkakus. A new attempt at the Sudeten strategy for Taiwan might also be contemplated.

If China's leaders are tempted to pursue high-risk strategies, they should think about the implications the role of Germany in Kosovo might have for Japan's future actions in a Taiwan crisis. NATO air strikes against Serbia saw the German air force flying combat missions for the first time since 1945 in the highly sensitive Balkans, with a left-wing government in Bonn and with a former anti-nuclear activist as foreign minister. Who would have predicted that, even a year previously?

Japan's security policy is also evolving quite quickly, even though Japan has not moved nearly as far as Germany has. Nor is Japan imbedded, like Germany, in wider frameworks such as NATO and the EU. But Japan has abandoned its long-running delusion that security problems can be ignored or left to others to solve. The North Korean threat has awoken the Japanese public to the fact that they live in a rough neighborhood. Japan, long focused on the risks of entanglement with the United States, has realized that it is now at much greater risk of abandonment if it is seen in the United States as an incorrigible free rider.

The new US–Japan defense guidelines have been passed by parliament, and Japan has agreed to cooperate in TMD. The next step will be for Japan to give up the absurd and self-serving notion that although Japan has the right to collective defense, its American-written constitution does not permit it to do so.[28] Another North Korean missile launch or spy ship incident could do the trick.

In the 1996 Taiwan Strait crisis, the United States acted forcefully, but apparently did not consider that its response could have been even more effective had it utilized the full potential of its alliance with Japan. In a future Taiwan Strait crisis, an American president might request Japanese naval escorts for an American carrier group deploying from Yokosuka. Japan's navy has minesweeping and anti-submarine warfare capabilities that would be invaluable in such a crisis. A combined US–Japanese task-force would be an effective deterrent to those factions in China seeking hegemony. By strengthening the hand of those who argue that China's greatest need is peaceful integration with the industrialized world, such a response might persuade China that pursuit of the Sudetenland solution for Taiwan will put at risk much more important national interests.

In the 1996 crisis, Japan said that it could not be neutral. Japan's prime minister might not say no to a US request for a combined task force in a future crisis. Japan has important interests at stake in the Taiwan issue, and it might argue that such a response was consistent with the legitimate right of collective defense under the UN charter. Those who think that such a US–Japan naval display might be too provocative should reflect on how belligerent China has been since the end of the Cold War. Taiwan's freedom is much more likely to be assured by evidence of US–Japan solidarity than by merely hoping that China's behavior will improve. Because of what Taiwan represents, and where it is, the maritime powers have a vital stake in the island's continued de facto independence. So do all those in the Asia–Pacific region who depend on maritime protection.

NOTES

1. By 1940, the Atlantic was no longer a friendly ocean for the United States. Hitler controlled the far shore, and Britain was barely holding out. As Roosevelt understood, if Germany came to dominate Eurasia, it would soon threaten the United States in its own hemisphere. In 1939, the laying of keels for 56,000-ton battleships suggested wider ambitions than Europe. Waldo Heinrichs, *Threshold of War: Franklin D. Roosevelt and American Entry into World War II* (London: Oxford University Press, 1988), p. 4.

2. Those who think that the First World War came about by miscalculation, or by ducal chauffeurs making wrong turns, should remember that 'the business of Prussia is war'. See 'The Sarajevo Fallacy', in Patrick Glynn, *Closing Pandora's Box: Arms Races, Arms Control, and the History of the Cold War* (New York: Basic Books, 1992).

3. For details on the Strait crisis, including the regional reactions, see John W. Garver, *Face Off: China, the United States, and Taiwan's Democratization* (Seattle: University of Washington Press, 1997).

4. See Ashton B. Carter and William J. Perry, *Preventive Defense: A New Security Strategy for America* (Washington DC: Brookings, 1999), especially Chapter 3.

5. For details of how this might be accomplished, see Garver, *Face Off*, Chapter 11.

6. The *Kitty Hawk* replaced the *Independence* in Yokosuka in 1998.

7. This was a three-stage, solid fuel missile, with an estimated range of 2,000 km. It was the North's first test of a multi-stage rocket, and all three stages separated successfully. Its effect on Japan was akin to the effect of the launch of Sputnik on the United States in 1957. In both cases, the payload did not matter. What was significant was the improvement in capability that had been revealed, and hence vulnerability to attack.

8. Former Defense Secretary Perry notes, 'China's leaders do not trust Japan and think that the United States is naive to do so'. Carter and Perry, *Preventive Defense*, p. 101.

9. 'Native' in this sense means a Chinese born on Taiwan rather than the mainland. It does not mean aboriginal, another distinct group on Taiwan. About 85 percent of the population is 'native' Taiwanese.

10. Ishihara's election is mostly a product of bumbling by the ruling Liberal Democratic Party. The election reflects the disillusionment of Japan's urban voters, rather than any national turn to the right.

11. Garver, *Face Off*, p. 138.

12. In the postwar period, China made two determined efforts to gain a foothold on the Malacca Straits. The first was in the early 1950s, when China tried to foment revolution in Singapore, which has a mostly Chinese population. In the mid-1960s, China came close to gaining control of Indonesia, with the Indonesian Communist Party as its instrument.

13. Whether or not Stalin wanted to install a communist government in China, he certainly wanted a compliant one. The example of too-independent Tito in Yugoslavia underlined the dangers of communists coming to power by their own efforts.

14. Sergei N. Goncharov, John W. Lewis and Xue Litai, *Uncertain Partners: Stalin, Mao and the Korean War* (Stanford CA: Stanford University Press, 1993), pp. 101, 211.

15. Goncharov *et al.*, *Uncertain Partners*, p. 136.

16. John Welfield, *An Empire in Eclipse: Japan in the Postwar American Alliance System* (London: Athlone Press, 1988), p. 248.

17. Garver, *Face Off*, p. 141.

18. See Nicholas D. Kristof, 'Jiang Trips over the Issue of Japanese War Apology', *International Herald Tribune*, November 30, 1998.

19. See Michael J. Green and Benjamin L. Self, 'Japan's Changing China Policy: From Commercial Liberalism to Reluctant Realism', *Survival* 38, 2 (Summer 1996).

20. These incursions are made regularly, for purposes of espionage and to take Japanese high-tech goods to North Korea. They are dangerous because the vessels are believed to be wired for self-destruction to deter boarders, and their crews are thought to be armed with Stinger-type surface-to-air missiles.

21. Brian Knowlton, 'No Harangue for Obuchi', *International Herald Tribune*, May 5, 1999.
22. AFP, May 30, 1999.
23. Since 1995, Vietnam has been a fellow member of ASEAN. ASEAN has been weakened by enlargement and cannot be expected to contribute much to broader regional security. See Robyn Lim, 'The ASEAN Regional Forum: Building on Sand', *Contemporary Southeast Asia* 20, 2 (August 1998).
24. 'The Philippines is proposing to establish a presence on three reefs just south east of Mischief – Second Thomas Shoal, Alicia Annie Shoal, and Sabina Shoal', *The Straits Times* (Singapore), May 31, 1999.
25. See Victor Cha, *Alignment Despite Antagonism: The United States–Korea–Japan Security Triangle* (Stanford CA: Stanford University Press, 1999).
26. No doubt the Chinese were particularly horrified by the famous balcony scene, where the Romanian dictator suddenly realized that the crowd was no longer applauding him, but was shouting abuse. The TV clips then usually move to the bodies of Ceauşescu and his wife lying in the snow.
27. Danzig (now Gdansk) was the Baltic terminus of the Polish Corridor, which afforded Poland access to the sea across Germany. By suggesting that Danzig was not worth a war, the Nazis did much to sap the will of the West, particularly France. Ironically, in 1939 Britain and France ended up going to war in defense of Poland, which they could not defend, especially when it was also attacked by the Soviet Union. In 1938, they had not honored their commitments to Czechoslovakia, which could have been more easily defended, given the defensive advantages of the Czech forces. But they lacked the will.
28. The Liberal Party, now in coalition with the ruling Liberal Democratic Party, is proposing new bills for constitutional amendment.

PART II
Chinese Perspectives

4

Mainland China's Military Pressures on Taiwan: An Assessment

Peter Kien-hong Yu

THREE CAVEATS

At the outset, it is important to be mindful of the following caveats: first, accurate information about CPLA capabilities and intentions are very difficult to obtain; second, there are significant differences of opinion as to whether and under what circumstances the United States would intervene on Taiwan's behalf in case of a CPLA attack; and third, there are uncertainties, such as the weather, which are unpredictable yet have an important influence on the CPLA's decision to attack Taiwan and the probability of its success.

Students of CPLA affairs have always encountered the problem of acquiring reliable and useful data. As John Caldwell stated, to this day, mainland China's penchant is to keep 'nearly all matters relating to the military a state secret'.[1] Due to Beijing's lack of transparency on its military matters, the proper way of handling isolated bits and pieces of information poses another problem. The end result of almost every analysis is, therefore, subjective and conjectural.[2]

Annual publications by the London-based International Institute for Strategic Studies (IISS), for instance, can only provide a rough idea as to how many tanks, naval vessels, fighter planes etc. the PRC possesses. In fact, it is doubtful that even ranking military officers below the level of the Central Military Commission (CMC) of the CPC are allowed to know the exact figures. Besides, different sources quite often provide different data. Similarly, by the time the US Defense Liaison Office in Hong Kong publishes its *Directory of People's Republic of China Military Personalities*, a new round of routine personnel changes could be under way, with some military officers retiring or being transferred. Moreover, that publication does not inform us whether, for example, General Zhang Wannian, the Vice Chairman of the CMC, has taken ill.[3] However, for an approximate comparison of forces between Taiwan and the mainland, see Table 3.

It is also very difficult for outsiders to tell which weapons can be operated with a reasonable degree of proficiency necessary for sustained military operations, as well as which systems are under repair or when the maintenance work will be completed.[4] Hence, one of the related questions which ought to be posed in assessments of the military balance in the Taiwan Strait is the following: As obsolete weapons are decommissioned and new equipment enters service, are the operational forces of the two sides becoming more familiar with combined arms warfare and tactical doctrine and thus able to absorb the infusion of advanced technologies?[5]

Beijing's high command has the tendency of concealing mainland China's best weapons and military facilities. It will not show or display such weapons until the time is ripe.[6] This way of dealing with the PRC's real and potential enemies is what I have called 'deterrence with Chinese characteristics'. In short, publications like *The Military Balance*, though authoritative, can also provide insufficient and even misleading data.

A second caveat centers around the United States. A discussion of whether the United States will involve itself in an armed conflict between both sides of the Taiwan Strait appears in the chapters written by Martin L. Lasater.[7] But two things should be borne in mind. First, during the March 1996 military tension in the Taiwan Strait, it was the US Defense Department, not the State Department, which succeeded in urging President Bill Clinton to dispatch two separate aircraft-carrier battle groups to be near the Taiwan Strait.[8] According to Xu Xinliang, who was the former DPP Chairman and who quit the party in May 1999, former US National Security Adviser Zbigniew K. Brzezinski told him that should there be war between the United States and mainland China in the next 30 years, the United States, with only 25 military personnel wounded, could devastate the PRC's military facilities within three days.[9]

Second, Republic of China Defense Minister General Jiang Zhongling, responding to former US National Security Adviser Anthony Lake's remark, said foreign military experts and Taiwanese military officials differed on what is meant by crossing the Taiwan Strait.[10] To Lake, it meant two- or three-dimensional attack. In Taibei's view, citing internal documents of the Nanjing Military Region and National Defense University, Beijing may also conduct an unconventional or unorthodox attack on Taiwan. It is very easy for the mainland to rely on the 'People's War Under Modern Conditions' doctrine to mobilize at any time 300,000–400,000 troops on junks, fishing boats, and so forth to accomplish its goal.

A third caveat is the unpredictable nature of the weather and its influence on conditions in the Taiwan Strait. For example, the El Niño (or even La Niña) weather phenomenon, which is caused by a body of warmer-than-normal water in the Pacific Ocean and which may stir up storms, typhoons and the like, may affect troop movement.[11] Normally, a good time to cross the Taiwan Strait is from March/April to June of every year. Thus, in May 1962 Chiang Kai-shek was fully prepared to launch a military recovery of mainland China.[12] However, El Niño has affected the weather pattern of the Taiwan Strait in recent years and that might cause a change in CPLA plans.[13]

Despite these caveats, which cause shortcomings in our forecasts, we can still offer an assessment of what we think is close to reality, often by citing relevant passages reported from March 1995 to December 1997 in a pro-Beijing publication in Hong Kong, *Guangjiaojing* (GJJ) (Wide Angle Mirror), which is close to or has good connections with the CPLA.[14]

TIMING AND REQUIREMENTS FOR CPLA ATTACK

Table 3 shows a general comparison between the armed forces of the PRC and the ROC on Taiwan.

Table 3
Overview of PRC and ROC armed forces

	Mainland China	Taiwan
Troops	3,000,000	420,000
Submarines	94	4
Fighters	5,200	450
Bombers	986	0
Surface ships	986	162
Medium- and long-range missiles	200,000	0

Source: *Guangjiaojing* (Hong Kong), December 1995, p. 24. For Western sources, see, for example, *The Military Balance*. It should be noted that rarely does the pro-Beijing publication provide information on the kinds of weapons that the mainland has.

In January 1980, Deng Xiaoping optimistically said that it should be possible to reunite mainland China and Taiwan in the decade of the 1980s.[15] In November 1990, ROC Lieutenant-General Liu Wenshu, who was in charge of military intelligence, for the first time publicly mentioned Deng's desire to resolve the Taiwan question in five years.[16] As a reminder, April 1995 marked the hundredth anniversary of the Shimonoseki Treaty between China's Qing Dynasty and Imperial Japan, by which Taiwan was ceded to the latter.[17] And just before the Fourteenth National Congress of the CPC in October 1992, Deng hoped that both sides of the Taiwan Strait could be reunited in the 1990s.[18] What all this suggests is that Beijing wants to resolve the issue of Chinese reunification at an earlier rather than later date. Furthermore, it has stated repeatedly that it has not ruled out and will never rule out its military option in resolving the Taiwan question.[19]

There are seven situations under which Beijing would probably use force against Taiwan. According to the ROC Ministry of National Defense's first edition white paper (the third edition, published in May 1996, did not list any), the conditions are:

1. If Taibei is making moves toward independence.
2. If there is internal chaos in Taiwan.
3. If the military capability of Taiwan's armed forces is relatively weak vis-à-vis the mainland's armed forces.
4. If foreign powers intervene in Taiwan's internal affairs.
5. If Taibei refuses to negotiate with Beijing on the reunification issue for a long period of time.
6. If Taiwan develops nuclear weapons.
7. If Taibei's strategy of peaceful evolution endangers Beijing's existence.[20]

And, of course, China may take certain situations more seriously at different times.[21]

Beijing realizes that the cost of taking over Taiwan by force would be enormous. Speaking in August 1992, Chiu Jinyi, then the ranking official of the ROC Straits Exchange Foundation (SEF) and later the Representative of the Taibei Representative Office in Singapore, revealed that Beijing itself estimated that it would cost *Renminbi* 550 billion ($66.2 billion) to attack Taiwan – about half of mainland China's gross national product.[22] Another expert on the CPLA from mainland China calculated that it would cost mainland China more than $100 billion.[23] Senior Minister Lee Kuan Yew of Singapore pointed out that a CPLA attack of Taiwan would mean that the mainland would not be able to become a modern, industrialized country within the next 25 years.[24] Another study by a research institute in Taibei noted that from July 1995 to March 1996 – the period of intense PRC military pressure on Taiwan following President Lee Teng-hui's visit to the United States in June 1995 – Taiwan suffered a loss of $23.7 billion in foreign exchange reserves.[25] (It should be noted that the Hanguang No.11 military exercise, which took place on Taiwan in September 1994 and which involved 13,936 military personnel, cost $1,189,394.)[26]

Different scholars and experts offer different views with regard to how long the CPLA would take to defeat Taiwan. These differences are summarized in Table 4.

In short, expert opinion of the time span needed to defeat Taibei varies from several hours to about six months. Several experts refer to missile attacks by the CPLA as its first offensive. If Taiwan can withstand these missile attacks, it will take a longer time for the CPLA to defeat Taibei.[27] Thus, whether or not to launch missile attacks on the first wave will be a

Table 4
Differing views on how long the CPLA would take to defeat Taiwan

Range (in terms of days or months)	Authority quoted
View 1: Undefined or between one and two days	During the March 1996 presidential campaign in Taiwan, the former Chief of the General Staff and later Defense Minister and Prime Minister, Hao Baichun, as a vice-presidential candidate, said something contrary to what he replied, for example, in December 1989 and October 1990 at the Legislative Yuan (branch): 'Should war break out between the two sides of the Taiwan Strait, Taiwan would *soon* be defeated.'[28]
	Taiwan's Defense Minister Jiang Zhongling said in March 1998 that in the missile age, war can be *quickly finished*.[29]
	Li Zenlin, former Taiwan Army Chief Commander and later the president of the Armed Forces University, said it would take only about *several hours* or *one or two days* at most for the air and naval forces of Taiwan and the mainland to finish fighting against each other.[30]
	Shen Fangping, a ranking Defense Ministry official and later the head of Zhongshan Institute of Science and Technology in Taiwan, said the war between Taibei and Beijing could be decided in *24 hours*.[31]
	Xiao Chuqiao, a former rear admiral of the Taiwan navy, said the CPLA will try to take over the Taiwan area within *30 hours*.[32]
View 2: Within a week	Reportedly, Deng Xiaoping hoped that seven divisions of paratroopers would take over Taiwan within *80 hours*.[33]
	An internal document of the mainland reportedly said the CPLA plans to take over Taiwan within *a week*.[34]
	I am of the view that it would only take about *seven days* for Taibei to surrender.[35]
	A former PRC diplomat working in the United States said that if the CPLA cannot succeed in reaching Taiwan shores in seven days, Taiwan would become independent since other countries would try to help Taibei within *seven days*.[36]
View 3: More than a week	Zhao Yunshan, a mainland military expert but working in Washington DC, said it will take the CPLA *12 to 15 days* to defeat Taiwan.[37]
View 4: Several months	John Zeng, an Australian expert on the CPLA, said the surrender of the Taiwan area would be perhaps *a month to six weeks*.[38]
	According to information obtained by the intelligence community in Taibei, the CPLA plans to use *20 days* to make Taiwan's air force surrender, *20 days* to defeat Taiwan's navy, and *40 days* to bring Taiwan's army to its knees (equivalent to a total of about *three months*).[39]
	According to Kanwa Translation Information Centre in Canada, should the ROC become the Republic of Taiwan (ROT), the PRC can probably win the protracted war in about *six months*.[40]
	Michael Pillsbury, an American expert on the CPLA, said in Taiwan that it would take *several months* for the CPLA to control Taiwan.[41]

125

decisive factor in the CPLA's calculations and in Taiwan's defense. Possibly because of the missile factor, the GJJ, citing some experts' views, states that, once a war breaks out, it will quickly escalate into a decisive one.[42]

In September 1994, the CPLA conducted an amphibious landing exercise code-named East Sea No. 4 on Dongshan Island, which is part of Fujian Province, 72 n.m. from Jinmen County waters.[43] The topography of Dongshan Island is very similar to the island of Taiwan in many aspects.[44] Suspicious of ROC President Lee Teng-hui's political intentions, the status of Nanjing Military Region was elevated to that of a war zone or region (*zhanqu*) in July 1995. In November 1995, another exercise was carried out on Dongshan Island, but under a war-zone banner for the first time.[45]

Under the pressure of the concept of a 'reunification timetable' (as opposed to the exact deadline of the reunification), Beijing certainly wants to finish off the war rather quickly. To do that is to its advantage; otherwise, a third party may intervene, thereby complicating the situation. The December 1995 issue of GJJ discussed how to end the war quickly.[46] The first wave of attack would be launching ballistic missiles, presumably at targets mentioned in the same issue – airports, military ports, wharves, military headquarters, power stations, the presidential palace and so forth. The December 1995 issue included nuclear-power plants and the command and control centers in Taiwan.[47] Another later issue noted as targets radar sites, ballistic-missile launching bases, military factories and warehouses, military positions where many troops are assembled, areas of heavy traffic etc.[48] One author said that to destroy the following 13 major targets, the Second Artillery Force of the CPLA – which is directly commanded by the CMC – needs only to launch 26 ballistic missiles: Taoyuan, Xinzhu, Jiayi, Gongguan, Tainan, Pindong, Taidong, Hualian and Magong airports as well as Zuoying, Jilong, Suao and Magong military ports.[49]

The next question is: Assuming that Taibei has not yet surrendered after the first wave of CPLA missile attacks, how many CPLA troops – now aided by satellites – are needed to cross the Taiwan Strait?[50] Again, there are differing assessments, as reflected in Table 5.

Some military officers view the strength required of the CPLA to invade Taiwan in slightly different terms. In the opinion of He Shitong, a former major-general of Taiwan, Taibei needs just 200,000 troops to defend itself, a total of 13 combat groups or combined brigades (*lianhe binzong hunhelu*). As for the air force and navy, what Taiwan has now in terms of quantity and quality should be maintained.[58] In the view of Hao Baichun, in an unconventional way the CPLA may send three waves of troops to attack Taiwan. On the first wave, Taiwan's troops can defeat 15 divisions of CPLA troops, some of which could come to Taiwan by way of fishing boats, motorized junks etc. The second wave, again about 15

Table 5
Estimated number of CPLA troops needed to cross the Taiwan Strait

Forces required (in terms of number of troops or divisions)	Authority quoted
Given in absolute figures	A captain on reserve in Taiwan, Song Zhaowen, believes that Beijing must be able to mobilize *30–40 divisions of regular troops and reserved units* for a full-scale invasion of the Taiwan area.[52]
	Hsieh Shu-yuan, who is a member of Taiwan's opposition DPP party, pointed out that mainland China has to send *1.4 million troops* across the Taiwan Strait. In addition, she noted that every soldier engaged in combat has to be supported by three other soldiers who, in turn, need ten logistic personnel.[53]
	A military reporter of the Japanese newspaper, *Asahi Shimbun*, estimates that it would require ten CPLA divisions in addition to *200,000–300,000 supporting troops* to cross the Taiwan Strait.[54]
	Former Taiwan Defense Minister General Cheng Weiyuan said in April 1989 that Taiwan's armed forces are capable of repelling the mainland's *2,000 fighters, 200 warships, and 20 divisions*.[55]
	Former Deputy Defense Minister General Guo Zongqing said at a closed-door hearing in Taiwan's Legislative Yuan in April 1989 that, generally speaking, the CPLA requires an armed force three to five times stronger than that of Taiwan. Should the CPLA send *more than two million troops* to attack the Taiwan area, it would need at least *20 million logistic personnel* to support the troops during the operation.[56]
Given in relative terms	John Caldwell is of the view that 'because of amphibious lift constraints and the need to maintain some forces along its other borders, China may be able to deploy only about *one-third to one-half of the ground forces*, and perhaps *half of the naval and air assets* could be brought to bear against Taiwan'.[57]
	A supporter of the DPP and the author of *Do Not Be Afraid of China: A Comparison of the Military Strengths Across the Taiwan Strait*, Chen Guoxiong, thinks that 'China requires an armed force *seven times* stronger than that of Taiwan, and its air force and navy must be *at least twice or three times* stronger than Taiwan's, to successfully invade Taiwan'.[58]

divisions, could come to Taiwan shores seven to ten days later.[59] In the view of General Chen Shousan, former Taiwan Deputy Defense Minister, the CPLA would dispatch five divisions of conventional troops on each wave in a two-dimensional or air-and-sea war.[60] (In passing, it should be pointed out that, starting from February 1962, Taiwan began to assemble 200,000–300,000 troops for the purpose of counterattacking the mainland.)[61]

In March 1996 the second wave of exercises conducted by the CPLA was two-dimensional: aerial and naval. The CPLA has acknowledged that controlling the airspace over the Taiwan Strait is very important to facilitate aerial bombardment.[62] From the report on the November 1995 exercise in Dongshan Island, we were told that, under the doctrine of the People's War Under Modern Conditions, the Chinese People's Armed Police Force and militia, as well as civilian vessels including fishing boats, took part.[63] More than 30,000 troops were involved in the third landing exercise in Pingtan Island of Fujian Province. GJJ reported that CPLA paratroopers can fight for more than three days,[64] and that on each wave 50,000 troops plus 500 tanks can cross the Taiwan Strait[65] – which is not, according to a CPLA general, the high seas.[66] Another report said the CPLA dispatched seven nuclear submarines during the March 1996 tension in the Taiwan Strait.[67]

It is also useful to have a rough idea as to the number of CPLA troops deployed opposite Taiwan; see Table 6.

If we add all the CPLA troops deployed in the three Military Regions – especially the marines, who can swiftly cross the Taiwan Strait – it seems

Table 6
CPLA Military Regions near Taiwan

	*Nanjing**	*Guangzhou*	*Jinan*
Group armies	3 (designations: 1, 12 and 31)	2 (designations: 41 and 42)	4 (designations: 20, 26, 54 and 67)
Infantry divisions (number of divisions)	11	6	13
Tanks (number of divisions and brigades)	Division: 2 Brigade: 2	Division: 0 Brigade: 2	Division: 2 Brigade: 2
Artillery (number of divisions and brigades)	Division: 1 Brigade: 3	Division: 1 Brigade: 2	Division: 1 Brigade: 2
Air defense (number of divisions and brigades)	Division: 1 Brigade: 4	Division: 1 Brigade: 2	Division: 0 Brigade: 4[68]

* The 31st Combined Group Army has about 80,000 troops. About 260,000 troops from other Military Regions can render support in the event of a war.[69] During the summer of 1998, troops from Beijing, Jinan, Nanjing and Guangzhou Military Regions were fighting floods in Changjiang (Chang River).

that Beijing does not have enough forces to make a smooth landing, despite mainland China's rhetoric to the contrary. Also, Taiwan can always spread mines in the Taiwan Strait. The August 1997 issue of GJJ reported that 10,000 mines could render Taiwan's submarines difficult to operate.[70] (In passing, it should be noted that it took the CPLA navy from August 1997 to January 1998 to get rid of the mines in a zone of more than 20 square kilometers in Xiamen Bay.)[71] Therefore, it is not surprising that the July 1997 issue of GJJ acknowledged that, before Lee Teng-hui's trip to the United States in June 1995, the troops in Guangzhou Military Region did not possess the capability to cross the Taiwan Strait – although its capability has since improved.[72] In June 1990, the *United Daily News* (UDN) in Taibei, quoting a mistaken assessment made by Taiwan's military intelligence community to the effect that Beijing would resume its Fujian Military Region, mentioned that the CPLA can assemble more than 600,000 troops in Nanjing and Guangzhou Military Regions.[73]

Niu Xianzhong, who is a noted professor of military strategy in Taibei, said in November 1994 that Taiwan has at least five to seven years to prepare for a CPLA attack due to the Hong Kong hand-over factor.[74] Lin Chong-Pin's paper, published in November 1995, pointed out that China 'is probably at least five or ten years away from being able to successfully take Taiwan intact'.[75] In his capacity as the Vice Chairman of the ROC Mainland Affairs Council, Lin made a similar remark in December 1997.[76] And, in February 1998, Michael D. Swaine of the RAND Corporation said that in ten years Taiwan would face a greater threat from the mainland, as the latter would possess, in addition to other capabilities, the ability to attack Northeast Asia, Southeast Asia and South Asia with more than 1,000 medium-range ballistic missiles.[77]

For the record, it should be mentioned that at the height of military tension in February and March 1996, the ROC Defense Minister, General Jiang Zhongling, estimated that Beijing had amassed about 150,000 troops within Fujian Province, including a regiment of the 15th paratroop corps or airborne army (*kongjiang jun*), and the 162nd division of rapid reaction troops or units which can respond to regional contingencies (*kuaishu fanying budui*) from Jinan Military Region. There were not 400,000 troops, as reported by a Hong Kong newspaper.[78]

How long would it take for the CPLA to mobilize and assemble the necessary troops to cross the Taiwan Strait? Chen Lian, former Taiwan Defense Minister, said it would take about four months.[79] A Taiwan colonel on reserve pointed out that from preliminary planning (*xianqi jihua*) to execution of the attack (*tuji denglu shishi*), it usually takes about six months.[80] By way of giving a concrete example, mobilization of CPLA troops in East Sea No. 4 military exercise began in April 1994. The exercise itself, which for the first time involved four basic Sukhoi-27s (the Chinese designation is Jian-11, the Western designation is Flanker), and was feared by ROC military officials as being able to transform suddenly into a war against the Taiwan area, actually started in September 1994 on Dongshan Island, Fujian Province. However, is also interesting to learn from GJJ that, in January 1996, Beijing began to reshuffle or redeploy some high-ranking military personnel, transferring many hawkish officers elsewhere.[81]

Needless to say, there are some experts – like Lin Chong-Pin – who do not think the CPLA can succeed in subjugating Taiwan militarily, but virtually all experts acknowledge that both Taibei and Beijing would suffer as a result of war.[82] Others, like some Japanese analysts, believe that, unless Beijing uses nuclear weapons, it would not be able to take over Taiwan.[83]

TAIWAN AND MAINLAND CHINA'S RESPECTIVE WEAKNESSES

As the ROC on Taiwan becomes more prosperous, it faces many new challenges and problems. First, by the year 2001, only 164,000 men will be drafted into Taiwan's armed forces.[84] Those who want to become professional soldiers are fewer still. One gets better pay in the civilian sector or in other public posts. The various military services are having a hard time recruiting talented young men and women into the military.

Second, as Taiwan society becomes more liberal and pluralistic and as the two sides of the Taiwan Strait engage in various types of exchange, some officers simply do not know what they are defending. This, despite General Tang Yaoming's statement in August 1996, the first native Taiwanese army chief commander serving from July 1996 up to mid-1998, that he stands for 'anti-Communism and anti-Taiwan's independence'.[85] But, are the troops fighting for the ROC? For the ROC on Taiwan? For the Republic of Taiwan (ROT)?[86] Or for a reunified China which could be under the Chinese communists in the foreseeable future? Besides, there are many illegal arms including hand grenades floating around the society,[87] as well as spies working for mainland China in Taiwan.[88] This leads one to wonder whether some ROC soldiers would join the underworld in plotting a coup.

After the historic defeat of the ruling party of Taiwan in the November 1997 local elections, Taiwan's Ministry of National Defense confirmed in January 1998 that members of the military were free to join any legal political party and to attend that party's activities, so long as they did not go against the ROC constitution, government policy, military regulations or combat preparedness.[89] In short, confusion could beget confusion within Taiwan's armed forces. For instance, should the DPP become the ruling party or take the presidency in the foreseeable future, would most pro-ROC military personnel quit the armed forces or gradually identify with the DPP or the ROT?

Third, signing a peace agreement or an agreement ending hostility between both sides of the Taiwan Strait is nowhere in sight, although a study on such an issue was commissioned by the ruling party of Taiwan and made public in November 1996.[90] Besides, Taibei has become increasingly inward-looking or defensive in its military strategy, as Hao Baichun and Jiang Zhongling admitted in public that the decision to attack or not to attack the Taiwan area rests in the hands of Beijing leaders.[91] Hao specifically mentioned that politics and other non-military factors determine the mainland's decision.[92]

During the Chiang Kai-shek era, ROC strategy was basically 'offensive–defensive' in words and deeds. According to mainland scholars, Chiang prepared for the military recovery of the mainland three times.[93] During the Chiang Ching-kuo era, it was 'attack as well as defend' (*gongshou yiti*). After President Lee Teng-hui's consolidation of power in May 1990, Taiwan's strategy became 'defensive defense' (*shoushi fangwei*), as it was mentioned for the first time in the second edition of the 1994 white paper on national defense published in Taibei.[94] In a word, Taiwanization of the ROC armed forces has become mainstream thinking since January 1988, and many military personnel have become inward-looking. Such behavior may also affect the outlook of common people on relations between Taiwan and the mainland.[95]

Taibei's posture is not entirely defensive, however. Just before the March 1996 presidential election in Taiwan, the Defense Minister, in a deterrent tone, said Taibei would react if Beijing's (unarmed) missiles violated Taiwan's territorial waters, that is 12 n.m. from Taiwan Island's baseline.[96] In such an event Taiwan would strike at the mainland's military targets. Hongshanqiao, former headquarters of Fujian Military Region and located in Fuzhou City, could be one of the targets. The five launching sites of M-class ballistic missiles in Fujian and Jiangxi Provinces would certainly be included.[97] Taiwan's Tiangong (Skybow) II missiles – which are installed at six military positions in Sanzhi Village, Taibei County, Penghu County, two places in Gaoxiong County, Taizhong County and Dongyin, Fujian Province – would play an important role.[98] When Hao Baichun was still in the army, he devised a strategy in which all radar stations along the southeast coast of the mainland would be destroyed, so that Chinese communist pilots would become deaf and blind.[99]

A fourth weakness is that Taibei is forced to buy expensive but obsolete weapons from abroad.[100] Also the ROC on Taiwan is unable to buy more submarines because they are usually regarded as destabilizing or offensive weapons. According to the former head of the Taiwan Defense Command, Admiral Edwin K. Snyder, the ROC needs at least six conventional submarines in order to fulfill its mission of protecting Taiwan.[101] According to another military observer in Taibei, Taiwan needs more than ten submarines to blockade ports in Zhejiang and Fujian Provinces.[102] In any case, by 2003 or 2005, according to a US assessment, the CPLA navy's strength will match that of Taiwan's navy.[103]

A further uncertainty is whether the United States will eventually end its arms sales to Taiwan, as stipulated in the August 1982 communiqué between the USA and the PRC. As a matter of fact, this question has been raised many times since the March 1996 missile tests by the CPLA.[104] Furthermore, Taibei cannot provide adequate logistical support to its troops. For example, in 1992, 510 tanks were supposed to be repaired, but only 227 tanks had been serviced as scheduled.[105] The ROC Control Yuan, through its powers of audit, itself has questioned whether Taiwan's military can service and maintain all of its military planes.[106]

Beijing also has its weaknesses. First, if the CPLA does not mind killing people in Taiwan, it will negate what CPC leader Jiang Zemin said in January 1995: 'Chinese won't attack Chinese.' On the other hand, if the CPLA does mind, it will have to think twice and thrice on the question of whether its attack might result in another February 28, 1947, incident.[107]

Second, after a conventional attack by the PRC, the Taiwan area would probably be devastated for the most part. This certainly would be the case if the people of Taiwan resisted and especially if a third party such as the United States – which led the North Atlantic Treaty Organization's (NATO) air bombardment against the Federal Republic of Yugoslavia from March to June 1999 – were involved in the conflict. What good, then, does the attack bring?

Third, should the CPLA attack any part of the Taiwan area, the ROC would most likely declare itself as the Republic of Taiwan, as some pro-independence activists have vowed they would do or would force the government in Taibei to do.[108] Needless to say, two additional questions ought to be posed: (a) Could the CPLA win and therefore nullify Taibei's '(special) state-to-state relationship', 'two states in one nation', or declaration of independence? and (b) Would other nations recognize the independent nation of Taiwan because the CPLA attacked, or would the attack cause these nations to shy away from recognizing Taiwan so as to avoid earning Communist China's wrath?

There are also other factors to take into consideration. For example, the CPLA has certain weaknesses in its ability to attack Taiwan successfully. These include the high cost of attacking Taiwan and the PRC's ability to absorb these costs without degrading CPLA ability to defend mainland China from its other threats; the negative impact of the likely Western embargo of arms and technology transfers to the CPLA; technological and qualitative differences between CPLA and ROC armed forces; greater training on the part of ROC forces in such areas as fighter pilots; and the impact of recent arms sales shipments to Taiwan from the United States, such as Patriot missiles, Stinger missiles, longer-range air-to-air missiles, advanced early detection systems and additional naval vessels.

WHAT DOES THE FUTURE HOLD?

Many analysts have pointed out that, generally speaking, both sides of the Taiwan Strait are qualitatively balanced. Some military experts, such as former US Assistant Secretary of Defense for International Affairs, Chas W. Freeman, Jr., in December 1996, say that, for the next ten years or so, Taiwan will continue to enjoy qualitative military superiority.[109]

However, between 2005 and 2010, the CPLA will gain a clear qualitative edge,[110] even though, by the year 2003, Taiwan's armed forces should be in a state of full readiness and preparedness for war (*quanzhanbei*), as opposed to the up-to-now status of contingency for repelling a CPLA invasion.[111] By that time, the CPLA will have more ballistic missiles, cruise missiles, and so forth. Needless to say, Taibei will try to further upgrade its electronic warfare capability. In August 1994, Taibei activated an upgraded and fully automated 'Strong Net' air defense network which replaced 'Sky Net'. This new network links 15 radar surveillance stations, air defense fighter bases, anti-air artillery, and surface-to-air missile units through a centralized, underground command and control center at Leshan Base, located in between Miaoli and Xinzhu Counties.[112] In November 1999 the last F-16 was tested, thereby ending the Peace Fenghuang project. By January 2000, 130 IDFs were also fully delivered to the ROC air force.

Taiwan is certainly interested in the development, testing and deployment of ballistic-missile defenses like the theater missile defense (TMD), which is part of the theater high-altitude area defense system (THAAD). But, it is doubtful that Taiwan's modified air defense system (MADS, or PAC-2 Plus system), already deployed in the Greater Taibei area in Nangang District, Linkou of Taibei County and Wanli of Taibei County, can intercept all incoming high-altitude ballistic missiles.[113] In March 1996, the CPLA tested its cruise missiles against Taiwan.[114] According to *Defense News*, such missiles could strike Taiwan's presidential palace in Taibei with pinpoint accuracy.[115] To be sure, the MADS cannot intercept cruise missiles,[116] even if the ROC buys three more sets of US-made Patriot missiles to be deployed in central and southern Taiwan.

As to the ROC air force, it will gradually lose its air superiority in three to five years, as admitted by a ranking air force official,[117] because the CPLA will possess more Su-27s or more advanced models.[118] The CPLA's first two light-weight aircraft carriers would have been launched by then.[119] It will also have more advanced destroyers, nuclear and conventional submarines, and other warships. In other words, Taiwan's Hualian County, especially the Jiashan air force base, and Taidong County's top-secret Jiupeng missile-testing base and air force base will be under threat for the first time, even though Taiwan possesses four E-2T AWACS which officially became part of its air force in November 1995. The AWACS can tract or see more than 2,000 airborne and seaborne targets – like the periscope of a submarine – at the same time, including enemy planes at a range of 640 km and missiles (although not ballistic missiles). AWACS can see targets as far as the historical battleground of Wuhansanzhen (comprising Wuchang City, Hankou City and Hanyang County in Hubei Province), some 1,000 km from the Taiwan area.[120] Of course, the success and pace of the mainland's military modernization program will depend on how large its defense budget is.[121]

Because the PRC does not have the intention of acquiring foreign territory, it can concentrate its efforts on peacefully re-embracing Taiwan. But misperception, misstep or miscalculation can always happen. For example, the Taiwan-controlled Wuqiu township[122] is often harassed by CPLA ships or PRC fishing boats.[123] In other words, it is very easy to create an incident.[124] The situation will be further complicated if and when the ROC's National Assembly constitutionally drops its sovereignty over the mainland or endorses President Li Denghui's 'two-Chinas' policy which was put forward in July 1999. For this reason, we cannot absolutely rule out the possibility of war in the Taiwan Strait. To justify a PRC attack of Taiwan, the CPLA probably would make the ROC fire the first shot. Even a small incident may escalate into a war.

NOTES

1. John Caldwell, *China's Conventional Military Capabilities, 1994–2004: An Assessment* (Washington DC: Center for Strategic and International Studies, 1994), p. viii.
2. According to Michael D. Swaine, it is tentative and speculative. See his *The Military and Political Succession in China* (Santa Monica CA: RAND, 1992), p. 201. Swaine wrote: 'information on an officer's exact rank, unit or department, date of service for each position held, specific military region or provincial district, etc., are rarely provided by official sources'. However, the Defense Liaison Office, US Consulate General, Hong Kong publishes an annual *Directory of People's Republic of China Military Personalities* which provides such information. It so happened that Swaine also cited this directory. On page 51 of his book, Swaine did not disclose the name of the source which provided him with information on Jiang Zemin's father, not knowing that the information is an open secret. As another example, during the flood fighting on the mainland in the summer of 1998, the *Jiefangjun Bao* (Liberation Army Daily) did not disclose the designation of military units involved, whereas the Hong Kong-based *Guangjiangjing* (hereafter GJJ) did.
3. *United Daily News* (hereafter UDN) (Taibei), April 4, 1998, p. 9; and *Straits Times* (hereafter ST) (Singapore), September 24, 1998, p. 16.
4. According to the *Asian Defence Journal* (ADJ), the PRC received its third Kilo-class submarine, its first Type 636, from Russia in November 1997. The CPLA has experienced difficulties in keeping its Kilo-class submarines in operational condition. This is because the submarines were equipped with batteries for operations in Russian northern waters, which are unsuitable for operations in the warmer climates of East Asia. See *ADJ News Roundup* (Malaysia) 2, 1

(January 1998), p. 7.

5. Taiwan's armed forces are facing such a problem. See, for example, UDN, July 13, 1996, p. 11 and July 19, 1996, p. 4.

6. In January 1998, US Secretary of Defense William S. Cohen visited mainland China's Air Defense Command Center, which is located in southeastern Beijing. The visit was arranged just days before he arrived. The center is responsible for defending the skies in a 200-mile radius around the capital. It has the ability to coordinate surface-to-air missile batteries, to track thousands of military and commercial flights in the region daily, and to generate an integrated response to a potential crisis. See *ADJ News Roundup*, p. 5, n. 4. See also the Christopher Cox report, dated May 1999 and cited in the book's bibliography under US Congress, House of Representation, *House Report 105-851*, also UDN, May 28, 1999, p. 2.

7. See *China Times* (hereafter CT) (Taibei), February 21, 1998, p. 9.

8. UDN, January 22, 1998, p. 11. At first, the US naval vessels were 100 n.m. from Taiwan Province. Later, upon learning that PRC submarines were ordered to 'challenge' those vessels, the US ships sailed away and kept a distance of 200 n.m. from Taiwan. See CT, January 6, 1998, p. 2.

9. CT, January 12, 1998, p. 4.

10. CT, March 6, 1998, p. 2 and March 7, 1998, p. 2; UDN, March 6, 1998, p. 2 and March 11, 1998, p. 9. See also GJJ (Hong Kong), December 1995, p. 19, April 1996, p. 24 and August 1997, pp. 79–81. In November 1984, at a CMC meeting, Deng said the strategy of preparing an early war, big war or nuclear war should be changed into that of economic construction during peacetime. When the CPLA put forward the doctrine of 'People's War Under Modern Conditions', it did not mean that 'People's War' – the real strategy – had been abandoned, as could be seen during the summer 1998 flood fighting on the mainland. This means that Jiang Zhongling is not wrong, and, depending on the situation, Lake also is not wrong. A former US diplomat, Harvey Feldman, said using fishing boats to attack Taiwan is absurd. See CT, January 24, 1998, p. 9.

11. El Niño's key feature is a warming of the eastern and central Pacific along the equator. There is also another problem, that of La Niña, which is characterized by unusually cold ocean temperatures in the eastern equatorial Pacific. La Niña usually follows a strong El Niño. See ST, August 31, 1998, p. 17.

12. Zhang Shan and Xiao Weizhong, *Erzhi Taidu* (Containing Taiwan's Independence) (Beijing: China Social Publishing House, August 1996), p. 166. See also Li Jian, *'Fangongdalu' mimoutouxi* (An Analysis of Chiang Kai-shek's Plot to Recover the Mainland) (Beijing: Huawen Publishing House, August 1996), pp. 185–96.

13. CT, February 22, 1998, pp. 5, 11 and March 4, 1998, p. 7. See also UDN, February 22, 1998, p. 5. El Niño has affected Changjiang (Long River) on the mainland. See CT, February 28, 1998, p. 9. Indeed, there was very serious flooding over there as well as Songhuajiang and Nenjiang during the summer of 1998.

14. Of course, sometimes the GJJ articles belittle what Taiwan has. See, for example, the June 1996 issue, pp. 58–66, and the January 1998 issue, pp. 74–7. They sometimes also exaggerate a bit. For example, one article said that, at night and during typhoons, Taiwan's armed forces will encounter greater difficulties in resisting the CPLA. What about the invading CPLA troops under such conditions? Are they not going to face even greater offensive obstacles when trying to cross the Taiwan Strait during those times? See the April 1996 issue, pp. 17

and 23, in which the author admitted that during typhoons the visibility is very poor. One can also discover the lack of consistency. The December 1995 issue, p. 19 mentioned 'People's War Under Modern Conditions', while the March 1996 issue, p. 7, referred to 'People's War'. As another example, one author mentioned that there were eight main air-force bases in Taiwan. The same author three months later said there were nine. (See April 1996, p. 15 and July 1996, p. 37.) The December 1995 issue, p. 16 mentioned that the Dongshan Island military exercise took place from November 23 to November 24, 1995. Another author in the March 1996 issue, p. 6, said the same exercise took place from late November to early December 1995. Contradictions can also be found. For instance, the December 1995 issue, p. 24, mentioned that one of the CPLA's targets is the presidential palace in Taibei (the March 1996 issue on page 50 said only 'government office buildings'), and yet the July 1996 issue, pp. 41–42, assured readers that Taibei will never be the target of an attack by the CPLA, accusing Taiwan's military for making such an assertion. Sometimes, GJJ misinforms readers. For example, the *dabiwu* (big military contest) in the CPLA was announced in January 1964 and began in June 1964, not 1962 as mentioned in the July 1996 issue, p. 10.

15. Parris H. Chang and Martin L. Lasater, eds, *If China Crosses the Taiwan Strait*, Chinese edition (Taibei: Asian Culture Co., 1995), p. 32.
16. *China Times Express* (hereafter CTE) (Taibei), November 14, 1990, pp. 1–2.
17. It is also called the Maguan Treaty.
18. UDN, October 14, 1992, p. 1.
19. Vice Chairman of the CPC's CMC, Zhang Wannian, reportedly said the year 2020 is the deadline for the Chinese reunification. See CT, December 22, 1997, p. 2.
20. See CT, January 30, 1992, p. 1.
21. UDN, February 6, 1996, p. 9.
22. *Taiwan Hsin Wen Daily News* (hereafter THWDN) (Gaoxiong, Taiwan), August 19, 1992, p. 3. In August 1991 the CPLA estimated that it would cost *Renminbi* 400–500 billion to carry out the invasion. See Zheng Yi, *Zhonggong juntou dianjianglu* (Recording the Military Heads of the Communist Party of China) (Taibei: Kaijin Cultural Enterprise Co., January 1995), pp. 64–5. The US-dominated multinational force spent between $40 and $65 billion in forcing Iraq to withdraw from Kuwait in January 1991. See *See Hua Daily News* (Sarawak, Malaysia), August 4, 1991, p. 19. From late 1997 to February 1998, the initial cost of the United States' four-month Gulf military build-up for 33,000 sailors, air crews and other forces, as well as 20 warships, including two aircraft carriers plus 350 warplanes, was $700 million. The US Defense Department asked Congress to approve another $600 million. See ST, February 25, 1998, p. 4.
23. Kanwa Translation Information Centre, Canada, *The Analysis of the Current Status of Relations Between Taiwan and China*, Kanwa Information No. 3 (April 1995), p. 18.
24. CT, March 5, 1996, p. 3.
25. *Lianhezaobao* (herafter LHZB) (Singapore), March 14, 1998, p. 30.
26. *Central Daily News* (hereafter CDN) (Taibei), October 21, 1994, p. 2. *Independence Morning Post* (hereafter IMP) (Taibei), September 30, 1994, p. 3. In April 1961, it cost the Central Intelligence Agency (CIA) $46 million to conduct an invasion of Cochinos Bay (or the Bay of Pigs). The original budget was $4 million. The invasion involved 1,500 anti-Castro Cuban rebels. See UDN, February 23, 1998, p. 10.

27. General Edward Anderson at US Army Space and Missile Defense Command said Taiwan can do that. See CT, May 7, 1998, p. 9.

28. Hao's remarks were repudiated by Commander Yan Zhongcheng of Jinmen Garrison Command. See *Commons Daily* (hereafter CD) (Gaoxiong, Taiwan), March 3, 1996, p. 1. In December 1989, Hao said the ROC can land 15 divisions of troops on mainland China. See CT, December 21, 1989, p. 3. In October 1990, Hao said the ROC armed forces are more than sufficient to defend the Taiwan area. See *Free China Journal* (hereafter FCJ) (Taibei), October 18, 1990, p. 1. The Defense Intelligence Agency (DIA) of the United States said: 'The brave Taiwanese could be expected to lose, if for no other reason, than attrition.' Quoted in *Guojiribao* (California), April 15, 1982, p. 20. John Caldwell wrote: 'The resultant conflict, between two qualitatively balanced, but quantitatively uneven, forces will probably result in a war of attrition, with the [sic] China prevailing.' See Caldwell, *China's Conventional Military Capabilities*, pp. 18–19.

29. CT, March 6, 1998, p. 2; and UDN, March 6, 1998, p. 2.

30. CT, May 6, 1996, p. 2.

31. CT, October 21, 1993, p. 4, 'Shen has been doing a good job'. See CT, March 29, 1998, p. 1.

32. CT, February 10, 1996, p. 23.

33. *Youth Daily News* (hereafter YDN) (Taibei), March 31, 1991, p. 1.

34. UDN, September 27, 1996, p. 9.

35. A retired ROC general, Wang Chengyu, also said seven days. See YDN, March 31, 1991, p. 3. A confidential PRC document also said a week. See UDN, September 17, 1996, p. 9. An ROC military expert also said within a week. See UDN, November 28, 1996, p. 11. Israel would not allow a war to take place for more than a week. See CT, December 1994, p. 11.

36. *Liberty Times* (hereafter LT) (Taibei), February 22, 1996, p. 3.

37. Zhao Yunshan, *Zhonggongjunshijingongtaiwanzizhanluezhanshu* (The Strategy and Tactics of Invading Taiwan by the PRC), as reprinted in *Straits Review* (hereafter SR) (Taibei) 61 (January 1, 1996), p. 49.

38. John Zeng, 'CPLA Thinking About an Invasion of Taiwan in the Year 2000', in Peter Kien-hong Yu, ed., *The Chinese CPLA's Perception of an Invasion of Taiwan* (New York: Contemporary US–Asia Research Institute, New York University, 1996), p. 154.

39. UDN, June 16, 1992, p. 5.

40. Kanwa Translation Information Centre, Canada, p. 18, n. 23.

41. CT, April 14, 1998, p. 4.

42. GJJ, March 1995, p. 15.

43. UDN, October 5, 1994, p. 1 and January 9, 1995, p. 2. See also CT, January 9, 1995, p. 1. In the early days of the Qing Dynasty, Shih Lang of Fujian Province also stationed his troops in Dongshan Island. See CT, December 4, 1995, p. 10. Dongshan Island has a casino on it, which might affect the mentality of CPLA officers and soldiers. See THWDN, November 15, 1995, p. 5. Sujianwan on Dongshan Island is suitable for practicing two-dimensional landing. Another suitable place is Dachenwan, which is near Shaoan County. See UDN, November 28, 1995, p. 11.

44. GJJ, December 1995, p. 17.

45. GJJ, December 1995, pp. 16–19.

46. GJJ, December 1995, p. 18.

47. GJJ, December 1995, p. 18.

48. GJJ, March 1996, p. 50.

49. GJJ, July 1996, p. 36.

50. LHZB, March 24, 1998, p. 2 (supplement).

51. CD, July 23, 1994, p. 1.

52. UDN, August 11, 1995, p. 11.

53. Shu-yuan Hsieh, *Jianqiangguofang* (Strengthening the National Defense) (Taibei: Central Committee of the Democratic Progressive Party, October 1995), p. 3. Hsieh's analysis was severely criticized by military experts. See, for example, *Central Monthly* (hereafter CM) (Taibei), December 1995, pp. 29–35; and CT, November 17, 1995, p. 11.

54. CT, January 20, 1996, p. 10.

55. CT, April 11, 1989, p. 2.

56. UDN, April 13, 1989, p. 3. Another figure who is a close friend of ROC President Li Denghui, Jeffrey L. S. Koo, said the PRC, if it wants to cross the Strait, needs at least three times the number of troops that Taiwan has. See UDN, December 9, 1995, p. 4. An ROC major-general on reserve said usually a division of troops requires two to three times the number of supporting troops. See CT, February 18, 1996, p. 11. Another military officer argues that at least five divisions composed of about 100,000 troops are needed in order to land on the island of Taiwan. See CT, May 4, 1993, p. 11. During the Second World War, the United States estimated that Japan had almost 100,000 troops on Taiwan. Under Operation Causeway, Washington planned to take Taiwan with 300,000 personnel and was prepared to have 24,000 casualties. See *Hearings Before the Committee on Foreign Relations, United States Senate, 96th Congress, First Session*, February 5, 6, 7, 8, 21 and 22, 1979, p. 754. In April 1960, the CIA projected an attack of Cuba. In April 1961, anti-Castro Cuban rebels launched an attack on Cuba, landing at the Bay of Pigs, south of Havana. The force of 1,500 Cuban refugees encountered unexpectedly strong resistance and was overwhelmed in little more than 48 hours. See UDN, February 23, 1998, p. 10.

57. Caldwell, p. 18, n. 1.

58. *China News* (hereafter CN) (Taibei), November 17, 1995, p. 2.

59. UDN, December 21, 1989, p. 2.

60. UDN, November 15, 1990, p. 1.

61. By winter 1962, the CPLA's emergency preparation for counterattacking the ROC armed forces ended. See Xu Caiwei, ed., *China Today: Political Work of the Chinese Army (Book One)* (Beijing: Dangdaizhongguochubanshe, June 1994), pp. 159, 162.

62. GJJ, March 1996, p. 46.

63. GJJ, December 1995, pp. 18–19, April 1996, p. 24.

64. GJJ, July 1997, p. 59.

65. GJJ, August 1997, p. 80.

66. GJJ, December 1997, p. 64. See Peter Kien-hong Yu, 'The Choppy Taiwan Strait: Changing Political and Military Issues', *Korean Journal of Defense Analysis*, Vol. XI, No. 1 (Summer 1999), pp. 39–66.

67. UDN, July 28, 1997, p. 3.

68. CT, May 18, 1996, p. 3. For a comparison of a previous year, see Andrew N. Yang, 'Taiwan's Defense Build-up in the 1990s', in Gary Klintworth, ed., *Taiwan in the Asia–Pacific in the 1990s* (Canberra, Australia: Allen & Unwin, 1994), pp. 74–7.

69. LHZB, March 25, 1998, p. 19.

70. See GJJ, July 1997, pp. 56–60, August 1997, pp. 78–83.

71. UDN, January 18, 1998, p. 9.

72. GJJ, July 1997, p. 56.
73. UDN, June 11, 1990, p. 1.
74. UDN, November 16, 1994, p. 39.
75. Lin Chong-Pin, 'Red Army', *The New Republic* (USA), November 20, 1995, p. 28.
76. CT, December 31, 1997, p. 9; UDN, January 3, 1998, p. 9.
77. CT, February 21, 1998, p. 9.
78. CT, February 14, 1996, p. 1. See especially December 30, 1996, p. 10; and UDN, February 13, 1996, p. 11 and February 18, 1996, p. 2. An ROC major-general on reserve countered Jiang's estimation: he thought that the CPLA did amass some 400,000 troops in Fujian Province. See CT, February 18, 1996, p. 11. An ROC scholar mentioned a figure of 150,000 troops in Fujian Province at that time. See UDN, July 29, 1997, p. 11. GJJ mentioned 150,000 troops in its April 1996 issue, p. 9.
79. IMP, July 19, 1992, p. 1.
80. UDN, August 11, 1995, p. 1.
81. GJJ, April 1996, p. 7.
82. Conversation with Yu Qifen, a CPLA major-general, October 20, 1998, in Beijing. CT, October 20, 1994, p. 1. For another expert's view, that both sides would suffer, see *Mainland China Monthly* (hereafter MCM) (Taibei), March 1995, p. 44.
83. CT, March 18, 1996, p. 11.
84. To be exact, 164,308. See UDN, January 30, 1992, p. 3. The figure may be 115,000 by the year 2004. See UDN, May 26, 1992, p. 1. By September 1996, after the first phase of reducing the number of troops, the ROC had 459,000 troops from the original 498,000. See UDN, September 25, 1996, p. 4. By the year 2000, the number will be reduced to 430,000. Finally, by June 2001, the number of troops will be 400,000. See UDN, August 30, 1996, p. 4, November 6, 1996, p. 4; and ST, March 4, 1998, p. 16.
85. UDN, August 31, 1996, p. 4.
86. Chen Lian, who was a presidential candidate in the March 1996 election, was criticized by another general for being silent on the issue of anti-Taiwan's independence during his services as the ROC Defense Minister. See UDN, February 29, 1996, p. 2. See also CT, December 27, 1994, p. 3. Tang Fei, the current ROC Defense Minister and former Chief of the General Staff, said he could not find a single military officer or soldier in Taiwan who is for the ROT. See CT, October 1, 1998, p. 4.
87. ST, February 27, 1998, p. 29. PRC-made bombs were found on one of the unoccupied Penghu Islands, Gupo Islet. See CT, February 3, 1998, p. 6.
88. ST, February 10, 1998, p. 18. By reading Zhang and Xiao's book (see note 12) and Li's book (see note 12), one gets the impression that there were many PRC spies in Taiwan in the early days. News reporters in Taiwan usually know when high-ranking officials in the ROC will go abroad. See, for example, CT, February 25, 1998, p. 1.
89. FCJ, January 9, 1998, p. 2.
90. UDN, November 19, 1996, p. 2. See also Peter Kien-hong Yu and Su Chia-hung, 'Drafting the Basic Provisions for a Bicoastal Chinese Peace Agreement', paper presented to the fortieth annual meeting of the American Association for Chinese Studies, 'China Entering the 21st Century', October 31–November 2, 1998, in New York.
91. UDN, December 21, 1989, p. 2 and July 6, 1995, p. 2.
92. CT, January 13, 1998, p. 4.

93. See Li Jian (see note 12). The first time was immediately after the outbreak of the Korean War. The second time was in the early 1960s when mainland China suffered from Mao's bad economic policy and natural disaster. Chiang planned to land in southeast Fujian Province. The third time was after the onslaught of the Great Proletarian Cultural Revolution. In July 1953, the United States had a Solarium Project, which covered the period from 1954 to 1965 as well as beyond, which aimed at eventually overthrowing the PRC. But in the early 1960s, the John F. Kennedy administration persuaded the elder Chiang not to militarily recover the mainland. See CT, December 6, 1984, p. 2 and September 22, 1996, p. 9.

94. UDN, March 9, 1994, p. 1 and August 11, 1995, p. 11. See also CT, March 23, 1994, p. 8, and former Defense Minister Sun Chen's remarks to the effect that the ROC was strategically defensive and tactically offensive. See THWDN, March 22, 1994, p. 4. In the early 1980s, former Defense Minister Song Changzhi for the first time reported to the ROC Legislative Yuan (branch) that the ROC was adopting a defensive strategy. See *National Policy Quarterly* (hereafter NPQ) (Taibei), March 15, 1990, p. 79.

95. See Peter Kien-hong Yu, '"Taiwanization" Programme in the ROC's Forces', *Jane's Defence Weekly* (hereafter JDW) (UK) (December 9, 1989), pp. 1288–9.

96. CN, March 6, 1996, p. 1. See also CT, March 18, 1996, p. 3. In April 1990, while referring to the *Goddess of Democracy* which was of St. Vincent and the Grenadines' registry and which planned to sail to the East Sea and broadcast to the PRC, an ROC Defense Ministry spokesman said the ROC would react should the radio ship face trouble in ROC territorial waters. See UDN, April 28, 1990, p. 4.

97. CT, February 25, 1998, p. 1.

98. CT, March 3, 1998, p. 2.

99. CN, November 16, 1990, p. 1; and UDN, February 16, 1996, p. 3. This strategy had not been changed as of the March 1996 crisis. See taiwansecurity.org/News/LT-01192000-1996-crisis.htm, dated January 24, 2000.

100. UDN, August 15, 1992, p. 4.

101. NPQ, March 15, 1990, p. 76. UDN reported that the ROC needs six to ten submarines. See April 21, 1998, p. 3.

102. UDN, November 22, 1990, p. 30. An ROC submarine captain said the ROC's submarines can threaten the mouth of Chang River and Qingdao waters. See GJJ, August 1996, p. 70. The same issue said that if Taiwan had eight to ten submarines, it could deploy only half of them at any one time. See pp. 68, 70.

103. CT, January 31, 1998, p. 2.

104. See, for example, CT, November 21, 1996, p. 1; and UDN, August 18, 1996, p. 10 and November 6, 1996, p. 10.

105. *Jianchayuantiaochabaogaohuibian* (*Shang*) (Compilation of Control Yuan Investigation Reports, Vol. 1) (Taibei: Control Yuan, February 1, 1995), p. 430.

106. CT, January 19, 1998, p. 4.

107. The incident began on that day. A great many Taiwanese and some residents from the mainland were killed by ROC policemen and troops. The incident created animosity between some native Taiwanese and the ruling party for many years. In the last few years, the Taiwan government has begun to compensate financially the relatives of those victims, thereby admitting the injustice. If the CPLA uses force to take over Taiwan, thereby resulting in casualities, the native Taiwanese will certainly not forget or forgive the mainlanders.

108. UDN, February 27, 1996, p. 4.

109. UDN, December 19, 1996, p. 4.

110. US Defense Secretary, William S. Cohen, said in January 1998 that by the year 2015, the PRC would pose a threat to the United States. See CT, March 3, 1998, p. 9. Admiral Joseph Prueher, commander of US forces in the Pacific, has repeatedly said: 'We do not expect a peer competitor [as the Soviet Union was during the Cold War] for at least the next decade and a half.' Quoted in *Free China Review* (hereafter FCR) (Taibei) 48, 3 (March 1998), p. 42.

111. UDN, July 10, 1996, p. 2; and CT, February 10, 1998, p. 7. The report said the CPLA will be in a state of full readiness and be prepared for war by 2007.

112. UDN, February 14, 1990, p. 1. See also Richard A. Bitzinger and Bates Gill, *Gearing Up for High-tech Warfare?* (Washington DC: Center for Strategic and Budgetary Assessments, 1996), p. 27; and Zhang and Xiao (see note 12), p. 355. During the March 1996 tension, Changbai Radar Station and the USS *Bunker Hill* (CG52) detected the CPLA missiles. See CT, February 25, 1998, p. 4.

113. GJJ, July 1996, pp. 36–46.

114. Zhang and Xiao (see note 12), p. 217.

115. *Defense News* (hereafter DN) (USA), March 4–10, 1996, p. 1. See also UDN, March 6, 1996, p. 2.

116. UDN, August 16, 1996, p. 11.

117. CT, March 29, 1998, p. 3.

118. Russia's Sukhoi Design Bureau tested its new fifth-generation fighter, the Su-37, in September 1997. The Su-37 has a unique ability of reaching a virtual standstill and rearing up in mid-air, like a cobra poised to conduct a strike. See *Jane's Intelligence Review* (hereafter JIR) (UK), February 1998, p. 5; and ST, February 21, 1998, p. 39. In March 1998 the ROC Defense Minister said Taiwan's air force had received 40 out of 150 F-16s and 30 out of 60 Mirage-2000s. By the year 2000, the ROC will have received all the new planes. See CT, March 6, 1998, p. 4.

119. Former ROC Deputy Defense Minister Zhiyuan Zhao said it would take the PRC five or six more years to construct its aircraft carrier. See UDN, April 26, 1996, p. 2. Another ROC official military publication said roughly by the year 2005 the CPLA would have its first aircraft carrier. See LHZB, March 25, 1998, p. 19. See also UDN, May 13, 1998, p. 13. On the other hand, Chas W. Freeman, Jr., said the PRC would not deploy an aircraft carrier within 30 years due to budget constraints. See UDN, December 19, 1996, p. 9.

120. CT, March 10, 1996, p. 2; UDN, November 30, 1995, p. 11 and November 22, 1996, p. 6; and THWDN, September 25, 1995, p. 4. It would take the CPLA 30 to 45 minutes to launch its M-class missiles. See CT, March 7, 1996, p. 2. See also Zhang and Xiao (see note 12), p. 350.

121. According to Tai Ming Cheung, the CPLA's total productivity in terms of its economic activities can be said to amount to the total productivity of Hainan Province or Gansu Province. See his lecture at the ROC's Mainland Affairs Council on January 6, 1998, p. 1.

122. It is located in Fujian Province's Putian County. The April 1996 issue of GJJ (p. 9) mentioned this islet along with Mazu and Jinmen Islands, which were under intensive threat from the CPLA in March 1996. For another incident related to Jinmen Island, see UDN, March 24, 1998, p. 9.

123. CT, March 1, 1998, p. 11. For another example, see UDN, March 24, 1998, p. 9; or ST, April 12, 1998, p. 13.

124. Dongding Island, part of the Jinmen Island group, was assessed as one of the targets of the CPLA's military harassment or seizure in March 1996. See UDN, May 4, 1998, p. 4.

5

Scenarios of CPLA Attack of the Taiwan Area

Peter Kien-hong Yu

According to historians in the West, out of more than 3,400 years of world history, only 268 years were peaceful.[1] In the early 1950s, the People's Republic of China (PRC) planned to attack the Republic of China (ROC).[2] January 1967 marked the 'last' battle between the ROC and the PRC. It took place in the airspace over northeastern Jinmen.[3] But, in February 1996, Taisheng Xu, Commander of the Marine Corps at Wuqiu, received a top-secret message exclusively for him from the ROC Defense Ministry saying that the Chinese People's Liberation Army (CPLA) might take Wuqiu. (Wuqiu is on the outskirts of Meizhou Bay, near the PRC-controlled Pingtan Island, 9 km from the eastern coast of the mainland, or 72 n.m. from Jinmen and 86 n.m. from Mazu. Wuqiu is composed of two islands.)[4] The CPLA also planned to launch nuclear-capable missiles over Taidong County, which has an ultra-secret missile base called Jiupeng.[5]

In this chapter, I will first outline major CPLA invasion scenarios; I will examine these in greater detail in the second section.

MAJOR SCENARIOS FOR CPLA INVASION

In July and August 1995, the PRC fired M-9-class ballistic missiles from the mainland into a sea area about 150 km north of Taiwan Island. In March 1996, its unarmed missiles dropped into waters even closer, code-named Strait 961. One of the test sites was 35 km off the northeastern tip of Taiwan Province, near the international port of Jilong, and the other test site was 51 km west of Gaoxiong Municipal City, another international port which ranks as one of the world's four busiest ports.

One of the presidential candidates, Lian Chen, referred to the March 1996 missile tests as a 'semi-military invasion' by the CPLA,[6] while *Wen Wei Pao* (WWP), a pro-PRC newspaper in Hong Kong, reported on March 10, 1996, that the March 12–20, 1996, live-fire exercise – covering a rectangular area of 17,000 square kilometers – was a 'mock invasion' of

Taiwan. James R. Lilley, former US Ambassador to the PRC, told the *New York Times* (NYT) that the PRC had virtually declared a partial blockade of the Taiwan Strait, even though the USS *Independence* aircraft carrier was deployed close to the eastern waters of Taiwan in March 1996.[7] According to a May 1996 study by the US Office of Naval Intelligence, the March 8–25, 1996, combined force operations or multi-service exercises were part of a series of rehearsals for an invasion – a series that began in September 1994 on Dongshan Island.[8]

ROC armed forces have been in a state of vigilance since retreating to the Taiwan area in the late 1940s. Their *zhanbeizhuangkuang* (status of war preparation) comes in three phases with scales 1 to 5:

- Normal phase – *jingchangzhanbei* (normal preparation), scale 5
- Alert phase – *jinjiezhanbei* (alert preparation), scales 4 and 3
- Battle/combat phase – *zuozhanzhandouzhunbei* (battle or combat pre-paration), scales 2 and 1.[9]

Should the CPLA attack the Taiwan area, the ROC air force can quickly enter the combat phase. One-quarter of the ROC navy can also quickly enter the combat phase. The ROC army on remote islands can enter the battle phase within four hours, while one-third of the army on the island of Taiwan can be prepared for combat within 12 hours.[10] In January 1988, when President Jingguo Jiang died, the island of Taiwan was put on scale 4, and the remote islands, 2. In the period from October 4 to the end of the National Day on Double Tenth, 1991, the ROC armed forces were on scale 4 instead of 5, due to the fact that the then opposition party, the Democratic Progressive Party (DPP), had just included in its manifesto a call for the creation of the Republic of Taiwan (ROT) through a plebiscite. In March 1996, Taiwan Island was still on scale 5, while air defense and *zuozhanguanli* (war management) troops on the island were on scale 4, and the rest of the troops, 5. As to the remote islands of Jinmen, Mazu and the lesser islands, before the end of the 1996 Chinese Lunar New Year, scale 4 was in effect during daytime and scale 3 from dusk to daybreak. As the CPLA began its first exercise on March 8, 1996, the islands were all on scale 3.[11] In February 1997, soon after the death of Xiaoping Deng, the remote islands of the ROC were put on scale 3.[12]

For a number of reasons, war between Taibei and Beijing can occur at any time:

- One side may overplay the game of threat or bullying, for example, Beijing is seen by Taibei as a hegemon.[13]
- Due to human error, high winds and technological malfunctions, a missile might not land in boxed target areas or might veer askew of the

targets as announced by Beijing or it could accidentally or inadvertently hit an unintended target or a third party, resulting in a military reprisal by the parties concerned. Thus, in July 1995, as reported by *Renmin-ribao* (People's Daily) and *Jiefangjunbao* (Liberation Army Daily), one of the CPLA's missiles malfunctioned before launching and another missed its target by more than 200 n.m.[14] In March 1996, Jinmen County Magistrate Shuizai Chen and a former US military official expressed their fear of miscalculation, misperception or misstep by either the PRC or the ROC.[15]

- In February 1996, ROC's Defense Minister Jiang said he perceived the possibility of a small-scale armed conflict between Taibei and Beijing in the Taiwan Strait.[16] But, would such a conflict develop into a war?

- Thinking that a third party would not intervene, an attack is launched. The Iraqi invasion of Kuwait in August 1990 is the finest example. In December 1996, a Hong Kong newspaper reported that the timing for the CPLA to attack the Taiwan area would be when US forces are attacking a third country.[17]

- Any exercise could be perceived as provocative by the other side. For example, on March 8, 1996 – the first day of the CPLA's missile-launch exercise – the ROC troops in northeast Jinmen still conducted their artillery fire.[18] But, under pressure from the United States, a company of Mazu troops postponed their military exercise, which was originally scheduled for April 7–11, 1996, even though the ROC presidential election had already finished.[19]

- Rumors and misinformation may trigger a pre-emptive war. For instance, ROC President Li himself revealed that he was informed that three months after his re-election the CPLA would attack the ROC on Taiwan.[20]

- Some observers point out that dogs which bark will not bite.[21] But, we also know that the PRC, before punishing the Socialist Republic of Vietnam with its 500,000 troops in February 1979, warned that country many times to stop playing the role of little ruler in Southeast Asia.[22]

- Anything could happen. Thus, in a document released publicly, we learned that even the Australian air force planned to bombard the PRC's Kunming air force base in the 1960s.[23]

- One side originally may think of bluffing but the situation may then develop in such a way that it is forced to fight a real war instead.[24]

- One needs just one excuse to start a war. Thus, in October 1994, the PRC accused the ROC of firing a shot at Xiamen on the mainland, from Xiaojinmen (Little Jinmen) which is under the ROC's juris-diction.[25] In March 1996, PRC Foreign Minister Qichen Qian told a news conference that the March 23, 1996, elections were merely a part of an independence ploy by Taiwan authorities.[26] In June 1996, an ROC destroyer accidentally or inadvertently sank a PRC fishing boat just outside Jinmen's Liaoluowan port.[27]

- According to a RAND Corporation study, misreading the other side's intention could trigger a crisis in the Taiwan Strait.[28] Robert Gates, who formerly headed the CIA, said in March 1996 that the United States, the ROC and the PRC all had misunderstandings and lacked communications.[29] As another example, Mingmin Peng, the DPP's presidential candidate in March 1996, said he had 'never met any expert who says China has the ability or the intention to attack Taiwan'.[30] In other words, if he were elected president, he could declare the *de jure* independence of Taiwan and think that eventually Beijing would accept the reality; for example, in November 1994, Iraq officially recognized Kuwait as a sovereign state.

- A war could break out at any time. As reported by *Wen Wei Pao* of Hong Kong in November 1995, when the CPLA was still conducting its exercise in the Dongshan Island area, an ROC plane which was spying on the exercise became a target of CPLA attack.[31] In March 1996, ROC radars tracked but did not lock on the movements of a Sukhoi-27.[32]

Because human beings perceive reality differently, various scenarios of Beijing's strategic options in reuniting the Taiwan area have surfaced over the years. Chong-Pin Lin came up with a spectrum of 11 levels, with the first level having the least violence:[33]

1. Sabotage of Taiwan's society: stowaways and weapons smuggling
2. Fishing flotilla harassment of Taiwan's ports
3. Show of force in Taiwan's vicinity
4. Unarmed missile testing near or in unpopulated Taiwanese territories
5. Occupation of remote and minor offshore islands
6. Verbal announcement of a forthcoming blockade
7. Execution of the blockade
8. Electro-magnetic pulse (EMP) bombing to paralyze Taiwan's military communications
9. Airborne infiltration to destabilize Taiwan's society and paralyze its military command
10. Air–sea battles and missile attack to destroy Taiwan's defense
11. Amphibious landing and occupation of Taiwan.

In November 1990, several months after the Iraqi invasion of Kuwait, ROC Lieutenant-General Wenshu Liu, appearing before the ROC legislators for the first time, said the ROC had to change its assessment of the CPLA's strategy of taking Taiwan. Originally, the Defense Ministry thought the PRC would blockade the Taiwan area and strangle its economy. After August 1990, the Defense Ministry began to think that the CPLA would first attack remote islands which are under the ROC's jurisdiction and then force the ROC to give up by waging war.[34]

Later in March 1991 in the wake of the Persian Gulf War, the ROC Chief of the General Staff, Shenling Chen, said the CPLA may also follow the footsteps of Iraqi troops by making the following moves:[35]

- Blockade Taiwan so as to strangle Taiwan's economy
- Take remote islands to make preparations for an eventual attack of Taiwan Island itself
- Wage war to force the ROC on Taiwan to surrender
- Carry out two-dimensional war and parachute paratroopers into Taiwan, if the third step (i.e. short of a full-scale war) did not succeed in forcing Taibei to give up.

In February 1992, the first edition of the ROC's defense white paper was published. It listed various military and non-military actions or moves which could be taken by the CPLA:[36]

- *Military*: (a) use force to seize remote islands; (b) conduct blockade on airspace and at sea for a long period of time so as to isolate the ROC on Taiwan; and (c) conduct aerial attack of the Taiwan area, launch missiles which are targeted on the Taiwan area, and land conventional and non-conventional troops at many places in the Taiwan area.
- *Non-military*: (a) sabotage the Taiwan area society and cause chaos; (b) isolate the ROC on Taiwan from the international society; (c) welcome businessmen from the Taiwan area to invest in mainland China so as to force them later on to tell Taibei to do what Beijing wants them to do; and (d) decrease antagonism between Taibei and Beijing so as to bring about an earlier negotiation between the two sides and to bring about a psychological collapse of the people of the Taiwan area.

In May 1992, the then ROC Defense Minister Chen said, strategically speaking, there is a greater possibility of the PRC secretly sending its people to the Taiwan area, harassing Taiwan, laying mines in the Taiwan Strait, and blockading Taiwan's ports than its conducting a large-scale attack of Taiwan from the air and sea, and landing paratroops on Taiwan.[37]

The second edition of the white paper was published in March 1994. Six possible CPLA military moves were listed:[38]

1. CPLA fighters may fly around the west of the Taiwan Strait's 'middle (as opposed to median according to international law) line' and even approach closer to the island of Taiwan, which will agitate the ROC's air defense as well as disturb its society and damage its morale.

2. The CPLA may use its M-class missiles, which would strike the western side of the island of Taiwan.

3. In a calculated move, the PRC would create fishery incidents. In the name of protecting its fishermen, the PRC's naval vessels and public security vessels would force the ROC's fishing vessels to refrain from operating in the Taiwan Strait. Gradually, the PRC would be in control of the Taiwan Strait.

4. The PRC would use motorized boats, naval vessels and airplanes to harass portions of the sea which are under the ROC's control or transport sea lanes leading to the ROC's remote islands. In this way, the ROC may fight back, resulting in a larger scale of incident.

5. Under the principle of refraining from using many troops, the CPLA would attack and seize Dongding, Wuqiu, Mazu or Jinmen Islands.

6. The CPLA would conduct a large-scale attack against the Taiwan area with its conventional and non-conventional troops.

In February 1996, the ROC Defense Ministry believed that the CPLA would take the following five actions: (1) increase the number of troops including the Second Artillery along the southeast coast of mainland China; (2) enlarge the scale of military exercise; (3) engage in bombardment of targets and launch missile tests; (4) use motorized fishing boats to harass remote islands of the ROC; and (5) stir up chaos on the island of Taiwan.[39]

Jason C. Hu, ROC Foreign Minister since October 1997, came up with the following continuum, although the elements need not be in sequence: (1) verbal threat; (2) internal sabotage; (3) blockade; (4) armed harassment; (5) local war; and (6) full-fledged war.[40]

As early as August 1995, the ROC began to think about how to deal with or react to the PRC's threat in 18 different scenarios, or 18-item repertoire, but the list did not include a PRC attack against Taiwan Island:[41]

- The PRC would engage in missile tests, resulting in its unilateral or temporary blockade of the Taiwan area.
- The CPLA's submarines would appear on the 'high seas' close to the island of Taiwan.
- The PRC would test its missiles at sea.
- The CPLA's naval vessels would cross the 'middle line' of the Taiwan Strait, trying to get closer to the island of Taiwan.

- The PRC would deliberately create fishery incidents.
- CPLA fighters, including Sukhoi-27s, would cross the 'middle line' of the Taiwan Strait.
- CPLA fighters during their military exercises would come in 'contact' with ROC military planes.
- Verbally, the PRC would announce its blockade.
- The CPLA's naval vessels would partially blockade the ROC's remote islands or maritime lanes of transport during exercises.
- The PRC would enlarge the scale of infiltration and stowaways.
- The PRC would provide misinformation and make up stories so as to disturb the peace and tranquillity of Taiwan society.
- The CPLA would take actions to 'punish' the ROC.
- The PRC would sabotage the internal stability of Taiwan.
- The PRC would use its financial power and money to disturb the Taiwan area's stock market and economy.
- The PRC would announce new rules and regulations which would not be favorable to businessmen from the Taiwan area in the mainland.
- The CPLA would legitimize its brink-of-war actions by saying that foreign powers had interfered in the internal affairs of the Taiwan area.
- The PRC would use money to develop mass media in the Taiwan area to spread untrue stories.
- The PRC would blockade the Taiwan Strait for a week or more.[42]

Paul H. B. Godwin believed that the PRC, with the help of its special operation forces or 'fist troops' (so labeled to signify their punch power) – created in June 1988, numbering 200,000 and trained to land on beaches, to parachute from the sky, to fight on mountains, and to engage in battle in urban and rural settings[13] – would first blockade or engage in military quarantine (which is not a military action) of Taiwan ports for three months. Second, it would paralyze the morale of ROC's armed forces. And third, if necessary, the CPLA would invade Taiwan.[44]

Yunshan Zhao asserted that the CPLA would take seven sequential steps: (1) the CPLA would use its missiles to attack the Taiwan area; (2) the PRC would seize control of the airspace; (3) once in control of the airspace, the CPLA would grab sea control in the Taiwan Strait; (4) it would land on the island of Taiwan; (5) the CPLA would encircle Taiwan and attack it; (6) it would attack cities in the Taiwan area; and (7) the PRC would consolidate its power in the Taiwan area and get rid of its opponents.[45]

Litai Xue, a senior research fellow at Stanford University, thinks the CPLA would first launch its missiles (such as Dongfeng-21), which are targeted at Taiwan's ports of Gaoxiong, Jilong and Taizhong.[46] In the second phase, the PRC would bombard Jinmen and Mazu. In the last phase, Beijing would use its cruise missiles targeted at important political and military places in Taiwan.[47]

A precondition of the above scenarios is that no upheaval would come about on the mainland in the post-Deng era. In other words, the CPLA would be able to concentrate its efforts in attacking the Taiwan area.[48] As a matter of fact, in May 1992, the then ROC Defense Minister Chen revealed that his ministry had engaged in PRC's threat simulations for more than 1,000 times.[49] In other words, the above-mentioned scenarios are a slight portion of those simulated.

Four additional caveats should be noted. First, in July 1985, Admiral Thomas H. Moorer, who served as Chairman of the Joint Chiefs of Staff, Chief of Naval Operations, and Commander-in-Chief of the US Pacific Fleet, observed:

> in fifteen or twenty years from now China could choose to engage in an all-out war of which a blockade would be just one component ... We have done studies of that in the U.S. Navy and have always concluded that any effort on the part of China to blockade Taiwan would *immediately* escalate into a full-fledged war that could spread throughout the entire area.[50] (emphasis added)

In other words, it may not be necessary for analysts to say what kind of steps the CPLA would take to invade the Taiwan area since the conflict would have its own momentum.

Second, even if there were steps in Beijing's invasion of the Taiwan area, which step would come first? Again, the answers vary. One ROC military analyst, Xiongbo Gao, pointed out that the PRC would not first engage in two-dimensional or three-dimensional (air, sea and land) war.[51] In their book, *Can China Win the Next War?*, Xiaobing and Qingbo predicted that the CPLA will try to take Jinmen first.[52] I am of the opinion that the CPLA will launch its missiles, aided by sophisticated gyroscopes, first and then try to take the Penghu Islands.[53] Like Zhao and others, former US Ambassador Harvey J. Feldman said, should the CPLA begin a large-scale attack of the Taiwan area, the first fight would take place in the air.[54] Another expert in Hong Kong believed that the CPLA would first use submarines to blockade Taiwan's ports and maritime shipping lanes.[55]

Third, with changing times and spaces, the invasion steps change as well. This can be seen even from ROC publications.

Lastly, the Chinese communists perceive reality in a dialectical way.[56] Are the above-mentioned scenarios conceived in a dialectical way? If not, would that cause a problem in understanding the PRC's real strategic intentions?

DETAILED DISCUSSION OF THE SCENARIOS

When in the positions of the ROC Chief of the General Staff, Defense Minister and Prime Minister, Baichun Hao stressed the importance of maintaining 500,000 troops, believing that the army was very important.[57] But criticism for having a large army grew.[58] After Baichun Hao stepped down from the premiership in February 1993, the structure of the ROC armed forces began to change. From that time, the ROC's army was officially regarded as oversized and it was scheduled to be reduced to 200,000 in the years ahead. On the other hand, the navy and the air force became more important in the eyes of President Lee Teng-hui.

However, the ROC's strategy vis-à-vis the PRC armed forces has not been fundamentally changed. The guiding principle is that taking control of the air space as well as the sea, and preventing a landing by the CPLA are of the utmost importance. The third edition of the ROC defense white paper pointed out the following: control of the air space and the sea is of first priority; a counter-blockade is very important; and repelling the CPLA at Taiwan's beachheads and coastal areas, by relying on fortified inland positions, is the key.[59] In the following, we will discuss the current guiding principle of the ROC.

Control of air space and the sea

Control of the air space and sea above and around Taiwan is crucial for ROC security. Thus, a key battlefield for the PRC and ROC will take place in the air and sea. In this battle, the trends point toward Beijing's favour. Taibei has generally been able to control the air space over the Taiwan Strait since 1949. It takes about five to seven minutes for a CPLA fighter to reach the sky over Taibei.[60] Should both sides of the Taiwan Strait be linked by air, the critical time of monitoring movements by CPLA airplanes would be cut by half.[61]

Decades ago, only once did the CPLA's bombers fly over the ROC's provisional capital Taibei and return to their mainland China base without dropping a bomb.[62] In November 1990, the then ROC Defense Minister Chen said the PRC could dispatch 800–900 military planes at any one time, but if it came to battle in the air space some 100 of such planes could be engaged.[63]

However, the former deputy chief commander of the ROC air force, Li Fan, said in a conference paper in January 1995 that, given that the air space over the western portion of Taiwan Island is limited, only 168 CPLA fighters could be accommodated, and that each time its air force attacks, the CPLA could only send 390 fighters.[64] Needless to say, the CPLA would bombard Jilong/Taibei, Taoyuan, Xinzhu, Taizhong, Jiayi, Tainan and Gaoxiong/Pingdong areas.[65] In addition to the major military and/or civilian domestic and/or international airports, Hualian and Taidong Counties' airports and bases could also be the targets, if the PRC wants to finish the war quickly.

According to one estimate, it would take between a week and ten days for the CPLA to exhaust the ROC air force.[66] The PRC will also try to destroy air fields in the Taiwan area, especially Qingquanggang Air Force Base in Dadushan, Taizhong,[67] and jam the ROC's *Qiangwang* (air defense network), which can monitor airplanes 600 km away.[68] Should the ROC lose its air control, it will sooner or later give up control of the Taiwan Strait.[69]

As to PRC civilian planes at 25 major airports,[70] if they enter Taibei Aviation Intelligence Zone, which will come under military control in war,[71] and come closer than 30 n.m. from the Taiwan coast, they will be intercepted by ROC fighters. Likewise, if they enter the 12 n.m. of areas under the ROC's jurisdiction, they will be fired upon.[72]

Before a mass invasion across the Strait, one question which ought to be asked is whether the CPLA would take remote islands that are easy to seize but difficult to defend. These include Jinmen (which is composed of 19 islands including Dongding Island); Mazu (12 islands including Dongyin Island of Lianjiang County, Fujian Province, which has Sky Bow I and II as well as Xiongfeng II missiles (the latter of which has a range of 170 km), and which will have a helicopter landing pad);[73] Wuqiu, as described at the beginning of this chapter; Dongsha Archipelago and Taiping (Itu Aba) Island in the South China Sea; and Penghu Archipelago (the Pescadores), which is close to Taiwan.

From Dongyin in the north to Dongding in the south, the distance is about 350 km. ROC troops with the strategic and operational depth described above can check the PRC from Sanduao to Xiamen – namely, the two ports of Xiamen and Fuzhou and seven large airports: Zhang-zhou, Jinjiang, Xiamen, Huian, Longtian, Fuzhou and Changle.[74]

Renewed arguments have been made by some politicians as to whether the ROC government should pull back its troops from Jinmen and Mazu, thus affecting the ROC's strategic depth and operational depth, because missiles on Dongyin Island could be used to fight against the CPLA's navy in the Taiwan Strait and, in the foreseeable future, the number of troops in Jinmen will be further reduced to fewer than 20,000.[75]

But we can rule out Jinmen, Mazu and Wuqiu, if the PRC wants to defeat the ROC, because those islands can be taken in a relatively short period of time. In late 1980s, a newspaper in Taibei said, unless attacked by the CPLA air force, Jinmen is secure.[76] In March 1996, Jinmen County Magistrate Chen (possibly with forcing Taibei to cancel its presidential election in mind?) said there was a 30 percent chance of the CPLA taking Jinmen, but he said the island can independently fight for its survival for three to six months, and his subordinate said daily supplies for civilians can last three months.[77] Meanwhile, the Mazu commander, Shirui Liang, said if his 10,000 troops were to perish 1 million CPLA troops would be killed.[78]

But, Yanggang Lin, one of the ROC presidential hopefuls for the March 23, 1996, election, said that, in three to five days, if the CPLA attacks Jinmen and Mazu, the islands would suffer a great deal.[79] Others like Casper Weinberger and Peter Schweizer in their 1996 book, *The Next War*, noted that in about four hours CPLA marines would have landed on Jinmen.[80] Still others said 24 hours.[81] As a matter of fact, in March 1996, the Xiamen fishing port, unlike other fishing ports, was still open to the people of Jinmen.[82] This is contrary to what a professor at the ROC's Sanjundaxue (Armed Forces University) said: except at the Minjiangkou and Xianmengangwan naval bases, which face Jinmen and Mazu, there is no naval base which can pack the kind of troops needed to attack Taiwan.[83] But there are also reports indicating that the CPLA marines have been trained to be packed by ships from beaches.[84]

During the 1950s, the major reason that Mao Zedong ordered the bombardment of Jinmen and Mazu was to test the extent to which the United States would help the ROC. Mao did not worry about Jieshi Jiang, who remained a staunch nationalist until his death. What Mao feared at that time was that some politicians in the West might help Taiwan to break away legally from China.

Dongsha Island group, which has been serviced by civilian planes since October 1996, and Taiping Island can be ruled out as well. This is because the PRC perceives that those two places can help bring about China's peaceful reunification. In other words, the armed forces of both sides of the Taiwan Strait could work together to defend Chinese interests in the South China Sea. According to one estimate, the CPLA has to send at least one battalion to take over Dongsha,[85] and it may take only 12 hours for the CPLA to seize Taiping Island.[86]

As early as May 1991, a PRC official of the State Oceanic Administration (SOA) in Beijing, at an academic conference held in Haikou, Hainan Province, proposed that the two navies cruise the South China Sea on an alternative basis. An article published in the May 1995 issue of *Mainland China Monthly*, a ruling-party publication in the ROC, responded favorably to such an idea.[87] Diaoyutai/Senkakus, which is a part of Yilan County, Taiwan Province, was also mentioned in July 1996 as a possible site for cooperation.[88] Of course, should the ROC become the ROT, the CPLA will take those two South China Sea islands right away.

Of all the above-mentioned islands, the CPLA can certainly take over Penghu, which is easy to take and difficult to defend and which has only two divisions (as a pro-DPP scholar concluded[89]), and which has a new missile base at Baisha Village.[90] On four occasions, Penghu was the first target of occupation by 'foreign powers' or émigré regimes.[91] Once the

CPLA had succeeded in taking over Penghu, Jinmen, Mazu and the lesser islands or islets would be sandwiched between the mainland coast and the CPLA-held Penghu. Before taking it, the CPLA's naval guns would probably pound coastal installations and its aircraft would bomb roads, bridges, airfields etc. The PRC's airborne troops would also be parachuted onto Penghu so as to disrupt ROC electronic communication systems. Remarks made by DIA analysts in the United States should be of interest to the CPLA: the Penghu Islands 'are generally flat and are fringed by cliffs and coral reefs. There are no landing beaches suitable for major amphibious operations in these islands'.[92] But some of the PRC's infiltrators could be hidden beforehand on those 20 islets (out of 65) where nobody lives, such as Jilong Islet and Xiji Islet.[93] A few fishing boats from the mainland that had no fish or fishing gear have been found sailing near Penghu in the past.[94]

Weather conditions should also be taken into consideration. From October to February of each year, stormy weather would not be favorable to landing CPLA marines. In other words, the best time to launch an amphibious attack is from March/April to June of each year.[95] Three days are required for the operation.[96] The ROC armed forces would certainly try to make counter-moves. In March 1996, the ROC opened a Sky Bow II missile base in Penghu, one month ahead of schedule.[97] If ROC military personnel think that they cannot repel the invading forces, they will destroy water reservoirs, military headquarters, installations and the like before leaving Penghu.

Needless to say, PRC fishing boats, motorized junks and so forth would harass remote islands, as the ROC Defense Ministry said in March 1996.[98] Should Jinmen and Mazu obtain a water supply from the PRC, as the PRC proposed to the ROC as early as March 1995,[99] those two ROC-held remote islands could be held hostage during a crisis.

The next question is whether the ROC would be able to control the Taiwan Strait. The Strait is 220 n.m. in length; it was surveyed by the China State Oceanography Bureau for the first time in June 1985. By now China should know the topography of the seabed, the thermal characteristics and the salinity of the Strait waters, enabling the PRC navy to use its weapons to the greatest advantage.[100] If the PRC decided to attack the ROC, the ROC would not be able to enjoy superiority at sea. A number of reasons can be given.

First, Taibei likes to remind the world, if not Beijing as well, that there is a tacit agreement between the two sides of the Taiwan Strait, that is there is a middle line in the Taiwan Strait. By repeating such a remark, Taibei is actually admitting that it is the weaker power of the two sides. According to some scholars, the middle line is unilateral thinking on the part of the United States and the ROC.[101] As ROC military officials argue, without the middle line, the PRC's naval ships can cruise just beyond the

12-mile territorial sea of the ROC on Taiwan.[102] But, as a standard political gesture and for the sake of inviting the ROC's oceanographic scientists and workers to take part in the survey work, Fujian Provincial Service in Fuzhou City reported the middle line with precise coordinates in January 1984: 26 degrees 40 minutes North and 121 degrees 10 minutes East; 26 degrees 10 minutes North and 121 degrees 10 minutes East; 25 degrees 31 minutes North and 120 degrees 43.5 minutes East; 24 degrees 46 minutes North and 119 degrees 52.5 minutes East; 23 degrees 27 minutes North and 118 degrees 26.5 minutes East; and 22 degrees 20 minutes North and 118 degrees and 25 minutes East.[103]

As a matter of fact, new ROC pilots have been trained in areas along the middle line.[104] And the ROC has also 'violated' this line. For example, its fighters normally escort civilian planes from Taiwan to Jinmen's Shangyi airport or Mazu's Beigan airport (Nangan airport's construction began in November 1998 and will take three to four years to complete) and its naval ships have also crossed the middle line.[105] In addition, the ROC air force said that during the March 1996 tension, its fighters still fly close to 15 n.m. of the mainland.[106]

Ironically, soon after the tension was over in July 1996, Taibei and Beijing's state-run oil companies signed a landmark agreement for the joint exploration of petroleum and gas in a tract of 15,400 square kilometers that stretched across the middle line of the Taiwan Strait.[107] President Yen Wang of the PRC's China National Offshore Oil Corporation specifically remarked that the middle line does not apply in their case.[108] In this connection, has Beijing denied the existence of the middle line after its March 1996 exercise?[109] An ROC vice admiral on reserve said the answer is yes.[110] Also related, the PRC has already announced that it has a plan for protecting fisheries in the Taiwan Strait and that the area for protection is measured 50 n.m. from the mainland's coast.[111] As another example, after launching its missiles on March 8, 1996, the PRC's naval ships were spotted in, for example, the outskirts of Gaoxiong waters.[112] Needless to say, PRC submarines – including nuclear ones since the spring of 1988 – often sail near the approaches of Taiwan Island waters, including Diaoyutai/Senkakus and Taidong County waters. This occurred in July 1996, for example, when the Diaoyutai/Senkakus incident flared up in large scale for the third time since the early 1970s.[113]

A second reason why the ROC could not enjoy superiority at sea is that ROC officials – including those in the navy – often refer to the Taiwan Strait as the high seas.[114] This is a deliberate mistake: part of the Taiwan Strait is the historic waters of the ROC, because of the existence of the U-shaped line with Chinese characteristics in the South China Sea. Moreover, in September 1979, the ROC declared its 200-mile Exclusive Economic Zone and the Taiwan Strait is some 70 n.m. wide at the narrowest length. So, what the ROC officials were referring to was actually international waterways. Thus, in January 1996, while expressing concern about the passage of the US aircraft carrier USS *Nimitz* through the Taiwan Strait, PRC Foreign Ministry spokesman Jian Chen said the Strait is a *guojihangxingdihaixia* (waterway for international transit) and foreign warships have the right of innocent passage (as opposed to transit passage) through the Strait.[115] And the CPLA has vowed that it will not let the United States dictate what the PRC can do in the Taiwan Strait.[116]

Third, would the ROC be able to stop the PRC's attempt to cross the Taiwan Strait, which is three times as wide as the English Channel which has a width of 12 n.m? [117] A reminder is first in order. From June 6 to July 1, 1944, the allied forces in Operation Overlord landed about 1 million troops (16 divisions within the first five days) on a 115-mile (185 km) front in Normandy stretching from the Cotentin Peninsula to the coast north of Caen.

However, several factors hinder a smooth CPLA crossing of the Taiwan Strait. On average, the depth of the Taiwan Strait is 50–70 m,[118] and the depth of waters surrounding the island of Taiwan ranges from less than 100 m to 1,000 m.[119] The Taiwan Strait is not suitable for practicing two-dimensional landing exercises – at least in February and March 1996 [120] – and it is 'too rough during the summer', especially when typhoons strike.[121] According to the US Office of Naval Intelligence, the CPLA has an amphibious lift capacity adequate to support only one infantry division.[122] If Jinmen and Mazu were in the hands of the PRC, however, the ROC would have a harder time in countering the PRC blockade of the Taiwan Strait.[123]

The ROC realizes that the PRC may launch its first aircraft carrier sometime between 2005 and 2010.[124] The ROC also conducts anti-submarine warfare in the eastern waters of Taiwan Island or nearby Suao port,[125] as PRC submarines can launch missiles from underwater.[126] To give one example, in May 1990, a CPLA submarine was spotted by the ROC navy in waters off Eluanbi, Pingdong County,[127] following the *Goddess of Democracy*, a foreign-registered ship which planned to broadcast pro-democracy messages to the mainland in the East China Sea. But, ROC S-2T anti-submarine warfare planes cannot be in the air for too long.[128]

Counter-blockade

For many years, the ROC has been preparing to counter a blockade by the PRC. The ROC navy assessment is that the CPLA will first impose a blockade against the ROC on Taiwan. The next step could be attack from the sea and from the air. The third possibility is to take over as many islands as possible or stir up incidents at sea.[129]

Shantou City and its outskirts, which have a system similar to the

Patriot system in the Guangdong Military Region, are places which will be involved in the blockade effort.[130] According to a newspaper report, as early as the 1950s, the PRC's Vice Chairman, Zhen Wang, called for the blockade of Taiwan.[131] In early 1985, if not earlier, Deng told a Japanese visitor that the CPLA had the capability to blockade the Taiwan area.[132] ROC Defense Minister Jiang and others admitted that the CPLA had the capability to blockade the Taiwan area.[133] To avoid being criticized by the international community and to avoid possible sanctions later on, the PRC may conduct 'military quarantine' – which is not an act of war – for three months.[134] In November 1954, US Secretary of State John F. Dulles referred to blockade as an act of war, and the Solarium Project of the United States was planning to use the ROC armed forces to blockade mainland China.[135]

In March 1996, besides conducting missile tests off Jilong and Gaoxiong, the CPLA held exercises at two different zones which were close to the middle line of the Taiwan Strait. From March 12 to 20, 1996, some 300 commercial daily flights and merchant vessels were affected by them. ROC military officials regarded the March 1996 exercises by the CPLA as 'a semi-blockade'.[136]

In the opinion of one engineer at China Shipbuilding Corporation (CSC) headquartered in Gaoxiong City, the CPLA would first use submarines and mines to blockade the Taiwan Strait.[137] Its nuclear submarines could sail to eastern waters off Taiwan.[138] In the assessment of the ROC navy, the CPLA navy needs only to deploy up to 28 submarines to blockade Jilong and Gaoxiong harbors,[139] not about 50 submarines as suggested by Godwin.[140] According to an ROC general, one destroyer is no match for a submarine. In other words, two destroyers can match one submarine. But, if there are two destroyers plus one anti-submarine helicopter which could be equipped with MK-46 MOD5 torpedoes, the submarine usually loses.[141] Of course, hostile merchant vessels can also lay mines after entering ports in the Taiwan area.[142]

In addition, Taibei wants to make sure that Jinmen and Hualian harbors would not be blockaded and, in its assessment, Taizhong harbor would not be easily blockaded due to poor weather conditions at sea for landing.[143] For this reason, the ROC must acquire or assemble at least six to ten diesel submarines, as submarines are the best weapons against submarines.[144] However, the ROC's harbors can be easily blocked due to protests by fishermen[145] or due to accidents.[146] For instance, in May 1996, an accident took place in Gaoxiong Port and, as a result, 24 merchant vessels could not enter or leave the port.[147]

Mining the Taiwan Strait, which is not difficult, has been mentioned in a pro-PRC monthly in Hong Kong, and the PRC may deploy about 12 destroyers to carry out the blockade.[148] But, according to a US study, the PRC mines may eventually drift to Japan in the north.[149]

According to *Xiandaijunshi*, a Hong Kong publication, the ROC's navy, with the help of the air force, can engage in *zhongdengguimo* (medium-scale) war at sea.[150] In February 1992, an anti-submarine warfare center was created[151] to track submarines in certain waters for 72 hours.[152] It is believed to have the capability to conduct anti-submarine warfare in waters off Hualian and Taidong Counties. According to Taiwan's navy, a war in the Taiwan Strait would be finished in one month.[153]

A modern submarine should be able to submerge to a minimum depth of 300 m so as to avoid being detected.[154] The depth of waters east of Taiwan Island could be 4,000–5,000 m.[155] But it should be noted that there is also a Luzon trough in the Luzon Strait which is suitable for submerged submarines.[156] William J. Durch also mentioned that the Bashi Channel is a choke point well suited for submarine warfare, with 1,000-fathom deeps on either side.[157] Of course, ROC fishermen have also helped their government in gathering intelligence.[158] For instance, they know when fishing harbors on the mainland side would be closed, the act of which would suggest that the PRC is preparing for exercises or launching a war. But, would that be adequate warning?

Counter-landing

By now, the CPLA must have photographed from its spy satellites every inch of the island of Taiwan.[159] If the ROC failed to control the air and the Strait or to maintain air supremacy, it would take about five to seven minutes for CPLA planes to reach the sky of Taiwan and its naval ships could sail to Taiwan in two to four hours.[160] Lilley said in September 1996 that the CPLA has 12–18 divisions of troops who are ready to fight overseas.[161]

The then ROC Chief of the General Staffs, Benli Luo, told ROC generals that the CPLA could land on Taiwan even under bad conditions.[162] Of course, Taibei does not want to see the island of Taiwan being attacked or become the battleground between the two sides of the Taiwan Strait.[163] Analysts on the mainland have pointed out that the PRC also wants to keep the armed conflict in the Taiwan Strait so as to avoid damaging the Taiwan economy.[164] But we cannot rule out the possibility that Beijing may decide to use neutron bombs.

The ROC faces many weaknesses. Morale is very important. In November 1990, the Deputy Defense Minister Chen said the ROC armed forces should be able to hold out for more than one year in order to resolve the crisis.[165] A military reporter of the *United Daily News* in Taibei asked how long could the people of the ROC hold out. In the face of a lightning war: one week? Of a blockade: three months?[166] Quoting an American military expert, the *South China Morning Post* reported that it is doubtful that the ROC armed forces want to engage in combat.[167] An ROC general on reserve also admitted that there exist problems of low morale and bad discipline.[168]

During the 1996 presidential campaign, ROC President Li said the southern people in Taiwan are relatively more courageous and braver than the northern people, in the light of the PRC's missile threat.[169] In March 1996, some foreigners in the Taiwan area contemplated leaving it, should a war break out, suggesting that their contributions to the island's economy might be diminished during a conflict with the PRC.[170]

Earlier in May 1992, the Defense Minister Chen revealed that there had been a record 1,000 mainland people caught 'illegally' entering Taiwan in one day.[171] Would some of those people – as many as 30,000 and among them 3,000 spies who succeeded in entering the Taiwan area – engage in sabotage or urban guerrilla warfare, as suggested by officials of the National Security Bureau, Investigation Bureau, and experts teaching at the ROC's Armed Forces University?[172] A *China Times* news reporter asked the following question: In a uniquely Chinese way, is it possible that one day a death unit would suddenly emerge in the streets of Taibei, consisting of 500 to 1,000 members, who would forcibly attempt to enter the ROC Presidential Palace?[173]

From July 1995 to March 1996, ROC foreign reserves dropped about $10 billion.[174] ROC fishermen lost about $40 million during the first round of the PRC's missile tests in 1995.[175] Other related pressures could be mentioned. As more and more people use air-conditioning systems,[176] an ROC military analyst pointed out that the CPLA could choose summer as the opportune time to attack the Taiwan area.[177] The Defense Minister Chen said in April 1991 that the PRC may bombard water reservoirs in Taiwan,[178] such as Zengwen, Nanhua, Wusantou and Baihe water reservoirs in Tainan County or Shimen water reservoir in Taoyuan County. To be sure, about two-thirds of the population in the ROC on Taiwan live in metropolitan areas of greater Taibei, Gaoxiong and Taizhong.[179] The three nuclear power plants in northern and southern Taiwan – which provide about one-third of Taiwan's electricity needs[180] and which were designed to cope with a single missile attack – may become targets of PRC attack according to the former Deputy Defense Minister Chen and former US Director of the CIA, James Woolsey.[181]

The island of Taiwan does not have natural resources. Its export–import business sustains the ROC's economic survival. The ROC government requires the Chinese Petroleum Corporation (CPC) to maintain at least a 90-day reserve supply of petroleum.[182] After Iraq's invasion of Kuwait in August 1990, the CPC said its oil reserves could last for 115 days.[183] To cope with the tense situation in the Middle East, another 50-day reserve supply was added to the 90-day requirement.[184] In March 1996, the CPC said its gasoline supply could last for 45 days, and its crude oil reserve for 15 days.[185] A Taiwan provincial official also noted that, in the event of a PRC blockade, rice reserves in the Taiwan area could last seven months.[186] Of course, flights will be affected as well. In November 1996, it was reported that mainland China's international airports can handle 8.8 million passengers per year. Among the passengers, 4 million were from the Taiwan area.[187]

Before landing, the CPLA will launch many missiles, including cruise missiles, as missiles can create the most decisive effects.[188] Some of the 50 or so major targets which are mostly concentrated in 10,000 square kilometers (roughly the size of Kuwait)[189] may include: Dazhibeian Special District in Taibei City, which is the headquarters of the Combined Operations Center for the armed forces, or Hengshan Command Headquarters; Gongguan in Taibei City, which is the headquarters of the Combat Air Command and Control Center; Sanzhi Village in Taibei County; Dagangshan in Gaoxiong County; and Dapingding in Xiaogang District of Gaoxiong City, which have missiles. ROC military officials also think that the PRC will strike Yushan, the highest mountain in Taiwan at 3,952 m.[190] PRC saboteurs may install beforehand electronic devices such as ring laser gyroscopic inertial guidance systems so as to improve the accuracy of PRC missiles in hitting the targets.

In any case, ROC military officials argue that, even if the CPLA's M-class missiles destroyed 20 percent of the army, the PRC cannot succeed in taking over the Taiwan area.[191] The ROC Premier Hao in February 1991 said the people of the ROC could withstand bombardment by PRC bombers.[192] During the 1995 tension, one major-general told the press that historically not a single country has been defeated by missiles alone.[193] Of course, the CPLA's rapid reaction forces will try to occupy airports and ports.[194] Assuming that were indeed the case, let us move on to the discussion of an actual landing by the CPLA.

Lian Chen, a presidential candidate for the 1996 election, said in September 1995 that the probability of the CPLA engaging in three-dimensional landing warfare is not high.[195] According to a *Commons Daily* reporter, the CPLA itself believes that the ROC armed forces can withstand the first wave of its attack,[196] as the ROC has five mechanized divisions and infantry divisions which are assigned to counter the CPLA's rapid reaction forces at places like Linkou of Taibei County, Hukou of Xinzhu County and Chaozhou of Pingdong County, all in Taiwan Province.[197]

Should the CPLA, which has the capability of sending only 30,000 marine troops according to a ranking US military official,[198] land on Taiwan, it will only choose places where it can succeed in landing, because it must concentrate its forces to quickly establish beachheads or land on coastal areas,[199] which average between 25 km[200] and 30 km in width.[201]

Moreover, there are more than 150 rivers, streams etc. on the island of Taiwan (30 of the 50 major rivers are polluted). Many rivers and streams such as Dansui river, Zhonggang stream, Dajia stream, Dadu stream and Zhoushui stream flow from east to west and vice versa. This means that it is difficult for the CPLA to land, as admitted by the mainland China authors of the book *Can China Win the Next War?*, who also pointed out that at any one time the CPLA can only deploy, at maximum, 100,000 troops.[202] For this reason, some military experts argue that the ROC only needs 200,000 officers and soldiers in the army, which means 13 combat groups or *lianhebinzonghunhelu* (combined strategic armored infantry and air cavalry brigades); and, in October 1997, the newly formed combined arms brigades formed at Xinzhu and Longtan bases.[203]

The same thing can be said for ROC troops, which would have equal difficulty in rendering the necessary support, from the south to the north,[204] for instance, or in engaging in large-scale tank battles.[205]

For this reason, some experts argue that, should war break out, the four *zhanqu* (war zones), namely, the east zone (that is, Hualian and Taidong 'corridor'), the north zone (which is under the command and control of the Sixth Corps), the middle zone (which is under the command and control of the Tenth Corps), and the south zone (which is under the command and control of the Eighth Corps), in addition to two *fangqu* (defense zones), namely Jinmen and Mazu, may have to fight independently.[206] (According to a *Commons Daily* news reporter, there are five war zones: Penghu is the first; Hualian and Taidong, the second; Northern Taiwan, the third; Southern Taiwan, the fourth ; and Central Taiwan, the last.[207])

Others suggested that expressways be built between the eastern and western coasts of Taiwan,[208] as the eastern coast could be flooded with people who are trying to flee in the event of a war.[209]

According to a DPP publication, the CPLA will try to cut Taiwan in half. This means that it will try to land in Yunlin and Jiayi Counties,[210] as the CPLA attempted to slice in half Changjiang (Chang River) in the late 1940s or Jinmen in half in October 1949, though it failed at Guningtou.[211]

The PRC may also drop its paratroopers onto Taiwan.[212] In November 1990, the 15th Corps, which has four brigades or about 28,000 soldiers and officers,[213] for the first time conducted an exercise involving several hundred paratroopers somewhere on an island in the South China Sea.[214] In June 1996, the CPLA engaged in a paratrooper exercise at night for the first time.[215] According to ROC generals, the CPLA believes that it can mobilize its 12 divisions and brigades of paratroopers who are stationed in Jinan Military Region to reach Taiwan skies within four hours,[216] and destroy power plants, bridges, oil tanks and so on in Taiwan.[217] And, in October 1996, Guangzhou Military Region ended its 15-night-and-day three-dimensional landing exercise in the early morning after having crossed more than 100 n.m.[218]

Needless to say, ROC ground forces are ready for them, as they conducted their first counter-CPLA paratroopers exercise in October 1994.[219] ROC military officials believe that the CPLA can only land two brigades of paratroopers at any one time, or two to four divisions all together, at places like the plains in Jiayi and Tainan Counties and the many golf courses throughout Taiwan.[220] In addition, Yilan County in northern Taiwan could also be targeted by the CPLA.

A word can also be said about Taibei, which is the symbolic political and economic center of the ROC on Taiwan. Is Taibei easy to defend but difficult to take? According to a military analyst in the ROC, this may not be the case, if the ROC cannot make sure that its maritime transport line is free from PRC harassment.[221] But, according to Hsieh of the DPP, after September of each year,[222] or in the fall and winter of each year,[223] a trench of *heishui* or *heichao* (in Chinese, literally black water or black current) or *kuroshio* (in Japanese, tidal current effect) occurs, in which the CPLA, with regard to taking Taibei, would have a harder time in crossing the Strait.[224] The *Far Eastern Economic Review* described the Strait and Pacific waters thus: 'The storm-tossed waters of the Taiwan Straits and the Pacific Ocean east of the island have lost none of their menace since the days of sail, when Formosa was known as a graveyard of ships.'[225]

The PRC may also use unconventional means to attack the Taiwan area. ROC Defense Minister Jiang said the ROC believes that the PRC is capable of mobilizing 30 divisions of unconventional troops,[226] while another Defense Ministry official said that the PRC can unconventionally land 16 to 17 divisions of troops.[227] Still another lieutenant-general said the PRC has about 30,000 fishing vessels which can transport 650,000 combat personnel.[228] And a captain on reserve pointed out that the Nanjing Military Region can mobilize 200 merchant vessels and 17,000 fishing boats which can carry five conventional troops.[229]

However, David G. Muller, Jr., a naval expert in the United States who may not understand dialectics, in the mid-1980s said the PRC's unconventional forces no longer pose a threat to the ROC.[230] In this connection, would Taibei (if it possessed them) as a last resort use lethal nerve agent GB in a binary form (two harmless elements mixed to form the lethal substance), mustard and tear gas – in that order – against the invaders?[231] (In November 1996, UN Secretary-General Boutros Boutros-Ghali said the Republic of Hungary became the sixty-fifth country ratifying the Chemical Weapons Convention; the treaty became international law in April 1997.[232])

The island of Taiwan has a 1,420-km-long coast, which is regularly patrolled by about 20,000 coastal troops.[233] In 1996, the then Army Chief Commander, Zhenlin Li, suspected that the PRC's conventional troops, with limited landing points, would feint its attack of the Taiwan area, while its unconventional troops would actually land on many points.[234] Indicating that such an opportunity exists, a news report cited the fact that more than 90 percent of stowaways did not enter Taiwan from its fishing harbors, numbering more than 300, or commercial harbors.[235]

The first 'direct' shipping voyage between the two sides of the Taiwan Strait took place in April 1997. The ROC plans to open the following fishing or small ports to its PRC counterpart in the future: Budai of Jiayi County, Mailiao of Yunlin County, Suao of Yilan County, Anping of Tainan County, Nanliao of Xinzhu County and Badouzi of Taibei County. However, more than 50 coastal locations have been designated as restricted areas, some of which are under 24-hour patrol.[236] In other words, ROC fishermen have to go along with the rules and regulations when sailing in or out. They will also be checked at 399 places throughout Taiwan.[237] As a matter of fact, the PRC conducted an exercise code-named 'No. 103 Exercise – *Wanchuanqifa*' (attack with 10,000 fishing boats, motorized junks and the like).[238] Of course, the ROC has also conducted exercises in preventing infiltration, smuggling and so on at fishing ports such as Xinda fishing port in Gaoxiong County.[239]

The ROC has many weaknesses. A newspaper report mentioned the weak positions from Xinzhu to Houlong of Miaoli County and Guishan Island of Yilan County; that is, from May to October of each year, small flotillas from the mainland can easily come and go.[240] Another report mentioned Huweiliao bordering Jiayi and Tainan Counties and Dongshi Bridge, which is nearby Donggang in Pingdong County, as no man's land.[241]

In June 1996, the ROC Defense Ministry for the first time confirmed that, in the period from January to March 1996, many groups of PRC steel-plated vessels appeared 17 n.m. from the mouth of Zhuoshui stream of Nantou, Zhanghua and Yunlin Counties.[242] Over the years, fishing boats on both sides have been smuggling weapons, drugs and so on.[243] Yet, given that the ROC's Seventh Peace Preservation Police Corps (PPPC), created in January 1990 and changed to the Maritime Police Bureau (MPB) in June 1998, has to patrol with 83 patrol boats about 35,000 square kilometers of its territorial sea surrounding the Taiwan Island,[244] ROC officials admitted that probably about every 20 km an ROC coastal patrol boat can be seen from the coast of Taiwan. They added that the ROC police force now has only seven helicopters but it needs at least 12 to monitor the coasts of Taiwan Island, day and night.[245]

CONCLUSION

In sum, the ROC may not have to counter the PRC's landing at day and night. This is because, before the CPLA lands, the winner and loser have already been decided in the Taiwan Strait.[246] The PRC has only one chance to subjugate the ROC; if it fails, the ROC will become the ROT. After a week or so of missile attack, most residents of Taiwan, who think of their families, property and so on, will ask their government to surrender to the PRC.

NOTES

1. UDN, November 4, 1996, p. 1.
2. UDN, February 5, 1997, p. 9. See also CT, September 4, 1996, p. 3.
3. See Chapter 5 in Peter Kien-hong Yu, *Bicoastal China: A Dialectical, Paradigmatic Analysis* (New York: Nova Science Publishers, 1999). On July 20, 1990, there was a close call between a F-104 fighter and four *Jian*-4 fighters. See www.udnnews.com/FOCUSNEWS/TAIWAN-CHINA/355524.htm, dated March 7, 2000.
4. Conversation with Taisheng Xu on December 2, 1996. For the Wuqiu map, see UDN, February 28, 1998, p. 6. Dongding Island was another probable target. See UDN, May 5, 1998, p. 4.
5. Conversation with Bosheng Xu, a retired ROC lieutenant-general, on May 24, 1997. See CT, April 23, 1998, p. 2; UDN, April 23, 1998, p. 2.
6. UDN, March 8, 1996, p. 2.
7. See www.udnnews.com/FOCUSNEWS/TAIWAN-CHINA/373913.htm, dated March 19, 2000.
8. CN, November 13, 1996, p. 1.
9. CT, March 15, 1990, p. 4 and October 17, 1991, p. 4; UDN, March 8, 1996, p. 1. For the CPLA, it comes in three levels, with the third level as the highest alert.
10. CT, October 17, 1991, p. 4.
11. UDN, March 8, 1996, pp. 1 and 3; CT, October 17, 1991, p. 4, February 27, 1996, p. 3, March 15, 1990, p. 4, and March 19, 1996, p. 3; and LT, February 22, 1996, p. 3. Penghu starting from March 11, 1996, was under scale 3. See CT, March 12, 1996, p. 4.
12. UDN, February 21, 1997, p. 2.
13. CT, February 15, 1996, p. 3.
14. UDN, January 27, 1997, p. 9; CT, November 7, 1995, p. 9; and CN, March 6, 1996, p. 1. See also UDN, July 27, 1995, p. 1 and November 5, 1995, p. 2; CT, July 27, 1995, p. 1 and July 30, 1995, p. 4. The ROC military acknowledged that the CPLA did not miss any. See www.mingpao.com/newspaper/2000125/cablh.htm, dated January 25, 2000. See UDN, July 30, 1995, p. 4. M-class missiles may miss targets by 300–600 m. See CT, March 7, 1996, p. 2 and December 12, 1996, p. 10. Surface-to-surface missiles, for every 1,000 km they travel, may miss targets by about 1 km. See CT, July 30, 1995, p. 4. But, according to the US record, the M-class missiles had not missed by more than 32 km. See CT, March 10, 1996, pp. 3 and 4. See also CT, March 7, 1996, p. 2. A misfired shell landed in a house in Hengchun, Pingdong County. See CN, October 29, 1996, p. 1 and UDN, September 10, 1996, p. 16. Veteran American newspaper reporter, Pierre Salinger, said he had a document proving that, in an exercise in July 1996, the US navy shot down Transworld Airways flight 800 off Long Island coast of New York State. See CN, November 9, 1996, p. 1.
15. UDN, March 9 and 19, 1996, p. 3. See also CT, March 10, 1996, p. 3.
16. CT, February 15, 1996, p. 3. A Japanese military reporter concurred with Jiang's remarks and said such a conflict may take place at sea. See CT, February 11,

1996, p. 25.

17. UDN, December 28, 1996, p. 10.
18. CT, March 9, 1996, p. 2.
19. *International Times* (hereafter IT) (Sarawak, Malaysia), April 4, 1996, p. 20.
20. UDN, January 25, 1996, p. 5 and February 8, 1996, p. 3. See also UDN, March 8, 1996, p. 3. Not until May 1996 did the public know that the CPLA would not conduct the fourth round of military exercises. See UDN, May 2, 1996, p. 2. Another good example is that Japan's *Sankei Shimbun* said it acquired a top-secret document of the CMC which said the PRC planned to attack the Taiwan area before 1996. See UDN, October 15, 1994, p. 11, and October 16, 1994, p. 10. For the analysis debunking this claim, see CT, December 17, 1994, p. 11. The ROC may also try to misinform its people. In July 1982, an ROC Defense Ministry official said the ROC had acquired a secret PRC document saying that the best time for the PRC to attack Taiwan was between 1985 and 1986. See *World Journal* (hereafter WJ) (New York), July 15, 1982, p. 1. However, the PRC officially denied it. See *Zhongbao* (hereafter ZB) (New York), July 17, 1982, p. 1.
21. See Denny Roy, 'To Bark or Bite? The Problem of Deception', in Peter Kien-hong Yu, *The Chinese CPLA's Perception of an Invasion of Taiwan* (New York: Contemporary US–Asia Research Institute, New York University, 1996), Chapter 4. For Yanggang Lin's remarks, see THWDN, March 16, 1996, p. 4.
22. UDN, January 25, 1996, p. 15.
23. UDN, January 16, 1996, p. 5. General Douglas MacArthur proposed an atomic bombardment of the mainland from 1950 to 1953 during the Korean War. In August 1958, such an idea was revived by the US Joint Chiefs of Staff. See CT, August 17, 1996, p. 9.
24. UDN, March 8, 1996, p. 3. Two former CIA directors feared that the United States and the PRC may fight against each other in the Taiwan Strait. See UDN, February 15, 1997, p. 9.
25. CD, November 18, 1994, p. 9. The ROC Ministry of National Defense denied a mainland China charge that the ROC troops had fired on the PRC-occupied Jiaoyu, which is very close to Jinmen in June 1984.
26. CN, March 12, 1996, p. 1.
27. UDN, June 27, 1996, p. 5. See also CD, July 6, 1995, p. 3.
28. UDN, December 8, 1995, p. 9.
29. CT, August 29, 1996, p. 2.
30. CN, November 13, 1995, p. 1.
31. UDN, December 4, 1995, p. 10.
32. UDN, November 18, 1996, p. 4, and April 13, 1997, p. 4.
33. Chong-Pin Lin, 'The Role of the People's Liberation Army in the Process of Reunification', in Richard H. Yang, ed., *China's Military: The CPLA in 1992/ 1993* (Taibei: Chinese Council of Advanced Policy Studies, 1993), p. 175. Originally, he said there are at least seven ways for the CPLA to attack the Taiwan area. See NPQ, March 15, 1990, p. 70.
34. UDN, November 15, 1990, p. 2.
35. YDN, March 16, 1991, p. 1. This kind of assessment was unveiled earlier by another military official. See UDN, November 15, 1990, p. 1.
36. CT, January 30, 1992, p. 3.
37. UDN, May 26, 1992, p. 1.
38. UDN, March 9, 1994, p. 1.
39. UDN, February 16, 1996, p. 3. See also LT, January 1, 1996, p. 6.
40. Jason C. Hu, '*Xianjieduantaihaianquanqingshizipinggu*' (Assessment of Current

Security in the Taiwan Strait), *Theory and Policy* (hereafter TP) (Taibei), July 31, 1989, p. 48. In October 1997, he said for the next three to five years, the Taiwan Strait would be most dangerous. See UDN, October 21, 1997, p. 2.

41. CD, November 13, 1996, p. 4; and CT, March 3, 1998, p. 2. In January 2000, the Legislative Yuan passed a law regulating the establishment of the stock market stability fund.

42. See *See Hua Daily News*, March 21, 1996, p. 12. See also CT, March 9, 1996, p. 2, and March 3, 1998, p. 2.

43. CT, September 4, 1994, p. 4; UDN, January 31, 1992, p. 11, and July 3, 1995, p. 1; and CD, March 28, 1995, p. 3. See also WJ, March 25, 1994, p. A18 and Chong-Pin Lin, 'The Military Balance in the Taiwan Straits', paper presented to the conference on 'The CPLA Towards 2000', sponsored by the Chinese Council on Advanced Policy Studies and the *China Quarterly*, July 13–15, 1995, Hong Kong. The National Defense University in the United States said the number of such troops is about 18–20 divisions. See LT, April 9, 1997, p. 4.

44. Parris H. Chang and Martin L. Lasater, eds, *If China Crosses the Taiwan Strait*, Chinese edn (Taibei: Asian Culture Co., 1995), pp. 60, 65, 68 and 74. See also UDN, July 30, 1995, p. 4, and July 22, 1996, p. 4.

45. SR, No. 61 (January 1, 1996), p. 49.

46. UDN, July 11, 1997, p. 9.

47. CT, July 22, 1996, p. 10.

48. For example, see Peter Kien-hong Yu, 'Potential Areas of Chinese Regional Military Separatism', *Contemporary Southeast Asia: A Journal of International and Strategic Affairs* (hereafter CSA) (Singapore) 15, 4 (March 1994), pp. 464–98.

49. UDN, May 26, 1992, p. 1.

50. Quoted in Martin L. Lasater, ed., *Beijing's Blockade Threat to Taiwan*, The Heritage Lectures, No. 80, 1986, pp. 5–6. In May 1985, Yaobang Hu, a potential successor of Deng, revealed that the PRC at that time might not be able to blockade the ROC. See CT, July 10, 1997, p. 9.

51. CT, March 4, 1996, p. 11.

52. Xiaobing and Qingbo, *Zhongguoshifonendayinxiayichangzhanzheng?* (Can China Win the Next War?) (Taibei: Zhouzhi Cultural Enterprise Co., 1995), p. 52. Other PRC analysts do not think that the CPLA will take Jinmen and other remote islands first. See IMP, September 30, p. 7; October 1, p. 7, October 2, p. 7, October 3, p. 6, October 4, p. 6, and October 5, p. 7, 1993.

53. See Peter Kien-hong Yu, 'Dangers Across the Taiwan Strait', *Armed Forces Journal International* (hereafter AFJI) (USA), April 1996, p. 38, and 'Taking Taiwan', JIR, September 1998, pp. 29–32.

54. Chang and Lasater, *If China Crosses the Taiwan Strait*, p. 152.

55. CDN, May 1, 1990, p. 3.

56. See Peter Kien-hong Yu, *Bicoastal China: A Dialectical, Paradigmatic Analysis*.

57. UDN, December 21, 1989, p. 2.

58. THWDN, October 16, 1990, p. 1.

59. UDN, May 18, 1996, p. 1. See also *Jane's Defence Weekly* (hereafter JDW), July 22, 1989, p. 105.

60. UDN, October 27, 1996, p. 11.

61. UDN, August 20, 1996, p. 9.

62. UDN, March 11, 1996, p. 3.

63. CT, November 15, 1990, p. 1.

64. UDN, January 8, 1995, p. 4 and January 10, 1995, p. 11. In April 1989, Weiyuan Cheng, then the ROC Defense Minister, said at any one time the CPLA could

only dispatch 300 fighters. See CT, April 11, 1989, p. 2.

65. UDN, January 8, 1995, p. 4.
66. UDN, November 21, 1990, p. 27, and December 1, 1995, p. 11.
67. UDN, October 21, 1995, p. 6.
68. UDN, November 30, 1995, p. 11, and December 1, 1995, p. 11. See also LHZB, March 18, 1999, p. 35.
69. UDN, October 21, 1995, p. 6. For Taibei's means of attaining the objective of retaining air superiority over Taiwan and the Strait involving defensive operations and tactical air requirements, see Martin L. Lasater, *Taiwan: Facing Mounting Threats* (Washington DC: Heritage Foundation, 1984), pp. 20–21.
70. CT, July 12, 1997, p. 9.
71. See FCJ, October 16, 1992, p. 1, and CDN, February 17, 1996, p. 2.
72. UDN, August 14, 1992, p. 41.
73. UDN, September 1, 1996, p. 1; September 30, 1996, p. 9, and December 15, 1997, p. 4.
74. UDN, October 29, 1994, p. 3, and June 24, 1997, p. 6; and CT, October 29, 1994, p. 11, and November 4 and 5, 1994, p. 3.
75. UDN, October 28 and 29, 1994, p. 11, and December 15, 1997, p. 4; CT, October 29, 1994, p. 11, November 4, 1994, p. 3, March 16, 1996, p. 1, and January 2, 1996, p. 4; and CD, April 14, 1997, p. 4.
76. IMP, April 13, 1989, p. 5.
77. IT, March 20, 1996, p. 16; UDN, March 11, 1996, p. 3; and CN, February 18, 1996, p. 3. On March 19, 1996, the ROC's Council of Agriculture said it would transfer 150 tons of rice to Jinmen and 30 tons to Mazu. COA officials also said that Jinmen had a rice reserve of more than 1,000 tons – about five months' supply. If including other grain supplies such as surghum, wheat and sweet potato, the grain reserves were sufficient for more than a year there. And Mazu had a rice reserve of 412 tons – enough for a year. See CN, March 20, 1996, p. 3. On March 22, 1996, a pro-PRC newspaper in Hong Kong said the chances of the CPLA attacking the ROC's remote islands were very slim, given the CPLA's success in its exercises. In other words, the CPLA does not have to first take those remote islands in order to defeat the ROC. See CT, March 23, 1996, p.7.
78. CT, February 27, 1996, p. 3. Mazu's troops have been nearly cut by half. See UDN, May 15, 1999, p. 8.
79. UDN, February 9, 1996, p. 2.
80. CT, December 14, 1996, p. 3.
81. WJ, February 25, 1996, p. A13; and IT, March 21, 1996, p. 14.
82. UDN, March 2, 1996, p. 3.
83. YDN, April 28, 1990, p. 2.
84. UDN, September 4, 1994, p. 2.
85. See UDN, January 29, 1996, p. 4, and January 30, 1996, p. 15.
86. IT, March 21, 1996, p. 14.
87. MCM, May 1995, p. 39. In February 1998, a CPLA navy monthly, *Modern Vessels*, for the first time called upon Taiwan and the mainland to cooperate and coordinate militarily in the Nansha Island group. See FCJ, February 27, 1998, p. 2.
88. CD, July 22, 1996, p. 3. See also FCJ, July 26, 1996, p. 1.
89. Shu-yuan Hsieh, *Jiaqianguofang* (Strengthening National Defense) (Taibei: Central Committee of the Democratic Progressive Party, October 1995), pp. 4 and 5. See also CD, October 27, 1995, p. 1; and UDN, February 16, 1996, p. 3.

90. UDN, November 19, 1996, p. 13. In March 1996, one of the PRC's missiles landed in waters not far away from Huayu (Hua Islet), Penghu. See CT, May 15, 1999, p. 4.
91. CD, March 11, 1996, p. 2.
92. Guojiribao (GJRB), April 5, 1982, p. 20.
93. UDN, July 10, 1996, p. 13; LT, February 3, 1997, p. 10; and THWDN, May 28, 1997, p. 7. The name of the sixty-fifth was given by the then Taiwan governor James C. Soong. See UDN, May 16, 1998, p. 4.
94. CN, February 20, 1990, p. 1. Important patrol places include Magong, Pengnan, Huxi and Baisa. See UDN, January 25, 1997, p. 13.
95. Hsieh (see note 89), p. 5; GJRB, April 3, 1982, p. 20; and CT, November 18, 1993, p. 6. See also *Report of the Damage Caused by Disaster in China, 1949–1995* (Beijing: Zhongguotongjichubanshe, December 1995), pp. 242–3.
96. Fu-chen Chen, *Juezhan 'Runbayue'* (The Decisive War in Intercalary August 1995) (Taibei: Golden Taiwan Publishing Co., July 1995), p. 147.
97. UDN, March 9, 1996, p. 3.
98. UDN, March 8, 1996, p. 3; CT, February 27, 1996, p. 3, and February 29, 1996, p. 2.
99. In July 1996, the PRC officially proposed three options. See UDN, July 30, 1998, p. 13. ROC President Li opposes the idea of Mazu getting water from the mainland, because the ROC plans to build a desalination plant on Mazu which can be built within a year and which can provide 500 tons of drinkable water to Mazu people. See CT, July 13 and 17, 1996, p. 4. See also UDN, August 5, 1996, p. 10, and CT, August 5, 1996, p. 10. Forty percent of Mazu's daily needs like garlic, mutton, vegetables and fruit come from the mainland. See CT, February 29, 1996, p. 2. Each day, Jinmen uses 17,200 tons of water but can only provide 16,400 tons; the figures for Mazu are 4,800 and 4,200, respectively. See UDN, July 7, 1996, p. 1, and August 23, 1996, p. 9; and CT, August 15, 1996, p. 9. Jinjiang City of Quanzhou County, Fujian Province, can provide water to Jinmen. See UDN, July 30, 1998, p. 13.
100. *Zhongguoxinwenshe* (China News Agency), Beijing, July 19, 1985, and William J. Durch, 'The Navy of the Republic of China', in Barry M. Blechman and Robert P. Berman, eds, *Guide to Far Eastern Navies* (Annapolis MD: Naval Institute Press, 1978), p. 256. See also IMP, October 3, 1993, p. 6.
101. CT, March 19, 1996, p. 3, and UDN, March 7, 1996, p. 11. See also CT, February 13, 1996, p. 2, and March 10, 1996, p. 11.
102. UDN, October 27, 1994, p. 2, and CT, October 28, 1994, p. 2.
103. Peter Kien-hong Yu, 'Fresh Options Needed to Calm the Strait', JIR, May 1999, pp. 28–33.
104. CT, July 26, 1996, p. 4.
105. UDN, March 20, 1996, p. 3, and CT, March 13, 1996, p. 11.
106. CT, March 10, 1996, p. 2. See also UDN, April 2, 1990, p. 2.
107. UDN, July 12, 1996, p. 1.
108. AWSJ, July 12, 1996, p. 3; THWDN, July 12, 1996, p. 4; and *Independence Evening Post* (hereafter IEP) (Taibei), July 12, 1996, p. 3. See also CT, March 17, 1996, p. 3.
109. UDN, March 11, 1996, p. 11.
110. UDN, March 6, 1996, p. 3.
111. CT, July 26, 1994, p. 2.
112. *Commercial Times* (hereafter ComT) (Taibei), March 9, 1996, p. 2. See also UDN, March 7, 1996, p. 11; and CT, March 9, 1996, p. 1.
113. See, for example, CT, June 5, 1994, pp. 3 and 4; and UDN, August 13, 1996,

p. 4. See also UDN, February 7, 1996, p. 3; and THWDN, June 5, 1994, p. 3. For PRC nuclear submarines, see LT, January 4, 1997, p. 4; and CD, February 12, 1997, p. 4.

114. UDN, March 6 and March 7, 1996, p. 3; and CN, March 6, 1996, p. 1.

115. CN, January 31, 1996, p. 1. The then Deputy Secretary of State, Warren Christopher, said the Taiwan Strait is international waters. See Chang and Lasater (note 44), p. 462. The October 28, 1988, issue of CD, p. 1, reported that the US Seventh Fleet passed through the Strait and ROC officials welcomed it. In November 1996, a US aircraft carrier was dispatched to protect President William J. Clinton, who was attending the APEC meeting. See UDN, November 25, 1996, p. 10.

116. UDN, January 31, 1996, p. 3; and CT, March 23, 1996, p. 11.

117. Chong-Pin Lin, 'Red Army', *The New Republic* (hereafter TNR) (USA), November 20, 1995, p. 28; and CT, March 10, 1996, p. 3. Another publication said the width of the Taiwan Strait ranges from 72 to 140 n.m. See UDN, January 30, 1992, p. 4. And an ROC lieutenant-general on reserve said the width of the English Channel is 20 n.m. See UDN, March 1, 1996, p. 11.

118. CM, December 1995, p. 35. Another publication said that for the most part, the depth of the Taiwan Strait is less than 40 m. See NPQ, March 15, 1990, p. 71. Durch said on average the Strait has a depth of 40 fathoms. See Durch (note 100), p. 218.

119. CT, November 25, 1992, p. 23.

120. UDN, February 13, 1996, p. 11.

121. CN, November 16, 1990, p. 1.

122. Office of Naval Intelligence, *Worldwide Threat to U.S. Navy and Marines Forces, Volume II, Country Study: China* (declassified version) (Washington DC: Office of Naval Intelligence, December 1993), p. 12.

123. CT, March 11, 1996, p. 4.

124. CN, February 25, 1995, p. 1, and May 22, 1997, p. 6; and UDN, January 5, 1997, p. 9. To maintain a 24-hour patrol, three aircraft carriers are needed. See WJ, March 16, 1997, p. A12. According to another expert, between 2015 and 2020, the PRC may possess two or three carriers. See CT, January 17, 1997, p. 9.

125. CDN (Taibei), February 7, 1995, p. 1; and UDN, May 15, 1997, p. 11.

126. CD, January 30, 1992, p. 2.

127. UDN, May 12, 1990, pp. 1–2.

128. CT, February 5, 1995, p. 4; and UDN, December 8, 1994, p. 39.

129. CD, December 22, 1996, p. 1.

130. UDN, July 27, 1993, p. 1 and February 4, 1997, p. 2. See also CDN, December 10, 1990, p. 6, which reported that Guangdong Military Region was conducting an exercise, with Taiwan as the target. Another analyst believed that Jinan Military Region will be relied on in the event of a PRC attack of the Taiwan area. See CT, December 1, 1993, p. 11.

131. CT, July 18, 1995, p. 2.

132. CT, March 9, 1996, p. 11.

133. THWDN, April 17, 1996, p. 2.

134. Chang and Lasater, *If China Crosses the Taiwan Strait*, pp. 65 and 68. Ronald Montaperto, a senior fellow at the Institute for National Strategic Studies at the National Defense University, said that at this stage the CPLA cannot conduct a naval blockade for a long period of time. See CD, August 5, 1995, p. 1.

135. *China: U.S. Policy Since 1945* (Washington DC: Congressional Quarterly, 1980), p. 104; and CT, December 6, 1984, p. 2.

136. UDN, March 6, 1996, p. 3; and CN, March 11, 1996, p. 2.
137. THWDN, February 29, 1996, p. 12.
138. THWDN, November 27, 1989, p. 12.
139. CT, November 22, 1991, p. 3. It is said that on the outskirts of Jilong harbor, the water's depth is no more than 20 m, which is not suitable for submarines. See *China Spring* (hereafter CS) (New York) 65 (October 1988), p. 52.
140. Chang and Lasater, *If China Crosses the Taiwan Strait*, p. 70. An article published in *Guangjiaojing Monthly* had a similar view. See *Guangjiaojing Monthly* (hereafter GJJM) (Hong Kong), November 1991, p. 19.
141. CT, February 10, 1995, p. 3.
142. CT, February 10, 1995, p. 3.
143. CT, March 11, 1996, p. 4.
144. CT, November 22, 1991, p. 3 and December 21, 1997, p. 1; UDN, August 14, 1996, p. 4, and January 18, 1999, pp. 1–2; *United Monthly* (hereafter UM) (Taibei) 60 (July 1986), p. 9; and *Yazhouzhoukan* (The International Chinese Newsweekly) (Hong Kong), March 3–9, 1997, p. 44. Some analysts point out that a country needs at least six submarines in order to deter: two for patrol, two for training and two for maintenance. See UM 60 (July 1986), p. 10.
145. CT, May 20, 1996, p. 7.
146. CT, October 3, 1996, p. 13.
147. CT, May 26, 1996, p. 1 and October 3, 1996, p. 13. See also CT, December 24, 1990, p. 5; and THWDN, November 16, 1996, p. 17. US defense officials had visited Gaoxiong port trying to get the necessary information regarding Gaoxiong waters. See UDN, December 10, 1995, p. 14.
148. GJJM, November 1991, p. 21.
149. UDN, October 21, 1995, p. 6.
150. *Xiandaijunshi* (Contemporary Military) (hereafter XDJS) (Hong Kong), August 1990, p. 81.
151. CT, February 10, 1992, p. 3.
152. THWDN, June 23, 1994, p. 2.
153. CT, December 21, 1997, p. 1; UDN, December 10, 1991, p. 1 and August 5, 1996, p. 6. Reportedly, a PRC Romeo-class submarine sank in the outskirts of Hualian County waters. See CT, December 5, 1991, p. 3.
154. CM, December 1995, p. 35.
155. CT, December 5, 1991, p. 3.
156. UDN, May 29, 1990, p. 4.
157. Durch (note 100), p. 228.
158. UDN, October 6, 1994, p. 16. Two spies working for the ROC's Defense Ministry were caught by the PRC. See UDN, November 17, 1996, p. 7.
159. CM, December 1995, p. 31.
160. UDN, January 30, 1992, p. 4.
161. CT, September 15, 1996, p. 9. Another source said the PRC has about 400,000–500,000 elite troops. See CT, January 16, 1997, p. 4.
162. CD, November 27, 1996, p. 5.
163. CT, December 21, 1989, p. 23 and November 22, 1991, p. 3.
164. CT, July 4, 1995, p. 4.
165. *The 1991 World Almanac* (Taibei: Central News Agency Publication Committee, 1991), p. 806. For a somewhat different wording of Chen's remarks, see FCJ, November 19, 1990, p. 2.
166. UDN, November 20, 1990, p. 27.
167. UDN, November 5, 1995, p. 2.

168. UDN, October 3, 1996, p. 1.
169. CT, March 8, 1996, p. 7. See also *Lifayuangongbao* (Legislative Gazette) (Taibei) 85, 28 (June 1, 1996), p. 272.
170. UDN, March 19, 1996, p. 4, May 4, 1996, p. 4 and June 10, 1996, p. 5. See also THWDN, February 28, 1996, p. 5.
171. UDN, May 26, 1992, p. 2; and CDN, April 19, 1992, p. 1. For a map of places where people from mainland China 'illegally' come to Taiwan Island, see CT, January 18, 1993, p. 6.
172. CT, March 15, 1996, p. 4; and CD, November 3, 1994, p. 4 and November 5, 1995, p. 2. See also LT, December 31, 1996, p. 3.
173. CT, November 2, 1992, p. 11. During the 1996 presidential campaign, several candidates were told they were targets for assassination. See CT, March 19, 1996, p. 1; CD, March 20, 1996, p. 3; and UDN, June 29, 1996, p. 2. To counter PRC death units, the ROC has been training special forces at Bajialiao, Pingdong County. See CD, November 27, 1996, p. 5.
174. CT, March 6, 1996, p. 10 and March 15, 1996, p. 4; and UDN, June 21, 1996, p. 1.
175. *Taiwan Times* (hereafter TT) (Gaoxiong, Taiwan), May 30, 1996, p. 20. See also Kuan-ming Sun, 'The East China Sea Missile Incidents', *Chinese Political Science Review* (hereafter CPSR) (Taibei) 26 (June 1996), pp. 135–6.
176. The use of electricity again reached a new peak in the summer of 1999. See CT, July 23, 1999, p. 9. In July 1999, Taiwan Province experienced a large-scale electrical blackout. See also radio broadcast, July 22, 1992. THWDN, July 25, 1996, p. 6. Harlan W. Jencks said the CPLA will use electronic nuclear weapons to blockade Taiwan, thereby cutting the civilian electricity supply. See CT, September 24, 1996, p. 10.
177. UDN, March 4, 1996, p. 11.
178. UDN, April 15, 1991, p. 2. See also a similar view written by a retired soldier in UDN, March 4, 1996, p. 11. A senior news reporter suggested that, should the PRC bombard water reservoirs in the Taiwan area, the ROC should attack, for example, the Three Gorges Dam on the mainland. See CT, December 19, 1994, p. 11.
179. CT, July 29, 1996, p. 7 and April 19, 1999, p. 6.
180. THWDN, March 6, 1996, p. 11.
181. CN, March 6, 1996, p. 1; UDN, November 15, 1990, p. 1; CT, March 6, 1996, p. 4, and June 1, 1996, p. 2. However, a military analyst pointed out that the probability is slim of radiation affecting people outside a nuclear power plant once it has been hit. See CT, June 10, 1996, p. 11. Another report said two missiles of more than 1,000 lb each must hit the nuclear power plant one after another before making an impact. See THWDN, March 27, 1994, p. 4.
182. THWDN, September 11, 1990, p. 3.
183. Ibid.
184. IMP, March 2, 1991, p. 1.
185. CT, March 8, 1996, p. 2; UDN, March 6, 1996, p. 5; and IMP, March 6, 1996, p. 4.
186. THWDN, November 4, 1995, p. 2. A graduate student pointed out that the ROC on Taiwan cannot be self-sufficient in food; yet, President Li wants to reduce acreage for farming from 800,000 to 160,000 acres. See UDN, February 13, 1993, p. 6.
187. CT, November 19, 1996, p. 2.
188. Jilang Lin, '*Zhonggongzhanlueyuzhanshudaodanduitaihaianquandiweixie*' (The Threat of Communist China's Strategic and Tactical Ballistic Missiles on the

Security of the Taiwan Strait), paper presented to the Conference of National Defense and Military Development in the Post-Cold War Era, sponsored by the Mainland Affairs Council and the ROC Air Force Academy, March 28, 1996, p. 24.

189. The ROC military first thought that the CPLA would attack about 100 targets. Later, it reduced that number to about 50 targets. See CT, December 23, 1998, p. 4. See also, CT, February 13, 1991, p. 3.

190. CT, July 19, 1995, p. 2.

191. CT, February 25, 1995, p. 3. See also CT, December 18, 1995, p. 4.

192. CT, February 13, 1991, p. 3.

193. UDN, March 7, 1996, p. 3.

194. UDN, December 23, 1996, p. 4; and LT, March 26, 1997, p. 6.

195. LT, September 28, 1995, p. 2.

196. CD, August 26, 1996, p. 1.

197. UDN, December 23, 1996, p. 4.

198. CT, February 17, 1996, p. 3. But, Angus M. Fraser, a former officer in the US marines, quoting a ranking US military official's 1980 fiscal year report, said the PRC has only a capacity to lift a force of not more than 30,000 troops. See WJ, January 6, 1983, p. 9.

199. LT, September 6, 1993, p. 1.

200. UDN, September 5, 1992, p. 10.

201. CT, October 21, 1993, p. 4.

202. CT, November 19, 1995, p. 3.

203. CD, July 23, 1994, p. 1, and October 20, 1997, p. 3; CT, April 27, 1997, p. 1, and August 19, 1997, p. 7. But, the then ROC Army Chief Commander, Tingchong Chen, argued that the army should not be reduced in size, given the large area that it has to defend. See CT, September 13, 1991, p. 3. Defense Minister Jiang said, if there is war, what the army has now is not enough. See CT, April 18, 1995, p. 4. A newspaper report pointed out that, in island defense, the defending side has to spread its forces; that is it cannot concentrate its troops on certain areas. See UDN, October 9, 1995, p. 11. On October 30, 1997, for the first time, the ROC President reviewed the arms brigades, the restructuring of which will continue until 2001. See LT, October 7, 1997, p. 2; and CN, October 31, 1997, p. 3.

204. UDN, September 5, 1992, p. 10. See also THWDN, March 22, 1994, p. 4.

205. IMP, April 13, 1989, p. 5.

206. UDN, August 2, 1996, p. 6. For the map of the ROC's deployment, see IT, March 19, 1996, p. 2.

207. CD, August 12, 1996, p. 4.

208. UDN, September 5, 1992, p. 10.

209. UDN, November 22, 1990, p. 30, and September 5, 1992, p. 10.

210. Hsieh (note 89), p. 5. Others say the CPLA will try to take Taizhong harbor area so as to cut Taiwan into half. See UDN, June 2, 1995, p. 2; and CT, June 3, 1995, p. 2. But Hsieh, note 125, said Taizhong harbor is not suitable for landing. According to an ROC air force secret document, the PRC built an airport in Dingxin County, Gansu Province, which is similar to the ROC's Qingquangang air force base in Dadushan, Taizhong. See CT, March 28, 1997, p. 9, and May 1, 1999, p. 15.

211. *Republic of China, 1987: A Reference Book* (Taibei: Hilit Publishing Company, 1987), p. 218. For firsthand information released by the PRC on its loss, see CT, February 16, 1990, p. 7.

212. CT, January 16, 1997, p. 4.

213. THWDN, July 12, 1991, p. 2. The PRC admitted that the major reasons for losing the 1949 Jinmen War were: the PRC took the ROC for granted; the telegraphic messages intercepted by the PRC were incomplete; and the PRC did not have enough logistical support.
214. CT, November 6, 1990, pp. 1 and 3.
215. UDN, August 4, 1996, p. 10. See also CT, August 26, 1996, p. 2.
216. CD, March 6, 1995, p. 2. According to another source, the PRC said its paratroopers could reach anywhere in mainland China within 24 hours. See CT, October 13, 1994, p. 11. The same source said the paratroopers are stationed at Xiaogan County and Huanggang County in the Hubei Provincial Military District of the Guangzhou Military Region. In February 1996, ROC Defense Minister Jiang said a regiment of paratroopers was sent from Hubei Provincial Military Region to Fujian Province. See UDN, February 14, 1996, p. 1.
217. CT, October 13, 1994, p. 11.
218. UDN, October 25, 1996, p. 9.
219. THWDN, July 12, 1991, p. 2; UDN, June 24, 1991, p. 9; and CT, October 13, 1994, p. 11.
220. CT, October 21, 1993, pp. 1 and 4; and CD, April 14, 1997, p. 4.
221. CT, November 17, 1995, p. 11.
222. Hsieh (note 89), p. 3.
223. I wish to thank Professor Arthur C. Chen and his student Shulun Wang of National Sun Yat-sen University for providing this piece of information in July 1996. See also LT, December 31, 1996, p. 2.
224. Hsieh (note 89), p. 3.
225. *Far Eastern Economic Review* (hereafter FEER) (Hong Kong), February 13, 1976, pp. 77–8. See also Durch (note 100), p. 218.
226. THWDN, October 14, 1995, p. 2.
227. CT, June 7, 1990, p. 5. But, former ROC Army Chief Commander Zhenlin Li said Taiwan's coast is only 1,100 km long. See CT, May 5, 1996, p. 2.
228. UDN, April 13, 1989, p. 2.
229. CT, October 21, 1993, p. 4. Another reporter said the PRC has more than 17,000 fishing boats along the coast. See CD, May 15, 1997, p. 1. During the 1982 Falkland Islands/Malvinas War, the United Kingdom used more merchant than naval ships in its campaign against Argentina. See UDN, November 16, 1994, p. 39. See also CD, November 13, 1996, p. 4.
230. ZB, September 17, 1984, p. 2.
231. GJRB, March 15, 1982, p. 20. See also UDN, August 17, 1997, p. 9; and CT, September 13, 1996, p. 4, and September 13, 1996, p. 4.
232. CN, November 2, 1996, p. 1.
233. *1996 Zhonghuaminguoguofangbaogaoshu* (The 1996 ROC Report on National Defense) (Taibei: Liming Cultural Enterprise Co., 1996), p. 27. See also UDN, August 11, 1995, p. 11. Each soldier is responsible for two meters of coast. See Chen (note 96), p. 209.
234. CT, May 5, 1996, p. 2. Jack Anderson, a columnist in the United States wrote: 'If the mainland should attempt a sea invasion, the DIA says their landing points can be predicted. Eastern and central Taiwan consist mostly of rugged mountains and hills with broad coastal plains in the west. Amphibious landing beaches are best in the north and northwest, giving access to Taibei and the major port of Chilung, and in the southwest near the major industrial center and port of Kaohsiung.' See GJRB, April 5, 1982, p. 20. See also UDN, September 29, 1996, p. 1.
235. CT, September 15, 1987, p. 3 and March 16, 1990, p. 6.

236. *The 1996 ROC Report on National Defense* (note 233), p. 253. See also CT, September 15, 1987, p. 3, and September 26, 1987, p. 3; THWDN, February 11, 1997, p. 3.
237. UDN, March 7, 1990, p. 6. Another source said 379. See CT, March 16, 1990, p. 6. Or, as NPQ said, 395. See NPQ 4 (December 1989), p. 140.
238. NPQ 4 (December 1989), p. 138.
239. THWDN, December 13, 1996, p. 18.
240. CT, June 7, 1990, p. 5; and UDN, December 22, 1998, p. 8.
241. CT, June 23, 1991, p. 4.
242. THWDN, June 28, 196, p. 3. See also CT, May 16, 1997, p. 4 and May 17, 1997, p. 3. PRC steel-plated vessels reappeared in waters off Yunlin and Jiayi Counties. See UDN, March 5, 1996, p. 9 and August 20, 1996, p. 9.
243. UDN, February 18, 1996, p. 7 and March 8, 1996, p. 9; THWDN, August 27, 1993, p. 6.
244. CT, June 18, 1998, p. 6; and THWDN, August 23, 1996, p. 4.
245. LT, December 31, 1996, p. 2.
246. CT, May 25, 1997, p. 4.

6

Taipei's National and Military Strategies and Policies

Kuang-ming Hsu[*]

In terms of the military threat posed by the People's Republic of China, the Republic of China must decide what to do, what it can do and how to do it. That is to say, when planning its national and military strategies, the ROC must first take into consideration the military means the PRC may utilize in its attack of Taiwan, and adjust itself accordingly. How the ROC perceives this military threat may lead to different national and military strategies. For example, in the days of Chiang Kai-shek, Beijing was a direct and open threat to the existence of the ROC. Later, when Chiang Ching-kuo was in power, the PRC threat remained a military one, but its scale was low-level and, as such, was not considered fatal to the existence of the ROC. In the meantime, the PRC shifted its strategy against the ROC from 'liberation of Taiwan' to 'peaceful coexistence', and confrontation between the two sides of the Taiwan Strait turned from a military to a diplomatic struggle. Under these circumstances, the ROC opted for a political strategy by highlighting its own existence in the international arena.

Today, President Lee Teng-hui does not have to fight like Chiang Kai-shek and Chiang Ching-kuo, who were facing an enemy that was prepared to conduct a limited conventional war, but not full-scale conventional warfare. Beijing opted for limited military action against the ROC so as to warn Taipei that it should never seek independence. The present PRC political objective is apparently different from the past. This means that the national and military strategies of the ROC should consider the PRC's political and not just military objectives. In other words, when planning its national and military strategies, Taipei should not merely deal with military threats. Instead, overall national power on both sides – including political, economic and military dimensions – should be taken into consideration in order to protect national interests and reach national objectives.

Ever since the political division of China, the leading variable affecting

174

the national strategy of the ROC has been the changing relationship between the two sides. The PRC still constitutes the major threat to the national security of the ROC, but in the process of changing cross-Strait relations, the interests and objectives of both sides have also changed. After the hand-over of Hong Kong to the PRC in July 1997, the relationship between both sides developed into a new stage; the PRC's 'one country, two systems' formula was elevated from theory to fact. Successful or not, the ROC leadership is now faced with a dilemma: (1) if it accepts the 'one country, two systems' formula, the sovereignty of the ROC would be at stake; and (2) if it rejects the formula, then the political confrontation between the two sides would continue and may even lead to military confrontation. Consequently, Taipei now finds itself in a passive and somewhat embarrassing position.

In this chapter, I will discuss four issues: (1) the relationship between national and military strategies and their meaning; (2) the kind of threat that exists to the national security of the ROC; (3) the strategic limitations of the ROC; and (4) the strategic choices of the ROC.

RELATIONSHIP BETWEEN NATIONAL AND MILITARY STRATEGIES

The concept of strategy has many definitions; most are linked solely to military affairs. However, modern strategies no longer involve officers and soldiers exclusively. Civilians may also apply strategies in their studies of national issues, making the first priority of strategy not to win a war in case of military conflict, but rather to integrate military planning with national diplomacy, national policy, and other related political and economic policies in order to deter, restrict or control direct military confrontations and conflicts. In the words of J. C. Wylie, 'Strategy is a scheme duly designed to accomplish a specific purpose; including a series of structures required for the accomplishment of an objective.'[1]

Modern definitions of strategy

Different countries adopt different strategies. For example, strategy in the United States is thought of in terms of national strategy, national defense strategy, military strategy, war-theater strategy and military service strategy. In the former Soviet Union, in addition to military strategy, there were national military policies and military doctrines. In the PRC, the different strategies are national strategy, national development strategy, national defense strategy, military strategy, military service strategy and war-theater strategy.[2]

In terms of classifying strategies, the United States, the former USSR, and even the PRC separated national defense strategy and military strategy. However, in the 1996 ROC white paper on national defense, national defense strategy was not included as a category. Moreover, it appeared that national defense strategy was almost the same as military strategy. That is to say, ROC strategy was classified in terms of grand strategy, national strategy, military strategy, military service strategy and battlefield strategy. Among them, military strategy is planned by the ROC Ministry of National Defense.[3] In the West, national security strategy, national strategy and national defense strategy are mostly mixed together. The 'grand strategy' of Great Britain, 'total strategy' of France, and the 'combined security assurance strategy' of Japan are all regarded as similar concepts.[4]

The so-called national strategy, according to John M. Collins, refers to an integration of all the resources which a nation can mobilize in order to accomplish the national interests and objectives in peace and war time.[5] Within this scope, there is a full-scale political strategy to deal with both international and local issues. National strategy includes military strategy, which is a means to accomplish the national strategy. Should a nation be able to accomplish its national security interests and objectives by means of political strategies or economic strategies, for example, it would not need to use military strategy. Nevertheless, this does not mean that a national strategy can exclude military strategy. On the contrary, military strategy constitutes the foundation and center of national strategy. This is why the Japanese strategist Koyoma Naiko said: 'In national strategy, the most important aspect is military strategy. Succinctly put, the execution of foreign policies of a nation is backed up by its military might and military forces.'[6] Clearly this indicates that, in understanding the relationship between military strategy and national strategy, we can see the strategic options and nature of a nation.

Collins defines national strategy as a combination of political strategy, economic strategy and military strategy as three strategies on the same level. Furthermore, to accomplish the national strategy, the three strategies should be properly applied. Collins' definition helps us to understand the national strategy of the ROC.

The so-called military strategy, according to PRC military experts, has the following features: (1) military strategy is subordinate to and serves the national strategy; (2) military strategy is not only applied to win wars but aims to stop wars as well; (3) military strategy is applicable both in peace time and war time; and (4) military strategy guides the use of armed forces as well as the build-up of armed forces.[7]

In the following pages, I will analyze the national strategy and military strategy of the ROC based on the above definitions of national strategy and military strategy.

Threat to the national security of the ROC

In late 1949, the ROC government retreated to Taiwan. Its national objective was aimed at defending Quemoy, Matsu, Taiwan and the Pescadores from attack by the PRC, while keeping itself prepared for a counterattack. The Chinese communists were planning to cross the Taiwan Strait and take Taiwan by force. Fortunately, the ROC managed to keep its air force and navy mostly intact. At that time, naval tonnage amounted to 100,000 tons and the air force had more than 200 fighter planes. In opposition, the PRC had only one flight squadron and its navy had only several dozen vessels which were earlier surrendered by the ROC forces. They had no air escort forces at all. Thus, the ROC enjoyed overwhelming air and sea superiority.

It goes without saying that Chiang Kai-shek opted for a *gongshifangwei* (attack for defense) strategy by conducting an aerial bombing campaign on coastal ports and vessels in mainland China. In January and February of 1950, a total of eight air raids were carried out on Shanghai, the major industrial city on mainland China, while other actions were directed at other ports in the East China Sea, downstream of the Yangtze river, in order to ruin the mainland economy and prevent the Chinese People's Liberation Army from assembling its vessels off the east coast. In the bombing campaign conducted on February 6, 1950, the ROC air force bombarded the Shanghai Power Company, southern Shanghai, and the Chiapei Power Company with 17 aircraft in four raids, causing Shanghai to lose over 90 percent of its electrical power and causing the majority of factories to stop production. On the other hand, the PRC navy continued sending troops to block the mouth of the Yangtze river while attacking the coastal area of Kiangsu and Chekiang Provinces.

Regarding the 'attack for defense' strategy launched by Chiang Kai-shek and the bombing of ports, vessels and industrial facilities on the mainland, we learned that the objective of the national strategy was not to win military war or to launch a counterattack. Instead, it aimed to prevent the Chinese communists from attacking Taiwan by crossing the Taiwan Strait, thus assuring the security of Taiwan and its offshore islands. That is why the elder Chiang once said: 'In the counterattack we launch against the mainland, we shall only move forward, as we cannot move back.'[8] The military strategy of 'attack for defense' may not have served to recover the mainland, but it did ward off the Chinese communists from launching assaults on Taiwan.

After the Taiwan Crisis of 1958, the PRC dropped the 'cleansing Taiwan with blood' propaganda campaign, and the prime national interest of the ROC – the existence of the nation – was assured. On October 21, 1958, the then US Secretary of State, John Foster Dulles, paid a visit to Taiwan. Two days later, a joint communiqué was signed with the ROC stating: the 'Restoration of freedom in mainland China is a sacred mission and we believe that the need for freedom exists in the hearts of all Chinese people and, to have it come true, executing it along the Three Principles of the People is the only means, and no force will be used'.[9] Since then, the ROC's national strategy has been to recover the mainland not by force but by the means of the 'Three Principles of the People'.

After June 1962, when the Taiwan Strait witnessed a third crisis, the United States did not endorse military action by the ROC against the mainland. Tension on both sides of the Strait then subsided. Since a dog-fight in the air over Quemoy in 1967, there have been no sea or air engagements between the two sides. On January 1, 1979, when the PRC established diplomatic relations with the United States, it dropped the policy of bombing Quemoy and Matsu on-and-off ('yes on odd days, and no on even days'), marking the end of the military conflict between the two sides.

On the other hand, the United States severed diplomatic relations with the ROC on January 1, 1979, and withdrew its Seventh Fleet. The 'attack for defense' strategy chosen by the ROC in the Chiang Kai-shek era was suspended. Adjustments had to be implemented and the national strategy of the ROC had to be changed.

With the disappearance of military conflict between the two sides of the Strait, the national security interests of the ROC – namely, national existence and the security of Taiwan, the Pescadores, Quemoy and Matsu – did not have to depend on military force alone. In other words, military strategy was no longer needed to maintain the national strategy. The ROC by that time had withdrawn from the United Nations; and its ties with the United States and other Western nations were severed. Since the PRC was recognized as the sole legitimate government of China with Taiwan as a part of China, the ROC was no longer a sovereign nation on the international stage. Due to the lack of space for political maneuvering, Taiwan's existence now relied on its ability to engage in economic and trade activities. Thus, the primary objective of the national strategy of the ROC changed to one of preserving its independence and survival in the international community.

To deal with this change, the military strategy of the ROC changed from 'attack for defense' to *zhuangshoufangwei* ('solely defense'). On March 16, 1982, Admiral Soong Chang-chih, Minister of National Defense at the time, replying to a query from Huang Huang-hsiung, an opposition party legislator, said: 'At this time, the national defense policy of the ROC is to reduce members of our armed forces. In terms of strategic guidance, we must maintain a strategic defense, that is to say, to defend the Taiwan Strait by reinforcing the air force and navy.'[10] Based on this 'solely defense' framework, the ROC attached importance to the geo-political situation of Taiwan and purchased appropriate kinds of weapons.

178

This was confirmed in an administration report by Prime Minister Lee Huan in 1989. He said:

> In order to maintain air superiority, full scale and active research should be carried out in making defensive fighters and missiles. Reinforcement should be made to upgrade the command, control, communications and information automated air defense system while increasing the electronic counter-attack capacity by deploying 3D radar for full coverage. The underground works in east Taiwan and the main bases on the west should be upgraded in terms of air combat capability. In terms of naval superiority, anti-air, anti-maritime, anti-submarine, sea mines and amphibious warfare shall be main points in rebuilding the force and the second generation naval force shall be expedited. The deployment shall be upgraded by reinforcing high-sea and offshore monitoring, so as to check Chinese Communist fishing boats activities. In terms of counter-landing, land and air combat fire and ground mobility shall be stressed and tank bunkers shall be erected, together with maintaining offshore islands' sea and air combat forces.[11]

The above suggests that in the late 1980s, the national defense policies of the ROC had dropped the objective of counterattacking the mainland. From the point of view of island defense and geopolitical science, such a 'solely defense' military strategy – that is putting the first priority on deploying air and naval forces and anti-landing forces – met the criterion of fighting with what one had in those days, when there was no significant gap between the armed forces on both sides of the Strait. However, such a passive defense strategy would not serve the national strategy objectives of the ROC when faced with a communist regime endeavoring to develop high-tech weapons and to widen the gap between the armed forces on the two sides of the Strait. To prevent a war, or to limit war or military conflict under modern conditions, requires strategic adjustment.

THE NATURE OF THE THREAT TO ROC NATIONAL SECURITY

Collins believes that national security interests, objectives and policies can only be meaningful if seen from the point of view of international and national threats.[12] Only by understanding the nature of a threat can we decide what should be done, what can be done and how to do it. Thus, by understanding the threat that the ROC faces regarding its national security, we should be able to understand its national and military strategies.

Basically, a threat may be understood as clear and present, or direct and potential, or indirect, as well as short-term or long-term. The PRC's threat to the security of the ROC varies from stage to stage.

Back in the Chiang Kai-shek era, the threat the PRC posed to the ROC was a direct, open and military one. It was an imminent and dire threat to the existence of the ROC, and only a corresponding military confrontation could have dealt with it, or the country would have met its demise. As a result, military strategy was the main element of national strategy at the time.

During the years when Chiang Ching-kuo was in power, the threat posed by the PRC to the ROC, although a military one, was a military or armed conflict of low intensity and only of short duration. It could not deal a fatal blow to the existence of the ROC. Then, after 1979, Beijing shifted its Taiwan strategy from 'liberation of Taiwan' to 'peaceful co-existence'.[13] In this situation, a full-scale diplomatic containment of Taiwan was adopted, and the two sides turned from military confrontation to diplomatic confrontation. This was amply illustrated after the PRC established diplomatic ties with the United States. Many other nations followed suit, and soon the PRC led the ROC in terms of countries with whom it had diplomatic ties by a large margin.[14] Launching a diplomatic blockade against the ROC, the PRC has insisted worldwide that the Taiwan issue is a domestic affair of China since Taiwan is a part of Chinese territory and the two political entities maintain a central–local relationship.

On August 17, 1982, the PRC and the United States signed a communiqué in which the PRC asked the United States to commit publicly to reduce arms sales to the ROC, both in terms of quality and quantity, until a final settlement. Today, the PRC is making major efforts in keeping the ROC from re-entering international organizations or new organizations in order to force the ROC to lose its sovereignty.[15] Such an indirect, potential political strategy is much more difficult to deal with than the direct, open, military threat the PRC adopted in earlier years.

To deal with the peaceful offensive of the PRC, the ROC dropped its approach of 'counterattacking mainland China' and instead supported peaceful reunification with the PRC.[16] On November 12, 1987, the ROC government lifted a ban on visits to relatives in the PRC by the people of Taiwan, thus putting an end to the 40 years of total isolation between the peoples on both sides of the Strait. This was an effective countermeasure against the peaceful attack waged by Beijing. The strategy of 'a great man will not brook his rival' adopted by Chiang Kai-shek remained entrenched in the administration of Chiang Ching-kuo, however, impeding efforts to counter the PRC diplomatically. This suggests that, at the time, the national strategy of the ROC was guided by political strategy, especially in terms of foreign political strategy.

In the 1990s, with the collapse of the Soviet Union, international politics entered the post-Cold War era. The strategy by which military came first, politics later, and then the economy last has been dramatically turned around. Now, it is the economy that takes first priority, followed by politics, and finally the military. Military power may not necessarily transform into political power. But economic power can gradually transform into political power. When over-emphasizing military technology and weapons development, military deployment may not solve the security issues of a nation if it creates a major burden on national finances and leads to economic collapse, as took place in the former Soviet Union. Therefore, the national strategy based on regional politics during the eras of Chiang Kai-shek and Chiang Ching-kuo had to be scrapped by Lee Teng-hui. The shift was clearly expounded in President Lee's State of the Union address made at the Second National Assembly, Fourth Plenum, on May 19, 1994: 'At the end of the Cold War, military confrontation worldwide has transformed into economic cooperation.'[17] On December 30, 1994, in his speech to the 1994 Party Works Review of the Kuomintang, further adjustments were noted by Lee:

> In view of the changing international situation, the 'a great man will not brook his rival' policy on which basis the ROC withdrew from the United Nations must be readjusted. The Cold War is over. A new world order is being built. We must adopt new thinking and tactics for the purpose of taking part in the international community so as to meet the needs and expectations of the people and the nation. Pragmatic diplomacy has to prevail, despite the obstacles. Major factors affecting international relations are no longer major factors. National sovereignty is changing as well. Our participation in international organizations is making progress and we shall move forward.[18]

Lee Teng-hui also pointed out 'interdependence between the economies and stability is becoming more and more important since the economy is where we seek prosperity. Without continued economic prosperity, we will have nothing in the end.'[19] This statement clearly shows that economic strategy is the first priority of Lee's national strategy.

In the mid-1990s, the PRC successfully engaged in economic reform.[20] On the one hand, this success has spurred the modernization of its national defense. On the other hand, since the mainland is a major world market, Beijing has been able to accelerate the ROC's diplomatic isolation. 'War Plan', a document prepared by Beijing and published in the *South China Morning Post* on September 8, 1994, contains the following strategic directives:

1. Allocate limited resources and foreign aid from the PRC to nations having formal relations with the ROC and those countries which could upgrade economic relations to political relations. Make sure those countries in the 'danger area' realize that maintaining relations with the PRC and not the ROC would be better to their interests.

2. For those countries that do recognize 'one China' but which still maintain non-official relations with the ROC, exchanges shall be upgraded to keep the ROC from strengthening its ties with those countries by taking advantage of economic difficulties they may face.

3. To those countries that recognize or are about to recognize the ROC and to those who support Taiwan independence, efforts shall be made to change the position of these countries. This shall only be applicable to developing nations, the United States and other developed nations. The principle must be held.

4. Embassies and consulates of the PRC shall make instant response and quick feedback regarding actions of the ROC and its foreign service agencies, especially on actions aimed to reintegrate the ROC into international organizations or activities.[21]

As early as July 21, 1994, the ROC Ministry of Foreign Affairs came up with seven strategies Beijing could use to step up its diplomatic blockade of the ROC:

1. *Political threat.* From time to time, the PRC has threatened newly established countries not to develop any official relations with the ROC, or else the PRC, as a permanent standing member in the Security Council, would use its veto power to block entry of new countries into the UN.

2. *Economic attraction.* Because of its huge market on mainland China, the PRC can use 'economic cooperation', 'major constructions' and 'joint ventures' to attract nations friendly with or that have diplomatic ties with the ROC.

3. *Buy-off.* By means of 'interest-free loans', the PRC has kept the Ivory Coast and Liberia from developing substantial ties with the ROC.

4. *Arms sales control.* By selling weapons systems, the PRC is damaging the foreign relations of the ROC, especially in term of foreign procurement.

5. *International blockade.* In international organizations and conferences, both at official and private levels, the flag, national title and national anthem have become a major issue and the PRC has threatened boycotts.

6. *Misleading propaganda.* When the Koo–Wang Meeting was held, the PRC launched a propaganda campaign claiming that the two sides had reached a detente.

7. *Omnipresent boycott.* The PRC has been sending its diplomats to undermine fair relationships between the ROC and its diplomatic allies. In 'The Taiwan Issue and Chinese Reunification' white paper, the PRC warned countries not to develop political ties with the ROC.[22]

The PRC has not only been using political and economic strategies against the ROC, but has also conducted military drills and launched unarmed guided missiles to warn the ROC's president not to go abroad to engage in diplomacy. This means that Lee Teng-hui is not dealing with an imminent threat as were Chiang Kai-shek and Chiang Ching-kuo. However, he is facing a full-scale economic, political and military threat, and the PRC has used them at the same time or with multiplied effects. For the ROC, it is not enough to fight back with only military, economic or political strategies: it needs a complete national strategy to compete with the PRC.

However, in formulating an effective and reasonable national strategy, the ROC may find itself restricted. I shall discuss some of these restrictions in the following section.

THE STRATEGIC LIMITATIONS OF THE ROC

All strategists may, while formulating a strategy, encounter limitations in various political, military, economic, cultural, geographical or technical aspects. By first understanding the strategic limitations of the ROC, we shall be able to see the content of its strategic thought.

National strategy is based on the concept of deploying the nation's political, economic, psychological, military or other strengths to ensure national security without engaging in war. However, for a small nation with limited potential and strength, its strategy may be restricted. Lin Cheng-yi, in his analysis of the national security strategy of the ROC, indicated that the ROC finds it difficult to strengthen its security by using collective security strategies or regional security strategies. Furthermore, exchanges between both sides of the Strait are subject to the PRC's political management. Lin believes that although a democratic ROC with an international economy may be a big help in strengthening Taiwan's security, the critical issue remains national defense.[23]

For the ROC, this would mean making military strategy the first priority in national strategy by deploying military forces or keeping them as a backup for foreign relations. However, since the issue of sovereignty remains a major focus of continuous interference by the PRC and international organizations control the proliferation of nuclear weapons, the ROC still faces restraints.

In terms of choosing pure military strategies, the most effective strategy for a small nation to fight against a large one is to possess nuclear weapons so as to deter the latter. A former British prime minister said that, although the United Kingdom was a small nation, it could compete with bigger countries because it possessed nuclear weapons.[24] Deng Xiaoping once said: 'I have what you have. If you want to destroy us, we will retaliate.' Possessing nuclear weapons would keep a large nation from using its own nuclear weapons on others.[25] Such a deterrence, backed by nuclear weapons, is called mutually assured destruction (MAD); and assured retaliation means an absolute deterrence by opting not to start a war.[26] The ROC has tried to develop its own nuclear weapons to act as a deterrent to the PRC's eventual attack, but it has failed in the effort because of interference from international organizations. Possessing nuclear weapons is the ROC's optimal defense strategy, but it cannot do so.

Following nuclear deterrence comes superior strategic deterrence. That is to say, the ROC should create a superior armed force to keep the PRC from considering military attacks. However, such a military strategy is restricted by limitations on arms sales by the United States and other Western countries, as well as by limits on the economic strength and arms research and development capabilities of the ROC.[27] Chiang Chung-lin, the ROC Minister of National Defense, in his report of April 17, 1996, to the National Defense Commission of the ROC Legislative Yuan, suggested that to prevent the relations between the two sides of the Strait from deteriorating into an arms race, the superior deterrence strategy must be abandoned. Instead, an effective deterrence strategy has to be chosen.[28]

The above analysis indicates that the strategic options of the ROC are still subject to international politics, international military affairs, the PRC's Taiwan policy, and the ROC's own economy, politics and military high-technology capabilities. The ROC may have thought of breaking through the international blockade imposed by the PRC by taking part in international organizations. This would ensure ROC security while preventing the PRC from starting a war, but none of these things has been easy in the face of PRC political and military assaults. The ROC must be very careful in planning its national strategy so as to ensure its own existence, while keeping relations with the PRC fairly stable.

THE STRATEGIC CHOICES OF THE ROC

Taiwan Professor Kai-huang Yang once said:

> Looking at things from the perspective of geographic security, Taiwan should have chosen the PRC rather than the United States, but the opposite happened. In terms of strategy, the ROC must opt for a friendly policy with its neighbors. But in fact, it has to make friends with far away countries to cope with the threat next door. From the point of view of the economy, Taiwan should have chosen mainland China for its development. But, should the tension between the two

sides of the Strait continue, the ROC would not have any choice but to become politically dependent on the United States.[29]

The fact that the ROC has to face the PRC as a strategic enemy is a product of history, and nothing can be done about that. In the future, however, a major issue will be whether the ROC should regard the PRC as a strategic enemy or a friend for the sake of its own security.

On April 30, 1991, ROC President Lee Teng-hui declared the termination of the 'counter-communist rebellion mobilization' at 0:00 May 1 in compliance with a resolution passed by the National Assembly whereby the 'counter-communist rebellion mobilization' provisions were abandoned. The major difference between this declaration and the 'reunification of China by the three principles of the people' announced by Chiang Ching-kuo is that the national goal is now legalized. The 1991 announcement has two implications: (1) the ROC government has officially dropped its goal of reunification by force; and (2) the ROC government will not fight to be the sole representative of China on the international stage.[30]

Regarding the first implication, the ROC has stated publicly that it will not seek the reunification of China by force. Such a move was intended to be a friendly or positive gesture to the PRC. In other words, the ROC is seeking a peacefully reunified China based on democracy, freedom and equity which is in contrast with the dictatorial, autocratic and poor communist China. This means that the ROC has transformed its military confrontation into political confrontation, especially when dealing with communist China in terms of internal affairs. In essence, the military strategy has turned into political strategy.

The second implication suggests that the ROC will not compete with the PRC to be the sole representative of China, instead recognizing the PRC as a political entity rather than a 'rebellious band'. In fact, the idea of 'political entity' proposed by the ROC is an attempt to seek equal status with the PRC on the international stage as a way to overcome Taipei's diplomatic impasse. Such a concept makes it clear that the ROC is not just a province of the PRC and, at the same time, downgrades the status of the PRC from a nation to a political entity. What is most important is that this political strategy dropped the 'a great man will not brook his rival' strategy. It does not signal anything amicable, but it is merely the beginning of a new confrontation with the PRC through pragmatic diplomacy.

From a series of political talks given by President Lee, we can tell that the ROC has not changed at all regarding its strategic objective: anti-communism. What has changed is its strategic means. The PRC remains a strategic enemy of the ROC. On December 20, 1994, during the review meeting of the Hankwang No. 11 Drill, Lee said: 'While conducting our pragmatic diplomacy, I have to emphasize that we have not changed our anti-Communism, anti-Taiwan independence, and for the reunification of China policy. Not a bit.'[31] He added:

> In terms of anti-Communism, we have opted for military force as a countermeasure to fight against the Chinese Communists. But, it is different now. We have put an end to the Counter-Communist Rebellion Mobilization period. We want to rely on more peaceful and reasonable methods to influence the Chinese Communist regime by promoting our free and democratic system as a way to get rid of the gap between the two sides in terms of thinking and ways of living and eventually accomplish the final objective of a free, democratic, equitable, and reunified China. We like to say that as long as China maintains its Communist and autocratic system, we shall maintain our national anti-Communism policy. As long as the PRC does not give up the threat of military force in reunifying China, we shall remain decisive in our anti-Communist efforts. As long as the PRC remains hostile vis-à-vis the ROC and its diplomatic pursuits, we shall not budge from our anti-Communism position.[32]

The 1996 ROC National Defense Report stated that military attack by communist China remains the number one threat to the security of the ROC.[33] Moreover, the report said that communist China is becoming an even more severe threat to the ROC. The PRC used to enjoy a quantitative advantage over the ROC in terms of military threat. However, its forces are becoming more and more superior to those of the ROC in terms of quality.[34] This suggests that Lee Teng-hui has not changed the national strategy of the ROC. What has changed is the strategic means. That is to say, the order of military first, politics second and economy last has become economy first, politics second and military last. The overall national strategy objective has turned from ensuring national security by means of military force to a peaceful change of mainland China for the assurance of the national security of the ROC.

In furtherance of this strategy, the ROC has made major efforts to promote better relations between the two sides of the Strait in the past few years. However, no friendly responses have come from Beijing. Instead, the PRC has launched military drills in order to stop the ROC's policy of pragmatic diplomacy.

Without security, the very existence of the ROC would be questionable. National security therefore remains the utmost consideration. To maintain national security, the ROC must have more diplomatic relations. In terms of the military, it needs a powerful army. In terms of the economy, it has to keep on developing. Needless to say, these policies conflict with and challenge the 'one country, two systems' policy of the PRC. As long as the ROC insists on being a sovereign nation, the PRC will continue to regard it as its enemy. Only when the ROC understands the national strategy of the PRC in the next century and finds specific issues that benefit Taiwan so as to enable it to cooperate with the PRC and refrain from irritating Beijing will relations between the two sides become warm. Only this will enable the ROC to find its own future in the twenty-first century.

At present, the national strategy of the ROC seems to be seeking possibilities for joining quasi-alliances or winning support from friends who maintain diplomatic ties with Taipei so as to resist the 'one country, two systems' policy of the PRC. On the other hand, it is engaging in economic, social and cultural exchanges with the PRC to settle the political confrontation on a mutually beneficial basis. In fact, the ROC has been promoting presidential diplomacy by making efforts to rejoin the United Nations and by seeking recognition from the international community. The PRC regards what the ROC has done as a severe violation of the 'one-China' principle. Sometimes, Beijing has even used military threats to make the ROC reel in its diplomatic efforts. As the ROC continues its pragmatic diplomacy, the political confrontation between the two sides will no doubt continue as well.

As a matter of fact, when formulating its national strategy, the ROC has to keep its sovereignty and territory intact; at the same time, it must urge the PRC to drop the idea of attacking Taiwan by force before the two sit down at the negotiation table. On the other hand, in building its own military strategy, it should prevent the PRC from starting a war or escalating a war. However, I do not see any sign of reconciliation of the existing political confrontation. On the contrary, the PRC is still keen on attacking Taiwan. Consequently, the national and military strategies of the ROC have to be duly reviewed and adjusted.

NOTES

*The author would like to express his appreciation to the following individuals who reviewed the first draft of this manuscript: Dr. Shiung-po Kao; Dr. Arthur S. Ding, National Chengchi University; Director Hsin-yao Hsieh, ROC Chinese Military Academy; and Mr. Fu-chen Chen, Office of Military Training, National Taiwan University.

1. John M. Collins, trans. by Niu Xianming, *Great Strategies*, 3rd edn (Taipei: Liming Culture Co., 1982), p. 40.
2. Lu Jingzheng *et al.*, *Guide on Contemporary Strategies* (Beijing: Defense University Publication Co., 1994), p. 52.
3. Ministry of National Defense, *National Defense Report, 1996* (Taipei: Liming Culture Co., 1996), p. 59.
4. John J. Kolout III *et al.*, 'Alternative Grand Strategy Options for the United States', *Comparative Strategy* 14, 4 (October–December, 1995), p. 362.

5. John M. Collins, *Great Strategies*, p. 40.
6. World Military Thoughts Database Compilation Committee, *World Military Thoughts Database* (Jinan City: Jinan Publication Co., 1992), p. 146.
7. Peng Guangqien and Wang Guangxu, *The Military Strategy in Summary* (Beijing: PLA Publishers, 1989), pp. 6–7.
8. Chiang Kai-shek, *Major Military Thoughts of President Chiang Kai-shek, Vol. IV* (Taipei: Ministry of National Defense, 1966), p. 1,595.
9. Lin Zhengyi, *Triangle of Taiwan's Security: Influence of the People's Republic of China and the United States* (Taipei: Laurel Book Co., 1989), p. 57.
10. *China Times*, March 17, 1982, p. 1.
11. *The Legislative Yuan Gazette* 78, 75 (September 20, 1989), p. 370.
12. John M. Collins, *Great Strategies*, p. 1.
13. On January 1, 1979, following the establishment of diplomatic ties with the United States, the chairman of the PRC, Ye Jianying, announced 'A Letter to Taiwan Compatriots', focusing on 'peaceful coexistence' with a proclamation to discontinue artillery shell attacks on odd days but not on even days.
14. Li Dengko, 'How to Break through the PRC's Blockage against Taiwan', in *'Academic Symposium on Mainland China Situation and Future Orientation in the Post-Deng Xiaoping Era' Essays*. Published by National Chengchi University, Chungshan Cultural Science Research Institute, January 1995, p. 186.
15. Ibid., pp. 191–2.
16. Lin Zhengyi, *Triangle of Taiwan's Security*, p. 57.
17. *Reference on Mainland China Operation* (Taipei: Mainland Affairs Council, the Executive Yuan, 1995), p. 12.
18. Ibid., p. 33.
19. Ibid.
20. Compared with 1980, total agricultural output grew 84.6 percent, posting a 6.3 percent average annual growth; industrial output grew 230 percent, or 12.6 percent in average annual growth; GNP grew from NT$447 billion to NT$1.77 trillion, around 140 percent when considered in peremptory prices, or 9 percent in average annual growth; national income up from NT$368.8 billion to NT$1.3 trillion, up 131 percent when counted in peremptory prices, 8.7 percent in average annual growth. In 1990, city dwellers recorded NT$1,387 average earnings while farmers had NT$630 average earnings, growing 68.1 percent and 123.9 percent respectively since 1980 and excluding price factors. During 1980–90, the average residential space of urban dwellers increased from 3.9 to 6.7 square meters, while for the rural population, it grew from 9.4 to 17.8 square meters.
21. *China Times*, September 9, 1994, p. 2; *Central Daily News*, September 9, 1994, p. 7.
22. *Liberty Times*, July 22, 1994, p. 6.
23. Lin Zhengyi, 'National Defense Strategy Orientations of the Republic of China in the Post-Cold-War Period', written under the joint auspices of the Mainland Affairs Council and the Air Force Academy, *'The Defense and Military Development by Taiwan and PRC during Post-Cold War' Seminar Essays*, June 30, 1996, p. 296.
24. Peng Guangqian and Wang Guangxu, *The Military Strategy in Summary*, p. 82.
25. Wang Shuchun, *et al.*, *Fundamental Theories of Military Strategies* (Beijing: Military Science Publication Co., 1990), p. 132.
26. Robert McNamara, the organizer of the American strategic designs, regarded 'definite destruction' as one of the duties of strategic forces. Later, during President Gerald Ford's administration, Defense Secretary Donald Rumsfield put

forward the 'definite retaliation' strategy.

27. Wu Chaowang, 'A Proof of Non-pure-military Deterrent Theories – Safe Defense Model of Thoughts', National Security Seminar Essay Compilation, Research Institute, Political Warfare Academy, June 7, 1996, p. 5.

28. Effective deterrence is such that enemies would be unwilling and dare not take the initiative to launch an armed offensive, or to continue conflict once a war begins. This is intended to cause the enemy to worry about possible consequences. Taiwan must be determined enough not to avoid a war and not to start a war, and must build military counterattack forces that the PRC will be unable to handle, before it can claim an effective deterrence against the PRC.

29. Yang Kaihuang, *Neither Side Loses – Taiwan and the PRC* (Taipei: Historical Database, 1996), p. 13.

30. Mainland Affairs Council, the Executive Yuan, *About Taiwan–PRC Relationships*, July 1994, p. 25.

31. *Reference on Mainland China Operation*, p. 21.

32. Ibid., pp. 21–2.

33. Ministry of National Defense, *National Defense Report, 1996*, p. 57.

34. Ibid., p. 51.

PART III
US Policy and Conclusions

7

The Taiwan Issue in Sino-American Relations

Martin L. Lasater

Thus far, we have examined several critical factors influencing the security of Taiwan in the post-Deng era. These include:

- Taiwan's value to China and evidence of Beijing's determination to use force to prevent Taiwan independence and to keep the island from being used by foreign countries as a base of operations against China
- US interests in Taiwan and evidence of American determination to ensure that the Taiwan issue is settled peacefully
- The balance of military power across the Taiwan Strait and the utility of using force to resolve the Taiwan issue
- US arms sales to Taiwan and the key future role to be played by military modernization on both sides of the Strait
- PRC and ROC proposals for unification, their commitment to 'one China', and their mutual refusal to approach the Taiwan issue from other than a zero-sum game
- Growing cross-Strait exchanges as evidence of the powerful forces of Chinese integration through cultural affiliation and economic advantage
- Various wild cards in cross-Strait relations, such as domestic political opposition to cooperation across the Taiwan Strait and track-II mediation efforts by well-known Americans
- The geostrategic importance of Taiwan in the post-Cold War era, which makes the Taiwan issue a vital international concern
- The role of the Chinese People's Liberation Army in pressuring Taiwan to enter political talks leading to unification
- Various scenarios by which the PRC might try to defeat Taiwan militarily and assessments of their probability of success or failure
- The national survival strategy of the ROC in response to the PRC threat to Taiwan's security.

This chapter will examine yet another critical factor in Taiwan's security: the management of the Taiwan issue in US relations with China.[1]

Certain key elements of US policy – American interests in the Taiwan issue, US arms sales to Taiwan, and American track-II diplomacy – have already been discussed. Other aspects of the US role in Taiwan's security need to be address, however. Some of the major ones reviewed in this chapter are: first, the American public's view of Taiwan; second, the role of Congress in US policy toward Taiwan and China; third, the principles governing the Taiwan issue in Sino-American relations; and, fourth, President Bill Clinton's evolving policy toward Taiwan, including the 'three-no's', proposals for 'interim agreements', and negative reaction to Lee Teng-hui's attempt to jettison Taiwan's one-China policy. Chapter 8 will discuss the possibility of the United States helping Taiwan to participate in a theater missile defense system for Northeast Asia, and the final chapter will summarize the book's arguments and offer policy suggestions to both Taipei and Washington.

AMERICAN PUBLIC OPINION

Like most highly politicized issues, US China policy is shaped not only by perceptions of US national interest but also by the moral convictions of the American people. Frequently, policy makers in the administration have tried to conduct China diplomacy in secret, but because of the decentralized and democratic nature of the policy process in the United States, these efforts have never been completely successful. The problem, from the policy maker's point of view, is that American values do not always support decisions on China policy based on *Realpolitik*. American values can be seen in newspaper editorials from around the nation, and these editorials consistently show a high regard for Taiwan and a decidedly mixed assessment of China. Overall, the editorials express support for a US policy of continued friendly, albeit unofficial, relations with Taiwan and cautious engagement with the PRC.

These reflections of public opinion could be seen, for example, in editorial comments surrounding the exchange of state visits between President Jiang Zemin and President Bill Clinton in 1997 and 1998. The goal of the state visits was to establish a 'constructive strategic partnership' between the two governments, but the public also held in mind the June 1989 Tiananmen Square incident and the firing of missiles into waters surrounding Taiwan in 1995–96.

Samples of editorials on Jiang Zemin's visit, which took place from October 26 to November 3, 1997, revealed a deep ambivalence felt toward the PRC and US relations with China. On the one hand, there was acknowledgment of the historic importance of Sino-American relations as China emerged as a great power; thus, a policy of engagement with the PRC was supported. On the other hand, engagement was seen, not as an end in itself, but rather as an instrument with which to deal pragmatically with Beijing and to effect positive change in China. There was also insistence that engagement not lead to appeasement on critical issues such as trade, proliferation, human rights and Taiwan. A few editorials will illustrate the point:

> The reality is that China is the world's most populous country, most rapidly developing military power and most rapidly expanding economy. Its capacity for disturbing the peace is immense ... These are the reasons why Washington needs a mature working relationship and candid communication with Beijing ... Engagement is needed not as a reward for any supposed niceness on China's part but because of China's importance in all spheres and the dangers inherent in a bad relationship. (*Baltimore Sun*, October 26, 1997)

> It's not just that Americans are disgusted by Chinese human rights abuses, including forced abortions, slave labor, orphans allowed to starve to death and ethnic cleansing in Tibet. These atrocities must inevitably impact on relations between our countries. How can a state that treats its own people so brutally be trusted to keep its international commitments? (*Boston Sunday Herald*, October 26, 1997)

> Not since the end of the Cold War has a foreign policy issue ignited passions the way U.S.–Sino relations have ... In a certain sense, our China debate is as much about American values as it is about China. Communist China stands for many things abhorrent to Americans, who are among the few true champions of human and religious rights on the planet. Americans feel strongly that U.S. foreign policy must have a moral component and become testy when the politics of pragmatism prevail ... China is no longer needed as a necessary strategic counterbalance to the Soviet Union, [so] the real trick here is to find a balanced position that serves the interest of human rights, trade and American national security. (*Washington Times*, October 29, 1997)

> In our relations with most other governments, our commitment to democratic values complements our economic and security interests. China should not be a huge exception to that rule. By combining good business with deft diplomacy, Washington can ensure that our expanding economic ties serve the larger purpose of helping to transform China into a more open society and a more trustworthy member of the world community. (*St. Petersburg Times*, October 30, 1997)

> China, with one-fourth of the world's population and a rapidly growing economy, is too big to ignore – and that's true whether or not you accept

the administration's thesis that trade and diplomatic engagement are likely to promote political openness inside China ... This relationship will continue to make Americans uncomfortable, because in the end human rights are not just one strand – as the administration maintains – among many in a complex bilateral relationship. Human rights is shorthand for the wretched condition of political dissent and unimpeded religious practice and freedom of speech in China. Until this situation changes all summits will have this same kind of asymmetry that will color whatever progress may be made. (*Washington Post*, October 31, 1997)

This search for balance between American values and national interests was also reflected in editorials commenting on President Clinton's state visit to China from June 25 to July 3, 1998. During his trip, the president had a unique opportunity to discuss the American political system and ideology before Chinese audiences, but he also made an unprecedented concession to Chinese leaders when he publicly announced in Shanghai the 'three-no's' in US policy toward Taiwan: 'We don't support independence for Taiwan; or two Chinas; or one Taiwan, one China. And we don't believe that Taiwan should be a member in any organization for which statehood is a requirement.' Samples of editorials follow:

One reason for Jiang's efforts to cultivate the United States is that after years of trying to deal with Taiwan directly, he has apparently come to the conclusion that the road to reunification with the breakaway Chinese province of 21 million people leads through Washington ... China expects that Washington will begin to pressure Taiwan to engage in reunification talks with China. Already, a string of former U.S. officials, including former defense secretary William J. Perry, have journeyed to Taiwan with a blunt message: If you declare formal independence, the United States might not be there to protect you from China's response. (*Washington Post*, June 23, 1998)

The weekend's unprecedented human rights debate between President Clinton and Chinese President Jiang Zemin put their summit on the right side of history [as] Clinton raised the issues of religious freedom and Tibet at the news conference and endorsed 'universal rights' in his speech at Beijing University. (*Los Angeles Times*, June 30, 1998)

Just when we were giving President Clinton credit for sounding the right notes in China, he managed to turn his visit into a fiasco after all. His kowtowing to China's 'three no's' over Taiwan is likely to set off a cycle of reactions and counterreactions that ultimately will damage rather than improve Sino-American relations ... President Jiang got his number one priority, Mr. Clinton carving the next slice of salami toward the Chinese goal of getting the U.S. to coerce Taiwan to join China, or alternatively to stand aside while China invades ... The issue of Taiwanese membership in international organizations is especially ridiculous, [and] the world's remaining superpower should be acting to curb this ongoing farce, not entrench it ... Congress, historically supportive of Taiwan and already restive over its foreign-policy prerogatives, will resist Mr. Clinton's unilateral change in long-standing American policy ... Taiwan is now plainly a democratic nation, and has every right to determine its own future. In the end, the U.S. will not resist this principle, whatever Mr. Clinton said in Shanghai this week. (*Wall Street Journal*, July 2, 1998)

The outlines of a deal are beginning to emerge. China gives President Clinton air time for his speech. Mr. Clinton says what China wants to hear on Taiwan. Then, in classic Clinton fashion, the White House tries to have things both ways, denying that U.S. policy has changed when in fact it has, and not for the better ... Recently officials of the Clinton administration have explicitly adopted a 'three no's' formula much more pleasing to the communist Chinese: no support for one Taiwan–one China; no support for Taiwan independence; no support for Taiwan membership in international organizations such as the United Nations. Now Mr. Clinton has given that policy a presidential stamp of approval – and on Chinese soil, to boot. Why does it matter? Because Taiwan's 21 million people have forged a prosperous democracy over the past decades. There is no justification for the United States to oppose their right eventually to determine their own future ... Mr. Clinton is trading away the human rights of Taiwan's 21 million people and sending an unfortunate signal to other democracies that might hope to rely on U.S. moral support ... Mr. Clinton has sided with the dictators against the democrats. To pretend this is no change only heightens the offense. (*Washington Post*, July 2, 1998)

From these editorial comments on the Jiang–Clinton summits, it is clear that the American public judges the correctness of US China–Taiwan policy from both moral and national interest perspectives. Morally, there was great concern over the lack of political freedom in China, human rights abuses, oppression in Tibet, and threats to Taiwan's security. The American people wanted these issues addressed by their government. For the sake of national interest, most Americans favored US engagement with China, but they insisted on hard bargaining with the Chinese over issues such as proliferation and trade. The maintenance of a strong American military force in the Western Pacific, backed up by US allies, was supported as well. Clinton's 'three-no's' policy was roundly condemned because it was unseemly for an American president to attempt to place limits on Taiwan's self-determination as a democracy.

These public views had not changed through the end of 1999. Editorials commenting on Lee Teng-hui's rejection of the ROC's traditional one-China policy were illustrative. The *Washington Post*, for example, editorialized on July 14, 1999, that President Clinton had 'aligned' US policy 'closer to Beijing's views, going well beyond "acknowledgment" to specifically rule out independence for Taiwan'. It continued:

> But instead of leading China's leaders to believe that the United States will help them force Taiwan into the fold, Mr. Clinton should help those leaders understand that the United States must support the Taiwanese people's right to determine their own future. He might also point out that if China's leaders would accord their own people that right, the chances of rapprochement between Taiwan and China would increase.

The *Wall Street Journal* of July 15, 1999, stated that Clinton was 'the first U.S. president to endorse China's unequivocal position of sovereignty over Taiwan'. Calling his administration 'weak and corrupt', the editors commented:

> By tilting so far in Beijing's direction of the past years, in fact, the Clinton Administration has decreased the chances for fruitful discussions or even detente between Beijing and Taipei. Washington has awarded China superior status, an acknowledged statehood; but Taiwan gets no status at all. What kind of bargaining position is that supposed to be?

A week later, the *Wall Street Journal* of July 21, 1999, said, 'when U.S. officials aren't echoing Beijing's line they are reinforcing it'. Examples cited were Assistant Secretary of State for East Asia Stanley Roth's 'heavy-duty pressure' on Taiwan 'to begin discussing reunification with Beijing'; Clinton administration efforts to ignore or hide evidence of Chinese espionage at American nuclear weapons laboratories; and Defense Secretary William Cohen's dismissal of concerns about China's nuclear weapons and possession of the neutron bomb.

The fact that the *Washington Post* was considered an American 'liberal' institution, while the *Wall Street Journal* was known for its conservatism, revealed the deep division between the American public and the Clinton administration over policies toward Taiwan and China. In a less democratic society, this lack of public support might not make too much of a difference in foreign policy; but, in the United States, where foreign policy is often public policy, such a gap between national leaders and the public can have important repercussions. One of the most obvious of these is the continuous friction between the executive branch and the legislative branch over the direction and conduct of US China–Taiwan policy.

The general public can do little about foreign policy issues, other than editorialize, speak out and vote. (Only rarely do Americans take to the streets on such issues, the Vietnam War being the notable exception.) However, the public does have the ear of its representatives in the Congress. And under the Constitution, Congress plays important roles in the formulation, implementation and oversight of American foreign policy. Among other things, Congress declares war, pays the bills, authorizes extended use of force, approves personnel appointments, passes laws, censures illegal or incompetent activities, commands the ear of the media and the public, demands accountability, and holds hearings. On foreign policy issues in which Congress takes special interest – like Israel and Taiwan – congressional opinion can be decisive at times.

Like the general public, Congress has been largely supportive of US engagement policy with the PRC – although certain aspects of that policy have come under intense criticism. At the same time, Congress has consistently supported US friendship with Taiwan. In part, this is because Taiwan is identified with American values such as democracy and free enterprise. In part, congressional support of Taiwan reflects institutional conflicts with the executive branch over a controversial foreign policy issue. In part, Congress feels an obligation to ensure that US interests in Taiwan are not undermined (or the Taiwanese people harmed) in the administration's pursuit of a strategic partnership with China.

As a result, compromise and confrontation are quite frequent between Congress and the administration over US policies toward China and Taiwan. The PRC has cultivated its close ties with the executive branch of the US government, while Taiwan has maintained close contact with members of Congress and key staff. The check-and-balance system in the United States has helped Taiwan to survive – and in some ways prosper – in the policy environment of Washington since the severance of diplomatic relations in January 1979. The best example of congressional involvement in policy toward Taiwan is the 1979 Taiwan Relations Act (S. 245/H. R. 2479).

1979 Taiwan Relations Act

Immediately after derecognition of Taiwan in January 1979, President Carter submitted draft legislation to Congress designed to handle unofficial US–Taiwan ties. Congress rewrote this legislation into the TRA. The

TRA was passed by both Houses of Congress in late March by more than two-thirds vote and signed into law by President Jimmy Carter on April 10, 1979, as PL 96-98.[2] There were several important congressional motivations for the TRA, many of which remain valid today.[3]

Correct inadequacies of draft legislation submitted by the executive branch. The administration's draft bill (H. R. 1614) provided for the continuation of commercial, cultural, economic and other non-diplomatic ties between the United States and the people of Taiwan. It further provided for the creation of the American Institute in Taiwan (AIT) as the non-governmental entity through which US ties would be administered. Provision was also made for a similar organization to be created by Taiwan to administer its non-governmental affairs with the people of the United States.

While accepting the essence of these provisions and not challenging the shift in US diplomatic relations from the ROC to the PRC, both the House and the Senate found the administration's proposal to be inadequate in several respects. In the case of the House, the Committee on Foreign Affairs concluded that H. R. 1614: (a) did not address the broader concern for the future peace and security of Taiwan, particularly in view of the president's announcement of intent to terminate, as of December 31, 1979, the US–ROC Mutual Defense Treaty; and (b) did not give sufficient emphasis to assuring a strong legal foundation for continuing – as if derecognition had not taken place – the broad scope of private commercial, cultural and other non-governmental activities that constitute the great bulk of relationships between the United States and Taiwan.

In the case of the Senate, the Committee on Foreign Relations found the administration's bill deficient in the following areas:

- While the administration took no position on the status of Taiwan under international law, it did regard Taiwan as a country for the purposes of US domestic law. The committee decided that it should spell out the specific manner in which relations with Taiwan would be maintained by the United States.
- The definition of the phrase 'the people of Taiwan' should be clearly defined and its meaning should include the governing authority of Taiwan as well as the people governed by it.
- Several matters dealt with implicitly in the administration's bill should be handled explicitly, for example, the legal standing of the people on Taiwan to sue and be sued in US courts, and the protection of property rights of entities and persons in both countries.
- The administration's bill made no provision for congressional oversight of the American Institute in Taiwan. The committee applied

the Case Act to the AIT, making agreements negotiated by the AIT subject to congressional notification, review and approval as if the AIT were a department or agency of the US government.

- The administration's bill made no provision for granting any privileges and immunities to members of the AIT and the Taiwan instrumentality stationed in the United States or Taiwan. The committee authorized and requested, but did not direct, the president to provide extensive privileges and immunities to Taiwan's representatives, subject to AIT officers being granted similar privileges and immunities in Taiwan.

- The administration's bill contained no reference to the interest of the United States in Taiwan's security, and lacked any reference to the sale of defensive arms to Taiwan. The committee was determined to remedy these deficiencies, and extensive discussions took place over the appropriate language necessary to reassure Taiwan without being inconsistent with recognition of the PRC. The language eventually approved was designed to make clear to the PRC that its new relationship with the United States would be seriously endangered if it resorted to force in an attempt to bring about the unification of Taiwan with the mainland.

Restore a sense of balance and fairness in US policy toward China and Taiwan. As mentioned by several members of Congress in their statements on TRA-related legislation then being considered, it was important for Congress to demonstrate through appropriate resolutions that the United States could both normalize relations with the People's Republic of China and at the same time provide for the future peace and well-being of Taiwan.

Establish a linkage between normalization of US–PRC relations and continued peace in the Taiwan Strait. The Congress felt it necessary to stress in the TRA that the normalization of US relations with China rested upon the expectation that the resolution of the Taiwan issue would be by peaceful means. The implication was that, should Beijing elect to pursue unification through non-peaceful methods, the United States would, at minimum, revisit its decision to establish diplomatic ties with the PRC.

Ensure Taiwan's security in the post-normalization period. Congress was especially concerned that the TRA provide for Taiwan's continued security and that US interests in Taiwan's security be protected – both of which were inadequately addressed in the administration's bill. The security provisions of the TRA will be noted below.

Reassure the people of Taiwan and other US friends and allies in East Asia. During congressional debate over the TRA, there was great concern that perceptions of the United States 'abandoning' Taiwan be countered. This was important for at least two reasons: (a) to reassure Taiwan that the United States remained its friend and would continue to make available an adequate supply of weapons for self-defense; and (b) to reassure US friends and allies in the Asia–Pacific region that the United States intended to remain in the region and that its commitments were credible.

Ensure a substantial role for Congress in US policy toward Taiwan. Congress did not trust the administration's handling of the Taiwan issue in Sino-American relations. The best way to remedy this was to craft a new piece of legislation to replace that submitted by the executive branch. This newly crafted bill – what became the TRA – addressed future US policy toward Taiwan as a package dealing with policy, security, the legal foundation for continuing business and other relationships with Taiwan, and providing for a non-governmental entity to handle matters previously handled by the American Embassy in Taipei.

Policy and security provisions of the TRA
In the TRA, Congress stated that the legislation was necessary to help maintain peace, security and stability in the Western Pacific. The TRA contains many policy guidelines that continue to govern the Taiwan issue in Sino-American relations. The legislation declared that it was the policy of the United States to:

1. Preserve and promote extensive, close and friendly commercial, cultural and other relations between the people of the United States and the people on Taiwan, as well as the people on the China mainland and all other peoples of the Western Pacific area
2. Declare that peace and stability in the area are in the political, security and economic interests of the United States, and are matters of international concern
3. Make clear that the United States' decision to establish diplomatic relations with the People's Republic of China rests upon the expectation that the future of Taiwan will be determined by peaceful means
4. Consider any effort to determine the future of Taiwan by other than peaceful means, including by boycotts or embargoes, a threat to the peace and security of the Western Pacific area and of grave concern to the United States
5. Provide Taiwan with arms of a defensive character
6. Maintain the capacity of the United States to resist any resort to force or other forms of coercion that would jeopardize the security, or the social or economic system, of the people on Taiwan.

To implement the above policy, Congress legislated specific guidelines for Taiwan's security. These policy directives specified that the United States will make available to Taiwan such defense articles and defense services in such quantity as may be necessary to enable Taiwan to maintain a sufficient self-defense capability; that the president and the Congress would determine the nature and quantity of such defense articles and services based solely upon their judgment of the needs of Taiwan, in accordance with procedures established by law; that the determination of Taiwan's defense needs would include review by US military authorities in connection with recommendations to the president and the Congress; that the president was to inform the Congress promptly of any threat to the security or the social or economic system of the people on Taiwan and any danger to the interests of the United States arising therefrom; and that the president and the Congress would determine, in accordance with constitutional processes, appropriate action by the United States in response to any such danger.

In many ways, the TRA was more specific than the 1954 US–ROC Mutual Defense Treaty, abrogated by President Carter in 1980 as part of the normalization agreement with the PRC. Although what constituted 'a sufficient self-defense capability' was left open to interpretation, Congress defined by law 'threats' to Taiwan's security to include not only military threats but also threats to the island's economic and social systems. Very importantly, Congress linked Taiwan's security to US security interests in the Western Pacific. Congress directed the executive branch to ensure that the United States maintained adequate forces to protect Taiwan from PRC attack. And Congress specifically linked the normalization of US relations with the PRC to continued efforts by Beijing to resolve the Taiwan issue by peaceful means.

Since the enactment of the legislation, Congress has carefully monitored the Taiwan issue to ensure that the TRA's provisions are enforced by the executive branch. Frequent oversight hearings are held by relevant congressional committees on the implementation of the TRA, and numerous bills are introduced during each Congress to voice continued support for the TRA. For instance, in the 104th Congress (1995–96), there were 59 bills directly referring to the Taiwan Relations Act; in the 105th Congress (1997–98), there were 66 bills directly referring to the TRA; and until mid-June 1999 in the 106th Congress (1999–2000), there were 17 bills introduced specifically referring to the TRA.[4]

Other legislation

In addition to the TRA, Congress has expressed its views on US policy toward Taiwan and China through numerous hearings, bills and resolutions. For example, the 103rd Congress (1993–94) considered 34 bills specifically dealing with Taiwan and 88 bills specifically dealing with the

People's Republic of China; the 104th Congress (1995–96) considered 38 separate bills concerned with Taiwan and 96 bills concerned with China; and the 105th Congress (1997–98) considered 48 bills dealing with Taiwan and 129 bills dealing with the PRC.[5] Generally speaking, the bills dealing with Taiwan were favorable or supportive, while bills dealing with China were critical of Beijing. A small sample of the bills concerning Taiwan and China that received wide support in the 103rd, 104th or 105th Congresses are listed below:

103rd Congress (1993–94)

H. Res. 188 expressing the sense of the House of Representatives that the Olympics in the Year 2000 should not be held in Beijing or elsewhere in the People's Republic of China. Passed by the House on July 26, 1993, by a vote of 287–99.

104th Congress (1995–96)

H. Con. Res. 53 expressing the sense of the Congress regarding [approving] a private visit by President Lee Teng-hui of the Republic of China on Taiwan to the United States. Passed by the House on May 2, 1995, by a vote of 396–0; passed by the Senate on May 9, 1995, by a vote of 97–1.

H. Con. Res. 117 concerning [supporting] writer, political philosopher, human rights advocate and Nobel Peace Prize nominee Wei Jingsheng [a well-known Chinese dissident]. Passed by the House on December 12, 1995, by a vote of 409–0.

H. Con. Res. 148 expressing the sense of Congress that the United States is committed to the military stability of the Taiwan Strait and United States military forces should defend Taiwan in the event of invasion, missile attack or blockade by the People's Republic of China. Passed by the House on March 19, 1996, by a vote of 369–14; passed by the Senate on March 21, 1996, by a vote of 97–0.

105th Congress (1997–98)

S. Con. Res. 107 affirming US commitments under the Taiwan Relations Act. Passed by the Senate on July 10, 1998, by a vote of 92–0.

S. Res. 187 expressing the sense of the Senate regarding [condemning] the human rights situation in the People's Republic of China. Passed by the Senate on March 12, 1998, by a vote of 95–5.

H. Con. Res. 270 acknowledging the positive role of Taiwan in the current Asian financial crisis and affirming the support of the American people for peace and stability on the Taiwan Strait and security for Taiwan's democracy. Passed by the House on June 10, 1998, by a vote of 411–0.

H. Con. Res. 301 affirming the United States commitment to Taiwan. Passed by the House on July 20, 1998, by a vote of 390–1.

H. Con. Res. 334 relating to [approving] Taiwan's participation in the World Health Organization. Passed by the House on October 10, 1998, by a vote of 418–0.

H. R. 2358 providing for improved monitoring of human rights violations in the People's Republic of China. Passed by the House on November 5, 1997, by a vote of 416–5.

H. R. 2570 condemning those officials of the Chinese Communist Party, the government of the People's Republic of China, and other persons who are involved in the enforcement of forced abortions by preventing such persons from entering or remaining in the United States. Passed by the House on November 6, 1997, by a vote of 415–1.

H. R. 2605 requiring the United States to oppose the making of concessional loans by international financial institutions to any entity in the People's Republic of China. Passed by the House on November 6, 1997, by a vote of 354–59.

Congressional sentiment toward Taiwan and China is not the product of partisan politics. During the 105th Congress, for example, there were 55 members of the Republican Party (GOP) in the Senate and 45 Democrats; in the House there were 228 Republicans, 206 Democrats and one independent. The very lopsided vote on many issues related to Taiwan and China during the 105th Congress demonstrates the fact that Congress is remarkably non-partisan in its evaluation of US policy toward Taipei and Beijing. Nor can congressional support for Taiwan or opposition to certain activities of the PRC be explained along a liberal–conservative spectrum.

As an institution, the Congress is favorably inclined toward Taiwan because it is a successful market democracy, and the Congress is repelled by PRC actions that deeply offend American values and harm US interests. In its demands for balance in US policy toward both sides of the Taiwan Strait, the views of Congress closely parallel those of the American people, as evidenced earlier from analysis of newspaper editorials. Congress brings both value judgments as well as assessments of national interest into its policy calculations, with special attention being paid to issues involving Taiwan's security.

Most resolutions express the 'sense' of Congress and are non-binding on the administration. More serious expressions of congressional concern are placed in amendments attached to binding legislation which the president must sign to authorize or pay for executive-branch activities. One example in the area of Taiwan's security is the Murkowski amendment attached to the FY 1994–95 State Department Authorization Bill, signed into law by President Clinton in April 1994.

Murkowski amendment to the TRA

In July 1993 the Senate Foreign Relations Committee adopted an amendment to the Taiwan Relations Act introduced by Senator Frank Murkowski. The amendment stated that the arms sales provisions of the TRA would supersede the August 17, 1982, Sino-American joint communiqué. This had important security implications, because the TRA specified that arms sales to Taiwan should be based on US determination of the security needs of Taiwan, whereas the August 17 communiqué placed qualitative and quantitative limits on future US arms sold to Taiwan – as long as the PRC followed a policy of peaceful reunification.

Although the State Department told Congress the communiqué would not adversely affect Taiwan's security – and further testified that the TRA took legal precedence over the communiqué[6] – over time the limitations on arms sales had a negative impact. Primarily this was because the amount of arms sold to Taipei was reduced each year by about $20 million. Thus, the so-called 'Taiwan bucket' for US arms sales was reduced from a 1982 high of $820 million to a level of about $580 million in 1993. By the early 1990s, Taiwan's military was becoming dangerously obsolete, a problem which became even more acute following the collapse of the Soviet Union in 1991, when Moscow began selling advanced Russian weapons systems to the PRC at very low prices. The decision of President George Bush in September 1992 to sell 150 F-16s to Taiwan was in large measure designed to remedy deficiencies in Taiwan's air defenses, but the sale was defined as being a one-time deal. Taiwan's long-term security needs were still not met.

The purpose of the Murkowski amendment was to do away with the Taiwan bucket altogether, clearing the way for other advanced defensive weapons sales such as anti-submarine warfare (ASW) submarines and longer-range air-to-air missiles. The Senate agreed with the reasoning of its Foreign Relations Committee and included the Murkowski amendment in the Senate version of the FY 1994–95 State Department Authorization Bill. Since the House version of the bill did not contain a similar provision, in April 1994 a congressional conference met to work out differences between the two bills. The conferees decided to include a non-binding sense-of-Congress substitute for the Murkowski amendment, Section 531, which read:

> In view of the self-defense needs of Taiwan, the Congress makes the following declarations:
>
> (1) Sections 2 and 3 of the Taiwan Relations Act are reaffirmed.
>
> (2) Section 3 of the Taiwan Relations Act take primacy over statements of United States policy, including communiqués, regulations, directives, and policies based thereon.

(3) In assessing the extent to which the People's Republic of China is pursuing its 'fundamental policy' to strive peacefully to resolve the Taiwan issue, the United States should take into account both the capabilities and intentions of the People's Republic of China.

(4) The President should on a regular basis assess changes in the capabilities and intentions of the People's Republic of China and consider whether it is appropriate to adjust arms sales to Taiwan accordingly.

In the conference report accompanying the State Department Authorization Bill, the conferees explained the intent of Congress in including Section 531:

> With this provision, the committee of conference expresses its continued concern for the security of Taiwan. It reaffirms the commitments made in the Taiwan Relations Act (TRA) to enable Taiwan to maintain a sufficient self-defense capability. Among the policy statements over which Sections 3(b) of the TRA takes precedence is the communiqué concluded between the United States and the People's Republic of China on August 17, 1982.
>
> The congressional statement reflects concern on the part of the committee of conference over the effect on stability in the Asia–Pacific region of China's military modernization, its increased military spending, and its territorial claims. If the President, in consultation with the Congress as provided in Section 3(b) of the TRA, finds that PRC capabilities and intentions have increased the threat to Taiwan, then a compensating adjustment in the transfer of defense articles and services to Taiwan should be seriously considered. Pursuant to the TRA, U.S. policy on arms sales to Taiwan should be based on Taiwan's defense needs and be formulated jointly by the Congress and the President.
>
> The Taiwan Relations Act is explicit that the nature and quantity of defensive articles and defensive services to be transferred to Taiwan shall be based solely upon the judgment of the President and Congress of the needs of Taiwan, in accordance with procedures established by law. Consequently, the transfer of particular defense articles and services – such as advanced ballistic missile defense systems and conventionally powered coastal patrol submarines – should be based on Taiwan's needs and not on arbitrary principles, such as prohibiting the incorporation of U.S. equipment on defensive platforms produced by other nations or the exclusion of entire classes of defensive weapons. The committee of conference calls on the Executive Branch to streamline and rationalize the procedures for implementation of U.S. policy concerning arms sales to Taiwan.

The conference bill, H. R. 2333, was passed by both Houses of Congress in late April 1994 and signed into law by President Clinton on April 30, 1994, as P. L. 103-236. In addition to the arms sales provision, the new law contained language urging high-level US official visits to Taiwan and US support for Taiwan in multilateral organizations.

Even though Clinton signed the bill to keep the State Department in business, the administration fought the Murkowski amendment every step of the way. The State Department, for example, warned the Senate Foreign Relations Committee that the amendment would set US–China relations back 20 years.[7] When Clinton signed the bill into law, the State Department said the non-binding language in the conference report would not change US policy toward Taiwan or China.[8] To dissuade further legislative attempts to modify US policy toward Taiwan, Secretary of State Warren Christopher wrote a private letter to Senator Murkowski reaffirming the TRA's legal precedence over the August 17 communiqué. His letter also promised to streamline the process of approving arms sales to Taiwan.[9] One immediate result of the Murkowski amendment was administration approval of the sale to Taiwan of advanced US naval electronic equipment for the six new LaFayette frigates Taipei had purchased from France.

Further examples of congressional action
Many other examples of congressional efforts to ensure greater balance in US policy toward Taiwan and China could be cited. Congress, for example, was instrumental in pressuring the administration to complete its Taiwan Policy Review discussed below. Also, Congress played a key role in persuading President Clinton in May 1995 to approve a visa for President Lee Teng-hui to visit Cornell University.

More recent examples of congressional influence over US policy toward China and Taiwan can be found in several influential reports required of the Pentagon. In the fall of 1998 the Pentagon submitted a congressionally mandated report on the modernization of the PLA. The report, excerpts of which are included in Appendix 1, noted that 'China's primary national goal ... is to become a strong, unified and wealthy nation that is respected as a great power in the world and is the preeminent power in Asia'. This goal 'will require the weakening of U.S. political influence in the region'. The report provided information on the PLA's development of new weapons, including many placing US military forces in danger.[10] Other Pentagon reports mandated by Congress for early 1999 included one dealing with the current military balance in the Taiwan Strait (found in Appendix 2) and another examining the possibility of including Taiwan in a theater missile defense system for Northeast Asia (see Chapter 8).

Another example of congressional involvement with Taiwan's security is the Helms–Torricelli bill, S. 693 (Taiwan Security Enhancement Act), introduced in March 1999 during the 106th Congress. The bill reaffirmed the security provisions of the TRA and its legal precedence over the August 17 communiqué, detailed the increased PRC military threat to Taiwan from recently acquired Russian weapon systems, directed the administration to submit annual reports to the Congress on Taiwan's request for defensive weapons, and specified that the United States should help Taiwan strengthen its defense through increased operational training and the sale of weapons such as missile defense systems, satellite early warning data, AIM-120 AMRAAM air-to-air missiles, AWACS, communications systems, diesel-powered submarines, improved ASW systems, naval anti-missile systems and Aegis destroyers.

Several generalizations can be made about the role of Congress in US China–Taiwan policy:

- Congress is far more critical of the PRC and friendly toward Taiwan than is the administration, which tends to pay greater heed to Beijing.
- Taiwan enjoys enormous support in the Congress, and Congress is extremely vigilant over administration policies and behavior toward Taiwan.
- Congress wants, expects and demands to play a central role in US policy toward China and Taiwan.
- Although the composition of Congress has changed over the years, its attitude toward Taiwan and China and its involvement in US policy toward Taiwan and China have remained fairly consistent, reflecting broad support among both Democrats and Republicans, liberals and conservatives.
- Congress is especially concerned over matters dealing with Taiwan's security and its democratic institutions.
- Congress is very concerned over PRC behavior in the areas of trade, human rights, military aggression, proliferation, Tibet, Hong Kong and Taiwan.
- Whereas Congress as a whole does not pay too much attention to the day-to-day implementation of US policy toward China and Taiwan (leaving these matters to relevant committees and subcommittees), there is close attention paid to the overall policy followed by the administration in these areas.
- Once congressional concern is aroused over an aspect of US policy toward Taiwan and China, then momentum quickly builds that can apply intense pressure on the executive branch for some specific action.
- Congress has many instruments through which to influence US policy toward China and Taiwan, and the Congress does not hesitate to use these instruments to exercise its power.

From all indications, Congress will continue to play a highly influential role in Taiwan's security in the post-Deng era. Although not directly responsible for the conduct of the nation's foreign policy, the appropriations and oversight powers of Congress give it enormous leverage over administration policy. Congress is unlikely to undermine the US policy of engagement with Beijing, but Congress also is unlikely to tolerate policies weakening Taiwan's security or threatening its survival as a free political entity.

PRINCIPLES GOVERNING THE TAIWAN ISSUE

Taiwan's security has become an international issue primarily because of the involvement of the United States. US support for Taiwan has enabled the island to maintain an effective self-defense, and American backing for Taipei has worked to deter most forms of PRC military adventurism toward Taiwan. At the same time, few in Washington doubt that Beijing would, under some circumstances, use force in the Taiwan Strait; by the same token, there is little doubt that the United States would intervene in a conflict in the Taiwan Strait under certain circumstances. Both China and the United States sought to prove this point in March 1996.

Since Taiwan's security is linked directly with the possibility of escalation into a Sino-American war – which neither Washington nor Beijing wants – one key factor in Taiwan's security in the post-Deng era is the effort by the United States and China to come to an understanding over the Taiwan issue. This effort has, in fact, been a central ingredient in Sino-American relations from the outset, but, since the early 1970s, mutual understanding has crystalized into a set of almost sacrosanct principles governing the Taiwan issue. As seen in President Bush's sale of F-16s to Taiwan in 1992 and President Clinton's statement on the three-no's in 1998, these principles do evolve over time; but they have also had remarkable continuity. This section will define the principles governing the Taiwan issue in Sino-American relations up to the end of the Bush administration, while the following section will summarize Taiwan security-related developments during the Clinton administration.

Sino-American joint communiqués

For the most part, the principles governing the Taiwan issue are found in the three US–PRC joint communiqués on which Sino-American relations are built: the Shanghai communiqué of February 28, 1972; the communiqué on the establishment of US–PRC diplomatic relations on January

1, 1979; and the communiqué of August 17, 1982. In every case, Taiwan was the central issue which had to be resolved before the agreement could go forward.

Shanghai communiqué

In the 1972 Shanghai communiqué, the two sides agreed to state separately their respective views of the Taiwan question.[11] Omitting paragraphs referring to US military personnel and installations on Taiwan, which were removed as part of the US–PRC normalization agreement, China set forth the following principles of its Taiwan policy:

- The PRC government is the sole legal government of China.
- Taiwan is a province of China which has long been returned to the motherland.
- The liberation of Taiwan is China's internal affair in which no other country has the right to interfere.
- China firmly opposes any activities which aim at the creation of 'one China–one Taiwan', 'one China, two governments', 'two Chinas', an 'independent Taiwan', or that advocate that 'the status of Taiwan remains to be determined'.

The United States declared the following as its principles on the Taiwan issue:

- The United States acknowledges that all Chinese on either side of the Taiwan Strait maintain there is but one China and that Taiwan is part of China.
- The United States government does not challenge that Chinese position.
- The United States reaffirms its interest in a peaceful settlement of the Taiwan question by the Chinese themselves.

These principles continue to reflect fundamental PRC and US interests over which little compromise is possible. China is firmly committed to ensuring that Taiwan remains part of China, while the United States is firmly committed to a peaceful settlement of the Taiwan question. Both sides agreed to adhere to a 'one-China' policy – that is, Taiwan is part of China. It is important to note, however, that the United States 'acknowledged' but did not 'accept', 'recognize' or 'agree to' the Chinese position that Taiwan was part of China. Also, the 'Chinese' position referred to in the US statement was the view held by both the PRC and ROC governments that Taiwan was part of China. Of course, 'China' to Beijing was the People's Republic of China, while 'China' to Taipei was the Republic of China. Moreover, the term 'Chinese' did not take into account the views of the majority population of Taiwan, the so-called 'Taiwanese'. This artful bit of ambiguity in 1972 enabled Sino-American relations to proceed and provided political cover for the United States to follow a dual-track policy of developing relations with Beijing even while maintaining close ties with Taiwan. The semantics of 'one China' did not really pose a problem until the late 1980s, when democratic reform on Taiwan allowed the Taiwanese to assume greater control of ROC policy. And, as will be seen, by the late 1990s Taiwan was trying to break away from the restrictions of the one-China principle altogether.

The United States and China established a liaison office in each other's capital in 1973 and extended diplomatic immunities and privileges to resident diplomats, but the Watergate affair and its aftermath in the United States and the leadership transition in China from Mao Zedong to the Gang of Four, Hua Guofeng and finally Deng Xiaoping did not allow much progress to be made toward normalization of Sino-American relations. After 1973 the PRC set three conditions for normalization: termination of official US relations with the ROC, termination of the 1954 US–ROC Mutual Defense Treaty and withdrawal of American troops and military installations from Taiwan. These demands were unacceptable to Presidents Richard Nixon and Gerald Ford; but they were accepted by Jimmy Carter, who came to office in 1977 with the intention of establishing diplomatic relations with Beijing.[12] Carter's election roughly coincided with the 1976 arrest of the Gang of Four by Hua Guofeng and the subsequent rehabilitation of Deng Xiaoping the following year.

At first, President Carter suggested that an American embassy be established in Beijing while a liaison office, similar to that existing in Washington and Beijing, be established in Taipei. The PRC rejected this proposal, and thereafter the United States abandoned attempts to broker a 'two Chinas' or 'one China–one Taiwan' solution to the Taiwan question.

Faced with a mutual threat from the Soviet Union, the United States and the PRC sought to expedite normalization. The administration informed China that Washington would not press Beijing for a pledge of the non-use of force in the Taiwan Strait but that it would continue to sell defensive arms to Taiwan. The administration further insisted that Beijing not contradict US statements that the Taiwan issue should be settled peacefully and with patience. In late November 1978 the Chinese accepted these conditions for normalization, and also reached key decisions consolidating the power of Deng Xiaoping and approving the use of force against Vietnam to punish it for the invasion of Cambodia, China's ally.[13]

212

Normalization communiqué

On December 15, 1978, the United States and the People's Republic of China announced they would exchange diplomatic recognition on January 1, 1979. In the joint communiqué on the establishment of US–PRC diplomatic relations on January 1, 1979, and the accompanying official statements, the United States and China further defined the principles governing the Taiwan issue. In the communiqué:

- The US government recognizes the PRC government as the sole legal government of China.
- Within this context, the people of the United States will maintain cultural, commercial and other unofficial relations with the people of Taiwan.
- The United States and the PRC reaffirm the principles agreed on by the two sides in the Shanghai communiqué, including the US acknowledgment of the Chinese position that there is but one China and Taiwan is part of China.

In its official statement accompanying the communiqué, the Carter administration agreed to terminate the 1954 US–ROC Mutual Defense Treaty, withdraw remaining American military personal from Taiwan, adjust US laws and regulations to permit the maintenance of non-governmental relations with the people of Taiwan, and reaffirmed that the United States had a continued interest in the peaceful resolution of the Taiwan issue, expecting that the issue would be settled peacefully by the Chinese themselves. In its official statement, Beijing again reiterated that the way of bringing Taiwan back to the embrace of the motherland and reunifying the country would be entirely China's internal affair.

The US Congress expressed dismay over the manner in which the Carter administration had normalized relations with the PRC and severed diplomatic ties with Taipei. The Senate in July 1978 had requested by unanimous consent that the administration consult with that body before any action was taken to abrogate the 1954 US–ROC Mutual Defense Treaty. This request was written into an amendment in the 1979 security aid authorization bill and signed into law by President Carter in September 1978. The administration chose to ignore the request and secretly moved forward on normalization while Congress was in recess and least able to react. When Congress returned from recess, it quickly focused on legislation to handle ties with Taiwan in the post-normalization period, the result of which was the Taiwan Relations Act.

The PRC has never accepted the TRA as a binding document in Sino-American relations. However, because the TRA is the law of the land, many of its provisions have become de facto principles governing the Taiwan issue. In terms of Taiwan's security, the most important of these are: (a) Taiwan's security is linked to American interests in peace, security and stability in the Western Pacific; (b) any effort to determine Taiwan's future by other than peaceful means is declared a threat to the peace and security of the Western Pacific and of grave concern to the United States; (c) the United States will make available to Taiwan such defense articles and defense services in such quantity as may be necessary to enable Taiwan to maintain a sufficient self-defense capability; (d) the President is required to inform the Congress promptly of any threat to the security or the social or economic system of the people on Taiwan and any danger to the interests of the United States arising therefrom; (e) the executive branch must ensure that the United States maintains adequate forces in the Pacific to defend Taiwan from PRC attack; and (f) the normalization of US relations with the PRC is linked to China's continued efforts to resolve the Taiwan question by peaceful means.

Arms sales and the August 17 communiqué
The PRC's reaction to the enactment of the Taiwan Relations Act was muted at first, in part because President Carter promised to implement the TRA in ways not contravening the normalization communiqué and because he placed a one-year moratorium on arms sales to Taiwan. During the 1980 presidential campaign, however, arms sales to Taiwan became a hot issue when Republican candidate Ronald Reagan indicated that he would provide advanced defensive weapons to Taiwan and 'would not pretend, as Carter does, that the relationship we now have with Taiwan, enacted by our Congress, is not official'.[14] Beijing reacted very strongly to Reagan's remarks, interpreting them as a retrogression in Sino-American relations. As a consequence, for much of the first two years of the Reagan presidency, Sino-America relations were bitter, with most controversy focused on arms sales to Taiwan.

Arms sales became a critical issue for several reasons. From the point of view of the new administration, there was genuine concern over Taiwan's security, especially in the post-normalization period when feelings of uncertainty and insecurity ran high on Taiwan. There was also considerable anger among Republicans over Carter's method of severing relations with Taiwan and a sense that some gesture of continued American support and goodwill was due. From the PRC perspective, the United States needed to be taught a lesson that it could not have its way over Taiwan after establishing diplomatic relations with Beijing. Also, in terms of cross-Strait relations, Beijing was concerned that renewed US arms sales would strengthen Taipei's resolve to resist the PRC's new policy of peaceful reunification. China thus determined to present the conservative US administration with a stark choice: choose either strategic cooperation with the PRC against the common Soviet threat, or improved US relations with Taiwan.

The hardline Chinese position precipitated heated debate within the United States, as well as within the new administration and among Reagan supporters. The debate tended to coalesce around the issue of whether the FX fighter should be sold to Taiwan. The FX was a unique defensive fighter designed to replace Taiwan's aging fleet of F-5Es and F-104s. The Carter administration approved the presentation of competing FX designs to Taipei by both Northrop and General Dynamics in June 1980, but when the Dutch government sold Taiwan two Zwaardvis submarines in November 1980, the PRC downgraded relations with The Hague. At the same time, the Chinese government said its action was intended to be an example to the incoming Reagan administration with reference to its pending decision on the FX sale to Taiwan.[15]

Although many supporters of President Reagan were inclined to sell Taiwan the FX, Republican policy makers were even more concerned about a growing threat from the Soviet Union. This pragmatic, anti-Soviet faction of the Republican party advised Reagan that a strategic partnership with China was necessary to protect American national security interests. Witnessing the PRC reaction to the Dutch submarine sale, the administration decided in January 1982, after a year of very intense debate, that the FX sale would not go forward. In announcing the decision, the State Department said 'no military need for such aircraft exists'.[16] The intense diplomatic confrontation over the FX led Washington and Beijing to undertake negotiations over a third communiqué, this one dealing specifically with the Taiwan arms sales issue.[17]

In the August 17, 1982, joint communiqué, the United States and China sought to resolve the issue of US arms sales to Taiwan by placing parameters around future sales. Both sides reaffirmed previous principles governing the Taiwan issue and added certain others:

- Respect for each other's sovereignty and territorial integrity and non-interference in each other's internal affairs constitute the fundamental principles guiding United States–China relations.
- Since January 1, 1979, the Chinese government has pursued a fundamental policy of striving for the peaceful reunification of the motherland, thus striving for a peaceful solution to the Taiwan question.
- China's policy of peaceful reunification has provided favorable conditions for the settlement of US–China differences over the question of US arms sales to Taiwan.
- Having in mind China's striving for peaceful reunification and the favorable conditions making possible the settlement of the arms sales issue, the US government states that it does not seek to carry out a long-term policy of arms sales to Taiwan, that its arms sales to Taiwan will not exceed, either in qualitative or in quantitative terms, the level of those supplied in recent years since January 1, 1979, and that it intends

to reduce gradually its sales of arms to Taiwan, leading over a period of time to a final resolution.

In its official statement on the August 17 communiqué, the PRC said US arms sales to Taiwan affected Chinese sovereignty. The final resolution referred to in the communiqué implied that US arms sales to Taiwan must be completely terminated over a period of time. The joint communiqué was based on the principles embodied in the joint communiqué on the establishment of diplomatic relations between China and the United States and the basic norms guiding international relations; it had nothing whatsoever to do with the Taiwan Relations Act formulated unilaterally by the United States. In fact, the TRA seriously contravened the principles embodied in the normalization communiqué, and the Chinese government had been consistently opposed to it. Thus, all interpretations designed to link the August 17 communiqué to the TRA were in violation of the spirit and substance of the communiqué and were unacceptable. Further, the agreement reached between the governments of China and the United States on the question of US arms sales to Taiwan only marked the beginning of the settlement of the issue.

In the US presidential statement accompanying the August 17 communiqué, Ronald Reagan stated that advancing the US–PRC strategic relationship was in the US national interest. The communiqué would make that possible, consistent with US obligations to the people of Taiwan. He was committed to maintaining the full range of contacts between the people of the United States and the people of Taiwan. Such contacts would continue to grow and prosper, and they would be conducted with the dignity and honor befitting old friends. Reagan said US policy in regards to arms sales to Taiwan, as set forth in the communiqué, was fully consistent with the Taiwan Relations Act. Accordingly, US arms sales would continue in accordance with the TRA, with the full expectation that the approach of the Chinese government to the resolution of the Taiwan issue would continue to be peaceful. He affirmed that the Taiwan question is a matter for the Chinese people, on both sides of the Taiwan Strait, to resolve. The United States would not interfere in this matter or prejudice the free choice of, or put pressure on, the people of Taiwan. At the same time, the United States had an abiding interest and concern that any resolution be peaceful.

The administration made clear in testimony before Congress that the United States reserved the right to increase arms sales to Taiwan should the PRC threat to Taiwan's security increase.[18] Moreover, the administration told Congress that the TRA, being the law of the land, took legal precedence over the joint communiqué, which was a statement of intended policy by the administration.[19]

Further insight into Reagan administration principles regarding the

Taiwan issue can be gleaned from the six assurances given Taipei on the eve of the communiqué. According to the ROC statement on the August 17 communiqué, the United States

1. has not agreed to set a date for ending arms sales to the Republic of China
2. has not agreed to hold prior consultations with the Chinese communists on arms sales to the Republic of China
3. will not play any mediation role between Taipei and Peiping [Beijing]
4. has not agreed to revise the Taiwan Relations Act
5. has not altered its position regarding sovereignty over Taiwan
6. will not exert pressure on the Republic of China to enter into negotiations with the Chinese communists.[20]

The Reagan administration's decision to proceed with the August 17 communiqué, and the justification for the agreement once it had been signed, were based on the need to preserve a strategic partnership with the PRC to counter the Soviet threat. Thus, there was some irony in the fact that one month later, in September 1982, General Secretary Hu Yaobang formally announced at the Twelfth CCP Congress that China had decided to improve relations with the Soviet Union as part of its 'independent' foreign policy.[21] The strategic partnership which justified the communiqué never materialized, as Beijing skillfully used Moscow's concerns over a potential Sino-American strategic alliance to gain Soviet concessions on removing the 'three obstacles' (large Soviet deployments along the Chinese border, Soviet assistance to Vietnam's occupation of Cambodia, and Soviet occupation of Afghanistan) as conditions to improve Sino-Soviet relations.

Although the PRC has tried on repeated occasions to get the United States to negotiate another joint communiqué – for example, during the Jiang–Clinton summits in 1997 and 1998 – the United States has refused. Therefore, the basic principles governing the Taiwan issue in Sino-American relations have been solidly in place since 1982. Nonetheless, a few refinements to those principles have come about through precedent-setting actions by President Reagan and his successors.

Precedents in US Taiwan policy under Reagan and Bush

As Senator S. I. Hayakawa observed, the August 17 'communiqué means either what you want it to mean or what you fear it means. There is enough ambiguity in the document, it seems, that no one need take offense … What we have in the communiqué is a situation not uncommon in human affairs: total ambiguity.'[22] That indeed seems to have been the administration's intent, as became apparent in March 1983, when the State Department announced it would set ceilings on arms sales to Taiwan at $800 million for fiscal year 1983 and $760 million for fiscal year 1984. These figures were much higher than actual sales in 1979, 1980 and 1981 (the base years referred to in the communiqué), but the State Department explained that an 'inflationary index' had been applied so that the $598 million in 1979 would be equivalent to $830 million in current, inflated dollars.[23] The administration then added a qualitative index to this quantitative index as well, when it replaced obsolete equipment in Taiwan's inventory with newer equipment. The Reagan administration also began to supply Taiwan with defense technology to build its own modern weapons.

Another important precedent of the Reagan administration was to reject Beijing's appeal that the United States 'do something' to help China's reunification. US policy toward China's reunification was described in December 1986 by Gaston Sigur, Assistant Secretary of State for East Asian and Pacific affairs, who explained that the United States viewed unification 'as an internal matter for the PRC and Taiwan to resolve themselves. We will not serve as an intermediary or pressure Taiwan on the matter. We leave it up to both sides to settle their differences: our predominant interest is that the settlement be a peaceful one.'[24] In March 1987 Secretary of State George Shultz further explained US policy toward China's unification: while the 'principles of one China and a peaceful resolution of the Taiwan question remain at the core of our China policy ... the situation [in the Taiwan Strait] itself has not and cannot remain static'. US policy was to 'support a continuing evolutionary process toward a peaceful resolution of the Taiwan issue'. The pace of that process, however, 'will be determined by the Chinese on either side of the Taiwan Strait, free of outside pressure ... Our steadfast policy seeks to foster an environment within which such developments [as indirect trade and increasing human interchange] can continue to take place.'[25]

Thus, toward the end of the Reagan administration, the United States had added to its fundamental principles the idea that Washington's role in the resolution of differences between the two sides would be to foster an environment making increased cross-Strait exchanges possible and likely. The United States did not take a position of supporting a *particular outcome* of the Taiwan issue, but it did support a *peaceful process* of resolving the issue by the two Chinese sides themselves. In other words, under the Reagan (and Bush) administrations, the US 'one-China' policy was simply this: first, the United States would not seek to divide China; and, second, the United States would support any resolution of the Taiwan issue agreed to peacefully by both sides of the Taiwan Strait. There were three principal reasons why the United States avoided the promotion of a certain outcome of the Taiwan issue:

218

1. There was no indication that the people of Taiwan wanted unification with the PRC anytime in the foreseeable future. The majority of Taiwan people favored a continuation of the status quo in the Taiwan Strait, if only because of great uncertainty as to future PRC policies. The 'one country, two systems' formula for Hong Kong was not deemed appropriate for Taiwan because the arrangement had not passed the test of time and because there were substantial differences between Hong Kong and Taiwan. Moreover, although China had started on the path of economic modernization and gradual social and political liberalization, the PRC remained a communist dictatorship subject to the whims of individual leaders and a single political party with no effective system of checks and balances.

2. Early unification was not necessarily in the US interest, especially if the people of Taiwan did not desire it. For one thing, the status quo in the Taiwan Strait had served US interests quite well since the 1950s. The US 'one-China' policy, which was based on the acknowledgment that both sides of the Taiwan Strait considered Taiwan to be part of China, enabled the United States to pursue mutually beneficial relationships with both Taiwan and the PRC. Given the political sensitivity of the Taiwan issue, any substantive change in US Taiwan policy would have to be approached very cautiously and only with adequate cause. Also, because of the important role the United States played in the Taiwan issue, any US backing of a particular outcome of the Taiwan issue would likely result in a significant weakening of Taipei's bargaining position. Moreover, the possibility existed that China would one day become a regional rival of the United States, perhaps even a threat. As long as this possibility existed, there was very little incentive for the United States to enhance Chinese power by 'giving' it Taiwan.

3. Although important, the Taiwan issue was not the central issue in US relations with China. From Washington's point of view, the main issues were long-term and strategic: whether the United States and China could coexist as major powers in East Asia; whether China would participate in or oppose an American-led security, political and economic system in the Western Pacific; and whether China would seek to replace the United States as leader of the Asia–Pacific region. A resolution of the Taiwan issue, even along lines favored by Beijing, would not alter the course of China in these strategic areas. So US compromise over Taiwan made little sense in the larger scheme of things.

President Bush during his four years in office largely continued the Taiwan policy of his predecessor. The most important addition Bush made to the principles governing the Taiwan issue in Sino-American relations was his determination that, if Beijing too dramatically upset the military balance of power in the Taiwan Strait, the United States would seek to redress that imbalance by selling more advanced arms to Taiwan. It was argued that such sales were consistent with both the TRA – which is true – and with the August 17 communiqué – which is debatable. The best example of this principle in action was President Bush's decision in September 1992 to sell Taiwan 150 F-16s, in large part (but not totally) in response to Beijing's purchase of Su-27s from Moscow.

It is important to know something of the background to the F-16 sale. One of the keys to Taiwan's defense is ROC air supremacy over the Taiwan Strait. If the ROC can control the skies, then a PRC amphibious invasion of Taiwan is impossible and an effective blockade of the island is prohibitively costly. For nearly two decades, Taiwan sought to replace the backbone of its air defense system, the F-5E Tiger II, with a newer and more advanced US fighter such as the F-16 Fighting Falcon, F-4C Phantom or F-5G Tiger Shark (later designated the F-20, one of the FX models). However, in January 1982 the Reagan administration decided not to sell a new fighter to Taiwan to avoid a possible rupture in Sino-American relations. The signing of the August 17 communiqué made it even more difficult for Taiwan to acquire an advanced fighter from the United States. Taiwan was also unsuccessful in purchasing a fighter from Israel or other foreign sources.

After 1982, Taiwan concentrated on building its own indigenous fighter (IDF), with considerable help from US companies such as General Dynamics, Lear Siegler and Garrett Engine. The first IDF prototype, dubbed the Ching-kuo fighter after President Chiang Ching-kuo, appeared in 1988. Despite initial engine and other design flaws, the ROC military eventually decided to produce 130 of the IDF fighters.

In the post-Cold War environment of the 1990s, Taipei redoubled its efforts to acquire foreign fighters, concentrating on the F-16 and the French-built Mirage 2000-5. Taiwan was able to purchase 60 Mirage 2000-5 fighters from France in 1992 at a price of about $6 billion, a deal that included some 1,500 Mica air-to-air missiles. The French may have offered Taiwan an additional 60 Mirages, but Taipei declined when the United States agreed to sell the F-16.

President Bush announced his decision to allow the F-16 sale to Taiwan in September 1992 in Fort Worth, Texas, home of General Dynamics. His decision was influenced by many factors: concern over maintaining Taiwan's capabilities to deter the Su-27s and other weapons being purchased by the PRC from Russia; the need to maintain a balance of power in East Asia and a military balance in the Taiwan Strait; the difficulty in supplying spare parts for the outdated aircraft in Taiwan's inventory; the desire to ensure that American companies got the ROC's arms business, not French enterprises or those of other countries;

mounting congressional pressure to sell Taiwan the F-16; to give a boost to American defense industries, on lean times after the Cold War; to preserve US influence over Taiwan's military; and to help Bush's presidential campaign in Texas, a critical state in the presidential primary.[26]

Taipei and Washington signed a letter of offer and acceptance for 150 F-16s in November 1992, with delivery of the first planes to occur in 1996. The F-16s initially offered to Taiwan were the older model A and B versions, in use by the US air force for over a decade. Since these strictly defensive models were considered inferior to the Su-27, Taiwan requested the more advanced C and D models; but the United States refused to sell these models because of their offensive capabilities. A compromise was worked out whereby Taiwan would receive new F-16 MLU (mid-life upgrade) aircraft similar to models scheduled to be flown by American and European air defense pilots. The F-16 MLU was a more advanced model of the F-16A/B, with some functions identical to the F-16C/D. The cost of the 150 MLU versions of the F-16A/B sold to Taiwan was about $6 billion.

Although the Chinese were upset by the F-16 sale, calling it a major retrogression, the effectiveness of their protests was considerably diluted in view of their purchase of Su-27s and other advanced Russian weapons. On the other hand, the sale was well received by most Americans. Even Democratic presidential candidate Bill Clinton approved the sale and promised to implement the agreement if elected.

Thus, at the time of the 1993 presidential transition between George Bush and Bill Clinton, a set of principles had evolved to manage the Taiwan issue in Sino-American relations. Essentially, these principles were:

- Washington recognized Beijing as the sole legal government of China.
- The United States acknowledged that Chinese on both sides of the Strait considered Taiwan to be part of China.
- The United States would continue to have close, friendly but unofficial relations with the people of Taiwan.
- The PRC would attempt to settle the Taiwan issue peacefully.
- Washington would sell only limited quantities of defensive weapons to Taiwan, but the United States would maintain something of a military balance in the Taiwan Strait.
- The United States would not seek to mediate differences between Beijing and Taipei.
- The United States would not support a particular outcome of the Taiwan issue, other than to insist that the outcome be arrived at peacefully in agreement between the two sides.
- The United States would not seek to divide China by supporting 'two Chinas', 'one China–one Taiwan' or 'Taiwan independence'.

These principles permitted the United States to pursue a 'dual-track' China policy that served American interests in both the PRC and Taiwan. Under this dual-track policy, the United States cooperatively engaged China, while at the same time met Taiwan's basic security requirements.

President Clinton inherited this arrangement, and there was every indication that his administration intended to continue existing policy. However, domestic and international circumstances caused a gradual shift in Clinton policy so that, by the end of July 1999, the administration had made important adjustments to the principles governing the Taiwan issue. For example:

- The United States now appeared to agree with Beijing's definition of 'one China'; in other words, accepting Beijing's view that Taiwan was part of the People's Republic of China.
- The United States now assumed a more active role in trying to persuade Taipei to enter into substantive political dialogue with the mainland to resolve their differences.
- The United States placed higher value on China's integration into the global and regional community of nations than it did on supporting Taiwan's desire for self-determination.
- While still willing to sell Taiwan advanced defensive weaponry and to intervene militarily to prevent an unprovoked PRC attack on Taiwan, the United States would pressure Taipei to avoid provoking Beijing into such an attack.

The emergence of these new principles during Clinton's second term in office will be explained in the next section. What is important to keep in mind is that these principles were largely a reaction to China's increased power. In other words, to preserve peace in the Taiwan Strait – and thus to avoid a serious Sino-American confrontation – the Clinton administration after 1996 thought it necessary to reduce somewhat its support of Taiwan.

TAIWAN POLICY UNDER PRESIDENT CLINTON

Although Bill Clinton criticized George Bush during the presidential campaign for 'coddling' China, when it became apparent he would win the election, Clinton began to adopt essentially the same policies toward China and Taiwan. This could be seen, for example, in the testimony of Winston Lord, designated Assistant Secretary of State for East Asian and Pacific Affairs, in his March 1993 confirmation hearing before the Senate Foreign Relations Committee.[27] Lord said one of the principal US goals in Asia under President Clinton would be 'restoring firm foundations for cooperation with a China where political openness catches up with economic reform'. To accomplish this, the administration would follow a 'nuanced' policy toward China, balancing US interests in maintaining cooperative relations with the PRC because of its geopolitical importance, while seeking improvement in China's record of human rights and the termination of policies harmful to US interests. Echoing an argument used earlier by George Bush in justifying his engagement strategy toward China,[28] Lord said Chinese 'leaders cling to an outdated authoritarian system' in which serious human rights and other abuses persisted. 'Chinese leaders are gambling that open economics and closed politics will preserve their system of control', but it will prove to be 'a gamble that sooner or later will be lost'.

Pinpointing the US policy conundrum with respect to Beijing, Lord said: 'Our policy challenge therefore is to reconcile our need to deal with this important nation with our imperatives to promote international values. We will seek cooperation with China on a range of issues. But Americans cannot forget Tiananmen Square.' This required the administration to 'conduct a nuanced policy toward Beijing until a more humane system emerges'. He cautioned: 'Shunning China is not an alternative. We need both to condemn repression and preserve links with progressive forces which are the foundations for our longer term ties.' Lord defined the fundamental elements of President Clinton's policies toward China and Taiwan in terms by now familiar:

1. The United States 'will continue to be guided by the three Sino-American communiqués that have provided a flexible framework for our relations'.
2. 'It is up to China and Taiwan to work out their future relationship; we insist only that the process be peaceful.'
3. 'Consistent with our undertakings not to challenge the principle of "one China", we will continue to build upon our unofficial relations with Taiwan based on the Taiwan Relations Act.'

Lord also pointed to several issues in Sino-American relations that would be addressed by the Clinton administration: widespread human rights violations on the mainland and in Tibet; Chinese exports of dangerous weapons and technology to volatile areas of the world; and the fastest growing trade deficit of the United States, second only to that of Japan. There was continuous need for collaboration at the United Nations and on regional conflicts, as well as on emerging challenges like the environment and illegal drugs. Accordingly, the United States and China would 'work together where our interests converge and bargain hard over differences'. In setting the tone for the relationship, Lord said: 'Our approach will reflect that China is a great nation. In response to positive movement by the Chinese, we are prepared to address their concerns and strengthen our ties.' He promised the new administration would support the democratic aspirations of the Chinese people, but 'without arrogance – recognizing that the Chinese people will determine their own destiny, but confident that we are aligning ourselves with the future'.

Thus, from the outset, the Clinton administration was concerned with the same issues as the Bush administration: trade, human rights, security, proliferation and Taiwan. The continuity of these issues, as well as the continuity of US interests in Asia and the Pacific, ensured the continuity of US policies toward China and Taiwan.

But, within this larger picture of continuity, there were some adjustments affecting the security of Taiwan. These included the Taiwan Policy Review in 1994, the Lee Teng-hui visit to the United States in 1995, the Taiwan missile crisis in 1996, the Jiang–Clinton summits of 1997 and 1998, track-II diplomacy and interim agreements proposals in 1998, and Lee Teng-hui's recasting of Taiwan's 'one-China' policy in 1999. Although some of these issues have been mentioned previously, all deserve brief discussion at this point within the context of Taiwan's security.

Taiwan Policy Review

Following the termination of diplomatic relations with the Republic of China on January 1, 1979, the United States instituted highly restrictive policies in terms of extending visas to top-level officials from Taiwan. In May 1994, for example, the State Department refused to allow President Lee Teng-hui to stay overnight in Honolulu or Los Angeles en route to Latin America, permitting him instead a 90-minute refueling stop in Honolulu and a brief, informal reception in a spartan airport lounge.[29] Congress was livid at this treatment of a friendly head of state, and comparisons were made to the respect accorded high-ranking Taiwan officials by many Southeast Asian governments – the implication being that the State Department was cowardly in the face of PRC threats as well as impolite.[30]

Congressional irritation over the State Department's humiliation of Lee prompted the introduction of several bills designed to revise US policy toward Taiwan. There was consensus in the Congress that the Clinton administration was needlessly compromising American values in dealing with Taiwan in order to pursue cooperative relations with Beijing, whose leaders repeatedly opposed US policies in areas such as trade, human rights and non-proliferation. To restore balance in US policy toward Taiwan and China, Congress considered a host of legislation such as the Murkowski amendment discussed above. Numerous hearings were held as well, all indicating a trend in Congress toward more vocal and active support for Taiwan.

Although the administration tried to resist moves by Congress to mandate changes in US Taiwan policy, congressional pressure gradually began to influence Clinton's views. In July 1994 the administration concluded a year-long inter-agency review of US policy toward Taiwan,[31] and the results were announced in September.[32] As explained by a State Department official, President Clinton had authorized certain 'refinements' in policy toward Taiwan to better serve America's increasingly extensive and complicated interests in Taiwan, while at the same time preserving the US one-China policy and unofficial relations with Taiwan. 'There is only one China', the official said, 'and Taiwan is a part of China.' He noted that US policy toward China and Taiwan was designed to help maintain stability in Asia, but that the policy involved a delicate balancing act.

One of the 'refinements' was designed to allow more effective meetings between US and Taiwan officials. The administration was 'willing to establish under the AIT [American Institute in Taiwan] auspices, a sub-cabinet economic dialogue with Taiwan. We will permit high-level U.S. government officials of economic and technical agencies to visit Taiwan ... All such meetings and visits will be focused sharply on solving practical problems and doing business. They carry with them no implication that we consider the relationship to be official and should not be interpreted by anyone as being so.' He explained that top-level US officials having no economic, commercial or technical portfolio would not be allowed to visit Taiwan. Similarly, Taiwan's top leadership – including its president and vice president – would not be issued permits to visit the United States. To avoid embarrassments such as that occasioned by Lee Teng-hui's stop-over in Hawaii, Taiwan's leaders would be allowed 'to transit the United States when necessary'. Exchange visits by cabinet-level officials with economic, commercial or technical portfolios would be considered on a case-by-case basis: 'We don't rule anything out.' Senior Taiwan officials would be able to meet with undersecretary-level US officials in the State and Defense departments in unofficial settings, while high-level economic and trade officials from Taiwan would be able to meet with the leadership of US economic, commercial and technical agencies in official settings.

The official said that Taiwan could change the name of its representative office in the United States from 'Coordination Council for North American Affairs' (CCNAA) to 'Taipei Economic and Cultural Representative Office in the United States' (TECRO). Further, as mandated by the Taiwan Relations Act, the United States would continue to provide material and training for Taiwan's self-defense, while at the same time adhering to the August 17 communiqué. The official noted that the US government acknowledged that Taiwan had a legitimate role to play in international organizations such as APEC (Asia–Pacific Economic Cooperation) and GATT (General Agreement on Tariffs and Trade) and that it was in the general interests of the world community that Taiwan's voice be heard in some additional international organizations. However, the United States would not support Taiwan's entry into the United Nations.

Even though the PRC was outraged over these adjustments – primarily because they allowed higher-level Taiwanese government officials to visit the United States and meet their American counterparts in official settings, in their view violating Sino-American normalization agreements – many members of Congress thought the adjustments were cosmetic. Senator Paul Simon, for example, called the policy refinements 'official pettiness', commenting: 'We continue to give Taiwan the cold shoulder ... Taiwan has a multiparty system, free elections, and a free press – the things we profess to champion – while we continue to cuddle up to the mainland government, whose dictatorship permits none of these.'[33]

Congress criticized the administration, not because of engagement with China or unofficial relations with Taiwan, but because of Taiwan's overwary treatment by an administration too focused on the hope of strategic cooperation with Beijing. As a body, the Congress shared the view of the American public that US policy toward China and Taiwan should be balanced, that both American values and US interests had roles to play, and that better treatment should be accorded Taiwan and its people by the US government. Growing congressional anger at the administration had a direct impact on President Clinton's 1995 decision to allow Lee Teng-hui to come to the United States to participate in a Cornell University ceremony.

Visit of Lee Teng-hui

President Lee Teng-hui's visit to the United States in June 1995 resulted in a major setback in Beijing's relations with both Taipei and Washington. PRC ballistic missiles were fired near Taiwan, and a significant military confrontation between the United States and China occurred in waters near Taiwan. As noted in Chapter 2, prior to Lee's visit triangular relations between Washington, Beijing and Taipei were being managed with moderate success through each side's version of comprehensive engagement. China's sharp, negative reaction to Lee's trip caused PRC relations with both the United States and Taiwan to spiral downward for more than a year. Sino-American relations did not return to normal until mid-1997, when President Jiang Zemin paid a state visit to the United States, while relations across the Taiwan Strait did not improve significantly until the Koo–Wang talks in the fall of 1998.

In early March 1995, Cornell University, from which Lee Teng-hui received his doctorate in agricultural economics in 1968, invited Lee to deliver the Olin Lecture at an alumni reunion to be held June 9–11 of that year. The ROC government requested a visa for Lee from the US government, despite the fact that the Taiwan leader had previously been denied a visa to receive an honorary degree from Cornell. Although the Clinton administration had adjusted its policy toward Taiwan in September 1994 to allow some high-level visits by ROC officials, top Taiwan leaders were only allowed transit visas. Thus, the State Department ruled out a visa for Lee to visit Cornell, arguing that it was inconsistent with US one-China policy. Secretary of State Warren Christopher and other top administration officials repeatedly assured Beijing that the trip would not happen.[34] In a controversial move, a KMT-controlled organization in Taiwan hired the Washington firm of Cassidy & Associates with a three-year $4.5 million contract to lobby Congress and the American public on Taiwan's behalf.[35]

Congress, however, needed little incentive to act since it was already angry over the State Department's refusal to allow Lee to rest in a Hawaiian hotel a year earlier. Noting that Taiwan had ended martial law, allowed a free press, and legalized opposition political parties, Senator Frank Murkowski bitterly complained to the press: 'Rather than rewarding Taiwan for these great strides, it remains the policy of the Clinton administration to deny entry into the United States to the democratic leader of Asia's oldest republic; in effect treating Taiwan like an international pariah.'[36] Congressional antipathy toward the administration hardened when Clinton allowed visits to Washington by Palestinian leader Yasser Arafat and Sinn Fein party leader Gerry Adams, both associated with known terrorist organizations.

Members of Congress introduced several resolutions urging President Clinton to allow the Taiwan president to attend the Cornell ceremony. One such resolution receiving wide backing in the House of Representatives was H. Con. Res. 53 ('Expressing the Sense of Congress Regarding a Visit by the President of the Republic of China on Taiwan'). The resolution said in part: 'Resolved by the House of Representatives (the Senate concurring), that it is the sense of Congress that the President should promptly indicate that the United States will welcome a private visit by President Lee Teng-hui to his alma mater, Cornell University, and will welcome a transit stop by President Lee in Anchorage, Alaska, to attend the USA–ROC Economic Council Conference.'

H. Con. Res. 53 passed the House on May 2, 1995, by a vote of 390–0. A week later, the Senate passed the resolution by a vote of 97–1. Congressional sponsors of these resolutions warned the administration that if it did not invite Lee to visit the United States, Congress would pass mandatory legislation to that effect. In this matter, Congress was backed solidly by the American public. A *Washington Post* editorial in May 1995 captured the mood:

> The State Department contends that admitting President Lee would 'unavoidably be seen' by Beijing as 'removing an essential element of

unofficiality' from U.S.–Taiwan relations. Excluding him is unavoidably being seen by Congress and many American citizens as removing an essential element of principle from American foreign policy ... The State Department embarrasses the country by barring the leader of the part of the Chinese people who already enjoy much democracy and are expert in free-market ways.[37]

China angrily denounced the congressional resolutions, warning that 'Lee's visit to the United States, under whatever name or form or whatever pretext, is bound to entail serious consequences'.[38] But mounting pressure from the Congress and national media in favor of Lee's visit – plus a serious move underway in Congress to pass bills containing dozens of mandated changes in foreign policy: in effect, placing more control over foreign affairs into the hands of Congress – persuaded President Clinton to allow Lee Teng-hui to make a six-day private visit to the United States. With extremely careful wording, the decision was announced in a State Department news briefing on May 22:[39]

> President Clinton has decided to permit Lee Teng-hui to make a private visit to the United States in June for the express purpose of participating in an alumni reunion event at Cornell University, as a distinguished alumnus. This action follows a revision of administration guidelines to permit occasional private visits by senior leaders of Taiwan, including President Lee. President Lee will visit the U.S. in a strictly private capacity and will not undertake any official activities.
>
> It is important to reiterate that this is not an official visit. The granting of a visa in this case is consistent with U.S. policy of maintaining only unofficial relations with Taiwan. It does not convey any change in our relations with or policies toward the People's Republic of China, with which we maintain official relations and recognize as the sole legal government of China. We will continue to abide by the three communiqués that form the basis of our relations with China. The United States also acknowledges the Chinese position that there is but one China, and Taiwan is a part of China.
>
> Americans treasure the rights of freedom of speech and freedom of travel and believe others should enjoy these privileges as well. This sentiment clearly motivated the Congress, in its recent actions, to support overwhelmingly permitting Mr. Lee to return to Cornell, his alma mater.
>
> Secretary of State Christopher has indicated that our relationship with China and Taiwan will continue to be governed by the three joint communiqués with the People's Republic of China and the Taiwan Relations Act. It is also Secretary Christopher's view that this decision to permit a private visit does not in any way reflect a change in the

fundamental nature of U.S. relations with Taiwan. We continue to maintain unofficial economic and cultural relations with Taiwan.

President Lee was in the United States from June 7 until June 10, with stop-overs in Los Angeles, Cornell University in Ithaca, New York, and Anchorage, Alaska. Lee's personal popularity soared back home, an important factor in the forthcoming March 1996 presidential elections, although many on Taiwan felt apprehension about the possible long-term negative impact the trip might have on Taiwan's relations with the United States and China. Lee explained while in the United States that the ROC did not seek the independence of Taiwan but rather the unification of a democratic China. But he also told Taiwanese-Americans at Cornell: 'The Republic of China (Taiwan) is definitely not a part of the People's Republic of China, and neither is it a province of that country.'[40]

The PRC was furious with Clinton's decision to permit the Lee visit, particularly in view of previous assurances from Secretary Christopher and other officials that no such visit would be approved. The PRC Foreign Ministry said: 'The Chinese government and people express grave indignation and lodge a strong protest with the US government over the announcement.' The invitation was 'an extremely serious act of brazenly creating two Chinas or "one China, one Taiwan", that damages China's sovereignty and undermines its cause for peaceful reunification'. The statement warned 'If the United States maintains this erroneous situation ... it will inevitably bring serious harm to Sino-U.S. relations, and all the consequences will be the responsibility of the U.S. government.'[41]

In addition to its formal protests, the Chinese government abruptly cut short the visit to the United States of PLA Air Force Chief of Staff Yu Zhenwu and canceled the visit of State Counselor Li Guixian. A few days later, the visit of Defense Minister Chi Haotian was postponed. Chinese consultations with US officials responsible for nuclear cooperation and controlling the spread of missile technology were also postponed. The PRC media vied with one another to heap condemnation on Washington and President Lee Teng-hui's past and future generations.

The Lee visit was important to Taiwan's security for several reasons. In the first place, it demonstrated that Congress and the American public, when aroused over some egregious treatment of Taiwan, will exert enormous pressure on the administration to change the objectionable policy. In the United States, no individual – whether president, secretary of state or former defense secretary – can cast into stone US policy toward Taiwan or China. It all depends on the circumstances.

Second, high-level visits to the United States by top political leaders on Taiwan cannot be ruled out in the future, although they will no doubt be infrequent, short and unofficial. These visits are difficult to deny because the American people view hospitality and freedom of travel as being more important than the loud protests of Beijing's communist leaders. The State Department's job is to bear the brunt of PRC anger, and thus it is understandably sensitive to appearances of officiality, but Congress and the public at large are neither intimidated nor impressed by expressions of Chinese outrage.

Third, the Lee visit had the effect of increasing American polarization between those concerned that the Taiwan issue might undermine US relations with the PRC and those who felt it wrong that US ties with Taiwan should be held hostage to Beijing's opinion. As a result, it became increasingly difficult for the Clinton administration to define a policy enjoying broad support in the United States; hence, the policy itself became increasingly inconsistent and unpredictable.

Fourth, the issue of Taiwan's security again moved to the fore in US policy circles. This became apparent a few months after Lee's visit, when the PLA began to exercise its military muscle in areas close to Taiwan and alarm bells began to sound in Washington over the implications of hostility in the Taiwan Strait.

Missile crisis in the Taiwan Strait

As illustrated in Chapter 2, PRC criticism of the United States and Taiwan increased dramatically after President Lee's trip to the United States. The Taiwan leader was condemned for his supposed efforts to create an independent Taiwan and the United States was castigated for its knowing or unwitting encouragement of Taiwan independence through arms sales and political support. For several months, roughly June 1995 to March 1996, Chinese policy toward Taiwan and the United States fell under the influence of hardliners within the PRC leadership who believed that China had to forcefully deter Taipei and Washington from further actions harmful to China's interests.

There was a series of six large military exercises held in the Taiwan area by the PLA between July 21, 1995, and March 25, 1996. Four of these involved missile exercises: July 21–26, 1995; August 15–25, 1995; and two during March 8–15, 1996. Major military exercises were held March 12–20 and March 18–25, 1996. During the late July 1995 missile firings, China launched M-9 tactical missiles at targets near Taiwan, the closest landing some 87 miles north of the island. On August 16, China tested two Dong Feng-21 intermediate-range ballistic missiles, launched from a base in northern China with a splashdown just north of the earlier M-9 target area. During March 8–15, 1996, Beijing conducted another series of M-9 missile tests in areas about 30 miles southwest of Kaohsiung and 20 miles northeast of Keelung – effectively imposing a week-long missile blockade of the island. Shortly after Taiwan's presidential elections on March 23, in which Lee Teng-hui won easily with 54

230

percent of the vote, all sides quietly backed away from the quasi-military confrontation.

Throughout the exercises, Taipei assumed a very low-key profile, being careful not to interfere with the PLA or to give cause for further escalation. At first, the United States also adopted a low-key public response to escalating tensions in the Taiwan Strait: 'we don't believe this [missile] test contributes to peace and stability in the area'.[42] As tensions increased, however, the United States – mostly through the Department of Defense – began to issue stronger warnings. Finally, and apparently catching some PRC strategists by surprise, President Clinton deployed a large armada to the Taiwan area in March 1996 to signal US resolve to defend its interests in a peaceful settlement of the Taiwan issue. The navy task force included the nuclear attack submarines *Portsmouth*, *Columbus* and *Bremerton*; the aircraft carriers *Independence* and *Nimitz*; the destroyers *O'Brien* and *Hewitt*, the guided missile frigate *McClusky*, the oiler *Pecos*, and the guided missile cruiser *Bunker Hill* with the *Independence*; and the cruiser *Port Royal*, the destroyers *Callaghan* and *Oldendorf*, the frigate *Ford*, and the replenishment ships *Willamette* and *Shasta* with the *Nimitz*.[43]

There were many lessons to be drawn from the 1995–96 missile crisis that had relevance for Taiwan's security in the post-Deng era. For the ROC, four principal lessons seemed to stand out: first, Beijing was willing and able to use force against Taiwan should it proceed too directly in a course of independence; second, despite its reluctance to become involved, the United States – for its own interests and in response to domestic political pressure – would likely come to Taiwan's aid should it be threatened militarily by the PRC; third, Taiwan was highly vulnerable to missile attack, not only physically but in terms of its economic stability; and, fourth, ultimately the security of Taiwan was almost totally dependent upon American support.

For the PRC, at least five lessons were apparent: first, the Taiwan issue was explosive in PRC politics, necessitating the greatest care in management to avoid a shift in the moderate–hardliner balance of power in the CCP leadership; second, the United States was unpredictable in its response, but its military intervention on behalf of Taiwan could not be ruled out; third, in terms of threats to China's security, none was greater than crisis in the Taiwan Strait; fourth, despite its ability to hurt Taiwan with missiles and blockades, the PLA was not yet ready to undertake major air, sea or land operations against Taiwan; and, fifth, the key to China's unification was not to attract Taiwan with sweet enticements but to reduce American support for Taiwan, thus giving Taipei no other choice than to reunify peacefully with the mainland or unify through conflict.

And for the United States, four lessons in US–China–Taiwan relations could be discerned:

1. The United States must not hesitate to intervene early and strongly to deter escalation of crises in the Taiwan Strait.
2. To prevent a possible war in the Taiwan Strait, the United States must not only deter military aggression by the PRC but also curtail political provocation by Taiwan.
3. The moderate–hardliner balance of power in Beijing was delicate and could be thrown in the direction of the hardliners – not in the US interest – if Taiwan issues were not handled carefully and correctly by Washington.
4. China increasingly was willing to confront the United States militarily over the Taiwan issue, and PLA capabilities were gradually becoming a greater threat to US military forces deployed to the Taiwan area.

The net effect of these lessons was a significant policy adjustment on the part of the Clinton administration: priority had to be placed on improving relations with China, even at the expense of becoming more circumspect in ties to Taiwan. This determination, which was strongly opposed by Congress and the nation's media, could be seen in the summit meetings of Jiang Zemin and Bill Clinton, not-so-subtle efforts by Washington to encourage Taipei to enter into political negotiations with Beijing, and the administration's quick reaction to Lee's renunciation of a one-China policy.

The Jiang–Clinton summits

The mixed reaction of the American media to the Jiang–Clinton summits was noted earlier in this chapter, and in truth not much of substance was accomplished – although the symbolic importance of the summits was noteworthy. From October 26 until November 3, 1997, President Jiang Zemin became the first Chinese leader in 12 years to make an official state visit to the United States. In addition to spending several days in Washington DC, Jiang visited Hawaii, Colonial Williamsburg, Independence Hall in Philadelphia, Harvard and the New York Stock Exchange. The accomplishments of the summit were cited in a joint statement issued from the White House on October 29.[44] From the point of view of the United States, the summit's major achievement was China's agreement to stop supplying nuclear technology to Iran, as well as a commitment from China to stop selling cruise missiles to Iran. Boeing was also pleased with another PRC multibillion order for 50 aircraft, while Westinghouse Electric and General Electric were cleared by the administration to compete for sales of nuclear power reactors to China.

In return, Jiang received renewed American assurance that it would not support the independence of Taiwan, a high-profile state visit that contrasted sharply with the limited trip of Lee Teng-hui in 1995, and a political boost at home by being recognized internationally as China's paramount leader. The establishment of a 'hot line' between Washington and Beijing also symbolized US perceptions of China as a major power, as did a maritime communications agreement to prevent accidental confrontations at sea between American and Chinese naval forces.

The Chinese seemed satisfied with Jiang's trip, primarily because it signaled an adjustment in US policy toward more accommodation to China's rising power. *Xinhua* editorialized on November 9, 1997, that Jiang's visit to the United States and Boris Yeltsin's visit to China later in November meant that a new multipolar world was developing in which China, the United States and Russia cooperated to ensure world peace.[45] Foreign Minister Qian Qichen expressed a similar view in mid-November 1997, when he observed that the Jiang–Clinton summit moved Sino-American relations into a new phase of cooperation in building toward a constructive strategic partnership. He said problems in the relationship remained, the most important of which was Taiwan, and developing bilateral ties would be a long and complicated process, but the framework and orientation for Sino-American relations in the twenty-first century were being laid.[46]

The conveyed sense that a Sino-American strategic partnership was moving forward was the dominant theme of President Clinton's state visit to China between June 25 and July 3, 1998. Eager to demonstrate success in its China policy, the White House provided a long list of achievements in the summit, including progress in non-proliferation and security issues, human rights, economic and commercial ties, energy and environmental cooperation, science and technology exchanges, cooperation in the field of law, law enforcement, and people-to-people exchanges.[47] One of the most memorable aspects of the trip, however, was the unprecedented opportunity for President Clinton to debate with Jiang Zemin publicly over human rights and democracy and to argue openly in favor of individual freedom as being the key ingredient for modernization. In his speech at Beijing University, for example, the president argued in a polite yet pointed way that freedom was the key to both stability and prosperity – two goals shared by Chinese leaders and the Chinese people.[48]

By far, the most controversial part of the president's trip was his three-no's comment in Shanghai in which Clinton said the United States did not support Taiwan independence, did not support two-Chinas or one China–one Taiwan, and did not support Taiwan's participation in international organizations requiring nation-state status for membership. The administration claimed that US policy had not changed, an interpretation also presented by AIT Chairman Richard Bush in Taipei on July 8. In a news conference just prior to his departure after having briefed Taiwan officials on the Clinton visit to China, Bush said the three-no's did not indicate a shift in US policy toward Taiwan and that the summit meetings between Clinton and Jiang did not harm Taiwan's interests. He said there was a difference between the words opposition and no support. '"Opposition" is on the negative side of the spectrum, "support" is on the positive side of the spectrum, while "no support" belongs to somewhere in the middle.' The US position, Bush said, 'is that cross-Strait differences should be resolved peacefully and that we don't support Taiwan independence'.⁴⁹

Once again, the PRC seemed very pleased with the summit. China's Foreign Ministry said the visit was 'crowned with success' and that 'new progress has been made toward the goal of establishing Sino-US constructive strategic partnership'.⁵⁰ Clinton's statement on the three-no's was specifically cited as a reaffirmation of the US commitment to the three joint communiqués and its 'proper handling of the Taiwan issue'.

The Jiang–Clinton summits reflected a desire on the part of Beijing and Washington to strengthen their strategic cooperation for the twenty-first century. For the United States, part of the cost of advancing that goal were more deliberate statements of assurance to the PRC that the United States had no intention of supporting Taiwan's bid for greater autonomy and a more prominent role in international affairs. In other words, the Clinton administration determined that Taiwan's self-determination and its efforts to expand its international representation were less important to US interests than the establishment of friendly, cooperative relations with China.

In essence, from 1997–98 the Clinton administration began to back down somewhat from the dual-track approach to US China–Taiwan policy adopted by the Reagan and Bush administrations, especially after August 1982. As indicated by continued arms sales and discussion of Taiwan's inclusion in theater missile defense programs for Northeast Asia, the United States was still committed to Taiwan's defense against an unprovoked PRC attack or threat to use force. However, the administration had also concluded that to reduce the risk of a military confrontation between China and the United States, Washington had to improve relations with Beijing and distance itself politically from Taipei.

In terms of Taiwan's security, such a US approach brought double danger. On the one hand, there was the possibility that Beijing would misinterpret the renewed American willingness to accommodate over Taiwan as a sign that the United States would not stomach a military defense of Taiwan if the island were attacked. On the other hand, Clinton's three-no's and subsequent pressure on Taipei to enter into political dialogue with the mainland posed a threat to the continued existence of the Republic of China and the de facto independence of Taiwan. This was because, unlike Washington or Beijing, Taipei was in no hurry to resolve cross-Strait differences as long as Taiwan's bargaining position was much weaker than that of the mainland.

Track-II diplomacy and interim agreements

The efforts of former Secretary of Defense William Perry in 1998 and 1999 to establish an informal, track-II channel of communications between Taipei and Beijing to help resolve their political differences were discussed in Chapter 2. Such efforts are one of the 'wild cards' that might affect Taiwan's security equation. In a positive sense, the track-II efforts of Perry and others are intended to reduce the possibility of conflict in the Taiwan Strait and the possibility of a future Sino-American war. Track-II initiatives can contribute to Taiwan's security. However, there are other implications to those efforts that are not so appealing to Taiwan.

In the first place, most track-II initiatives come from individuals and organizations with much closer ties to Beijing than to Taipei. This is not to cast doubt on their even-handedness, but it might suggest that their understanding of Taiwan's point of view is not as well developed as their understanding of the PRC. Thus far, the PRC has encouraged track-II efforts as a way to get Taiwan to the negotiating table. The ROC, on the other hand, has politely rejected track-II intercession because it does not want to negotiate a political settlement with Beijing under current circumstances. Taiwan's political position, especially in the international community, is simply too weak; and Beijing has refused to accept Taipei as an equal partner in the negotiations.

Also, the Republic of China's experience with American intercession and mediation has not been all that good. The well-meaning remarks of Kurt Campbell, Deputy Assistant Secretary of Defense for Asian and Pacific affairs, is illustrative. He praised Perry's track-II efforts, saying, 'Bill Perry is a latter-day George Marshall', apparently forgetting that Marshall threatened to cut off American military assistance to the Nationalists if they did not negotiate with the Chinese communists on the mainland. Marshall had hoped to find an equitable and just end to the Chinese civil war, but every child on Taiwan is taught that Marshall's efforts were one of the major factors leading to the Nationalists' defeat. And it goes without saying that the DPP found Perry's efforts disturbing, especially after he told Chen Shui-bian and Hsu Hsin-liang not to count on American support in the event of a declaration of Taiwan independence. One DPP journal said Perry 'gave the impression that the U.S. would sacrifice a democratic Taiwan when convenient to appease China' and then asked rhetorically: 'How can there be an effective "track 2" diplomacy when these "unofficial" messengers don't understand the subject at hand?' The article noted that Perry, Brent Scowcroft and Henry Kissinger all had private business interests with China: 'How can

America's national interests be best served by former officials who, at a minimum, have the appearance of being partial to China?'[51]

In short, the United States and China may be willing to give track-II diplomacy a try, but Taiwan does not yet seem ready to shoulder the risks involved.

Nonetheless, the search is on in the United States to find a way out of the Taiwan impasse. This seems to have been the good intention of Stanley Roth, Assistant Secretary of State for East Asian and Pacific Affairs, who told an audience at the Woodrow Wilson Center in Washington DC, on March 24, 1999:

> this administration has great confidence in the creativity of the people of Taiwan and the people of the mainland, working together, to identify the necessary human contacts and the most comfortable processes to give the dialogue [between the two sides] real meaning. Using a phrase that has garnered much favor in Washington of late, I could imagine that 'out of the box' thinking within this dialogue might contribute to *interim agreements*, perhaps in combination with specific confidence building measures, on any number of difficult topics. But, as the U.S. has steadfastly held, we will avoid interfering as the two sides pursue peaceful resolution of differences because it is only the participants on both sides of the strait that can craft the specific solutions which balance their interests while addressing their most pressing concerns.[52] (emphasis added)

Roth did not repeat his suggestions for 'interim agreements' to the Senate Committee on Foreign Relations the next day,[53] but his public comments were widely interpreted as deliberately putting pressure on Taiwan to become more accommodating to Beijing's demands for political talks. Richard Bush, Chairman of the American Institute in Taiwan, took pains to explain the US meaning of interim agreements in a speech to the Taiwan Chamber of Commerce of North America in Taipei on June 26, 1999.[54] Bush said the key word in Roth's statement was 'creativity', that is, 'we hope that both sides will demonstrate creativity to find ways to foster more stability and less tension and to take advantage of the opportunities for cooperation'. In this sense, Roth's interim agreements referred to agreements that offer less than an ultimate resolution, are less than comprehensive, and are not total. These agreements would be objectively achievable, meaningful and lead to a significant reduction in tensions. Bush asked: 'We agree that a total solution to the Taiwan Strait issue won't occur overnight. But even without a full agreement, would not the people of Taiwan be served by agreements that are possible and which reduce tensions, expand cooperation, and build mutual trust?' Bush then said that Washington's one-China policy consists of five principles:

1. The United States insists that the Taiwan Strait issue be resolved peacefully.
2. The [Clinton] administration believes that constructive and meaningful dialogue and cross-Strait exchanges are the best way to resolve cross-Strait differences.
3. Differences should be resolved by the two sides themselves.
4. The United States will remain even-handed in its approach to cross-Strait dialogue, and will not apply pressure to either side.
5. The administration believes that any arrangements concluded between Beijing and Taipei should be on a mutually acceptable basis.

Bush added that, because Taiwan is a democracy, it is the Taiwan public that ultimately must approve any such arrangements. He then once again explained that the long-term US strategy toward China was (a) to encourage the right kind of development at home in China – to become 'a strong, prosperous, and open society, coming together, not falling apart' – and (b) to 'integrate China into institutions that promote global norms on proliferation, trade, the environment, and human rights'.

Not mentioned by Bush was the relationship between a peaceful settlement of the Taiwan issue and the success of American strategy toward China. Increasingly, the Clinton administration was coming to view the success of its China policy as being at least partially dependent on a successful cross-Strait dialogue. In other words, the moderation of China and its peaceful integration into the world community – important strategic goals of the United States as it neared the twenty-first century – could not be achieved if Taiwan pursued policies likely to precipitate a war in the Taiwan Strait or even Sino-American confrontation.

It would not take Sun Tzu to understand that this US perception, in fact, gave Beijing the edge it needed in its political competition with Taipei for favorable attention in Washington. All the PRC would have to do is to follow a dual-track approach of its own: first, appear reasonable in its demands that Taiwan enter political negotiations aimed at an equitable resolution of cross-Strait differences; and, second, appear willing to go to war if Taipei seemed to be leaning in the direction of independence or unreasonably delayed dialogue. In 1998–99 Taiwan began to feel the box tightening as the United States – indirectly perhaps and certainly not with the intent to harm – began to cooperate with China to leave Taipei with no choice but to become part of the People's Republic of China. To some observers on Taiwan, such as scholar Ho Szu-yin, it was the pressure from Roth's 'interim agreements' and the Clinton administration's impatience over 'constructive and meaningful dialogue' that influenced the timing of Lee Teng-hui's renunciation of the ROC's one-China policy in mid-July 1999.[55]

Lee rejects one-China policy

As noted in Chapter 2, Lee told a German radio station in July 1999 in a prepared statement that Taiwan's relations with the mainland had been redefined as state-to-state or special state-to-state relations. A top ROC official a few days later said that Taiwan's ties with mainland China constituted special relations and that the term 'one China' would no longer be used to describe Taiwan's policy. Shortly thereafter, the ROC government announced that its official policy toward the mainland would henceforth be 'one nation, two states' or 'special state-to-state relations' rather than 'one China, two political entities' in place since 1991. (In that year, the ROC constitution was revised to define the area of ROC jurisdiction as being Taiwan proper and the offshore islands of Penghu (Pescadores), Kinmen (Quemoy) and Matsu. The revisions also acknowledged the existence of the PRC.) If the PRC could accept Taiwan as a diplomatic equal, ROC officials said, they were willing for the first time to talk to the PRC about unifying the country.[56]

ROC officials said the new terminology did not mean an actual change in Taiwan's policy – or total abandonment of the one-China principle – but rather represented a clarification of existing policy. Such a change in terminology was necessary, it was explained, because the term 'one China' had been used by Beijing to isolate Taiwan internationally, that is, by having other countries accept 'one China' as meaning the People's Republic of China – an interpretation the ROC categorically rejected. By no longer using the term 'one China' to describe its mainland policy, the ROC claimed its position was merely descriptive of reality: Taiwan and the mainland were de facto states, governed independently, and equal in the eyes of international law.[57]

In addition to the many other considerations behind the change in ROC mainland policy, there was deepening concern within the Taiwan government that the Clinton administration had evolved its interpretation of 'one China' from an ambiguous concept left to be defined by both sides of the Taiwan Strait to a determination that the PRC was the 'one China'. Indeed, Taiwan's negative reaction to Clinton's three-no's pronouncement in Shanghai, Perry's track-II efforts, and Roth's interim agreements could all be explained by this concern. If this perception were true, then the US 'one-China' principle now meant that Taiwan should become part of the People's Republic of China.

Such a shift in definition on the part of the Clinton administration would make all the difference in the world, as far as Taipei was concerned. Under the previous American understanding of the term, 'one China' could be the PRC or the ROC or some other mutually acceptable definition of 'China'. Under the new Clinton definition, 'one China' would mean the PRC, and the principle that Taiwan was part of China would mean Taiwan was part of communist China. This US interpretation of 'one China' would be a disaster for the Republic of China and for the people of Taiwan. The change in definition would (a) place the United States on the side of the PRC in holding that Taiwan was a local government under the CCP central government in Beijing; (b) greatly reduce the possibility of Taiwan remaining a symbol of democracy and freedom that one day might take hold on the mainland; and (c) dramatically increase international pressure on Taipei to enter into political talks with Beijing. The change in US definition would also seriously weaken Taiwan's security by:

- Giving the PRC greater justification to use force against Taiwan if it pursued pragmatic diplomacy or delayed political talks
- Reducing American incentives to intervene on Taiwan's behalf in case of conflict since US policy was not just 'acknowledgment' of Taiwan being part of an undefined 'China', but now 'acceptance' of Taiwan being legally part of the PRC.

Washington's reaction to Lee's announcement did little to dispel this rather conspiratorial interpretation of US one-China policy. The administration dispatched Richard Bush to Taipei to gain a greater understanding of what Lee Teng-hui had in mind, while Stanley Roth and the National Security Council Asian affairs specialist, Kenneth Lieberthal, were sent to Beijing to urge the PRC government not to use force in response to Lee's pronouncement.[58] Roth and Lieberthal also assured their PRC hosts that the United States continued to uphold its 'one-China' policy, a position both President Clinton and Secretary of State Madeleine Albright made clear as well. Clinton stated in a news conference on July 21: 'Our position is clear. We favor the one-China policy. The understanding we have had all along with both China and Taiwan is that the differences between them would be resolved peacefully. If that were not to be the case, under the Taiwan Relations Act, we would be required to view it with the gravest concern.'[59] Albright went somewhat further, using her talks with Chinese Foreign Minister Tang Jiaxuan in an ASEAN regional security forum in Singapore to gently chastise Taiwan, telling reporters that Richard Bush had told Lee 'that there needs to be … a peaceful resolution to this and a dialogue. And I think that the explanations offered thus far don't quite do it.'[60]

An even stronger signal of administration displeasure over Lee's remarks was postponement of a trip to Taiwan by a group of US military experts who were to discuss Taiwan's air-defense needs. The discussion was part of a quiet program of consultation between the Pentagon and Taiwan which began after the missile crisis of 1996 to assess Taiwan's defense requirements.[61] According to several US and Taiwan sources, such consultation was as important as military hardware in helping the ROC plan its future defense,[62] highlighting the vulnerability of Taiwan's military without US hardware and software assistance.

China reacted strongly to Lee's pronouncement, with threats and condemnation. Even though the United States urged China not to react with force, the general feeling within the administration was that Lee Teng-hui, not the PRC, was responsible for the new cross-Strait crisis. The US and Japanese reaffirmation of their one-China policy has been noted, and ASEAN's foreign ministers also reaffirmed the organization's one-China policy following their meeting in Singapore in late July.[63] In the view of most Asia–Pacific governments, the issue was not whether Taipei was describing the reality in the Taiwan Strait – which Taiwan claimed – but rather whether its actions unnecessarily provoked the PRC. Whatever legitimacy Taiwan might claim, maintaining regional peace and stability was more important to its neighbors. This required that Taipei not 'rock the boat' by taking actions likely to be interpreted by Beijing as moving the island further in the direction of independence. Given the PRC's distrust of Lee, it did not take much to arouse this suspicion.

Still, there were no doubt other motivations behind Beijing's harsh verbal reaction – its military response seemed at the end of July to be limited to naval exercises, fighter sorties in the Taiwan Strait, and the test firing of a Dong Feng-31 long-range ballistic missile within Chinese territory. Perhaps most important was the annual Beidaihe policy conference in which top leaders ironed out their differences and set the course for policy for the forthcoming year. The meeting in late July 1999 had many key decisions to make, including how to reform China's state-run enterprises, the implications of the spiritual challenge to communism presented by the recently outlawed Falun Dafa group,[64] whether to expand military exercises in the Taiwan Strait in response to Lee Teng-hui, and to what extent China's membership in the WTO should be pursued. The 1999 meeting was thought to bring into sharp conflict the views of moderates under Jiang Zemin and Zhu Rongji and hardliners rallying around Li Peng. At minimum, it was believed that the hardliners would insist upon a tougher policy toward the United States and Taiwan in exchange for their support of continued economic reform.[65]

Another important motivation on the part of the PRC was probably the unprecedented opportunity the crisis presented to improve Sino-American relations, severely challenged throughout most of 1999 due to allegations of Chinese spying, the Kosovo conflict and the bombing of the PRC embassy in Belgrade. The prompt US affirmation of its one-China policy and slap on the wrist of Lee Teng-hui had the effect of thawing US–China relations. Talks were suddenly resumed on China's entrance into the WTO; the Congress approved Clinton's request to extend MFN to China one more year; and the Albright–Tang talks in Singapore were described in near flowery terms ('the restoration of communication over a very friendly lunch', as the secretary phrased it).[66] As the *Wall Street Journal* headed an article outlining the improved atmosphere: 'Taiwan Flap Brings China Closer to U.S.'[67]

President Lee Teng-hui may not have anticipated the mostly negative international reaction to his comments, and certainly the ROC government did not welcome the response, since it made life more, not less, difficult for the struggling democracy. Still, Lee's statements were praised by most Taiwanese, seemingly caught in a euphoria of self-discovery of their Taiwan roots[68] and perhaps impervious to the security implications of renouncing the 'one-China' principle that made their autonomous existence tolerable to moderate leaders in Beijing and supportable to China-hands in Washington.

CONCLUSION

US support is a vital factor in Taiwan's security in the post-Deng era. That support, in turn, is highly dependent on several influences: American public opinion, congressional involvement in the Taiwan issue, the management of the Taiwan issue in Sino-American relations, and US policy toward Taiwan, most recently that of the Clinton administration. Each of these influences is itself a variable, subject to such things as American values, perceptions of US interests, domestic and international circumstances, and strengths and weaknesses of individual policy makers. Because of the complexity of all of these variables, and their even more complex interaction, US support for Taiwan has been remarkably consistent yet vulnerable to change.

Overall, it can be said that Americans support Taiwan primarily because of values (although many strategists see important US interests involved as well), while relations with China are dictated primarily by *Realpolitik* considerations (with some values involved, such as hope for China's evolution into a market democracy). To date, the Taiwan issue in Sino-American relations has been managed successfully through a combination of ambiguity, American national power, skillful diplomacy, Chinese (both mainlander and Taiwanese) flexibility, and more than a little good luck. This generally has worked to Taiwan's security advantage: Taiwan has not been attacked and Taipei has received large amounts of US weapons, technical advice and political–military support in times of crisis in the Strait. But in the eyes of those who believe US relations with China are the highest priority, US support for Taiwan has come at great cost. (One is reminded of Richard Holbrooke's statement: 'The strategic relationship with China, not Taiwan, is the main issue, with global and historic importance. That it has been submerged under the Taiwan issue only illustrates anew that trivia can command center stage while great issues wait in the wings.')[69]

Taiwan needed to be concerned in 1999 over the growing PRC military threat. But far more ominous – and perhaps underestimated – was the challenge posed by growing Clinton administration impatience over finding a solution to the Taiwan issue. If true, such 'fatigue' on the part of Washington could have disastrous results for Taiwan as it seeks to expand its presence in the international community and redefine its image as a Taiwanese, not Chinese political entity.

The next chapter will bring into focus another critical issue for Taiwan's future security: the question of whether, or to what extent, Taiwan should participate in theater missile defense in East Asia.

NOTES

1. For a more complete examination of this issue, see Martin L. Lasater, *The Taiwan Conundrum in U.S. China Policy* (Boulder CO: Westview, 1999).
2. See especially US Senate, Committee on Foreign Relations, *Taiwan: Hearings on S. 245*, February 5, 6, 7, 8, 21 and 22, 1979 (Washington DC: Government Printing Office, 1979); Louis W. Koenig, ed., *Congress, the Presidency, and the Taiwan Relations Act* (New York: Praeger, 1985); William B. Bader and Jeffrey T. Bergner, eds, *The Taiwan Relations Act: A Decade of Implementation* (Indianapolis IN: Hudson Institute, 1989); Ramon H. Myers, ed., *A Unique Relationship: The United States and the Republic of China under the Taiwan Relations Act* (Stanford CA: Hoover Institution Press, 1989); and appropriate sections in Stephen P. Gibert and William M. Carpenter, eds, *America and Island China: A Documentary History* (Lanham MD: University Press of America, 1989). In addition, many congressional hearings have dealt extensively with the implementation of the Taiwan Relations Act, most of which have been published by the Government Printing Office.
3. The best collection of congressional views on the formulation of the TRA can be found in Lester L. Wolff and David Simon, eds, *Legislative History of the Taiwan Relations Act: An Analytic Compilation with Documents on Subsequent Developments* (Jamaica NY: American Association for Chinese Studies, 1982).
4. According to the Thomas search engine of the Library of Congress, using the term 'Taiwan Relations Act' for the 104th, 105th and 106th Congresses.
5. According to the Thomas search engine of the Library of Congress, using the terms 'Taiwan' and 'China' in the legislative history of the 103rd, 104th and 105th Congresses.
6. State Department Legal Adviser Davis R. Robinson told Congress in September 1982: '[The communiqué] is not an international agreement and thus imposes no obligations on either party under international law. Its status under domestic law is that of a statement by the President of a policy which he intends to pursue ... The Taiwan Relations Act is and will remain the law of the land unless amended by Congress. Nothing in the joint communiqué obligates the President to act in a manner contrary to the Act or, conversely, disables him from fulfilling his responsibilities under it.' Prepared statement of Davis R. Robinson, Legal Adviser, Department of State, given before US Congress, Senate,

Committee on the Judiciary, Subcommittee on Separation of Powers, September 27, 1982, ms.

7. *Far Eastern Economic Review*, August 5, 1993, p. 15.
8. See Robert G. Sutter, 'Taiwan: Recent Developments and U.S. Policy Choices', Library of Congress, Congressional Research Service *Issue Brief* IB94006 (updated May 26, 1994), p. 12.
9. Statement of Senator Murkowski before the US Senate on May 3, 1994, from *Congressional Record* reprint provided by the Senator's office.
10. See *Far Eastern Economic Review*, December 10, 1998, pp. 28–9.
11. For American diplomatic background on the Shanghai agreement and formulation of statements on Taiwan, see appropriate sections in Richard M. Nixon, *RN: The Memoirs of Richard Nixon* (New York: Grosset & Dunlap, 1978); Henry A. Kissinger, *White House Years* (Boston MA: Little, Brown and Co., 1979); and Marshall Green, John H. Holdridge and William N. Stokes, *War and Peace with China: First-Hand Experiences in the Foreign Service of the United States* (Bethesda MD: Dacor Press, 1994).
12. For his views on China, see Jimmy Carter, *Keeping Faith: Memoirs of a President* (New York: Bantam Books, 1982), pp. 186–211.
13. Carter, *Keeping Faith*, p. 197.
14. 'Ronald Reagan on U.S. Policy Toward Asia and the Pacific', Reagan for President Press Release, Los Angeles CA, August 25, 1980.
15. *Xinhua*, January 17, 1981, in *FBIS-China*, January 19, 1981, p. G2.
16. 'No Sale of Advanced Aircraft to Taiwan', *Department of State Bulletin* 82, 2059 (February 1982), p. 39.
17. For details regarding the US–PRC confrontation over arms sales to Taiwan, see Martin L. Lasater, *The Taiwan Issue in Sino-American Strategic Relations* (Boulder CO: Westview Press, 1984) and *Policy in Evolution: The U.S. Role in China's Reunification* (Boulder CO: Westview Press, 1989).
18. See the August 18, 1982, testimony of Assistant Secretary of State John Holdridge in US Congress, House of Representatives, Committee on Foreign Affairs, *China–Taiwan: United States Policy* (Washington DC: GPO, 1982), pp. 2–29.
19. The comments of State Department Legal Adviser Davis Robinson can be found in his prepared statement before the US Congress, Senate, Committee on the Judiciary, Subcommittee on Separation of Powers, September 27, 1982. See note 6 in this chapter.
20. 'ROC Statement on August 17 Communiqué, August 17, 1982', issued by the Coordination Council of North American Affairs, Washington DC. The Coordination Council of North American Affairs was the private corporation created by the ROC government to handle its affairs in Washington after January 1, 1979. The corresponding US corporation was the American Institute in Taiwan, created by the Taiwan Relations Act.
21. Hu Yaobang, 'Create a New Situation in All Fields of Socialist Modernization', *The Twelfth National Congress of the CPC* (Beijing: Foreign Languages Press, 1982), pp. 58–9.
22. S. I. Hayakawa, 'Ambiguity: The China Syndrome', *New York Times*, August 30, 1982, p. A17.
23. *Washington Post*, March 22, 1983, p. A12.
24. Gaston J. Sigur, Jr., 'China Policy Today: Consensus, Consistence, Stability', US Department of State, *Current Policy* 901 (December 1986), p. 4.
25. 'Remarks by the Honorable George P. Shultz, Secretary of State, Shanghai Banquet, Shanghai, China, March 5, 1987', Department of State, *Press Release* 59 (March 10, 1987).

26. For further details on the F-16 sale, see Dennis Van Vranken Hickey, *United States–Taiwan Security Ties: From Cold War to Beyond Containment* (Westport CT: Praeger, 1994), pp. 77–93; also, several references in Martin L. Lasater, *The Changing of the Guard: President Clinton and the Security of Taiwan* (Boulder CO: Westview, 1995).

27. Winston Lord, 'A New Pacific Community: Ten Goals for American Policy', opening statement at confirmation hearings for Assistant Secretary of State, Bureau of East Asian and Pacific Affairs, Senate Foreign Relations Committee, March 31, 1993, ms.

28. In a 1991 policy speech to Yale University explaining why the United States should pursue constructive engagement with China, President Bush said: 'If we pursue a policy that cultivates contacts with the Chinese people, promotes commerce to our benefit, we can help create a climate for democratic change. No nation on Earth has discovered a way to import the world's goods and services – while stopping foreign ideas at the border. Just as the democratic idea has transformed nations on every continent – so, too, change will inevitably come to China.' See 'Remarks by the President in Commencement Address to Yale University', (Kennebunkport ME: The White House, Office of the Press Secretary, May 27, 1991).

29. For an account of the May 4, 1994, incident and its repercussions, see James Mann, 'Between China and the U.S.', *Washington Post*, January 10, 1999, p. C1; and his book, *About Face: A History of America's Curious Relationship with China, from Nixon to Clinton* (New York: Knopf, 1999).

30. *Far Eastern Economic Review*, June 9, 1994, p. 18.

31. For background to the Taiwan Policy Review, see James Mann, 'U.S. May Ease Limits on Ties with Taiwan', *Los Angeles Times*, July 6, 1994, p. 1.

32. The results of the Taiwan Policy Review were presented in a background briefing to reporters by a senior (unnamed) State Department official on September 7, 1994. The summary of the official's remarks were taken from a CNA report from Washington DC, on the same day. For a much briefer but formal explanation of the policy adjustments, see 'Statement of Assistant Secretary Winston Lord, Senate Foreign Relations Committee, Hearing on Taiwan Policy', September 27, 1994, ms.

33. For congressional and public reaction to the policy review, see *New York Times*, September 8, 1994, p. A5; *Washington Post*, September 8, 1994, p. A10; CNA report from Washington DC, September 8, 1994.

34. See *Wall Street Journal*, July 14, 1995, p. A8. Later, Christopher would explain that he tried to warn the Chinese that congressional support for Lee's visit might be a factor in the president's eventual decision. He told reporters while en route to Brunei in late July 1995: 'I think it's well understood I did try to signal to Foreign Minister Qian Qichen the very strong congressional attitudes that existed with respect to Lee. If I was unable to do so or not articulate enough to let him know of that risk, I hope he now understands better the basis on which the visit was made.' See Reuters report from Andersen air force base on Guam, July 31, 1995.

35. James Mann, 'Between China and the United States', *Washington Post*, January 10, 1999, p. C1.

36. Reuters report from Washington DC, March 6, 1995.

37. 'A Visa for Taiwan's President', *Washington Post*, May 10, 1995, p. A24.

38. UPI report from Beijing, May 11, 1995.

39. 'Daily Press Briefing' (Washington DC: US Department of State, Office of the Spokesman, May 22, 1995).

40. Quoted by Jason Hu, ROC government spokesman, in Reuters report from Ithaca NY, June 9, 1995.
41. Reuters report from Beijing, May 23, 1995.
42. Reuters report from Washington DC, July 20, 1995.
43. Reuters report from Washington DC, March 14, 1996.
44. 'Joint US–China Statement' (Washington DC: White House Office of the Press Secretary, October 29, 1997).
45. Lu Jin and Liu Yunfei, 'Major Powers Reshape Their Relations', *Xinhua*, November 9, 1997, in *FBIS-China*, November 9, 1997.
46. Qian's report to departments under the CCP Central Committee, November 19, 1997, as reported in *Xinhua*, November 19, 1997, in *FBIS-China*, November 19, 1997.
47. 'Fact Sheet: Achievements of US–China Summit' (Beijing: White House Office of the Press Secretary, June 27, 1998).
48. 'Remarks by the President to Students and Community of Beijing University' (Beijing: White House Office of the President, June 29, 1998).
49. Taiwan Central News Agency, July 8, 1998, in *FBIS-China*, July 8, 1998.
50. *Xinhua*, June 30, 1998, in *FBIS-China*, June 30, 1998.
51. See several such articles in *Taiwan International Review* 4, 1 (January–February 1998).
52. Stanley O. Roth, 'The Taiwan Relations Act at Twenty – and Beyond', presentation to the Woodrow Wilson Center and the American Institute in Taiwan, March 24, 1999, Washington DC, ms.
53. 'Testimony of Stanley O. Roth, Assistant Secretary of State for East Asian and Pacific Affairs, Before the Senate Committee on Foreign Relations, March 25, 1999: 'Twenty Years of the Taiwan Relations Act', ms.
54. Richard Bush's speech was quoted extensively in 'Deteriorated U.S.–PRC Ties Harmful to Taiwan: AIT Chairman', Central News Agency (Taipei), June 26, 1999.
55. See Julian Baum *et al.*, 'Upping the Ante', *Far Eastern Economic Review*, July 22, 1999, pp. 18–19. This view was certainly shared by *Washington Post* editors: see 'Taiwan Tensions', *Washington Post*, August 4, 1999, p. A20.
56. *Wall Street Journal*, July 19, 1999, p. A10.
57. For elaboration of Lee's shift in policy, see *Free China Journal*, July 23, 1999, pp. 1, 2.
58. *Washington Post*, July 21, 1999, p. A15.
59. Quoted in *Washington Post*, July 22, 1999, p. A2.
60. See *Wall Street Journal*, July 26, 1999, p. A19; *Washington Post*, July 26, 1999, p. A13.
61. An insightful report on Taiwan's vulnerabilities in military preparedness can be found in John Pomfret, 'Chinese Threat Tests Taiwan's Preparedness', *Washington Post*, July 27, 1999, p. A13.
62. See Jim Mann, 'U.S. Has Secretly Expanded Military Ties with Taiwan', *Los Angeles Times*, July 24, 1999, downloaded from Taiwan Security Research website.
63. Reuters report from Singapore, July 23, 1999; BBC report, July 26, 1999.
64. For China's harsh crackdown on the non-political, spiritual *qi gong* sect, see many articles appearing in the *Washington Post* and *Wall Street Journal* during the June–July period of 1999.
65. See, for example, *Washington Post*, July 18, 1999, p. A23; ibid., July 19, 1999, p. A13; and *Wall Street Journal*, July 27, 1999, p. A19.
66. *Washington Post*, July 26, 1999, p. A13.

67. *Wall Street Journal*, July 28, 1999, p. A18.
68. See Matt Forney, 'Cultural Revolution: Taiwan Breaks Free of China Syndrome', *Wall Street Journal*, July 27, 1999, p. A1.
69. Richard Holbrooke, 'Reagan's Foreign Policy: Steady As She Goes', *Asian Wall Street Journal*, April 8, 1980, p. 4.

8

Theater Missile Defense and Taiwan's Security

Martin L. Lasater

As demonstrated by the 1995–96 crisis in the Taiwan Strait, one of the most serious military threats faced by the ROC is a PLA missile attack. The PRC has several kinds of missiles that might be used in such an attack, including cruise missiles, M-class missiles and various longer-range ballistic missiles armed with conventional warheads (or perhaps neutron bombs, as China hinted following Lee Teng-hui's one-China comments in July 1999[1]).

Because of Taiwan's vulnerability to PRC missile strike, Beijing seems to have placed great reliance on this threat for intimidation purposes, moving some 200 M-class missiles within range of Taiwan by early 1999. As a result of this shift in emphasis to missiles in the Taiwan Strait, one of the most controversial issues to appear in Sino-American relations during 1999 was the possibility of Taiwan participating in a US-proposed theater missile defense (TMD) system for Northeast Asia. Although the project is years away from full development and deployment, China reacted strongly to TMD because it posed serious challenges to its interests, not only toward Taiwan but also toward China's strategic posture as a global power. Beijing issued dire warnings to Taipei, Washington and Tokyo over the proposed TMD system, and began consultations with Moscow – which also opposed TMD on the grounds that it violated the 1972 Anti-Ballistic Missile (ABM) Treaty – over how the two countries might cooperate to defeat TMD. In the United States, Congress pressed for early deployment of a ballistic missile defense system, calling for either the amendment of the ABM treaty or the scrapping of it altogether in view of new threats that had emerged. Of these new threats, China was one of the most important, with 19 ICBMs deployed, 13 of which were aimed at the United States.[2]

The TMD issue will probably be debated for at least a decade, but several dimensions of the TMD program should be examined here in the context of Taiwan's security. These dimensions include (a) US interests in deploying TMD; (b) a description of the TMD system itself; (c) Taiwan's possible involvement in the program; (d) Beijing's adamant opposition to TMD; and (e) the strategic implications of TMD.

US INTERESTS IN MISSILE DEFENSE

With the end of the Cold War, the United States perceived one of the major threats to its security to be the proliferation of nuclear, biological and chemical weapons of mass destruction and the missiles that can deliver them to US territory, American troops deployed overseas, and US friends or allies. As of early 1999, more than 20 nations were capable of producing these weapons of mass destruction and nearly 30 countries possessed theater ballistic missiles or cruise missiles. While not posing a major direct threat to the continental United States, these weapons did pose an immediate threat to deployed American forces and US friends and allies. The development and deployment of an effective missile defense system was viewed as essential to counter the immediate threat in areas such as Northeast Asia and to prepare for the possibility in the twenty-first century of a major theater war or smaller-scale contingency with an enemy possessing advanced weapons such as missiles.[3]

The United States had for many years been interested in missile defense. The Reagan-era 'Star Wars' program was an early example, and the American experience in attempting to destroy Scud missiles launched by Iraq in the 1991 Gulf War made the issue of theater missile defense even more urgent. The United States began intensive study of missile defense in 1994, but little enthusiasm was felt for the system because of its expense and repeated failures to overcome the tremendous techno-logical challenges of intercepting and destroying incoming ballistic missiles. However, political support for a ballistic missile defense system grew in the Republican-controlled Congress during the second term of the Clinton administration, and the August 1998 launch of the North Korean Taepo-dong 1 ballistic missile, capable of reaching Japan and Okinawa, galvanized renewed urgency in developing missile defenses. The cost of missile defense will be enormous, in excess of $15 billion, with $4 billion for research and development already approved by Congress, and an additional $6.6 billion to be spent on deployment of a national missile defense system from 1999 to 2005.[4]

The United States established three priorities in its missile defense program: the highest priority was the development and deployment of an effective theater ballistic missile defense and cruise missile defense; the second priority was to develop and deploy an effective national missile defense; and the third priority was to continue to develop the technology to improve missile defenses. As an indication of the missile defense deployment schedule, the Department of Defense estimated that it would be able to begin system deployment for the national missile defense program during fiscal year 2005, with construction to begin in 2001 and weapons production to commence in 2003. Congress has overwhelmingly supported the administration on missile defense and its scheduled deployment.

DESCRIPTION OF THEATER MISSILE DEFENSE

In terms of the higher-priority TMD program, the United States sought to merge both missile defense and advanced air defense systems to protect its forward deployed forces, as well as those of friends and allies. The interoperable missile and air defense systems will comprise a multi-tiered capability against both ballistic and cruise missiles. The theater air and missile defense (TAMD) system will include an integrated architecture consisting of individual weapon systems, sensors, and battle management/ command, control, communications, computers and intelligence capabilities.

The lower-tier elements of this architecture are the initial top priority, designed to destroy shorter-range ballistic and cruise missiles. The Patriot Advanced Capability-3 (PAC-3) and navy area systems are the core elements of this initial lower-tier TMD program. The PAC-3 system will provide air defense for ground combat forces and high-value assets against cruise missiles and theater ballistic missiles. The navy area program, built around Aegis ships, will provide an active defense against theater missiles on a more mobile basis. A follow-on system for lower-tier missile defense is the highly mobile, medium-extended air defense system (MEADS), being built cooperatively with Germany and Italy.

Upper-tier systems are designed to defend larger areas and to defeat medium-range and intermediate-range ballistic missiles. The army's theater high-altitude area defense (THAAD) system and the navy theater wide program are such upper-tier systems. THAAD is designed to protect broad and dispersed areas and population centers, while the navy theater wide system will represent an evolution of the navy area program, again built upon the existing Aegis weapon system.

An additional layer of missile defense is designed to attack theater missiles during their boost phase. The primary boost-phase defense system is the air force airborne laser program. Boost-phase defenses are intended to attack a missile soon after its launch, probably over the adversary's own territory. Other programs, such as the joint land-attack cruise missile defense elevated sensor system, are being designed to destroy land-attack cruise missiles over the adversary's territory. In addition, missile launching sites will be targeted for counterattack and possibly

249

preemptive strike. One example is the Israeli boost-phase launcher intercept concept, involving unmanned Israeli attack vehicles armed with sophisticated sensors and heat-seeking missiles that would remain over enemy territory to strike launchers that had fired ballistic missiles.[5]

Thus, as summarized by the INSS 1998 strategic assessment study, the current theater missile defense system will incorporate four layers: first, strikes against enemy missile launch sites; second, destruction of missiles in their boost phase; third, destruction of missiles in their high-altitude trajectory phase; and, fourth, destruction of missiles in their terminal phase. Of these four layers, capabilities now exist for effective strikes against enemy missile sites; initial research is being conducted on laser strikes against missiles in their boost phase; the navy area Standard missile and army THAAD programs are being tested for the trajectory phase; and terminal defense systems, such as PAC-2 and PAC-3, are being deployed and upgraded.[6]

The 1997 *Proliferation: Threat and Response* document of the Department of Defense included the following in the TMD system planned by the United States:

• Patriot Advanced Capability-3 (PAC-3)
• Navy Area Defense
• Theater High-Altitude Area Defense (THAAD) System
• Navy Theater Wide Defense
• Medium Extended Air Defense Systems (MEADS)
• HAWK Air Defense System
• Airborne laser programs being researched.[7]

To enhance US security and that of its friends and allies, and to further US non-proliferation strategies, the United States decided to develop and deploy theater ballistic missiles defense systems in cooperation with friendly governments. The objectives in this cooperation were to strengthen US security relationships, enhance US counterproliferation strategies, share the cost burden of R&D and deployment, enhance interoperability between US forces and those of its friends and allies, and to share knowledge of benefit to the United States and its partners. Early on, these partners included American NATO allies, Israel, Japan and South Korea.

Secretary of Defense William Cohen's trip to the Far East in early November 1998 was intended in part to secure Korean and especially Japanese cooperation on TMD – cooperation which had gained much momentum as the result of North Korea's launch of a Taepo-dong 1 medium-range ballistic missile in August, which crossed Japanese territory and, surprisingly, contained a third stage which fizzled but nonetheless indicated the missile was approaching ICBM capabilities. A Pentagon spokesman indicated that the United States actually had been discussing TMD with Japan for almost five years and with South Korea and Taiwan for several years.[8]

TAIWAN'S INVOLVEMENT IN TMD

Although military-to-military discussions between the United States and Taiwan had been going on quietly for several years, the US Congress formally opened the door for Taiwan's participation in TMD in November 1997, when the House of Representatives passed H. R. 2386, the 'U.S.-Taiwan Anti-Ballistic Missile Defense Cooperation Act', by a vote of 301–116. The bill directed the Secretary of Defense to study and report to the Congress on: (1) the architecture requirements for the establishment and operation of a theater ballistic missile defense system in the Asia–Pacific region capable of protecting Taiwan from ballistic missile attacks; and (2) cooperative United States measures which would provide Taiwan with an advanced local-area ballistic missile defense system. The bill further expressed the sense of Congress that the president, upon the request of the Taiwan government, and in accordance with such study results, should transfer to Taiwan defense articles or services for the purpose of establishing and operating a local-area ballistic missile defense system to protect Taiwan and specified islands (Pescadores) against limited ballistic missile attacks. Further, the bill declared that it was in the US national interest that Taiwan be included in any effort at ballistic missile defense cooperation, networking or interoperability with friendly and allied nations in the Asia–Pacific region.

Although H. R. 2386 did not pass the Senate, its contents resurfaced in the National Defense Authorization Bill for Fiscal Year 1999 (Public Law 105-261). The conference report on the Bill stated:

> The Senate amendment contained a provision (sec. 1086) that would require the Secretary of Defense to conduct a study of architecture requirements for the establishment and operation of a theater ballistic missile defense system in the Asia–Pacific region that would have the capability to protect key regional allies of the United States. The House bill contained no similar provision. The House recedes with a clarifying amendment. The conferees understand the phrase 'key regional allies of the United States' to include Japan, South Korea and Taiwan.

This congressionally mandated study, originally due at the beginning of January 1999, was delayed by the administration, reportedly because it risked inflaming Sino-American relations at a time when the relationship

251

was already troubled over possible Chinese espionage activities to acquire American nuclear warhead technology, human rights abuses, and myriad other issues discussed elsewhere in this book.

There was ample evidence of a PRC missile threat to Taiwan. According to leaked portions of a classified report to Congress on Chinese missile deployments, by February 1999 Beijing had 200 M-9 and M-11 ballistic missiles in southern China aimed at Taiwan and the mainland planned to raise that number to around 650 over the next several years.[9] The 1999 Pentagon report on the security situation in the Taiwan Strait noted that Taiwan's active missile defense would 'not sufficiently offset the over-whelming advantage in offensive missiles which Beijing is projected to possess in 2005'.[10] According to a Pentagon spokesman, PRC ballistic missiles targeting Taiwan had been in place near the Taiwan Strait for at least five or six years (1993–94) and were used during the missile crisis of 1995–96.[11] At the time of the missile crisis, it was estimated that China had between 30 and 50 M-class missiles facing Taiwan.[12] Thus, at minimum, the PRC had doubled the number of ballistic missiles aimed at Taiwan in the 1996–98 period. Taiwan's reaction to the increased missile threat and the possibility of joining TMD illustrate the complex security situation faced by the ROC in late 1998 and early 1999.

The ROC considers TMD

An overview of Taiwan's missile defense needs and perceptions of TMD was provided in November 1998 by General Tang Fei, ROC Chief of the General Staff.[13] General Tang said the type of missiles probably available to Taiwan would be PAC-3 missiles for low-altitude defense. These might be obtained by Taiwan in three years (2002) and would probably be deployed in Kaohsiung, Taichung and perhaps Taoyuan and Keelung. The cost for the missiles would be about $1 billion. According to Tang, there was no need for Taiwan to have a complete TMD system as being developed by the United States, since Taiwan was less than one-twentieth the size of the US West Coast. He did not seem especially worried about the PRC missile threat, because the M-9 carried only 500 km of explosives and its accuracy was not entirely reliable. The missiles would not be very destruc-tive, but they would affect the nation's economy and the morale of soldiers and civilians. Tang also indicated that Taiwan's Chungshan Institute of Science and Technology was about five years behind the West in terms of scientific and technological development. The cost of the institute building missiles was about three to ten times greater than that of the West. Thus, the ROC would probably make an initial purchase from the United States, then ask for the technology, and the institute would then build the remainder of the missiles needed for Taiwan's defense.

In a report issued at about the same time as General Tang's interview, *Defense News* said that ROC government officials were withholding full support for Taiwan's participation in TMD because the program was too conceptual and too costly. The report further indicated that Taiwan would initially focus on the acquisition of radar and sensor platforms, including satellites, to assist its existing PAC-2 system and possible future TMD systems.[14] Three batteries of the so-called PAC-2-Plus system were already deployed in northern Taiwan to protect the Taipei metropolitan area. The batteries were purchased in 1992 from the United States at a cost of about $706 million.

Further insights into the ROC military's preferences for TMD were gained in interviews reported in Taipei newspapers in December 1998. Taipei's *Tzu-Li Wan-Pao*, for example, reported in mid-December that Taiwan's military would propose the procurement of three to six sets of PAC-3 anti-missile systems from the United States during their 1999 annual Taiwan–US military sales conference.[15] The military favored the PAC-3 system because the earlier Patriot system was already proven and the alternative US army THAAD system was too costly for Taiwan's military budget. The PAC-3 system would be supported by at least four Aegis-class destroyers and Taiwan's locally produced Tien-kung (Sky Bow) anti-missile system developed by the Chungshan Institute. The combined missile defense system deployed by Taiwan would have both anti-air and anti-missile capabilities and would build upon the existing PAC-2 system in place around Taipei. According to Taiwan press reports, at least two successful live-fire tests were made with the Tien-kung 2A anti-missile in mid-1998 from Chiupeng Base in Pingdong.[16]

While the military seemed to prefer the PAC-3 system, President Lee Teng-hui and ROC legislators saw political and strategic advantages in exploring the possibility of Taiwan formally joining TMD and taking part in the more advanced anti-missile program. President Lee in late December 1998, for example, reportedly took the unusual step of instructing his military leaders to 'actively deliberate on joining the TMD system'.[17] Possibly because of political pressure to join TMD, the ROC military by early January 1999 had shifted its position somewhat – as described by Vice Minister of Defense Wang Wen-hsieh – from one of not joining the 'high-priced but doubtful efficiency' TMD program to one of 'wait and see' if the system works. Wang said the military was still studying the costs and benefits of TMD to Taiwan's security.[18] As a further indication of President Lee's preferences on the issue, the KMT's official newspaper reported that Lee told the Japanese monthly journal *Shokun* on January 14, 1999, that the TMD 'program is conducive to safeguarding the Asia–Pacific regional stability and security. Consequently, the Republic of China will be happy to witness its success and is willing to cooperate in this regard.'[19] The same report in the KMT newspaper noted that the ROC military had dropped its initial reservations over TMD and instead was concentrating on whether the United States and Japan would be willing to cooperate with Taiwan 'in an air defense system involving the most advanced technology and to facilitate technological transfer'.

As will be seen in the next section, PRC protests over possible Taiwan participation in TMD began to grow in intensity during this period, prompting the ROC Foreign Ministry to call the mainland's objections 'uncalled for and unpropitious to bilateral ties' and 'extremely excessive'.[20] Nonetheless, Taiwan backpedaled somewhat. On January 19, ROC Foreign Minister Hu Chih-chiang (Jason Hu) emphasized two points: first, TMD was a defensive system and posed no threat to mainland China; and, second, Taiwan would not decide whether to participate in TMD until after the United States decided whether to develop the system – a process that might take as long as five years. In the meantime, Taiwan would study the issue more closely.[21]

In early February, General Tang Fei became Defense Minister. In a press conference on February 1, Tang further explained the military's perspective on TMD. First, he noted that TMD had a deterrent power for Taiwan but not an offensive power. Consequently, its political significance was larger than its military significance. Taiwan was being asked by the United States, along with Japan, to participate in TMD in order to share the financial burden of the expensive system. Tang said if some other means can be found to lessen mainland China's military threat to Taiwan, the ROC military would firmly support it. In the meantime, the military was 'assessing the feasibility of joining the TMD system from the points of view of technology, cost and benefits, as well as possible sources of finance'. Actually, he said, the ROC military had been studying the TMD issue since 1996 and 'currently considered it appropriate for the ROC to join a "lower-altitude" defense system, the technical requirements of which are already well-developed. Further study is required on whether to join the "higher-altitude" TMD defense system.'[22]

Second, Minister Tang noted that mainland China posed two kinds of missile threats to Taiwan: guided missiles and cruise missiles. He said 'The question of how to eliminate the threat posed by the two kinds of Chinese missiles is a major focus of our military buildup.' He said that the land-based Patriot anti-missile missile and the warship-based Aegis anti-missile systems, 'when used in combination', are 'the only efficient systems to date to counter low-flying missiles'.[23]

In response to reports in the *Financial Times* (February 11, 1999) that Beijing had deployed 150–200 M-9 and M-11 missiles in southern China targeting Taiwan, ROC military spokesmen confirmed that its intelligence agencies knew of more than 100 M-group missiles aimed at Taiwan.

Defense Minister Tang Fei put the figure at 120 missiles to the DDP caucus at the Legislative Yuan, and the caucus promised to support him in funding the TMD system.[24]

Following the release of the Pentagon report on the security situation in the Taiwan Strait in late February 1999, an ROC general commented in an interview with a local newspaper that since Taiwan had previously purchased a Patriot anti-missile system, it already participated in TMD. The question was 'to what extent Taiwan should participate in the system'. The general noted that a complete TMD system included long-, middle- and short-range missiles used by the army, navy and air force. Taiwan's purchase of three sets of the PAC-2 system, and its expectation to purchase six sets of the PAC-3 system, comprised the lowest-altitude anti-missile system within TMD. The Patriot system enabled Taiwan to counter both planes and missiles. For Taiwan to participate in a complete TMD system, however, would depend greatly on agreements reached between the United States and China. Taiwan will reap political benefits from being involved in the low-altitude TMD program with the United States, but Taiwan 'should not be over-optimistic about the plan for the establishment of a complete TMD system'. Moreover, there was the issue of whether Taiwan could afford a complete TMD system, which would require 'a huge national defense budget'.[25]

In early March, Defense Minister Tang Fei met with former US Joint Chiefs of Staff Chairman, General John Shalikashvili, to discuss Taiwan's plans for TMD. General Shalikashvili was part of a delegation led by former Secretary of Defense William Perry which was visiting Taiwan to promote a 'track-II' dialogue between Taipei and Beijing. Tang told the delegation that Taiwan was forced to consider the feasibility of joining TMD because of mainland China's development and deployment of ballistic missiles in the southeastern coastal region opposite Taiwan. He said Taiwan would have no need to consider TMD if the PRC discontinues its Taiwan-targeted military development programs and curbs missile deployments.[26] Tang said Taiwan was considering working with other countries to build a TMD system because it requires a huge budget and very high risk; nonetheless, 'We are capable of building a defense system against missile attacks.'[27]

In a later meeting with DPP Chairman Lin Yi-hsiung, General Shalikashvili was reported as saying: 'The TMD is defensive weaponry, and if Taiwan wants to take part in it, it would be difficult for Washington to reject.' The DPP chairman remarked that his party had not yet decided whether to support Taiwan joining TMD because the system was still in its appraisal stage.[28]

In a speech in Hong Kong later in March, William Perry indicated that he was becoming pessimistic about the prospects for peace in the Taiwan

Strait. Citing declining support for reunification in Taiwan, the shift in PRC military attention from Russia to Taiwan, and the PLA missile build-up opposite Taiwan, Perry predicted more missile tests in the Taiwan Strait and crises similar to those of 1995 and 1996. Asked about Taiwan's participation in TMD, the former secretary said the system could only protect a limited area against a small number of incoming missiles.[29]

The ROC military was aware that the TMD issue was as much a political question as a military question. In responding to Legislative Yuan interpellations on March 9, Minister Tang Fei said:

> The TMD matter is not simply a military issue; it is rather a political issue. Recently, when the Chinese communists' President Chiang Tse-min [Jiang Zemin] mentioned the timetable for reunification, his tone has sounded more urgent that before. On top of this, the Chinese communists are deploying missiles along the coast ... There is no specific figure on the cost of TMD. However, since the Chinese communists have already posed a threat to us, obviously we cannot wait three or five years when their missiles are hitting us and then begin. At present, we can proceed with the basic projects that can be incorporated into the traditional weaponry systems.[30]

Other ROC military officials echoed Minister Tang's remarks. Spokesman General Kung Fan-ding said on March 23: 'Intelligence gathered by ROC security units show that communist China has stored more than 100 M-class missiles, including M-9 and M-11 guided ballistic missiles, in its southeastern coastal province of Fujian, which is opposite Taiwan.' The PLA had set up several mobile missile bases which could 'complete combat preparations and deployments in three to four hours'. The range of the missiles covered the entirety of Taiwan. Kung also addressed remarks by former American defense officials that the PLA did not have the capability of attacking Taiwan now or in the foreseeable future. He pointed to several areas of PLA modernization:

- Downsizing, adjustment and modernization of several PLA units
- Forming rapid-reaction forces
- Installing new military facilities in China's southeastern coastal regions
- Stepping up research and development in areas of advanced defense technologies and weapons
- Intensification of training especially designed to attack Taiwan
- Establishment of command, control, communications and intelligence systems related to operations against Taiwan
- Preparing for partial or localized war under high-tech conditions
- Allocating enormous energies to developing ballistic missiles, cruise missiles and weapons for information and electronic warfare.

General Kung said that, according to ROC military estimates, by 2005 the mainland's air and naval forces will have been fully modernized and will pose a grave threat to Taiwan.[31]

During the same news conference, Air Force Major-General Wang Chih-ke told reporters that Taiwan planned to purchase a long-range radar system from the United States (reported value $785.7 million), capable of tracking both aircraft and missiles, which would become operational in about six years. Taiwan's existing Strong Nets radar systems reportedly could identify aircraft within a range of 600 km or 370 miles.[32]

Debate over TMD continues in Taiwan, but most Taiwan analysts express the view that the TMD question would never have been raised had the PRC not threatened Taiwan with missiles. Since Taiwan has a right to defend itself, participation in TMD is viewed as a legitimate policy choice for Taipei, although one that deserves more study.[33] One of the most pertinent comments came from the Mainland Affairs Council, which issued a report, 'Whether the Republic of China Will Join the TMD', on March 19. The document concluded: 'There are many factors determining our participation, but the mainland's current arms expansion and its military self-control in the future will finally determine whether our country should join the TMD.'[34]

On March 24, Defense Minister Tang Fei told the Legislative Yuan's Defense Committee that it will cost Taiwan an estimated NT$300 billion (US$9.23 billion) over eight to ten years to establish a low-altitude missile defense system. According to Tang, such a system would be able to destroy about 70 percent of missiles launched against the island. Despite the fact that TMD is still merely a proposed system, Tang said Taiwan should begin to lay the ground work for joining TMD. 'It would be too late for us to consider whether to join four or five years later.'[35] In the same legislative hearing, the defense minister said Taiwan would be able to match China's armed forces until 2005. However, if the PLA's military modernization program continues at its presence pace, 'the military threat to Taiwan is highly likely to be beyond control after 2005'. Tang said 'In light of this undesirable development, any measures which can replace military means to break out of the current cross-Taiwan Strait impasse will be most welcome.'[36]

Thus, by early March 1999, Taiwan had determined to proceed with a local missile defense system, concentrating on low-altitude interceptions by a combined Patriot, Sky Bow, Aegis system. It was beginning to purchase the radar and other equipment necessary to put the missile defense system into operation within five or six years. Yet to be determined was whether Taiwan would or could participate in the research, development and deployment of the higher-altitude components of TMD and the region-wide system being contemplated by the United States and Japan.

BEIJING'S OPPOSITION TO THEATER MISSILE DEFENSE

China's reaction to Taiwan's possible participation in TMD began in early October 1998, soon after the US Congress passed the National Defense Authorization Bill for Fiscal Year 1999, signed into law by President Clinton as P. L. 105-261. The bill called upon the Department of Defense to study the feasibility of establishing a theater missile defense system to protect US forces in Northeast Asia, as well as American friends and allies – defined by Congress as being Japan, South Korea and Taiwan. The PRC Foreign Ministry issued a statement condemning Taiwan's inclusion in TMD and asked the US government to 'abide by the principles in the three Sino-US joint communiqués and honor the relevant commitments made by the United States on the Taiwan question by not transferring the TMD system and related technology and equipment to Taiwan and not selling sophisticated weapons to Taiwan'.[37]

As TMD discussion gathered momentum in the United States, Japan and Taiwan, the PRC began to take a more serious view of TMD. Beijing's objections to deployment of the system centered around several themes: (a) opposition to Taiwan's participation; (b) concern that TMD would increase Japanese militarism; and (c) fear that TMD would tip the regional balance of power too heavily in US favor. In a January 12, 1999, press conference in Beijing, the Foreign Ministry referred to these objections, saying:

- The United States should not transfer the TMD system and relevant technology and equipment to Taiwan, or sell other advanced weapons to Taiwan so as to avoid damaging Sino-U.S. relations.
- [Speaking of Japan's recent decisions to launch military surveillance satellites and to jointly research TMD with the United States]: The Chinese side is deeply concerned over the possible military and political impact of those moves taken by the United States and Japan on regional and global security.
- We consider that peace and development are the mainstream of our time after the end of the Cold War, and under these circumstances the deployment and spread of strategic-weapons systems may trigger a new round of the arms race, thus affecting world balance and stability.[38]

Some of the strategic objections of China were expressed more clearly by the PLA in *Jiefangjun Bao* on January 24, 1999.[39] Stating that TMD 'will exert a far-reaching negative influence on global and regional strategic balance and stability in the 21st century', the article said missile defense was an effort by the United States 'to seek its strategic superiority' and 'hegemonic status'. Such ambition by the United States 'inevitably will lead to a new round of the arms race, which will jeopardize security and stimulate missile proliferation rather than increase safety and prevent proliferation' due to a 'perpetual contradiction' in the offensive and defensive capabilities of major nations. On a regional level, the TMD program will introduce many weapons systems with both 'missile defense as well as offensive potentialities'. Because of the expense involved in developing these advanced systems, the United States is seeking to co-operate with Japan and Taiwan, actually going 'beyond the military cooperation level of the United States and its allies during the Cold War period'. In fact, 'this move is tantamount to a proliferation of strategic military technology, which undoubtedly constitutes a new threat to the regions and countries concerned'.

A six-part series appearing in *Jiefangjun Bao* February 4–12 examined TMD in some detail, concluding that TMD would have three major negative consequences:

1. By violating the ABM Treaty with Moscow, TMD might threaten Russia's acceptance of the SALT-II guidelines and precipitate a new arms race between the United States and Russia, probably also involving Asia.
2. The TMD program would lead to the proliferation of missile technology, involving China, Japan, Taiwan, the Middle East and South Asia.
3. Bringing Taiwan into TMD would damage the Sino-American strategic partnership planned for the twenty-first century.[40]

Many of these same points were stressed in a March 22, 1999, *Jiefangjun Bao* article written by Ouyang Haisheng, but with added emphasis on the negative impact of involving Japan in TMD: 'What is of most concern at the moment is that Japan's enthusiasm for joining TMD has surged up to an extraordinary extent … U.S.–Japanese cooperation in developing TMD is bound to further strengthen the military forces in Japan and stimulate a further surge of … militarism.'[41]

The mouthpiece of the CCP Central Military Commission, *Zhongguo Guofang Bao* (China Defense News) in March 1999 contained an article by Zheng Jian of the Academy of Military Sciences' Strategic Research Department, arguing that the United States was seeking to set up a multi-national anti-missile system to form an Asian–Pacific military security mechanism under US control. In essence, this would establish a military alliance, similar to US-led military security mechanisms set up in Europe, and would be part of an American attempt to establish a new world order following the Cold War.[42]

Several PRC strategists voiced opposition to TMD being extended to Taiwan. The *China Daily* warned: 'Should the United States bring Taiwan into its proposed anti-missile scheme, Sino-US relations would suffer a setback unprecedented since the normalization of bilateral ties.'[43] Ouyang Liping of the China Institute of Contemporary International Relations said: 'By bringing Taiwan in, the U.S. would forge a de facto military alliance with Taiwan', while Sa Benwang of the China Institute for International Strategic Studies claimed that the TMD system would 'add fuel to separatist attempts for "Taiwan independence" and will also encourage Japan's ambitions for military expansion'. Jian Taojie with the Center for Peace and Development Studies described TMD as an 'extension of efforts to contain China militarily'.[44]

In an interview with an unidentified 'senior Chinese official', the *Financial Times* reported on February 26, 1999, that China might link TMD to Beijing's agreement to abide by the terms of the Missile Technology Control Regime. 'Since the U.S. can lead the way in breaking this regime, other countries have an absolute right not to follow the rules of this regime and undertake cooperation on missiles and missile technology with third countries', the official said – a veiled reference to China's missile cooperation with Pakistan and Iran.[45]

The release of the congressionally mandated Pentagon reports on Taiwan's security situation and prospects for including Taiwan in TMD programs prompted a quick and bitter response from the PRC. A Foreign Ministry spokesman said the reports were attempts to justify advanced arms sales to Taiwan and thus constituted 'serious interference in China's internal affairs'. Taiwan leaders were warned not to attempt to use TMD to purchase advanced weapons, since it would 'surely affect the security situation of the Taiwan Strait'. Concern was expressed that Taiwan would use involvement in TMD to obstruct reunification further and a stern warning was issued: 'We advise Taiwan authorities not to go too far in the road of obstructing reunification with the motherland.'[46]

Reuters reported on March 5, 1999, an interview with a 'senior Chinese official' who had harsh words for the United States and its TMD program. The official said Tokyo already had rockets, so TMD would give that nation 'both the spear and the shield', adding that TMD would 'enhance military cooperation between Japan and the United States, and we don't like it'. Noting US reports that China had deployed missiles opposite Taiwan, the official retorted: 'Whether we should deploy missiles on our own territory is our own business' and warned Washington to keep its 'hands off'. Warning of 'serious consequences' should Taiwan be included in TMD, the official said that the system would give the pro-independence lobby on Taiwan a 'false sense of security'. Furthermore, since TMD was a regional system, Taiwan's inclusion in TMD would be tantamount to a 'semi-military alliance' with the United States and the command, communications and control systems established on Taiwan would constitute 'a U.S. military presence on Taiwan' – all in violation of US agreements with China.[47]

Similar concerns were expressed by PRC Foreign Minister Tang Jiaxuan on March 7, 1999. Noting that China was 'very concerned' about the development of TMD, Tang said Taiwan's inclusion in the program with the United States and Japan would meet with 'strong opposition' from China, because it would amount to an encroachment on China's sovereignty and territorial integrity and interfere with reunification. The foreign minister also criticized TMD in general for going against 'the trend of the time'; not being 'conducive to the international disarmament efforts'; exerting a 'negative impact on regional and global strategic balance and stability into the next century'; harming 'the peace and stability in the Asia–Pacific region'; enhancing 'the overall offensive and defensive ability of the military alliance' between Washington and Japan; and going 'far beyond the legitimate defense needs that [Japan] has repeatedly indicated'.[48]

A week later, Chinese Premier Zhu Rongji, scheduled to visit the United States in April 1999, also addressed the TMD issue: 'We oppose the TMD and we are firmly and particularly opposing to include Taiwan into the TMD.' Zhu also downplayed Pentagon reports of PRC missiles being aimed at Taiwan. Somewhat contradictorily, he said 'We are by no means to target missiles at our brothers and sisters in Taiwan, and we will not use these missiles very lightly and easily.'[49] The next day, the Foreign Ministry dismissed reports of Chinese missiles targeting Taiwan: 'These rumors are groundless and without foundation and utterly irresponsible', claiming that 'some people have been spreading rumors ... to increase tension across the Taiwan Strait'.[50]

Rather than denying the existence of the missiles or their intended target, a more reasonable explanation for the PRC deployments was offered by Hong Kong's *Wen Wei Po*: 'the mainland's military deployment against Taiwan changes at all times in light of the situation of Taiwan independence. In recent years, the boat has gone up with the rising level of the river. The fact is that the "boat" goes up after the "rising level of the water".'[51] In other words, the missiles were deployed against Taiwan to prevent Taiwan independence – sentiments for which were perceived to be on the rise.

In assessing the PRC reaction to TMD, it is important to keep in mind that TMD poses significant, potential threats to Chinese interests. These include:

- Delaying China's unification under terms favorable to the PRC
- Increasing Taiwan's ability to deter or defeat a PLA attack
- Increasing the possibility of Taiwan independence
- Reducing the offensive and deterrent effectiveness of PRC ballistic missiles

- Necessitating greater resources to be dedicated to the PLA's modernization, thus limiting resources available to economic modernization
- Removing restraints on American and South Korean incentives for war against North Korea
- Forcing Beijing to align more closely with Moscow and possibly co-operate more with Pyongyang to counter TMD
- Contributing to Japan's rearmament and militarism
- Strengthening the US position as regional hegemon in Asia
- Disrupting the current balance of power in a direction favoring the United States
- Reducing the possibility of the Asia–Pacific region becoming multipolar with China playing a more important leadership role
- Exacerbating political tensions within the CCP leadership.

For these and other reasons, TMD – although a defensive system intended by the United States to protect its forward deployed forces and its friends and allies against missile attack – is seen in Beijing as threatening fundamental PRC interests. The development and deployment of TMD would in effect place the PRC onto the horns of a dilemma: to try to counter TMD could bankrupt China, much as the arms race in the Cold War had bankrupted the Soviet Union and led to its collapse; to try to stop TMD would require either threatening the United States – which might backfire in an era of increased American perceptions of a 'China threat' – or removing the reasons for TMD deployments – that is persuading North Korea to give up its ballistic missile program (unlikely) or to withdraw PRC missiles from threatening positions along the coast of China opposite Taiwan (an affront to Chinese sovereignty and encouragement for Taiwan independence).

However, as China no doubt realized, the United States had decided to develop TMD for more reasons than the potential threat from Chinese missiles. Even if China did not possess a single ballistic missile, other countries would possess them (between 25 and 30, according to former Defense Secretary Donald Rumsfeld, chairman of a government panel studying missile defense).[52] In other words, despite the profound impact on Chinese interests and PRC vigorous protests, there was very little Beijing could do to stop the US missile defense program.

STRATEGIC IMPLICATIONS

Despite its defensive nature, a revolutionary weapons system such as ballistic missile defense is bound to have wide strategic implications, since, as the Chinese like to say, it provides a shield as well as a sword to countries possessing both ballistic missiles and ballistic missile defense. Certainly one of the most important strategic results of TMD would be increased military cooperation between China and Russia, as well as perhaps North Korea (although Beijing and Moscow are wary of unpredictable Pyongyang).

Thus, it is noteworthy that the *Wen Wei Po* revealed stepped-up Chinese and Russian cooperation in developing laser technology and 'wave frequency weapons' to attack US satellites in orbit during time of war.[53] Since much of US strategy revolves around space-borne intelligence and pinpoint accuracy of various strike munitions, such a Sino-Russian capability would degrade the US ability to find and destroy PLA targets.

It should be remembered that both China and Russia support a multipolar world in which the United States would not be the sole superpower but rather one of several centers of power, including Moscow and Beijing. Often in the United Nations (Kosovo being a recent example), the conflicting interests of the United States on the one hand and China and Russia on the other lead the two sides to adopt opposite positions on global and regional issues. In recognition of their mutual interest in counterbalancing US dominance of the international system, Beijing and Moscow have formed a strategic partnership much stronger than that being pursued by Clinton and Jiang. The Sino-Russian strategic partnership is not a military alliance, but it is an agreement to consult and, where possible, coordinate on issues of mutual interests.

By March 1999, Beijing and Moscow were consulting on how best to counter the US theater ballistic missile program in Asia and the proposed US national missile defense program. These missile defense programs, while not necessarily targeted against Russian and Chinese ICBMs or SLBMs, would seriously weaken the backbone of Russian and Chinese strategic postures. An effective US missile defense system, for example, would lower the deterrent value of the Russian and Chinese ballistic missiles, reduce the probability of their victory in war, and weaken perceptions of their national power.

The Sino-Russian consultations were announced by the Chinese Foreign Ministry on March 11 and by Russian officials the next day.[54] Colonel-General Leonid Ivashov, head of the Russian Defense Ministry's International Military Cooperation Board, said on March 12, 1999, that the TMD system 'will undermine stability in the Far East and spur up the rocketry race ... This is the reason why we are holding consultations on this issue with our Chinese colleagues and will continue them at a higher level.' Similar programs, the general said, were being constructed in Norway, thereby undermining 'strategic stability'.[55] In addition to Sino-Russian military consultations on TMD, the missile defense system and its security and stability implications were being discussed by the two foreign ministries.[56] At the same time, it was announced that an unusually high-level meeting between Chinese and North Korean foreign ministers was scheduled for April, with special attention to be paid to the problems associated with the US plan to deploy a theater missile defense system in Northeast Asia.[57]

As it has done in the past, China tried to link American policy it did not like (in this case, TMD) with PRC behavior toward Taiwan. Hence, a secondary strategic implication of TMD *may* be damage to cross-Strait dialogue. The word 'may' is emphasized here, since – unlike almost certain Sino-Russian cooperation to oppose TMD – Beijing's decision to hold dialogue with Taiwan hostage to TMD is more problematic (the PRC may be able to limit TMD deployment by reducing tensions in the Taiwan Strait by encouraging cross-Strait talks). But the TMD–Strait dialogue linkage has been established, as indicated by Wang Daohan (China's chief negotiator with Taiwan) in an interview with the *New York Times* on March 23, 1999. Wang said that, if the United States deployed TMD on Taiwan, 'it is like playing with fire'. Such deployment would 'completely disrupt the current world situation, and instead a new Cold War will appear'. Wang said China would regard the inclusion of Taiwan in a theater missile defense system as tantamount to the establishment of a military alliance between Washington and Taipei and would precipitate an arms race.[58]

There are two possible types of arms race that might be of concern to the United States and which would have an impact on Taiwan's security. First, China might – with some Russian assistance – improve its strategic missile capabilities to the point where Beijing could threaten more dramatically the continental United States. And, second, the PRC might – again with Russian assistance – greatly improve its shorter-range ballistic missiles and anti-ship and anti-air weaponry, thereby placing American forces deployed in the Western Pacific at increased risk. Both of these improvements in PLA capabilities would strengthen the Chinese deterrence against American intervention in the Taiwan Strait and thus, possibly, broaden the options available to Beijing in applying pressure to Taipei. Whether that deterrence would be adequate to overcome US incentives to intervene, of course, is another question.

The United States dismissed both Russian and Chinese concerns over TMD – in part because TMD was a defensive, not an offensive, system and therefore not a direct threat to anyone. Moreover, the TMD program and the national missile defense system were theoretical concepts, not deployable systems. Also, missile defense, like its Star Wars predecessor, was an excellent bargaining tool for Washington in tough security negotiations with major potential adversaries. And, equally important, missile defense was a favorite program in the Republican-controlled Congress.

During a March 2, 1999, press conference in Beijing, Secretary of State Madeleine Albright emphasized the theoretical nature of TMD but also hinted that the US decision to include Taiwan in the missile defense program would be strongly influenced by Chinese efforts to control missile proliferation. She said:

> During my discussions this week, Chinese officials expressed concern about the possible deployment in the region of systems for theater missile defense. I replied that, instead of worrying about a decision that has not been made to deploy defensive technologies that do not yet exist, China should focus its energies on the real source of the problem – the proliferation of missiles. Nothing would be more stabilizing for the region than North Korean restraint on missile development and testing. Nothing would better serve China's interests than using its developing dialogue with Taiwan to build mutual confidence and reduce the perceived need for missiles or missile defense.[59]

On March 9, the State Department spokesman reiterated this message, saying: 'Instead of worrying about a decision that has not been made to deploy defensive technologies that do not yet exist, the Chinese should focus on the regional and global proliferation of missiles.'[60] The US position was further explained by Assistant Secretary of State Stanley Roth in testimony before Congress on March 25, 1999:

> The question of Taiwan and a theoretical theater missile defense – TMD – strategy, has of course been a topic of much discussion recently. First, let me set out some important technical points. TMD is a defensive system for which no deployment decisions, other than for protection of our own forces, have been made. This high-altitude system technology is in the early stages of development with potential deployment at least some years away.
>
> But, that said, I think it is critical to emphasize that the PRC's actions are a key factor in the region's, and Taiwan's, interest in TMD. We have urged the PRC to exercise restraint on missiles, to work toward confidence-building measures with Taiwan, and to press North Korea to forgo its missile ambitions. These factors are under the PRC's direct control or considerable influence, and the PRC's actions can affect perceived need for TMD. Put differently, we do not preclude the possibility of Taiwan having access to TMD. Our decisions on this will be guided by the same basic factors that have shaped our decisions to date on the provision of defensive capabilities to Taiwan.[61]

Despite the largely theoretical nature of TMD research, by mid-1999 the technology of missile defense was at least promising, with some success being registered. An improved Patriot missile slammed into a target missile high over the White Sands missile range in New Mexico in mid-March 1999,[62] and an army THAAD interceptor collided with a test missile in space in August 1999, again above White Sands.[63] Reportedly, there was considerable debate within the Clinton administration over the merits of proceeding with TMD, particularly with Taiwan's participation in the program. The Department of Defense was said to be strongly in favor of TMD and believed Taiwan should be included; whereas the State Department and the National Security Council were hesitant about including Taiwan so as to preserve the strategic dialogue with China begun with the Clinton–Jiang summits in 1997 and 1998.[64]

CONCLUSION

The 1998–99 debate over TMD came at a difficult time for Sino-American relations. There was a long list of other divisive issues to be addressed: human rights violations in the PRC – violations which appeared to be increasing against both political dissidents and the spiritually faithful; China's growing trade surplus with the United States, around $57 billion in 1998, with no sign of reduction; frustratingly little progress in negotiations with the Chinese to open more of their markets in anticipation of joining the World Trade Organization; allegations of Chinese espionage activities in the Los Alamos National Laboratory, resulting in the theft of designs for the W88 warhead, enabling China to place multiple warheads on its ICBMs and SLBMs; concern that China had obtained illegal information from American companies contracting the PRC to launch sensitive satellites; in China itself, central planners seemed to be making a comeback; several major Chinese purchases of American commercial jets were canceled; Chinese financial institutions were having difficulty repaying foreign loans; in contrast to China's wishes, the United States was considering a more hardline approach to North Korea to contain Pyongyang until it collapsed; harsh criticism in the United States and China of their leaders' policies in Sino-American relations; Congress was seeking a much stronger role in US China policy; and so on.

Because of all of these existing problems in Sino-American relations, PRC protests over Taiwan's possible inclusion in TMD were mostly ignored in the United States. Little attention was paid, for example, when a senior Chinese official told foreign journalists in early March 1999 that providing Taiwan with military equipment to defend against missile attacks would be 'the last straw' in Sino-American relations. He also warned that the sale of Aegis ships to Taiwan would be treated more seriously than the sale of F-16s.[65]

Still, some took the PRC threats seriously. US Marine Corps General Charles Bolden, Deputy Commander of US Forces Japan, said in late January 1999 that he was against US–Taiwan cooperation on TMD because it could cause unwanted friction in the increasingly strained

US–China relationship.[66] But most Western analysts believed that China had brought the TMD issue on itself, having threatened Taiwan with M-class missiles during the Taiwan Strait crisis and having deployed nearly 200 M-9 and M-11 missiles opposite Taiwan since 1996. Gerald Segal of the Institute of International Strategic Studies, for example, said in an interview in January 1999 that the United States is committed to defend Taiwan, as the 1996 crisis in the Taiwan Strait had demonstrated. Instead of learning that lesson, China chose instead to increase its missile threat against Taiwan and to strengthen its ability to attack US forces, believing that it could overwhelm both Taiwan defenses and American willingness to intervene. But, Segal warned, that is a competition China cannot possibly win: if it tries to compete with the United States it will bankrupt itself in the same way the Soviet Union did when it attempted to compete militarily with the United States. The TMD program was an expected American response to the PRC missile threat, and China will have to change its policies if it expects to be a major player in East Asia.[67] And Colonel Larry M. Wortzel of the US Army War College's Strategic Studies Institute wrote in February 1999 that 'China's use of missiles against Taiwan may well have the effect of destroying China's own strategy'.[68]

Perhaps the most interesting aspect of TMD is that it is a near-perfect reflection of the larger conundrum of the Taiwan issue in Sino-American relations: the United States is justified in developing and deploying both national and theater missile defenses; Taiwan has a right to incorporate TMD research and development into its defense since PRC missiles are obviously a threat of the first order; and China's opposition to TMD and Taiwan's inclusion is certainly understandable because missile defense will change China's strategic environment in ways probably not to its advantage. And, despite the vicious circle, TMD will likely go forward.

In its big-power competition with the United States, China has very few options other than to proceed with its ballistic and cruise missile deployments in eastern and southern China. From Beijing's point of view, the US presence in the Western Pacific is an obstacle to China's future greatness. The US navy is the world's strongest, capable of being deployed anywhere in open ocean. US alliances and quasi-alliances form a barrier to China's freedom of movement in its own backyard. The US techno-logical advantage over the PRC is almost unchallengeable, especially when combined with the technological strengths of American friends in Asia such as Japan, South Korea, Taiwan and Singapore. A similar US advantage exists financially, with the strength of the combined US–Japanese–South Korean–Taiwanese–Singaporean economies being unas-sailable. At the same time that these strengths exist within the American quasi-alliance system, the countries China can look to for assistance are few in number and relatively weak; the strongest 'friend' is Russia, which might implode on any given day. Reunification with Taiwan, especially under peaceful terms, seems a fading goal as long as democratization precedes Taiwanization of the island. CCP reforms that could attract Taiwan do not appear forthcoming, because they would threaten the leadership role of the CCP itself. If reunification is to be achieved through forceful means, then the prospects of American intervention are at least moderately high – making the PLA's ability to defeat the ROC questionable, at least for the next ten years. Given this unfavorable strategic environment, China's decision to deploy M-class missiles opposite Taiwan was inevitable, particularly in the context of political competition in Beijing. Being strongly assertive of Chinese territorial and sovereignty rights and protective of a proper Chinese role in regional and global affairs are absolute prerequisites for leadership survival in China today. No current or foreseeable Chinese leader can afford to appear weak on the Taiwan issue.

However, this assertion of Chinese national power – including the right to use force against Taiwan – is viewed by a great many Americans as a threat to US interests in regional peace and stability. US strategy is based on the maintenance of a favorable balance of power in the Western Pacific in which no regional hegemon will be allowed to threaten the preeminent position of the United States. The fact that China rejects the US vision of a new world order and seeks to replace the existing US security architecture in East Asia contributes to growing perceptions that China is challenging the United States for the position of regional leader. That, increasingly, China is cooperating with Russia to accomplish this reordering of the American-backed architecture cannot be lost on Washington. Without a major revision of US strategy and policy toward Asia, this is a challenge no administration can long ignore. There has been no indication of a willingness in the United States to redraw the lines of US interests in the Pacific to give China a free hand in establishing its own sphere of influence.

In short, the United States and China are engaged, however reluctantly, in a power struggle for influence in Northeast Asia, East Asia and Southeast Asia – regions in which the United States maintains a presence due to its history of needing to project power forward to avoid peer challenges closer to home, and regions in which China believes it has a vital interest because of proximity, a long history of being the dominant power, and experiences of aggression from the east. The reconciliation of security interests between the United States and China is very difficult, and ultimately may prove impossible without a conflict.

Thus, at its heart, the TMD issue is part of the major power competition between the United States and China. As usual, Taiwan is caught in the middle – destined to be a minefield over which Washington and Beijing are careful to traverse, lest all sides be drawn into a conflict none wants but none can confidently avoid.

268

NOTES

1. For reference to the neutron bomb, see *Wall Street Journal*, July 16, 1999, p. A12.
2. For an argument to scrap the ABM treaty, see Senator Jesse Helms, 'Amend the ABM Treaty? No, Scrap It', *Wall Street Journal*, January 22, 1999, p. A10.
3. For a discussion of missile defense in US strategy, see Chapter 6 in William S. Cohen, *1998 Secretary of Defense Annual Report to the President and the Congress* (Washington DC: Office of the Secretary of Defense, 1998).
4. *Wall Street Journal*, January 21, 1999, p. A20; *Washington Post*, January 21, 1999, p. A1.
5. See Barbara Opall-Rome, 'Israel Proposes Mission to Target Missile Launchers', *Defense News Online*, March 29, 1999.
6. Institute for National Strategic Studies, *1998 Strategic Assessment: Engaging Power for Peace* (Washington DC: National Defense University, 1998), pp. 246–7.
7. *Proliferation: Threat and Response* (Washington DC: Office of the Secretary of Defense, November 1997), pp. 64–5.
8. Department of Defense Background Briefing, October 27, 1998, in DOD's information website, *DefenseLink*.
9. Mure Dickie, 'Taiwan: Vigilance pledge on missiles', *Financial Times* online edition, February 11, 1999.
10. *The Security Situation in the Taiwan Strait: Report to Congress Pursuant to the FY99 Appropriations Bill* (Washington DC: Department of Defense, 1999), as reported in *DefenseLink*.
11. Department of Defense News Briefing, February 11, 1999, reported in *DefenseLink*.
12. 'More than 100 PRC Missiles Targeted on Taiwan', Hong Kong AFP, in *FBIS-China*, February 11, 1999.
13. 'Taiwan: Chief of General Staff on Joining US TMD System', Taipei *Chung-kuo Shih-Pao*, November 24, 1998, in *FBIS-China*, December 3, 1998.
14. Barbara Opall-Rome, 'Taiwan Resists Call to Embrace TMD', *Defense News Online*, November 30, 1998.
15. 'Taiwan: Taiwan Favors Patriot Anti-Missile System', Taipei *Tzu-Li Wan-Pao*, December 11, 1998, in *FBIS-China*, December 16, 1998.
16. 'U.S. Considers Selling Taiwan Patriot PAC-III', Taipei *Lien-Ho Pao*, February 7, 1999, in *FBIS-China*, February 7, 1999.
17. 'Taiwan: Military Studying Possibility of Joining TMD', *Lien-Ho Pao*, December 28, 1998, in *FBIS-China*, January 2, 1999. For various views expressed on Taiwan about the pros and cons of joining TMD, see 'Taiwan: Legislature Hearing Discusses Joining TMD', *Tzu-Li Wan-Pao*, January 7, 1999, in *FBIS-China*, January 11, 1999.
18. 'Taiwan: MND: ROC Not Yet Decided to Join U.S. TMD System', Taiwan Central News Agency, January 11, 1999, in *FBIS-China*, January 11, 1999.
19. 'Taiwan: Lee Teng-hui Hails TMD System', *Chung-Yang Jih-Pao*, January 15, 1999, in *FBIS-China*, January 18, 1999.
20. 'Taiwan: Foreign Ministry Denounces PRC "Interference" in TMD', Taiwan Central News Agency, January 13, 1999, in *FBIS-China*, January 13, 1999.
21. 'Taiwan: Foreign Minister: US-Led TMD Not to Pose Threat to PRC', Taiwan Central News Agency, January 19, 1999, in *FBIS-China*, January 19, 1999.
22. 'Taiwan: New Defense Minister says TMD System would be "Deterrent"', Taiwan Central News Agency, February 1, 1999, in *FBIS-China*, February 1, 1999.

23. 'Taiwan: Defense Minister: Taiwan to Study Missile Defense System', Tokyo *Kyodo*, February 1, 1999, in *FBIS-China*, February 1, 1999.

24. 'Defense Ministry Confirms Beijing's Missile Deployment', *Lien-Ho Pao*, February 11, 1999, in *FBIS-China*, February 11, 1999; see also 'AFP: More Than 100 Missiles Targeted on Taiwan', Hong Kong AFP, February 11, 1999, in *FBIS-China*, February 11, 1999.

25. 'Taiwan Needs Low-Altitude Anti-Missile System', *Tzu-Li Wan-Pao*, March 1, 1999, in *FBIS-China*, March 1, 1999.

26. 'Defense Minister Meets Gen. Shalikashvili, Discusses TMD', Taiwan Central News Agency, March 9, 1999, in *FBIS-China*, March 9, 1999.

27. 'Defense Minister Tang: Taiwan "Forced" to Consider TMD', *Lien-Ho Pao*, March 9, 1999, in *FBIS-China*, March 9, 1999.

28. 'Expert: "Difficult for US to Reject Taiwan's TMD Entry"', Taiwan Central News Agency, March 9, 1999, in *FBIS-China*, March 9, 1999.

29. 'Perry Comments on TMD', Taiwan Central News Agency, March 22, 1999, in *FBIS-China*, March 22, 1999.

30. 'Defense Minister Tang on Starting "Basic" TMD Projects', *Lien-Ho Pao*, March 10, 1999, in *FBIS-China*, March 10, 1999.

31. 'Ministry Reiterates Warning on Mainland Missile Threat', Taiwan Central News Agency, March 23, 1999, in *FBIS-China*, March 23, 1999.

32. 'AFP: General Confirms Policy on "Long-Range" Radar', Hong Kong AFP, March 23, 1999, in *FBIS-China*, March 23, 1999.

33. See, for example, 'PRC Military Threat Major Concern for Taiwan Joining TMD', Taiwan Central News Agency, March 20, 1999, in *FBIS-China*, March 20, 1999; 'SEF Official: PRC Military Threat Encourages Study of TMD', Taiwan Central News Agency, March 20, 1999, in *FBIS-China*, March 20, 1999; 'Taiwan Officials Comment on TMD Participation', Taiwan Central News Agency, March 23, 1999, in *FBIS-China*, March 23, 1999; and 'Taiwan's Hand Forced by China's Missile Stance', Reuters, March 23, 1999.

34. For a summary of the MAC document, see 'MAC: Taiwan Has Right to Decide Whether to Join TMD', *Chung-kuo Shih-Pao*, March 20, 1999, in *FBIS-China*, March 20, 1999.

35. 'Defense Minister Says TMD to Cost Taiwan $9.23 Billion', Taiwan Central News Agency, March 24, 1999, in *FBIS-China*, March 24, 1999.

36. 'Tang Fei: Taiwan Can Match PRC's Armed Forces Until 2005', Taiwan Central News Agency, March 25, 1999, in *FBIS-China*, March 24, 1999.

37. 'China: Spokesman Denounces US Defense Authorization Bill', *Xinhua Domestic Service*, October 6, 1998, in *FBIS-China*, October 6, 1998.

38. 'China: Spokesman on Taiwan Joining TMD, Japan Issues' and 'Transfer of TMD to Taiwan "Violation"', *Xinhua*, January 12, 1999, in *FBIS-China*, January 12, 1999.

39. Gao Junmin and Lu Dehong, 'A Dangerous Move', Beijing *Jiefangjun Bao*, January 24, 1999, in *FBIS-China*, February 1, 1999.

40. Zhang Zhaozhong, 'Resurgence of the "Star Wars" Program', *Jiefangjun Bao*, February 4–12, 1999, in *FBIS-China*, various issues between February 4 and February 14, 1999.

41. Ouyang Haisheng, 'Negative Factors for World Security and Stability – Commenting on the U.S. Theater Missile Defense Program', *Jiefangjun Bao*, March 22, 1999, in *FBIS-China*, March 22, 1999.

42. Zheng Jian, 'Can Foreign Weapons Protect Taiwan?', *Zhongguo Guofang Bao*, March 21, 1999, reported in 'Army Paper Attacks TMD', Hong Kong *Ming Pao*, March 21, 1999, in *FBIS-China*, March 21, 1999.

43. Quoted in 'China Warns of Unprecedented Setback to Sino-US Relations', *Inside China Today* website, reported from Beijing, January 27, 1999.
44. Ibid.
45. James Kynge, 'Threat of Missile Transfer', *Financial Times* online edition, February 26, 1999.
46. 'Spokesman on U.S. Defense Department Report on Taiwan', *Xinhua*, March 1 and 2, 1999, in *FBIS-China* issues, March 1 and 2, 1999.
47. Reuters report, March 5, 1999. See also, Han Hua, 'Taiwan's Participation in TMD Will Lead to Serious Consequences', Hong Kong *Wen Wei Po*, March 6, 1999, in *FBIS-China*, March 6, 1999; 'Beijing Accuses the United States of Forming "Paramilitary Alliance" with Taiwan', *Ming Pao*, March 8, 1999, in *FBIS-China*, March 8, 1999.
48. 'Tang Jiaxuan: PRC "Very Concerned" about TMD Development', *Xinhua*, March 7, 1999, in *FBIS-China*, March 7, 1999.
49. 'Further on Zhu Rongji on TMD', *Xinhua*, March 15, 1999, in *FBIS-China*, March 15, 1999.
50. 'Spokesman Dismisses Taiwan Missile Threat as "Groundless"', Hong Kong AFP, March 16, 1999, in *FBIS-China*, March 16, 1999.
51. Fan Chiang, 'What is the Motive Behind US–Taiwan Theater Missile Defense System?', *Wen Wei Po*, March 16, 1999, in *FBIS-China*, March 16, 1999.
52. *Washington Post*, March 19, 1999, p. A8.
53. Fan Chiang, 'What is the Motive Behind US–Taiwan Theater Missile Defense System?', *Wen Wei Po*, March 16, 1999, in *FBIS-China*, March 16, 1999.
54. 'Spokesman: China, Russia Oppose Development of TMD', *Xinhua*, March 11, 1999, in *FBIS-China*, March 11, 1999.
55. 'Russia Opposes U.S. Anti-missile Systems in Asia', Moscow Interfax, March 12, 1999, in *FBIS-China*, March 12, 1999.
56. 'Russia: Official to Raise US Missile Issue in PRC Talk', Moscow Interfax, March 12, 1999, in *FBIS-China*, March 12, 1999.
57. 'PRC Official on US Missile Plan; DPRK Plans PRC Visit', Moscow ITAR-TASS World Service, March 18, 1999, in *FBIS-China*, March 18, 1999.
58. 'Forget Taiwan Missile Shield, China Warns', *New York Times*, March 24, 1999, in Taiwan Security Research website.
59. 'Press Conference by Secretary of State Madeleine K. Albright' (Beijing: US Department of State, Office of the Spokesman, March 2, 1999).
60. 'U.S. Rejects Beijing's Warnings on Taiwan', Associated Press, March 9, 1999.
61. 'Twenty Years of the Taiwan Relations Act: Testimony of Stanley O. Roth, Assistant Secretary of State for East Asian and Pacific Affairs, before the Senate Committee on Foreign Relations, March 25, 1999', ms.
62. *Washington Post*, March 16, 1999, p. A7.
63. *Washington Post*, August 3, 1999, p. A6.
64. See, for example, 'Asia–Pacific: Big Powers Flex Muscles over Taiwan: Pentagon Reports China Missile Build-Up Raises Military Stakes in Asia and Fuels Fears in Washington', *Financial Times*, online edition, February 10, 1999.
65. For a summary of the important briefing, see *Washington Post*, March 6, 1999, p. A1.
66. Bryan Bender, 'USA is Likely to Tread Slowly on Taiwan Theatre Missile Defence', Jane's Information Group, January 25, 1999.
67. For a transcript of the interview, see 'A Wise Decision for Taiwan to Join the TMD', *Chung-kuo Shih-Pao*, January 30, 1999, in *FBIS-China*, January 30, 1999.
68. Colonel Larry M. Wortzel, 'The Danger of No Theater Ballistic Missile Defenses', Strategic Studies Institute Newsletter, February 1999.

9

Conclusions and Policy Suggestions

Martin L. Lasater

The overall conclusion reached in this study is that Taiwan's security situation in the post-Deng era is complex and unpredictable. However, on a scale of 1 to 10, with 1 being ensured peace in the Taiwan Strait and 10 being ensured war, one would have to conclude that the prospects for war are greater than the prospects for peace. Perhaps a 6 or 7 on the 10-point scale would reflect the probability of some form of conflict occurring in the Taiwan Strait before 2010 – and that might be optimistically biased in favor of peace.

It is not that peace is impossible to sustain; it is that peace is so difficult to maintain in a situation, like that of the Taiwan issue, in which all concerned parties have vital or important interests at stake with relatively little room for compromise. Taipei, Beijing, Washington and their various domestic audiences (some supporting existing policy, some opposed) all have in common a desire to find a peaceful resolution of the Taiwan issue that is relatively fair and serves the interests of all. But, barring some change in the fundamental positions of the ROC, PRC or the United States, the hope for peace may give way to the exigencies of conflict. The outcome of such violence is becoming harder to predict, but under most circumstances it would seem that Taiwan would lose and China would win in an internal Chinese conflict, but that Taiwan would win and China would lose if the conflict involved the United States.

Thus, the circumstances under which the United States would intervene become all important. This issue will be addressed in some detail below, but first it might be useful to summarize the most important factors bearing on Taiwan's security in the post-Deng Xiaoping era, as these have been discussed in the previous chapters.

SUMMARY OF MAJOR FINDINGS

China is willing to go to war over Taiwan
The PRC seems most likely to use force against Taiwan (a) if the island seeks to become an independent nation-state, separate from Chinese

272

territory; or (b) if the island is to become a base of military operations for a foreign power such as the United States. Of the two circumstances, the former is more credible; however, China's historical experiences do not discount the second possibility. Indeed, a common perception in Beijing is that Washington uses the Taiwan issue to keep China divided and weakened. Within the PLA, there is a growing consensus that Taiwan must be reunited with the mainland if China is ever to achieve its great-power status in Asia. Thus, Chinese nationalism and a powerful strategic rationale are combining to strengthen PRC resolve to fight over Taiwan, even it means a military confrontation with the United States. Moreover, as this resolve firms, Beijing's patience over a resolution of the Taiwan issue seems to be wearing thin.

The United States probably will defend Taiwan against PRC aggression
The security of Taiwan is linked to many important US interests, including the maintenance of a favorable balance of power in the Western Pacific. American willingness to defend Taiwan against an unprovoked PRC attack (a) strengthens perceptions of American credibility in the Asia–Pacific region; and (b) demonstrates US determination to prevent China from becoming a regional hegemon. The United States would probably accept any solution to the Taiwan issue arrived at peacefully between the two sides of the Strait. However, as China increases its national power and seeks to expand its sphere of influence beyond its borders, thereby becoming a peer competitor of the United States in the Western Pacific, American recognition of Taiwan's geostrategic importance may be growing. The PRC's increased power does add to its deterrence against American intervention, but US interests in maintaining a favorable balance of power are far more important than the risks associated with China's increased threat.

The PLA, already quantitatively superior to ROC armed forces, is gaining qualitatively as well
The ROC probably can defeat a PRC attack until around 2005, at which time the PLA's modernization – with Russian assistance – will pose a quantitative and qualitative threat difficult for Taiwan to match, even with purchases of American weapons and technology. A major arms race is under way in the Taiwan Strait, with both sides trying desperately to leverage their respective military advantages into a decisive checkmate.

US arms sales to Taiwan are critical and will probably continue
Despite the many restrictions on US arms sales to Taiwan, enough flow through the pipeline to provide the ROC with defensive capabilities against most forms of PRC aggression. Without these sales, Taiwan would be extremely vulnerable to Chinese intimidation; with the sales, Taipei can be moderately autonomous, if not quite independent. The level of US

arms sales fluctuates with both the nature of the PRC threat to Taiwan as well as the political relationships existing between Washington, Taipei and Beijing. Although these sales might increase as the PLA modernizes and as the PRC exercises its growing national power, US arms sales in themselves are no guarantee of Taiwan's security.

To date, there is no political solution to the Taiwan issue in sight, but the situation is fluid
In the final analysis, a resolution of the Taiwan question must come from the Chinese themselves on both sides of the Taiwan Strait. Thus far, however, neither side has been able to formulate a proposal acceptable to the other. In many respects, the political confrontation across the Strait is a continuation of the Chinese civil war, since in early 2000 the CCP and the KMT control the two sides' respective governments. This political competition is a zero-sum game – with hot and cold tactics – in which each side's proposals are in effect a demand that the other side surrender. Both sides seek to use the United States to their advantage, and both sides have had success and failure in these efforts. As the security climate in the Taiwan Strait becomes more pressurized, various 'wild cards' are emerging that might break through the political impasse and result in peaceful or non-peaceful resolution. These wild cards include track-II diplomatic efforts, the policy influence of the DPP on Taiwan and hardliners in Beijing, growing economic and cultural exchanges across the Taiwan Strait, and unexpected moves by political leaders, such as Lee Teng-hui's moving away from a 'one-China' policy.

The security of Taiwan is of international strategic concern
Taiwan's geostrategic importance has increased, not decreased, as a result of the collapse of the Soviet Union and the end of the Cold War. As China's geopolitical importance has grown relative to that of the United States and other great powers in the 1990s, Beijing increasingly has looked to the East and South Chinas Seas – and to the Pacific and Indian Oceans beyond – as areas into which it would like to project power and influence. This ambition, as natural as it may seem from China's point of view, runs counter to the maritime security interests of Japan, much of ASEAN, Australia, India and, most importantly, the United States – the current 'offshore balancer'. In the Asia–Pacific region, the island chain is a natural barrier to China's expansion of influence; and, in this island chain, Taiwan occupies a central position. From a strategic point of view, therefore, the security of Taiwan is of grave concern, since the island can either contribute to or impede the projection of Chinese power into the Western Pacific Basin. The revised US–Japan defense guidelines almost guarantee that, should Washington become involved in a future conflict in the Taiwan Strait, Tokyo will play a supportive role.

The military situation in the Taiwan Strait is increasingly volatile
It is difficult to gather accurate information on the PLA or its strategies to attack Taiwan. There also is no consensus on the duration of a conflict in the Taiwan Strait or the number of PLA troops and equipment necessary to defeat Taipei. Both sides have their strengths and weaknesses, but the overall trends point to both a quantitative and qualitative advantage accruing to the PRC no later than 2010. Since both Taipei and Beijing constantly prepare for conflict in the Taiwan Strait, and the two militaries are in close proximity, even a small incident may spark a war.

PRC missiles pose the greatest threat to Taiwan, since they may suffice to break the will of the Taiwanese people
War may break out at any time in the Taiwan Strait, and there are many scenarios by which the PLA may try to defeat Taiwan. In most conventional scenarios, the first priority for Taiwan's defense is to establish control over the air and sea surrounding Taiwan. The ROC is strongest in terms of air defense, but its air force can be exhausted by repeated PLA sorties. In terms of sea control, Taipei is somewhat weaker and may not be able to control the Taiwan Strait, although Beijing may not be able to control the waters to the east of Taiwan. The second priority for Taiwan's defense is to counter a blockade. The PRC can use submarines, mines, blocking ships and other devices to close Taiwan's harbors and restrict shipborne movement into and out of Taiwan ports, but this is a long and difficult process. By itself, a blockade of Taiwan would probably not bring Taipei to its knees, although it would cause severe economic dislocation. A third priority for Taiwan's defense is to counter PLA ground forces attempting to land on the island. Land operations on Taiwan present major problems for both the attacker and the defender; therefore, other factors – such as the effectiveness of special operations forces and the determination of local defense forces – would probably make the difference between victory and defeat for either side. However, the critical determinant in a war in the Taiwan Strait is probably the effectiveness of PLA missiles in breaking the will of the Taiwan people to resist. In this respect, Taiwan may be vulnerable.

The national and military strategies of the ROC are evolving but they have not yet solved the problem of long-term survival
Due to the nature of the modern PRC threat to Taiwan – unrelenting political confrontation and preparation for attack – the ROC must continually review and adjust its national strategy and its military strategy. Of the two types of threat faced by Taiwan, the political is more severe than the military at present, but the PLA's preparation for military conflict under modern conditions will require a strategic adjustment on the part of Taipei. Unfortunately, the restrictions under which Taiwan must

operate – such as no nuclear weapons – makes an effective defensive strategy difficult to conceptualize and implement.

Congress and the American public will probably continue to be supportive of Taiwan
Because Taiwan is a market democracy and friend of the United States, the American people and their representatives in Congress favor a US policy of continued friendship and support for Taiwan. Congress exercises considerable influence on US policy toward both Taiwan and China, and there is little or no inclination on Capitol Hill to compromise Taiwan's security interests for improved relations with Beijing. Indeed, Congress will act to ensure – through law if necessary – the continued implementation of the TRA's arms sales requirements and act as a brake on administration efforts to move 'strategic partnership' with China beyond the talking phase.

The principles on which Sino-American relations are built are under severe strain because of developments in China and Taiwan
The Taiwan issue has long been at the center of US–PRC relations – at least from the point of view of Beijing. The three joint communiqués and various administrative precedents gradually developed a set of principles governing the Taiwan issue in Sino-American relations. Since the mid-1980s, but especially since the beginning of the 1990s, these principles have been challenged by a series of trends: (a) the growing national power of the PRC, accompanied by a stronger sense of Chinese nationalism, including a desire for early unification with Taiwan; (b) democratization and Taiwanization within the ROC, giving voice to stronger demands for Taiwan's political separation from China; and (c) a dramatic shift in the international security environment of the United States, with China replacing Russia as the nation most likely to challenge US global and regional interests in coming decades.

The probability of a Sino-American confrontation over Taiwan is growing
Neither Beijing nor Washington wants such a confrontation, but the 1995–96 Taiwan Strait crisis proved to both countries that war is possible if the Taiwan issue is not handled carefully. Among the lessons learned from the crisis were: (a) the PRC will use force to intimidate Taiwan if ROC leaders move the island toward greater political autonomy; (b) the United States will intervene on Taiwan's behalf to prevent PRC intimidation; and (c) actions by the Taiwan government can bring the United States and China to the brink of war. Since 1997 the Clinton administration has tried to adjust its policies toward the Taiwan issue, but the 'three no's', 'interim agreements' and 'track-II' efforts may have had unintended effects. Taipei suspects the United States is now pushing

Taiwan to become part of communist China, pressure resulting not in capitulation but rather stronger Taiwanese expressions of separation from a communist-dominated China. At the same time, hardliners in Beijing are now more convinced than ever that the United States would not intervene to protect Taiwan. Despite their positive motivation, Clinton's policies seemed to be increasing the prospects for war in the Taiwan Strait and a Sino-American conflict.

Taiwan will benefit from TMD, but its overall security will become more dependent on external factors in the early twenty-first century
In all likelihood, the ROC will acquire PAC-3 and Aegis-based systems for point missile defense over the next several years. This will increase Taiwan's ability to defeat some, but not all, PRC cruise and ballistic missiles that might be launched should war occur in the Taiwan Strait. The ability of China to produce large numbers of guided missiles and to acquire state-of-the-art conventional offensive weaponry from Russia and other sources means that Taiwan's narrow technological advantage over the PRC will probably be overwhelmed in five to ten years (2005–10). At that time, without intervention by the United States, Taiwan could probably be defeated by a determined PLA attack. Whether the United States intervenes or not will be likely to have less to do with Taiwan policies than (a) domestic American politics; (b) international circumstances such as global demands on American military forces; and (c) perceptions by US policy-makers of China's threat to American interests at the time.

Other than military preparedness, the most important contribution Taiwan can make to its own security is political astuteness
It is Taiwan's destiny to be caught in the middle as great powers compete for influence in the Western Pacific. Historically, small nations in such positions have either been absorbed by larger countries or have prospered by learning how to play the power game to their advantage. There is no reason to be unduly pessimistic about Taiwan's future, unless the Taiwan people and their elected officials contribute to their society's demise by alienating both their enemies and their friends, while at the same time weakening the island's social cohesion.

US RESPONSE TO PRC USE OF FORCE

In concluding this study, it is important to examine the probability of American intervention on Taiwan's behalf. Indeed, as demonstrated repeatedly in this work, American intervention is one of the most important determinants of whether the PRC would or would not be successful in the employment of force against Taiwan. Without US intervention, the PRC might well be successful in defeating Taiwan; with US intervention, the likelihood of Taiwan's defeat could be reduced to near nil proportions. However, whether the United States decides to intervene would be greatly influenced by the circumstances surrounding the crisis. No doubt, the first and preferred US option would be political: that is, diplomatic entreaties to try to stop the use of force before it began, to limit its escalation, and to end it as soon as possible. These efforts at diplomatic containment would continue throughout the crisis and may or may not be successful. But, assuming military intervention became a necessary option, three factors would be critical in the US decision: first, the reason the PRC elected to use force against Taiwan; second, the type of force being used; and, third, the circumstances in place at the time.

Table 7 lists various reasons which the PRC might use to justify force against Taiwan and speculates whether the United States would likely intervene on Taiwan's behalf.

Table 7

Justifications for PRC use of force and the American response

Reason PRC might use force	Likelihood of US military intervention
Taiwan moves toward independence	Uncertain; likely disagreement between administration and Congress over Taiwan's right of self-determination
Internal chaos on Taiwan	Uncertain but unlikely; USA does not want to be involved in chaotic Taiwan domestic political situation
Foreign intervention in Taiwan affairs	Likely, since this is an invalid justification; USA, Japan and Russia will not interfere in Taiwan domestic affairs
Taipei refuses for long period of time to negotiate terms of unification	Likely; unless ROC seen to provoke PRC attack
Taiwan develops nuclear weapons	Perhaps; USA fairly confident ROC will not use nuclear weapons against mainland
Taiwan's model of democracy threatens to undermine CCP rule on mainland	Likely; PRC seen as unprovoked aggressor
Taiwan acquires theater ballistic missile defense system	Likely; PRC seen as unprovoked aggressor
ROC gains wider diplomatic recognition at expense of PRC	Likely; PRC seen as unprovoked aggressor
Taiwan rejects 'one-China' policy	Likely; as long as Taiwan does not declare independence
World community accepts idea of 'two Chinas'	Likely; PRC seen as unprovoked aggressor

As can be seen in Table 7, there are few justifications for the PRC to use force against Taiwan that would not risk American military intervention. The exceptions might be (a) Taiwan moving in the direction of independence, in which case the US response would be uncertain because of probable disagreement between the Congress and the administration over conflicting American interests – such as support for Taiwan's right of self-determination versus conflict avoidance with the PRC; (b) internal chaos on Taiwan, in which case the United States might be hamstrung due to the lack of a viable government in Taipei with which to coordinate; and (c) Taiwan developing nuclear weapons, in which case the United States might impose sanctions on Taipei for proliferation. Most of the other justifications Beijing might use to attack Taiwan would be rejected by the United States. In these cases, the United States would see the PRC as an aggressor and probably respond with military intervention.

The probability of American intervention becomes a little more difficult to determine when considering the many different kinds of force the PRC might threaten or use against Taiwan. For example, an unprovoked, land–air–sea missile PRC attack would probably result in quick and decisive American intervention. Chinese sabotage of Taiwan's electrical system, however, probably would not draw the Seventh Fleet into nearby waters. Table 8 displays the various types of force which the PRC might use, with an accompanying assessment of the probability of American military intervention.

As Table 8 shows, the type of force being threatened or used against Taiwan can have an important impact on the likelihood of American military intervention. Significant uses of force are more likely to result in US intervention: for example, missile testing on Taiwan territory, enforced blockade of Taiwan, any use of nuclear weapons, any direct attack on Taiwan or the Pescadores, attacks or threats against ships in international waters around Taiwan, attacks on ROC offshore islands, and mobilization of the PLA for an apparent war against Taiwan.

Low levels of force are least likely to result in American intervention: for example, agitation or sabotage, verbal threats, Chinese fishing-boat nuisance, economic or political pressure, accidents in the Taiwan Strait, harassment of ROC fishing vessels, increases in PLA strength in the Taiwan region but not mobilization, and propaganda attacks.

Still more complexity is introduced in the US decision to intervene when the circumstances under which the threat or use of force occurred are factored in. For example, Washington would be more inclined to assist Taipei if the PRC initiated an attack with no provocation than if Taipei deliberately caused a crisis in the Taiwan Strait to secure US backing for its independence or US forces were busy elsewhere. Table 9 lists various circumstances surrounding the use of force in the Taiwan Strait and speculates on whether the United States would be inclined to intervene militarily on Taiwan's behalf.

Table 8
PRC use of force and the US response

Type of force used by PRC	Likelihood of US military intervention
Agitation or sabotage on Taiwan through infiltration of spies and other agents	Unlikely
Fishing boat flotilla harassment of Taiwan's ports	Unlikely
Massive show of PLA force in Taiwan area	Perhaps; US show of force to show determination and to deter escalation
Unarmed missile testing near Taiwan	Unlikely; unless landing too close to Taiwan, then perhaps show of force
Unarmed missile testing on unpopulated Taiwan territory	Likely; strong US show of force to show determination and deter escalation
Occupation of ROC-claimed remote or minor offshore islands	Unlikely, but perhaps; show of force to show US determination and deter escalation
Verbal announcement of blockade	Unlikely; but heightened alert status and signal readiness to deploy
Execution of blockade	Likely
Electromagnetic bombing to paralyze Taiwan's military communications	Likely, if nuclear weapon used; but this scenario improbable
Airborne landings on Taiwan	Likely
Missile attacks on Taiwan	Likely
Air–sea battles over and around Taiwan	Likely
Amphibious landing on Taiwan	Likely
Use of economic or political means to isolate Taiwan	Unlikely
Staged 'accidents' in Taiwan Strait between fishing fleets or naval units	Unlikely; but would monitor closely to see where it leads
Naval harassment of ships in international waters surrounding Taiwan or calling at Taiwan ports	Unlikely; but would monitor closely since freedom of the seas important US interest
Attack of Kinmen and Matsu	Likely; but deployments intended to deter threat to Pescadores and Taiwan, not necessarily to save offshore islands
Attack of Pescadores	Likely; island group viewed as being essential to defense of Taiwan
Dramatic increase in PLA capabilities in military regions opposite Taiwan	Unlikely; but monitor closely and heighten preparation to deploy
Large-scale military exercises in Taiwan Strait region	Unlikely; unless exercises too close to Taiwan, then deploy show of force
Verbal threats to use force	Unlikely; but monitor closely
Submarine and other naval activity near Taiwan ports but no use of force	Unlikely; but monitor closely and prepare to deploy
PLA aircraft deliberately crossing the middle line of the Taiwan Strait, prompting repeated ROC air alerts	Unlikely; but monitor closely
Great increase in PRC propaganda attacks against Taiwan or its leaders	Unlikely; but monitor situation
PLA mobilizes forces in Taiwan Strait in apparent preparation to attack Taiwan	Probably; deployments intended to signal US determination and deter escalation
Mining the Taiwan Strait or Taiwan ports	Likely
Use of nuclear or other weapons of mass destruction	Likely; although scenario is improbable
PLA harassment of Taiwan fishing boats	Unlikely

Table 9 demonstrates that the circumstances surrounding the outbreak of violence in the Taiwan Strait would play an important and perhaps decisive role in the US decision to intervene militarily on Taiwan's behalf. The likelihood of US intervention would be strongest if the PRC attacked Taiwan without provocation or under circumstances such as: a PRC leader sought to use the Taiwan issue to firm up his or her political authority; Beijing sought to become a regional hegemon; the PRC adopted an anti-American strategy and policy; the PRC retreated on its economic and political reforms; China was disintegrating; the USA changed its policy from engagement to containment of China; the PRC applied political or economic pressure on Taiwan to push it into an incident; or the PLA was seeking to take advantage of ROC armed forces weakness.

The likelihood of US intervention would be weakest under circumstances such as: political instability on Taiwan or in the United States; if Taipei deliberately tried to precipitate a crisis in the Taiwan Strait; if China were embarked on a clear path of democratization; if the United States became isolationist; or if the United States redrew its Pacific line of defense eastward to Guam or Hawaii.

A great many circumstances would have a significant but uncertain influence on the US decision to intervene: for example, sharply divided opinion in the United States over intervention; the US military was heavily overextended; the US alliance with Japan was in deep trouble; Congress or the American people were far less supportive of Taiwan; Taipei formally declared Taiwan an independent nation-state separate from China; the conflict began accidentally; or it was clear the two Chinese sides had determined to fight the war to the finish despite American entreaties.

Theoretically, the combination of these factors – China's justification for the use of force, the level of force employed by the PRC, and the circumstances surrounding the use or threat of force in the Taiwan Strait – creates various scenarios of likely, unlikely or uncertain American military intervention. Tables 10, 11 and 12 contain the elements of these scenarios – but not the scenarios themselves – for the purpose of trying to pinpoint better the conditions under which force might be used in the Taiwan Strait and the United States might become involved.

Since Taiwan's ability to resist PRC force would be vastly improved if the ROC were aided by the United States, it follows that Beijing would prefer to use force against Taiwan under conditions least likely to bring American intervention: these conditions are reflected in Table 11. However, there are at least five problems which PRC strategists face in trying to take advantage of these conditions: first, the PRC has limited ability to control levels of social stability or instability on Taiwan; second, Beijing has no influence over political stability or instability in the United States; third, the levels of force unlikely to precipitate American intervention may be inadequate to defeat the ROC; fourth, the CCP does

Table 9
Circumstances of war and American intervention

Circumstances surrounding conflict	Likelihood of US military intervention
Sharply divided opinion in the US government over intervention	Uncertain due to nature of American political system
Few American military resources to send to Taiwan area, e.g. one or more regional crises already underway	Uncertain due to American military caution not to be overextended
Political instability in PRC leadership; Taiwan issue being used to gain political advantage in CCP power struggle	Likely; but will try to avoid helping ultranationalists coming to power in Beijing
Political instability in Taipei, with one major faction in Taiwan power struggle asking for PRC intervention	Uncertain, but unlikely; difficult decision in a highly fluid situation
Political instability in USA: e.g. crisis in American presidency, severe economic dislocation, executive–legislative deadlock	Unlikely due to American political system
Taipei deliberately precipitates crisis in Taiwan Strait to gain US support for independence	Unlikely at first; but domestic US pressure for intervention may overcome administration's reluctance
PRC honestly believes that Taiwan is slipping away with no future chance of unification	Likely; but reluctantly since USA does not support Taiwan independence
Beijing trying to teach Taiwan a lesson but not attempting to defeat Taiwan	Uncertain, depends on circumstances and level of force: if too strong a military threat and too long a duration, probably yes; if moderate and short, maybe no
US alliance with Japan in jeopardy or in shambles	Uncertain; entire American Far Eastern strategy needs reexamination
PRC seems intent on becoming regional hegemon	Likely
PRC adopts anti-USA strategy and policy	Likely
PRC retreats on reforms and becomes more inward looking and xenophobic	Likely; but cautious so as to avoid worsening conditions in China
China disintegrating with Beijing attempting last-ditch effort to gain control of Taiwan	Likely; but not for purposes of dividing China
US change of policy from engagement to containment or some other hostile policy toward China	Likely
US change of policy to one of actively supporting Taiwan's unification with mainland	Likely; not to separate Taiwan from China but to compel Beijing to use peaceful means of reunification
US Congress far less supportive of Taiwan	Uncertain; administration's decision to intervene based on other circumstances at the time

Circumstances surrounding conflict	Likelihood of US military intervention
American people far less supportive of Taiwan	Uncertain; depends on administration and congressional assessment of US interests at the time and circumstances of conflict
DPP assumes control of Taiwan government through elections	Likely; but reluctantly since USA does not support Taiwan independence
Referendum held on Taiwan with results showing large majority of people want independence	Likely; but reluctantly since USA does not support Taiwan independence
Taiwan government formally declares Taiwan an independent nation-state	Uncertain; perhaps only with great public and congressional pressure; USA does not necessarily extend diplomatic recognition to Republic of Taiwan
Accident at sea, errant early-warning alarm, misreading of military exercises, or wayward missile causes exchange of fire between PRC and ROC	Unlikely; try to stop the fighting as soon as possible and return to *status quo ante bellum*
Too much PRC pressure causes Taipei to lash out in some incident	Uncertain but likely; try to stop the fighting as soon as possible and return to *status quo ante bellum*
Determination by both sides to fight it out to the end	Uncertain; reluctant to be involved but bitter policy debate in Washington with results unknown
PLA seeks to take advantage of weaker ROC armed forces	Likely
China becoming more democratic	Unlikely; vital US interest in not reversing that trend
USA becomes isolationist	Unlikely
USA withdraws from forward presence in Western Pacific	Unlikely

not want China to become democratic; and, fifth, the PRC has very limited influence over whether the United States becomes isolationist or redraws its line of defense in the Western Pacific.

But, in addition to the factor of American intervention, there is also the strongly determining factor of whether Taiwan's society is strong and unified in the face of the PRC threat or divided and weak. If Taiwan is strong and unified – even in the absence of US intervention – then the only certain way to defeat the ROC would be a successful PLA amphibious invasion, no doubt accompanied by blockade, missile attack, airborne invasion and air–sea battles over the Taiwan Strait and Taiwan Island. Without US intervention, this kind of attack might defeat Taiwan. However, these circumstances – a strong, unified Taiwan and massive PRC

Table 10
Conditions of likely US intervention

PRC justification	*PRC levels of force*	*Circumstances*
Foreign intervention in Taiwan affairs	Unarmed missile testing on Taiwan territory	PRC leader using Taiwan to further his/her political power
Taipei refuses for too long to negotiate	Imposition of blockade of Taiwan	Taipei lashes out because of too much PRC pressure
Taiwan's democracy threatens CCP rule	Electromagnetic attack on Taiwan's communications	PRC seeking to become regional hegemon
Taiwan to acquire theater ballistic missile defense system	Airborne landing on Taiwan	PRC adopts anti-US strategy and policies
ROC gaining too much diplomatic recognition	Missile attacks on Taiwan	PRC retreats on reforms and reverts to extremism
World community accepting idea of 'two Chinas'	Air–sea battles over and around Taiwan	China disintegrating
Taiwan abandons 'one-China' principle but does not declare independence	Amphibious landing on Taiwan	USA changes policy to one more hostile toward China
	Naval harassment of shipping in international waters around Taiwan	PLA seeks to take advantage of ROC military weakness
	Attack of Kinmen or Matsu	
	Attack of Pescadores	
	Mobilization of PLA in preparation for attack of Taiwan	
	Mining Taiwan Strait or Taiwan harbors	
	Use of weapons of mass destruction against Taiwan	

Table 11
Conditions of unlikely US intervention

PRC justification	PRC levels of force	Circumstances
Internal chaos on Taiwan	PRC infiltration and sabotage	Political instability on Taiwan; one side invites PRC to intervene
	PRC fishing boats creating incidents in Taiwan's ports	Political instability in USA
	Announced but not enforced blockade	Taipei deliberately precipitates crisis in Taiwan Strait to gain US support for independence
	Economic and political isolation of Taiwan	China becoming democratic
	Staged 'accidents' in Taiwan Strait	USA becomes isolationist
	PLA harassing Taiwan fishing boats	USA redraws Pacific line of defense far eastward
	Increase in numbers of PLA in regions opposite Taiwan	
	Verbal threats to use force	
	Submarine or other PLA naval activity near Taiwan	
	PLA aircraft crossing middle line of Taiwan Strait	
	Increase in PRC propaganda against Taiwan or its leaders	

Table 12
Conditions of uncertain US response or intervention

PRC justification	PRC levels of force	Circumstances
Taiwan moves toward independence	Show of force in Taiwan area	Sharply divided opinion in US over intervention
Taiwan develops nuclear weapons	Unarmed missile testing near Taiwan	US military resources stretched thin due to other regional crises
	Occupation of ROC-claimed islets far away from Taiwan	Beijing teaching Taipei a lesson but not intending to attack Taiwan
	Large-scale military exercises in Taiwan Strait region	US alliance with Japan in jeopardy
		Congress not supportive of Taiwan
		American people not supportive of Taiwan
		Taiwan government formally declares Taiwan independence
		Accidental cause of conflict in Taiwan Strait
		Both Chinese sides determined to fight it out to the end

285

use of force – are the precise conditions most likely to draw American intervention.

On the other hand, if Taiwan were unstable due to social chaos or political paralysis, then many of the possible uses of force against Taiwan could result in Taipei's capitulation – perhaps even with American intervention. Under conditions of social or political weakness, coordination of the island's defenses and summons to resist could be ineffective. Taiwan might be able to survive with US support, but social chaos on Taiwan is one of the very few conditions under which American intervention is improbable. The United States would not want to become involved in a situation risking war with China when Taiwan was unstable. Since China has at least some influence over social stability on Taiwan, it probably should be assumed that one of Beijing's principal strategies is the undermining of social and political stability on the island – a strategy consistent with Chinese methods of indirect approach.

Since there is no guarantee that China can be successful either in undermining Taiwan's social stability or in preventing American military intervention, Chinese leaders must be prepared to fight the United States if they are sincere in their determination to prevent Taiwan from becoming an independent state. Several conclusions relative to PRC strategy and policy can be drawn from this analysis:

1. Beijing can safely maneuver in a 'low-risk' threat environment to try to pressure Taipei and Washington and can be expected to do so.
2. The PRC will probably do more to undermine social, economic and political stability on Taiwan.
3. China will prepare to use higher levels of force and accept more risks to achieve its goal of national unification.
4. Beijing might well conclude that a military confrontation with the United States may be necessary to achieve unification.
5. Chinese leaders will try to bide their time on the Taiwan issue, waiting for circumstances which might weaken Taiwan internally and reduce the probability of American military intervention.
6. At the same time, PRC leaders are under a great deal of pressure – both from hardliners within the party and PLA and indirectly from independent advocates on Taiwan – to prevent Taiwan independence before it is too late.
7. To deter or defeat the United States, China will design and deploy the PLA to inflict unacceptably high losses on US forces.
8. As China develops these capabilities, its political leaders will attempt to neutralize American opposition to China and its unification objectives.

In some ways, these conclusions are the logical extension of current trends, which are not overly promising in terms of a peaceful resolution of the Taiwan issue. However, as the next and final section suggests, there is still time for all sides to reconsider their views and perhaps find a new equilibrium in the Taiwan Strait.

POLICY SUGGESTIONS

Taiwan's security in the future will be heavily influenced by three inter-locking factors: developments on Taiwan itself, cross-Strait relations and the level of American support for Taiwan. Taiwan's policy choices right-fully reside with its people and their elected representatives because it is a democracy; however, insofar as Taiwan's security is dependent on continued American support, those choices should take into consideration the interests and views of the United States. This is a fact of life for Taiwan, unless it wants to face the PRC threat alone.

From an American perspective, Taiwan is closely tied to China cultur-ally, historically and geographically. And since China is an international actor of strategic proportions, US policy toward Taiwan has to take into account the nature of Sino-American relations. Most Americans do not approve of the communist government of Beijing; and a long-term US goal is to see China become a market democracy, as Taiwan now is. However, the United States cannot function as a global leader without dealing extensively with the PRC across the entire spectrum of security, political, economic, environmental and other international issues.

Since the United States must deal with China, it is important to Washington that cooperative relations with Beijing be maintained. And because the Taiwan issue is so important to Chinese leaders, the United States must seek to manage the Taiwan issue in ways least likely to disrupt Sino-American relations. This was accomplished with some success through the mid-1990s, at which time two developments began to disrupt the US 'dual-track' policy and the basic principles governing the Taiwan issue. These two developments were the growing power and rising nation-alism of mainland China, and trends toward independence on Taiwan. Together, these two forces have increased tension in the Taiwan area, loosened the one-China 'glue' that held US–PRC–Taiwan relations together in relative stability, and deepened divisions within US policy-making circles over how best to respond.

Taiwan bears considerable responsibility, in the view of many Americans, for growing tensions in the Taiwan Strait. Lee Teng-hui in particular is singled out for criticism because of his 'pushing the envelope' in lobbying for a trip to the United States in 1995, and his redefinition of Taiwan's one-China policy caused the mini-crisis in 1999. But, in reality, President Lee is but the tip of the iceberg of Taiwanese nationalism; and that sense of unique identity will not be suppressed by Beijing or Washington or even Taipei – at least not without considerable force. Some way has to be found to allow expression of Taiwanese nationalism, even if it is not allowed to precipitate a war in the Taiwan Strait.

Beijing has sought by way of threat and intimidation to stifle Taiwanese nationalism, while the Clinton administration has sought to restrict Taiwan's freedom of international movement toward the same end. Such policies will not result in Taiwan's acceptance of local status under the PRC, but rather result in a vicious circle of increased tensions in the Taiwan Strait and added pressure on Taiwan – all of which will contribute to probable conflict involving the United States.

The challenge for Beijing and Taipei is to find an escape from the zero-sum game in which only one side can win. With mutual distrust running so high, it is doubtful such an opportunity will emerge under the Lee Teng-hui government. But perhaps a new government in Taipei after May 2000 will discover both the will and the flexibility – on both sides of the Taiwan Strait – to find a new equilibrium. Such is the hope for peace, and it can only occur if all sides act responsibly.

The role for the United States is both crucial and secondary. Washington cannot control the outcome in the Taiwan Strait, but it can pursue policies which encourage both sides to find a peaceful and fair settlement – even while the United States protects its own interests. These interests are important to identify:

- The United States has interests in a peaceful resolution of the Taiwan issue, but not at the cost of pressuring Taiwan to become part of a communist-dominated China.
- The United States has interests in a cooperative, friendly relationship with the PRC, but not at the cost of abandoning the people of Taiwan, violating American values, and bypassing the TRA.
- The United States has interests in supporting Taiwan and maintaining friendly, unofficial relations with its authorities, but not at the cost of defending Taiwan's independence with American lives and treasure.
- The United States has interests in integrating China into the world's council of great powers, but not at the cost of allowing Chinese hegemony.
- The United States has interests in more humane, democratic and free-market institutions in China, but not at the cost of ignoring pragmatism and courtesy in dealing with Beijing.

It may well be – as this book has demonstrated – that war will occur in the Taiwan Strait; and, if this happens, the probability of a Sino-American conflict is quite high. War is a price all sides must be willing to pay, if their principles and interests are to be protected. On the other hand,

288

peace is possible, even if a sudden resolution of the Taiwan issue may not be forthcoming. Decision-makers in Beijing, Taipei and Washington have an excellent opportunity over the next five years to devise a new framework for their relationship. At minimum, it would seem that

1. The interests of China must be protected by firm commitments from Taipei that Taiwan is part of China and that it will not seek to become an independent country, separate from China, and from Washington that the United States will not support Taiwan independence.
2. The interests of Taiwan must be protected by guarantees of its autonomy from communist rule, a respectful place in the international community, security from threat or intimidation, and freedom from US pressure to enter into negotiations with Beijing.
3. The interests of the United States must be protected by peace and stability in the Taiwan Strait region, relations with both the mainland and Taiwan in a manner consistent with the joint communiqués and the TRA, and assurances that both sides of the Taiwan Strait are committed to a gradual, peaceful and mutually beneficial resolution of their differences.
4. The interests of the Asia–Pacific community must be protected by assurances from Beijing that it will not seek regional hegemony, and from Taipei that it will not precipitate a war with the mainland by rejecting the idea of a united China in the future.

Is such a framework possible? At this point in time it is premature to say. However, it can be reliably forecast that without such a framework, or one similarly designed to protect the interests of all concerned parties, Taiwan's security in the post-Deng Xiaoping era will progressively become more tenuous and war in the Taiwan Strait will become more likely.

Appendix 1

Excerpts from Report of the US Secretary of Defense on the Pattern of Military Modernization in China, November 1998[1]

1. The goals of Chinese security strategy and military strategy

Security Strategy

China's primary national goal is to become a strong, unified, and wealthy nation that is respected as a great power in the world and as the pre-eminent power in Asia. The Chinese see their country as a developing power whose nuclear forces and seat on the UN Security Council already bestow some of the attributes of a great power. They look forward however, to achieving a status of parity in economic, political, and military strength with the world's leading powers by the middle of the next century.

China's grand strategy for achieving this national goal is to promote rapid and sustained economic growth; raise the per capita income of its people to the global norm for advanced nations; improve the social quality of life for its people including heath and education on a par with the leading nations of the world; raise technological levels in sciences and industry; maintain the political unity and stability of the nation; protect national sovereignty and territorial integrity; secure China's access to global resources; and promote China's role as one of the five, or six major poles in a new multipolar world.

Although China continues to promote the notion of national self-sufficiency and independence, its strategy also encompasses greater integration into global affairs. This involves commercial policies in order to gain maximum benefits from foreign trade and investment, which have served as the twin engines of China's economic development. Politically, there is a greater willingness to participate in multinational fora and a public relations effort to foster a benign image of a China interested in peaceful development and progressing toward meeting international norms. China does not seek hegemony in Asia or elsewhere, although its leaders hope to achieve a position where Asian countries and those with interests in Asia take no actions which conflict with China's interests.

290

This strategy also encompasses a domestic political component, namely the continued government of China by the Chinese Communist Party (CCP). China's strategic vision is that of the CCP and its leaders remain firmly committed to its realization. The CCP has ruled China for nearly half a century and, during that period, its leaders have exhibited no inclination to share their monopoly of power. China's leaders, however, are beset by a host of internal problems – some the result of the country's economic success, others the legacy of the planned economy they are gradually dismantling – which could threaten the stability and longevity of the regime if unresolved over time. Large-scale unemployment (likely to grow as reform of state-owned enterprises proceeds), separatist and human rights agitation, worker migration from rural to urban areas, an ever growing population, environmental and ecological concerns, and widespread corruption within both state and Party entities are contributing to popular discontent and disillusionment over the future of both China and its Communist Party.

China's security strategy strives to enhance the military, political, and economic components of national power. Beijing places top priority on continued economic growth and industrial sector development. China's National's Defense Law identifies six military tasks that underlie this objective:

(1) Modernize the People's Liberation Army (PLA);
(2) Defend China's territorial sovereignty;
(3) Deter and resist aggression by global and regional hegemons;
(4) Support the Party's reunification policies;
(5) Ensure domestic security and stability;
(6) Support the national economic modernization program.

China seeks to take advantage of the current relatively benign international environment, in which there are no major external threats to China's security, by selectively modernizing its military forces in a measured and fiscally responsible manner. Beijing assesses that, barring a declaration of independence by Taiwan, the chance of a large-scale unavoidable conflict is almost negligible over the next decade and a half.

Military Strategy

Since the early 1990s the focus of China's military strategy has been on preparing for potential military contingencies along China's southeastern flank, especially in the Taiwan Strait and South China Sea. Thus China's goal is to field forces capable of rapidly deploying to fight and win a future regional war under high-technology conditions along China's periphery. The Persian Gulf War underscored for Beijing the need to improve the PLA's ability to fight against an adversary which possesses advanced information technologies and long-range, precision-guided weapons. Chinese perceptions of an emerging military–technological revolution have increased the urgency of gaining the capability to fight a high-technology war. To realize this goal, the PLA has undertaken a long-term military modernization program which currently is focused on reducing the overall size of the force by some 500,000 personnel; equipping it with more modern weapons, either acquired from abroad or produced domestically; and developing a better educated and technologically skilled force, both in the officer and enlisted ranks. To support and sustain these forces, China is trying to establish a more effective national mobilization system for shifting the military, government and industry from peacetime to war footing. If war were to become inevitable, China's military strategy would be to contain and limit the conflict, and to fight with sufficient force and tactics to win as quickly as possible, achieving a military solution before outside powers could intervene and before vital trade and investment were disrupted.

2. **Trends in Chinese strategy regarding the political goals of the People's Republic of China in the Asia–Pacific region and its political and military presence in other regions of the world, including Central Asia, Southwest Asia, Europe, Middle East, and Latin America**

China's strategy to establish itself as the leading political power in Asia is based an the premise of expanding Chinese influence throughout the region through active diplomacy and the development of cooperative economic ties, political support for initiatives to maintain regional peace and stability, and an expanded role in supporting multilateral organizations. This strategy has led China to participate in multilateral organizations such as the ASEAN Regional Forum, in an effort to defuse territorial disputes with the ASEAN nations by diplomacy rather than through force. In addition, China has sought to reduce the potential for conflict by resorting to confidence building measures with some of its most important Asian neighbors, including Russia and several of the Central Asian republics. This political strategy also is reflected in China's efforts to reduce tensions and maintain stability on the Korean peninsula.

The Chinese realize, however, that attaining recognition as the preeminent political power in Asia will require the weakening of US political influence in the region. Although China has no plan to lead a faction or bloc of nations in directly challenging US power, its international political activities and certain of its economic and military policies are designed to achieve the same result. Beijing espouses a multipolar view of the world where power is split equally among five or six nations or blocs and is engaged in gathering political support for this view.

Outside of the Asia–Pacific region, China is pursuing an assertive, world-wide diplomatic campaign aimed at promoting Beijing's positions on such issues as Taiwan, human rights, proliferation and trade. In recent years, China's goals have turned increasingly to the support of economic and commercial interests as exemplified by China's participation in the Asia–Pacific Economic Cooperation (APEC) forum and its efforts to join the World Trade Organization (WTO). Beijing remains committed to maintaining if not expanding, its political and economic presence in such areas as Central and Southwest Asia, Europe, Latin America, and Africa; however, China has no ambitions to establish a military presence in these regions.

3. **Developments in Chinese military doctrine, focusing on (but not limited to) efforts to exploit the emerging Revolution in Military Affairs or to conduct preemptive strikes**

China's military doctrine – commonly referred to as 'local war under high tech conditions' – while still defined by the precepts of People's War and active defense is focused on preparing Chinese military forces to fight small-scale, regional conflicts along China's periphery. Execution of this doctrine requires smaller, more specialized quick-reaction forces capable of rapidly dealing with border incursions or striking outside China's borders. By implication, this doctrine, although defensive in nature, requires that the PLA possess a limited offensive and force projections capability; it also includes the option of preemptive military action.

Chinese military planners are working to incorporate the concepts of modern warfare attributed to the Revolution in Military Affairs to Chinese military doctrine, particularly as they relate to information operations and strike warfare. Beijing is engaged concurrently in a weapons modernization program intended to fill short-term gaps in its defense and to improve, over the longer term, the military's capability to counter more powerful forces. For example, Beijing is developing or seeking to acquire such force multipliers as mobile ballistic missile systems, land-attack cruise missiles, and advanced surface-to-air missiles. China also is working to ameliorate weaknesses in C4I, training, and logistics so as to improve gradually the PLA's overall warfighting capability.

4. **Efforts by the People's Republic of China to enhance its capabilities in the area of nuclear weapons development**

China has embarked on a ballistic missile modernization program and is gradually replacing its liquid-propellant missiles with solid-propellant missiles. A warhead modernization program probably exists to complement the missile program and the evaluation of new warhead technologies likely was completed by July 1996, when China announced its nuclear test moratorium. However, China's experience with the presumed newer warhead technologies is very limited and China could, in the future, encounter difficulties in its development or maintenance programs.

5. **Efforts by the People's Republic of China to develop long-range air-to-air or air defense missiles designed to target special support aircraft such as Airborne Warning and Control System (AWACS) aircraft, Joint Surveillance and Target Attack Radar System (JSTARS) aircraft, or other command and control, intelligence, airborne early warning, or electronic aircraft**

Air-to-Air Missiles

China is not developing an air-to-air missile (AAM) specifically designed to counter special mission aircraft such as the Airborne Warning and Control System and the Joint Tactical Surveillance Targeting and Reconnaissance System. However, there are AAMs in China's inventory which could be used against these aircraft and Beijing is acquiring more modem missiles which could threaten them, to include indigenous versions of an advanced medium-range air-to-air missile (AMRAAM).

Surface-to-Air Missiles

The capabilities demonstrated by coalition forces against Iraq during the early stages of Operation Desert Storm provided a vivid demonstration to Beijing that its vision of an adequate air defense fell woefully short in the face of precision weapons, cruise missiles, and stealth aircraft. In the aftermath of the Persian Gulf War, Beijing embarked on a measured effort to procure a modern integrated air defense system. To date, China has purchased from Russia two variants of the SA-101/GRUMBLE long-range surface-to-air missile (SAM) system, as well as the SA-15/GAUNTLET short-range tactical air defense missile system. China also is developing a number of indigenous air defense systems, including the HQ-9 advanced long-range SAM and the HQ-7 short-range tactical SAM. The HQ-9 is intended to counter high-performance aircraft, cruise missiles and tactical ballistic missiles. The HQ-7 – also known as the FM-80 – includes both land-based and naval variants. China's air defense capability is expected to improve over time as it develops its own SAM system and procures additional missiles and technology from foreign sources with the ultimate goal of integrating these systems into a cohesive infrastructure. While it may take several decades to realize this goal, Beijing already has demonstrated a rudimentary local integrated air defense capability with its mobile, Tactical Air Defense System.

6. Efforts by the People's Republic of China to develop a capability to conduct 'information warfare' at the strategic, operational, and tactical levels of war

In recent years, the PLA has shown an exceptional interest in information warfare (IW) and has begun programs to develop IW capabilities at the strategic, operational and tactical levels as part of its overall military modernization effort. The PLA's interest in IW is reflected particularly in the number of articles which appear frequently in military publications and in the use of IW-related scenarios in exercises and wargames.

The PLA's desire to develop a capability to conduct IW at the strategic level is best mirrored in the numerous articles and papers on military strategic and doctrinal issues as they relate to IW. These articles suggest that the PLA, at a minimum, understands the requirements involved in integrating the technical and operational elements of IW in order to attack the enemy's decision-making systems, apply military deception, and conduct operational security, psychological operations, and electronic warfare. There also are recurring references to innovative training and education programs designed to prepare China's military forces for 'local war under high tech conditions,' which includes an IW dimension.

At the operational level, Chinese military writers often have noted that the information gathered by the US prior to and during the 1991 Gulf War provided the coalition forces with a critical advantage over the forces of Saddam Hussein. In an effort to counter this advantage, the PLA is improving its indigenous capabilities to collect, process and disseminate information. The PLA also is said to be incorporating IW – including concepts learned from exploiting US military doctrine – in studies and exercises aimed at improving its staff planning process and moving the PLA toward 'jointness.' Recently, a series of articles in the official Liberation Army Daily described military exercises which incorporated such IW concepts as computer network attack and computer network defend exercises at both the operational level and tactical levels. These exercises also included elements of electronic warfare, psychological operations, military deception, operations security, and physical destruction, representing the full spectrum of IW at the operational level.

At the tactical level, the Chinese military appears to be focused largely on information warfare as it relates specifically to electronic warfare (EW). China recognizes that the army which is capable of achieving 'information superiority' on the battlefield in future high-tech wars will seize the initiative and attain victory. As such, the PLA views EW as in integral part of its IW planning and is currently emphasizing improvements in EW training and acquisitions of more modern EW equipment.

7. Development by the People's Republic of China of capabilities in the area of electronic warfare

China views electronic warfare (EW) as a fourth dimension of ground, naval, and air combat. It currently is engaged in an extensive program to upgrade its EW technology, equipment and training, China's current inventory of EW equipment includes a combination of 1950s to 1980s vintage technology. This equipment appears to be fielded haphazardly, with a few 'select' units receiving the most modern equipment. China is seeking to procure state-of-the-art intercept, direction finding, and jamming equipment to upgrade poorly equipped ground-based, ship-borne and airborne forces, and to serve as a template for a robust reverse-engineering effort. In so doing, China has established close commercial ties with electronic companies in numerous foreign countries.

Ground Forces

The PLA ground forces consider EW a critical area for modernization efforts, as it can act as combat multiplier whether on offense or defense. The PLA will employ EW assets to support all echelons through the use of electronic countermeasures (ECM) consisting of active and passive jamming of communications and non-communications targets, and electronic support measures (ESM) consisting of intercept and direction-finding systems. Physical destruction of the enemy's communications and non-communications systems also is considered a component of EW.

EW is employed to disrupt the enemy's use of the electromagnetic spectrum during time frames critical to enemy operations to render the enemy ineffective in achieving his objectives. EW also serves to protect critical friendly point targets, such as command posts, key weapons sites, troop formations, and logistics nodes.

The PLA will attempt to establish EW dominance on the battlefield during the early, critical stages of battle. The PLA would use EW to support military operations by denying or degrading enemy use of radar and communications systems, as well as protecting friendly use of the electromagnetic spectrum. PLA ground force EW capabilities likely will increase qualitatively and quantitatively over the next 20 years.

Although the Chinese have written about applications of radio frequency (RF) weapons and a Navy official has been quoted as stating that RF weapons are among those weapons that the Chinese military will need in the 21st century, the Chinese do not have an RF weapon capability at this time. They are, however, developing high-power microwave (HPM) sources that could form the basis for some types of RF weapons. They also are conducting studies of electronics susceptibility to HPM pulses and of HPM propagation through the atmosphere.

An analysis of publications in technical journals suggests that one RF weapon concept the Chinese are investigating is the HPM Missile warhead. This is an explosively powered RF system that would be delivered to the vicinity of a target and, upon detonation, would emit a single intense pulse of HPM energy to upset or damage electronics in enemy equipment. If this type RF weapon is feasible – and it is at present unclear whether it is possible to produce enough energy to negate electronics at a greater range than a high-explosive warhead of the same size would cause blast damage – then the Chinese should be able to deploy such weapons by 2015.

Another possibility is a directed-energy RF weapon in which an RF beam is propagated over kilometer ranges against targets such as manned aircraft and guided missiles. Chinese deployment of such RF weapons by 2015 is assessed to be technically feasible, although as with the RPM warhead the critical unresolved issue is whether these RF weapons would be more effective at accomplishing the desired military mission than would more conventional weapon systems. A less stressing RIF weapon concept for which the requisite technology is now mature and that therefore could be deployed in the near term is a countermine system on a ground vehicle to dud or predetonate mines with electronic fuses.

Naval Forces

The PLA Navy's (PLAN's) main combatants (frigates, destroyers, and eventually aircraft carriers) are expected to have an extensive electronic warfare (EW) suite. The suite will have intercept systems designed to detect and locate enemy radar and communications signals, along with the capability to employ various types of countermeasures against radar, communications. and electro-optical/infrared threats. Minor combatants (missile patrol boats) will have at least radar intercept systems and capabilities for countering radar and electro-optical/infrared threats. Shipboard EW equipment will be integrated together via automated data exchange interfaces between the intercept and jamming systems. Intercept systems against radar signal could cover from 500 MHz to 40 GHz. Some combatants could have intercept capabilities against communications and data signals. Jamming capabilities will consist of both active and passive methods for targeting airborne surveillance and fire control radars and missile seekers. Some ships may have jamming capabilities against communications and data transmissions. Submarines (attack and ballistic missile) are expected to carry passive intercept systems for detecting and locating enemy radar emissions. These systems will cover from around 500 MHz to 40 GHz.

PLAN combat aircraft could have self-protection jamming systems for use against enemy fire control radars and missile seekers. Some aircraft will be modified to conduct offensive EW missions in support of anti-surface warfare. Unmanned aerial vehicles may be used for surveillance and jamming support missions.

The Chinese are expected to produce the majority of the naval EW systems; however, some foreign systems or components will be imported from various sources, mostly likely in Europe and Russia. However, the performance of Chinese naval EW systems probably will continue to lag behind state-of-the-art Western EW systems.

The PLAN will emphasize multiple methods and techniques for protecting its own radar and communications from enemy electronic attack operations. For radars, electronic protection (EP) features will include frequency agility (RF hopping), antennas designed to significantly reduce signal sidelobe levels, digital processing for sidelobe canceling, trackers operating in the millimeter wave region, and electro-optical/infrared trackers. Communication EP features will emphasize the use of frequency hopping signals and extensive use of fiber-optic cabling for shore-based communications networking. Strict communications security (COMSEC) and emission control (EMCON) procedures will be emphasized.

Air Forces

The PLA Air Force (PLAAF) is in the process of upgrading its EW capability through technology acquisition, reverse engineering, and indigenous research and development. At present, the capabilities of most airborne EW equipment in the PLAAF inventory are extremely limited by Western standards. China's new designs, often offered for sale at air shows, while displaying significant improvements over older systems, remain simple by modern standards. Moreover, China's current inventory of deployed EW assets is inadequate both in size and capability to significantly influence the outcome of combat against a more modern adversary. China is developing a number of new standoff EW aircraft which are likely to enter the inventory over the next 20 years. These assets may be augmented by escort jamming aircraft. Additionally, China is expected to increase the capabilities of self-protection jammers on all of its new tactical aircraft. The PLAAF also can be expected to pursue new airborne SIGINT collection platforms in various EW configurations.

8. **Efforts by the People's Republic of China to develop a capability to establish control of space or to deny access and use of military and commercial space systems in times of crisis or war, including programs to place weapons in space or to develop earth-based weapons capable of attacking space-based systems**

China is said to be acquiring a variety of foreign technologies which could be used to develop an anti-satellite (ASAT) capability. Beijing already may have acquired technical assistance which could be applied to the development of laser radars used to track and image satellites and may be seeking an advanced radar system with the capability to track satellites in low earth orbit. Beijing also may have acquired high-energy laser equipment and technical assistance which probably could be used in the development of ground-based ASAT weapons. The Chinese also may be developing jammers which could be used against Global Positioning System (GPS) receivers. In addition, China already may possess the capability to damage, under specific conditions, optical sensors on satellites that are very vulnerable to damage by lasers. However, given China's current level of interest in laser technology, it is reasonable to assume that Beijing would develop a weapon that could destroy satellites in the future.

Exploitation of space – to include manned space operations – remains a high priority. Although nearly all major aspects of China's manned space program began within the last five years or so, the Chinese are still aiming for a possible first manned launch before the end of the decade. While one of the strongest motivations for this program appears to be political prestige, China's manned space efforts could contribute to improved military space systems in the 2010–2020 time frame.

9. **Trends that would lead the People's Republic of China toward the development of advanced intelligence, surveillance, and reconnaissance capabilities, including gaining access to commercial or third-party systems with military significance**

China has the capability to launch military photoreconnaissance satellites; however, the technology employed is outdated by Western standards. The Chinese do not possess a real-time photoreconnaissance capability. China eventually may deploy advanced imagery reconnaissance and earth resource systems with military applications. The Chinese also may attempt to deploy a near-real-time electro-optical imaging satellite within the next decade, as well as a high-resolution film-based photoreconnaissance satellite. In the interim, the Chinese can be expected to exploit commercial SPOT and LANDSAT imagery. Use of other commercial satellite imagery also can be anticipated as it becomes available. China already has launched two low-orbit meteorological satellites and a geosynchronous weather satellite. Although China has received some degree of foreign technological assistance in the areas of reconnaissance, surveillance and targeting capabilities, much of its system development effort appears to have a substantial indigenous component. In the future, however, Beijing could be expected to acquire and incorporate greater amounts of foreign technology and hardware to expedite program development.

10. **Efforts by the People's Republic of China to develop highly accurate and stealthy ballistic and cruise missiles, including sea-launched cruise missiles, particularly in numbers sufficient to conduct attacks capable of overwhelming projected defense capabilities in the Asia–Pacific region**

Over the past decade, China has invested heavily in its infrastructure to develop and produce new ballistic and cruise missiles. Beijing currently is upgrading and expanding the size of its ballistic missile force, as well as developing new types of ballistic and cruise missiles.

SRBMs/MRBMs

China's CSS-6 (DF-15) or M-9 road-mobile short-range ballistic missile (SRBM) has been operational since 1994. This missile can deliver a 500-kilogram payload to a maximum range of 600 kilometers, enabling Chinese forces to attack with conventional firepower areas which previously were unreachable, even by air platforms. The 300-kilometer range CSS-X-7 SRBM – better known by its export designator, the M-11 – has not yet been deployed by Chinese forces. However, an improved, longer-range version of this missile already may be under development. Application of satellite-assisted navigation technology would improve the accuracy of both missiles. China's first road-mobile, solid-propellant ballistic missile is the CSS-5 (DF-21) medium-range ballistic missile (MRBM). It has been operationally deployed since around 1991. With an estimated range in excess of 2,000 kilometers, it can strike most of China's neighbors. Development of a longer-range version may be underway.

ICBMs/SLBMs

In the first decade of the twenty-first century, China is expected to begin deployment of two new road-mobile solid-propellant intercontinental ballistic missiles (ICBMS) currently in development: the DF-31 will have an estimated range of about 8,000 kilometers; the other ICBM will have an estimated range of some 12,000 kilometers. China's first generation submarine-launched ballistic missile (SLBM), has not yet reached initial operational capability (IOC), even though a follow-on SLBM already may be under development.

Cruise Missiles

China is seeking foreign cruise missile and production-related technologies; it already may have acquired engine, guidance and control, and low-observable technologies. This high level of investment could allow China to increase the pace of cruise missile development; however, Beijing could encounter problems with propulsion systems and mass production capabilities.

China is attempting to purchase from Russia two SOVREMENNYY-class destroyers, together with SS-N-22/SUNBURN antiship cruise missiles (ASCMs). The requisition of two SUNBURN-equipped SOVREMENNYYs would have marginal impact on the balance of power in the region; however, were China to obtain a significant number of additional missiles, it could retrofit them on other major combatants and improve the PLA Navy's offensive punch against surface naval targets. Any attempt to reverse-engineer the SUNBURN, however, likely would take ten years or more. In the interim, technological improvements that the Chinese are said to be making to the C-801/SARDINE and the C-802/SACCADE could provide a modest upgrade to China's antiquated ASCM force. In addition, the Chinese are said to be working on a submerged-launch version of the C-802.

China is developing land-attack cruise missiles (LACMs) for theater warfighting and strategic attack. These missiles appear to have a relatively high development priority. Chinese research and development of LACMs is aided by an aggressive effort to acquire foreign cruise missile technology and subsystems, particularly from Russia. The first LACM to enter production probably would be air-launched from bombers and could be operational early in the next century. A second generation, longer-range LACM probably would be fielded several years later.

11. **Development by the People's Republic of China of command and control networks, particularly those capable of battle management of long-range precision strikes**

China has an extensive network of hardened, underground shelters and command and control facilities for both its military and civilian leadership. Fear of a possible war with the former Soviet Union in the 1960s and 1970s prompted Beijing to expend considerable resources constructing national level command posts, civil defense facilities and associated communications. These facilities are intended to ensure survival of China's leadership and provide a refuge from which it can maintain control over the country's military forces. These facilities are supported by both civil and military communications networks. Chinese military national level command and control communications are carried over multiple transmission systems in order to create a military communications system that is survivable, secure, flexible, mobile and less vulnerable to exploitation, destruction or electronic attack. China's communications networks are capable of supporting PLA military operations within China's borders. While they could be degraded by an enemy, they could not be denied completely.

C4I modernization and automation has been a top Chinese priority since at least 1979. This effort has produced a command automation data network capable of rapidly passing operational orders down the chain of command and moving information to national and theater level decision makers. However, China's C4I infrastructure, including the command automation data network portions, is not capable of controlling or directing military forces in a sophisticated, Western style joint operating environment. The command automation data network is capable of supporting PLA peacetime operations – within China's borders. The command automation data network also can support limited preplanned conventional attack options along China's periphery. However, China's C4I infrastructure cannot support large scale, joint force projection operations at any significant distance from the country's borders. China still lags far behind Western standards for controlling complex joint military operations and lacks the robust C4I architecture required to meet more effectively the demands of the modern battlefield.

12. Efforts by the People's Republic of China in the area of telecommunications, including common channel signaling and synchronous digital hierarchy technologies

Currently, Chinese telecommunications cable networks use primarily Plesiochronous Digital Hierarchy (PDH) architecture, with maximum transmission rates of up to 140 Mbps. Western telecommunications firms have installed a small number of Synchronous Digital Hierarchy (SDH) fiber optic cable systems, with transmission rates ranging from 2.5 to 10 Gbps. Western involvement is critical for Chinese adoption of SDH technology. Western firms not only design and install SDH networks, but they also transfer the required manufacturing and technical knowledge through joint venture companies. After 2002, SDH will entirely replace the existing PDH network and China's fiber optic cable systems will be composed entirely of SDH systems. China also will expand the capacity of existing and newly installed SDH fiber networks through the use of Wave Division Multiplexing (WDM). WDM increases the capacity of optical fiber cable by splitting the light signals into different wavelengths and sending them simultaneously through the cable. WDM will transmit two (or more than 40) signals of different wavelengths in the same direction over a single strand of fiber. This combined signal is separated at the receiving end. For example, a variation of WDM, 'Quad-WDM,' can increase the transmission capacity of a 2–5 Gbps cable to 10 Gbps. WDM uses erbium doped fiber amplifiers (EDFA) instead of repeaters. Further, China is employing Asynchronous Transfer Mode (ATM)/frame Relay technology in provincial and communications links. Adoption of ATM technology will increase the capacity of Chinese data networks and is well suited to meeting future increases in demand.

Chinese telecommunications switching is now almost entirely digital, relying on Digital Stored Programmed Controlled (DSPC) equipment. China produces its own DSPC equipment for export as well as civil and military users. Common Channel Signaling Number 7 (SS7) is used widely for both domestic and international service. Out of band SS7 signaling allows the Chinese to use their voice grade circuits in a more efficient manner than previous in band signaling methods. By 2000, SS7 will be the standard long distance signaling protocol in China.

13. Developments of the People's Republic of China of advanced aerospace technologies with military applications (including gas turbine 'hot section' technologies)

China is engaged in a number of programs aimed at developing advanced aerospace technologies which have military application.

Turbine Engine Technology

China has designed, manufactured and tested, but never entered into production, an indigenous turbine engine system. Whatever recent progress China has made in this area is due, in large part, to foreign assistance, particularly from Russia.

Hypersonic Research

China is conducting limited hypersonic research including vehicle studies and ramjet development. With respect to ramjet activities, materials development, fuel injection, mixing and combustion studies appear to be receiving the greatest attention with limited research on management and fuels also being pursued. Research papers indicate that the Chinese are keenly aware of hypersonic efforts in the United States, Europe and Russia, and that they leverage this research to support their programs. The hypersonic vehicle studies are essentially paper studies at present, with the primary application being an advanced launch vehicle. Overall, the level of these research efforts is relatively small compared to Western and Russian programs.

Focal Array and Infrared Technologies

China is mainly active with research and development programs in focal array technology using materials such as platinum silicide (PTSI), mercury cadmium tellunide (MM), indium antimonide (DWI) and gallium arsenide/ aluminum gallium arsenide (GAAS/ALGAAS). These materials are used in the manufacturing of advanced technology focal planar array detectors. China is not a world leader in infrared detector technology.

Microelectro Mechanical Systems (MEMS)

Chinese MEMS development capability lags behind that of other leading MEMS-producing countries like the United States, Japan, South Korea, and several European countries. China, however, has been active in its efforts to acquire MEMS devices and related technologies. There are a number of organizations in China – mostly affiliated with universities – which conduct research related to MM technology; however, Chinese MEMS technology lags the state-of-the-art by five years or more.

14. Programs of the People's Republic of China involving unmanned aerial vehicles, particularly those with extended ranges or loitering times or potential strike capabilities

Over the years, Beijing has produced a variety of unmanned aerial vehicles (UAVs), principally for use as target drones; others have been built for reconnaissance and surveillance purposes. Most of China's early UAVs were reverse-engineered versions of either Russian or American models. China's most advanced UAV is the ASN-206. This UAV, capable of both day and night reconnaissance, can be used for border patrol operations; artillery targeting positioning and adjustment; nuclear radiation probing or sampling; aerial photography; prospecting and surveying; and traffic monitoring and control. It can carry a still camera, an infrared camera or a real-time television camera. The ASN-206 has a ceiling of 5,000–6,000 meters, a maximum level air speed of 210 kilometers per hour, and an endurance time of 4–8 hours. It has a control range of 150 kilometers from the ground control station.

Beijing is said to be developing a rotary-wing UAV, apparently for use as a reconnaissance platform. It also may have concluded an agreement with a foreign supplier to acquire a high altitude, long endurance UAV, together with a ground control station, and either production or co-production rights. This UAV would provide China with the capability to conduct extended imagery and surveillance, electronics signals collection, and electronic warfare missions; tactical ground force commanders also could use the platform for intelligence collection, artillery spotting, or communications.

15. **Exploitation by the People's Republic of China for military purposes of the Global Positioning System or other similar system (including commercial land surveillance satellites), with such analysis and forecasts focusing particularly on those signs indicative of an attempt to increase accuracy of weapons or situational awareness of operating forces**

Numerous organizations within China's military–industrial complex are believed to be using the Global Positioning System (GPS) and Global Navigation Satellite System (GLONASS) to improve the accuracy of Chinese weapons and the situational awareness of Chinese operational military forces. Since at least the early 1990s these organizations have tried to obtain civilian GPS technology and equipment for use in a variety of weapons systems. China my be engaged in an effort to use satellite navigation to improve the accuracy of its missile force. GPS updates would provide the potential to improve missile accuracy through mid-course guidance correction and increase the operational flexibility of road-mobile platforms.

The Chinese aerospace industry also is seeking to integrate GPS guidance technology into fighters and helicopters. The China Aerospace Corporation displayed a GPS receiver at an exhibition in Beijing in September 1996 and provided brochures advertising both a 12-channel GPS receiver and a 12-channel GPS/GLONASS receiver. One brochure showed a space launch vehicle, suggesting GPS use in missile applications. Information obtained at a more recent air show indicates that all of China's new fighters will incorporate GPS navigation systems. China's military-backed industries also have entered into joint ventures with foreign firms to produce GPS receivers, which may find their way to military weapons. To complement GPS/GLONASS navigation aids, the Chinese have been attempting to acquire commercial satellite imagery from various foreign countries. This widely available satellite imagery could be used in conjunction with imagery GPS/GLONASS to develop digital terrain maps for targeting, missile guidance, and mission planning.

16. Development by the People's Republic of China of capabilities for denial of sea control, including such systems as advanced sea mines, improved submarine capabilities, or land-based sea-denial systems

Beijing can be expected to rely heavily on its naval forces to develop an effective active offshore defense capability and enhance its military stature in the region. China considers the safeguarding of its sovereignty along coastal waters, to include the East and South China Sea, an essential component of its national security and intends to improve the ability of its Navy to exercise sovereignty rights throughout these waters. However, the Chinese Navy will be unable to perform comprehensive sea-denial operations in its coastal waters for at least the next decade. The Navy has made some improvements in its sea-denial military capabilities, particularly with respect to sea mines and submarines; however, it has placed a lesser emphasis on the development of its land-based sea-denial systems such as land-based cruise missiles due to its strategy of active, offshore defense.

Sea Mines

The Chinese Navy maintains an inventory of naval mines and is capable of conducting operations within the country's coastal seas. Most of China's surface ships are equipped with mine tails and are capable of laying mines as a secondary mission. The Navy conducts mine training exercises using surface ships, submarines, and aircraft in coastal areas and can conduct both laying and operations. Although the Navy does not train outside coastal areas routinely, it could conduct mine laying and mine sweeping operations further offshore. In an apparent effort to improve the mine warfare capabilities of its Navy, China is attempting to acquire state-of-the-art mine warfare technology, to include micro-processors, rocket propulsion, remote, control, and mine counter-countermeasures.

China currently produces numerous types of naval mines, to include the MI 1 bottom-influence mine; the EM31 moored mine; the EM32 moored influence mine; the EM52 rocket-propelled rising mine; and the EM53 ship-laid bottom influence mine which is remotely controlled by a shore station. China is believed to have available acoustically activated remote control technology for its EM53. This technology probably could be used with other Chinese ship-laid mines including the EM52. Application of this technology could allow mine fields to be laid in advance of hostilities in a dormant condition and activated when required or deactivated to allow safe transit for friendly ships. Over the next ten years or so, China likely will attempt to acquire advanced propelled-warhead mines as well as submarine-launched mobile bottom mines, to expand the Navy's stand-off mining capabilities.

Submarines

There are approximately 70 submarines of all types in the Chinese naval inventory. This number is projected to decline to about 40 ships over the next 20 years, as older platforms are retired and replaced by smaller numbers of more modern boats. However, the quality and capabilities of China's submarine fleet are expected to improve as China begins constructing more modern ships with Russian assistance. Individual submarines likely will become more difficult to detect and will be better armed. China's submarine force is expected to improve its offensive anti-surface warfare capability with the deployment of submarine-launched cruise missiles, but realize only minor improvements in its ability to conduct anti-submarine warfare.

China's most modern, indigenously-built diesel attack submarine is the SONG-class. It is said to incorporate a significant amount of foreign technology. China also has continued construction of the older, but proven, MING-class submarine in order to maintain the numbers in its inventory as obsolete ROMEO-class boats are retired. Beijing may be planning to build a new class of nuclear-powered ballistic missile submarine (SSBN) and a new class of nuclear-powered attack submarine (SSN). Beijing has contracted with Moscow to purchase four KILO-class attack submarines. Three boats already have been delivered, the fourth is scheduled for delivery later in 1998. Beijing's acquisition of the KILO could provide sophisticated submarine technology of selected subsystems for reverse-engineering.

17. Efforts by the People's Republic of China to develop its anti-submarine warfare capabilities

Beijing realizes that its anti-submarine warfare (ASW) capabilities are poor, especially relative to modern naval standards. PLA Navy ships have only rudimentary ASW equipment and the PLA Naval Air Force has a shortage of ASW helicopters. China is attempting to improve its ASW shortcomings, primarily by acquiring new equipment and technology from foreign sources, including Russia and France. France probably delivered dipping sonar to China in 1997. Beijing reportedly will acquire 12 KA-28/KAMOV ASW helicopters as part of the probable SOVREMENNYY destroyers deal. These helicopters would improve the Navy's airborne ASW capability, especially if they also are used on other combatants such as LUHU destroyers and JIANGWEI frigates. The KILO-class submarines acquired from Russia likely will have a secondary ASW mission. Purchase of modern ASW-related equipment affords China the opportunity to modernize its capabilities relatively quickly and possibly to reverse-engineer technology for use in its own indigenous systems.

18. Continued development by the People's Republic of China of follow-on forces, particularly a form capable of rapid or amphibious assault

The development of Rapid Reaction Forces (RRFs) is an important component of China's military modernization program. These forces are responsible for a variety of missions and tasks, many of which require that they possess the capability to mobilize and deploy quickly; however, they are hampered by inadequate C4I and logistics – to include transportation – support. Currently, they comprise about 15 percent of the total PLA strength; this figure is expected to double by about 2010.

China has designated the 15th Airborne Corps as its primary strategic-level rapid reaction unit for deployment during national contingencies. It is organized into three airborne divisions subordinate to the Chinese Air Force but controlled operationally by the Central Military Commission. Each airborne division is supported by a dedicated and co-located military transport regiment composed of a wide variety of transport aircraft from the Air Force's 13th Transport Division. However, at present, this unit only has sufficient lift capability to transport about 6,000 troops or two airborne regiments. China may be acquiring additional military transports to improve the mobility of its airborne forces but probably does not intend to increase the overall number of airborne units over the next 10 years.

China is continuing to improve its capabilities to conduct amphibious operations within the region. China's fleet of about 60 amphibious ships conducts training exercises in coastal regions and is capable of landing 1–3 infantry divisions, depending on the mix of equipment and stores for resupply. China probably has never conducted a large-scale amphibious exercise which has been fully coordinated with air support and airborne operations. If China were to use its civilian merchant fleet, its ability to move forces likely would increase. Inadequate air defense, poor command and control, together with lack of experience and training in cross-beach movement of forces, however, would be critical shortcomings. The size of the amphibious fleet most likely will decline to about 5 units over the next 20 years, although its lift capacity will increase albeit slightly.

China's naval marine force consists of one marine brigade numbering some 5,000 personnel based in the South Sea Fleet. Its size is projected to remain fairly stable over the next 20 years. Certain regular ground force units appear tailored, equipped and trained for maritime operations and to augment the marine force as needed.

NOTE

1. Source: *Defense News* Online, Special Report.

Appendix 2

US Department of Defense Report on the Security Situation in the Taiwan Strait[1] March 1999

I. The Security Situation in the Taiwan Strait

Nearly three years after the People's Republic of China (PRC) conducted provocative military exercises opposite Taiwan on the eve of that island's first popular presidential election, the security situation in the Taiwan Strait remains calm with no threat of imminent hostilities. There has been little change in the military balance; Beijing has limited its military activity in the region to routine training; Taipei has reduced the size and scope of its military exercises and played down other activities which Beijing might misconstrue as provocative and destabilizing. Within the political arena, senior negotiators from the two quasi-official organizations responsible for managing cross-Strait relations – Taiwan's Straits Exchange Foundation (SEF) and China's Association for Relations Across the Taiwan Strait (ARATS) – met in China in mid-October 1998 and resumed direct contacts – suspended since 1995 – aimed at reducing tensions and improving bilateral relations. Although they agreed on future SEF–ARATS dialogue, cooperation, and visits, there was little movement on resolving the more substantive political issues which divide the two sides.

Beijing views Taiwan as a province of China and demands that Taiwan accept the principle of 'one China' as a basis for negotiations aimed at eventual reunification. The PRC insists that Taiwan should engage in 'political talks' which would set the stage for the island's eventual reunification with the mainland under the 'one country, two systems' formula. China also has condemned Taipei's activities aimed at broadening international recognition. For its part, Taipei rejects Beijing's concept of 'one China,' arguing that China currently is a divided nation and demanding that Beijing deal with Taiwan on an equal basis. Taipei has predicated unification on the condition that China attain levels of economic development and political freedom comparable to those enjoyed on Taiwan; in the interim, Taipei believes that the two sides should focus on 'technical' or procedural issues, such as cultural and educational exchanges, law enforcement cooperation, and the resolution of commercial disputes arising from Taiwan's extensive trade and investment interests on the mainland. Taipei also has condemned Beijing's efforts to isolate Taiwan internationally.

Both Beijing and Taipei have stated they seek a peaceful resolution to the reunification issue. Chinese leaders, however, have refused to renounce the option of using force against Taiwan, stating that a formal declaration of independence by Taipei or foreign intervention in Taiwan's internal affairs relative to the reunification issue would provoke China to take up arms against Taiwan. Beijing recently resurrected a third previously stated circumstance, namely, Taipei's acquisition of nuclear weapons.

Taiwan remains concerned over the continuing modernization and professionalization of China's People's Liberation Army (PLA) and the potential threat that it poses to the island's security. Taipei points to the series of military exercises in July 1995 and March 1996 which the PLA conducted opposite Taiwan – exercises that included ballistic missile launches into waters near the island – and the acquisition of advanced weapons systems from Russia, like the Su-27 fighter and the KILO-class submarine, as clear indications of China's focus on defeating Taiwan militarily.

II. Defense Strategy and Force Planning

Traditionally, China's defense strategy and force planning priorities have been determined by the need to maintain a large armed forces structure capable of responding to a wide range of internal and external missions. This tradition continues to be reflected in China's reliance on a force structure comprised of three elements: the more than 2.5 million member PLA; the one million member People's Armed Police (PAP); and a reserve-militia component numbering well over 1.5 million personnel. However, in recent years, there has been growing evidence that China's force development strategy is being influenced, in part, by its focus on preparing for military contingencies along its southeastern flank, especially in the Taiwan Strait and the South China Sea.

Over a decade ago, the PLA shifted its strategic focus from preparing to fight a large-scale, 'total war' to preparing to fight limited, 'local wars.' Several developments sharpened the PLA's focus and sense of purpose in preparing for this new kind of warfare. They include the military success of the US-led coalition in the Persian Gulf War; Beijing's perception of an unfolding revolution in military affairs; Chinese suspicions over perceived US efforts to 'contain' and militarily 'encircle' China; the deployment of two US naval aircraft carrier battle groups near Taiwan during the 1996 missile crisis; and China's fear that Taiwan was moving toward *de jure* independence. These developments have reinforced China's desire to size and structure PLA forces capable of fighting and winning 'local wars under high-tech(nology) conditions.'

Although the PLA is still decades from possessing a comprehensive capability to engage and defeat a modern adversary beyond China's boundaries, Beijing believes that the PLA can develop asymmetric abilities in certain niches – such as advanced cruise missiles and conventional short-range ballistic missiles (SRBMs). Asymmetric warfare generally is defined as attacks by a weaker or more technologically backward opponent on a stronger foe's vulnerabilities using unexpected or innovative means, while avoiding the adversary's strengths. China's effort to 'leap-frog' generations of technology in weapons programs is often times perceived as an effort to develop new and surprising capabilities, but most of the actual programs are derivative of efforts already well underway in more developed countries. Rather than technological breakthroughs, Beijing's military modernization effort could more accurately be described as a focus on asymmetric engagement capabilities. China is seeking to identify innovative tactics and employment parameters for systems and technologies which the PLA has successfully employed or can be reasonably expected to employ in the next two decades.

With respect to Taiwan's defense strategy and force planning priorities, Taipei long ago renounced its intention to 'recover' the mainland militarily. Taipei's force development plan focuses on three specific areas: maintaining air superiority over the Taiwan Strait and the waters contiguous to Taiwan; conducting effective counter-blockade operations; and defeating an amphibious and aerial assault on the island. Taipei hopes that sufficient technological and tactical advantage over the mainland in these areas will buy time for the forces of change in China to render the future political and security landscape more amenable to Taiwan's long-term interests.

Force modernization programs on both sides of the Taiwan Strait are interactive in nature. Just as Taiwan's military acquisitions are intended to address PLA military modernization programs, PRC force planning takes into account emerging capabilities on Taiwan.

III. A Comparison of Military Forces to 2005

An Overview of the PLA

Beijing's military modernization program, underway for the past two decades, is designed to prepare the PLA to conduct regional active defensive warfare in support of Chinese economic interests and sovereignty claims – a doctrinal shift away from a focus on the large-scale, land-based guerrilla warfare of Mao's classic 'People's War.' Chinese doctrine and tactics, however, still bear the indelible mark of Mao's teachings, particularly as they apply to concentration of power by a technologically inferior force at select times and places on the battlefield to overcome a foe armed with superior weapons.

Rather than shifting priority resources from civil infrastructure and economic reform programs to an across-the-board modernization of the PLA, Beijing is focusing on those programs and assets which will give China the most effective means for exploiting critical vulnerabilities in an adversary's military capabilities. This approach potentially will give Beijing the 'credible intimidation' needed to accomplish political and military goals without having to rely on overwhelming force-on-force superiority. China's modernization programs thus seek to realize short-term improvements in anti-surface warfare (ASuW) and precision strike and longer term advances in missile defense, counter-space, and information warfare (IW). Concurrently, the PLA is acquiring weapons that would be useful in countering potential adversaries operating on naval platforms or from bases in the East and South China Seas, particularly stand-off weapons such as anti-ship cruise missiles (ASCMs) and long-range land-attack cruise missiles (LACMs), as well as SRBMs. Beijing also is working to address problems associated with integrating advanced weapons systems into their inventory; and weaknesses in command, control, communication, computers, and intelligence (C4I); training; and logistics, so as to improve the PLA's overall warfighting capability.

In comparing PLA and Taiwan military strengths, the PLA has clear quantitative advantages. However, only a portion of the PLA's overall strength could be brought to bear against Taiwan at a given time. Primary forces likely to be involved in an operation directed against Taiwan would include conventional short range ballistic missile units in Jiangxi and Fujian provinces; air and ground force units subordinate to the Nanjing Military Region; and naval assets subordinate to the East Sea Fleet. Depending on operational requirements, however, additional air, naval, ballistic missile, and ground force assets from other parts of China could be involved in operations against Taiwan.

An Overview of the Taiwan Military

For more than a decade, Taiwan's military modernization effort has focused on acquiring modern weapons systems and associated equipment to deter – and, if necessary – defeat Chinese aggression. Billions of dollars have been spent on domestic programs like the Indigenous Defense Fighter (IDF) and the *Tien Kung* air defense system, as well as on foreign purchases like the US-made F-16 fighter and the French-built Lafayette-class frigate. Many of these newer systems are in the process of being assimilated into the active inventory. In addition, in the early 1990s, Taiwan's Ministry of Defense publicly announced plans to trim the size of the island's armed forces by 40,000 personnel by 2003, reducing the overall size of the force to around 400,000. Most of the cuts are occurring in the Army, which will number about 200,000. The Air Force and the Navy reportedly will remain at about 60,000–70,000 personnel for each, while the number of personnel assigned to the military police, the coast guard, logistic units and military schools will number between 50,000 and 60,000.

The primary reason for this reduction is to create a smaller army with more mobility and firepower. Another reason is the military's competitive disadvantage in recruiting and retaining highly-trained and techno-logically proficient personnel to handle modern weapon systems. A third factor is the desire to reduce the number of general officers, especially in the Army. By 2005, Taiwan will have a fighter force of about 400 aircraft and an armor force of about 1,500 tanks. The Navy's fleet will number some 30 major surface warships, as older destroyers are phased out of the inventory and replaced with newer combatants. Additionally, the ratio of advanced weaponry to older systems within each of the service inventories will increase.

Chinese Conventional Missiles

As demonstrated in military exercises in the Taiwan Strait in 1995 and 1996, China views its growing conventionally armed ballistic missile force as a potent military and political weapon to influence Taiwan's populace and their leaders. New LACM designs, when operational, will increase China's capability to strike regional targets accurately with conventional warheads. These kinds of weapons systems will play an increasingly important role in modern combat. By 2005, the PLA likely will have deployed two types of SRBMs and a first generation LACM. An expanded arsenal of accurate, conventional SRBMs and LACMs targeted against critical facilities, such as key airfields and C4I nodes, will complicate Taiwan's ability to conduct military operations.

Short-Range Ballistic Missiles (SRBMs)
Within the next several years, the size of China's SRBM force is expected to grow substantially. The PLA currently has one regimental-sized CSS-6 (DF-15/M-9) SRBM unit deployed in southeastern China. The CSS-6 is a solid propellant, road-mobile missile which can deliver a 500-kilogram conventional payload to a maximum range of 600 km. The CSS-X-7 SRBM – better known by its export designator, the M-11 – also is a solid

propellant, road-mobile SRBM with an estimated range of 300 km. This missile, however, has not yet entered the PLA's inventory; and an improved, longer range version may be under development. Moreover, both the CSS-6 and the CSS-X-7 are expected to incorporate satellite-assisted navigation technology to improve their accuracy. In an armed conflict with Taiwan, China's SRBMs likely would target air defense installations, airfields, naval bases, C4I nodes, and logistics facilities.

Land-Attack Cruise Missiles (LACMS)

China also is developing LACMs. These missiles appear to have a relatively high development priority. Chinese research and development of LACMs is being aided by an aggressive effort to acquire foreign cruise missile technology and subsystems, particularly from Russia. The first LACM to enter production probably would be air-launched and could be operational early in the next century.

Antiship Cruise Missiles (ASCMs)

Technological improvements to the C-801/SARDINE and the C-802/SACCADE are providing a gradual upgrade to China's current force of antiquated, first generation, CSS-N-1/SCRUBBRUSH ASCMs. Despite the obsolescence of many of its ships, its lack of operational experience and its inability to resupply ASCMs at sea, the PLA Navy could assemble a sizeable ASuW force against Taiwan and, most likely, saturate the Taiwan Navy with barrages of ASCMs. In addition, B-6D bombers subordinate to the PLA Naval Air Force (PLANAF) are capable of firing the C-601/KRAKEN ASCM. The Navy's new FB-7 bomber likely will carry C-801/C-802 ASCMs. China's ASCM capability is expected to improve further with the planned acquisition of two Russian-built SOVREMENNYY-class destroyers armed with the SS-N-22/SUNBURN ASCM.

Taiwan Missile Defense

Taiwan's most significant vulnerability is its limited capacity to defend against the growing arsenal of Chinese ballistic missiles. These missiles pose a serious threat to non-hardened military targets, C2 nodes, and Taiwan's military infrastructure. As an initial response to this emerging threat, Taiwan has purchased the Modified Air Defense System (MADS), an improved variant of the PATRIOT surface-to-air missile (SAM) system which was used during DESERT STORM. The MADS, which began arriving on Taiwan in 1997, is expected to be deployed around heavily populated Taipei. Exclusive reliance on active missile defenses and associated BM/C3I, however, will not sufficiently offset the overwhelming advantage in offensive missiles which Beijing is projected to possess in 2005.

314

PLA Air Force

The PLA Air Force (PLAAF) currently numbers over 400,000 personnel with approximately 4,500 combat aircraft organized in some 30 air divisions. The PLAAF also maintains about 150 transport aircraft in two air divisions. The PLAAF inventory includes over 2,200 obsolete F-6/FARMER fighters, several hundred F-7/FISHBED and F-8/FINBACK fighters, and over 40 Su-27/FLANKERs. In addition, it has some 500 A-5/FANTAN ground attack aircraft and about 500 bombers, including the obsolete B-5/BEAGLE. Both its aerial refueling and airborne early warning (AEW) programs are behind schedule, as are several of its indigenous aircraft development programs. By 2005, the PLAAF will possess nearly 2,200 tactical fighter aircraft, 500 ground attack aircraft, and 400 bombers, as older aircraft are retired. The majority of the mainland's air fleet still will be composed of second and third generation aircraft augmented by a limited number of fourth generation platforms. Command and control constraints and constricted airspace would limit the number of aircraft which the PLAAF could deploy at one time in an air battle over the Taiwan Strait.

Fighters

The F-10, China's first domestically-produced fourth-generation fighter, reportedly is still undergoing testing and evaluation. The aircraft most likely will be armed with advanced beyond-visual-range (BVR), active radar (AR), air-to-air missiles (AAMs), and may be air refuelable. Domestic assembly of Su-27 kits has begun, with assistance from Russian technicians. Follow-on phases will involve assembly of an undetermined number of aircraft from a mixture of Russian- and Chinese-produced parts and, later, full domestic production of all but the aircraft's avionics and engine. The Su-27s originally purchased directly from Russia are the only fighter aircraft in the PLAAF inventory with sufficient combat radius to allow extended operations beyond China's borders. China will have made modest strides in its aerial refueling program by 2005. The F-8-II, other third generation aircraft modified to incorporate some fourth generation technology, as well as the F-10 are expected to possess aerial refueling capabilities.

Air-to-Air Missiles (AAMs)

The PLAAF currently has in its inventory a number of AAMs which are superior to those in Taiwan's inventory. The Russian-built AA-11/ARCHER infrared (IR) AAM carried on the Su-27 is superior to Taiwan's AIM-9/SIDEWINDER and indigenously produced *Tien Chien-I*/SKY SWORD-I IR AAM. China's AA-10a/ALAMO missiles, on the other hand, are roughly comparable to, or slightly less capable than, Taiwan's AIM-

7/SPARROWs. China's F-7 is capable of carrying the PL-2A and PL-5B IR AAMs, as well as the all-aspect PL-8 IR AAMs, while its F-8-IIs are capable of carrying the PL-2A, PL-5B, PL-8, and the BVR semi-active radar (SAR) PL-4 and PL-10 AAMs. All of these missiles are comparable to Taiwan's AAMs. By 2005, Beijing likely will have an AR AAM in its inventory and could adapt it for use on a larger number of platforms than Taipei could match. The PLAAF also is developing BVR AAMs for use aboard its fourth generation fighter aircraft.

Bombers
China's bomber aircraft include the B-6/BADGER and the B-5/BEAGLE. The B-5's slow speed and lack of standoff capability make this platform an extremely vulnerable target. The B-6 also is an aging aircraft. However, it is being produced in several versions. One variant is designed to carry an ASCM while another is being developed to carry an air-launched cruise missile (ALCM). The B-5 is being phased out of the inventory but it is still used in training and would probably be employed along with the B-6 bomber during a military conflict against Taiwan. However, both bombers would have limited success against Taiwan's air defense assets; the newer BADGER models incorporating cruise missile technology likely would have better success.

Transports
One of the PLAAF's combat missions is to provide airlift in support of PLA operations. However, until just recently, the PLAAF was unable to transport ground forces rapidly to distant parts of the country or sustain ground operations for extended periods due to antiquated aircraft and the lack of large-capacity aircraft. The PLAAF transport force now is capable of supporting the PLA at increased levels for a limited time and rapidly deploying to internal trouble spots. However, the PLAAF's current complement of large transport aircraft is limited to about a dozen IL-76MD/CANDIDs and about 50 Y-8/CUBs; the remainder of the transport force consists of smaller aircraft like the AN-24/COKE, AN-26/CURL, and Y-5/COLT. The MD variant of the CANDID is a military model specially configured for airborne operations. Beijing can be expected to purchase additional Russian IL-76 or similarly-sized foreign aircraft. The ongoing expansion of China's civil aircraft fleet will allow the PLAAF to use the country's civil airlines to supplement its transport capability during crises.

Airborne
China's 15th Airborne Army consists of three airborne divisions, each with about 10,000 troops. The 15th is China's primary quick reaction force and has been designated as a strategic rapid reaction unit. However,

China's airborne units remain handicapped by insufficient lift. Acquisition of additional aircraft and modern equipment, together with the increased emphasis on utilizing airborne forces during training exercises, will improve – albeit marginally – the 15th's combat capabilities.

Ground-Based Air Defense

Beijing is expending tremendous effort establishing an Integrated Air Defense System (IADS) at both the strategic and tactical levels. China's air defense technology currently lags behind western standards and its current IADS capability lacks many crucial components. Beijing probably could establish a fully operational national IADS within the next twenty years, but clearly not by 2005. China has a rudimentary tactical IADS capability in the form of its mobile Tactical Air Defense System (TADS).

Taiwan Air Force

The Taiwan Air Force (TAF) has about 70,000 personnel and over 400 combat aircraft. The current inventory includes approximately 180 older F-5E/F fighters and over 100 more modern Indigenous Defense Fighters (IDFs).

Fighters

The IDF has faced numerous developmental and operational problems since its inception in the 1980s. Nevertheless, its technical sophistication, with its fly-by-wire controls and blended wing-body design, is believed to be superior to any aircraft produced and deployed by China to date. Production of all 130 IDFs is scheduled to be completed by early 2000. Most of the IDFs are expected to be armed with the indigenously-produced, BVR *Tien Chien-II* (Sky Sword-II) AR AAM. Taiwan also has purchased 150 F-16 fighters from the United States: 120 single-seat 'A' models and 30 two-seat 'B' models. On-island deliveries, which began in April 1997, are continuing and should be completed by year's end. These aircraft are armed with upgraded AIM-7M/SPARROW SAR and AIM-9P4 and AIM9S SIDEWINDER IR AAMs. Deliveries of 60 French-built Mirage 2000-5s also began in April 1997 and were completed by October 1998. With its four MICA active radar (AR) and two MAGIC II infrared (IR) AAMs, the Mirage 2000-5 is Taiwan's most formidable air defense fighter. The TAF's current strategy is to employ the IDF for low altitude interception and ground attack; the F-16 for mid altitude offshore interception and ground attack; and, the Mirage 2000-5 for high altitude offshore interception. Taiwan also is planning an upgrade program for about 100 F-5 fighters. The systemic integration and generational problems that affect Taiwan's overall forces with respect to modernization apparently are having the greatest impact on the TAF, where the technology curve is highest.

Air Defense Early Warning

Taiwan has established an air defense early warning network which, when used in conjunction with its ground-based SAMs and fourth-generation tactical aircraft, appears to pose a credible deterrent against an air attack from the mainland. Taiwan has replaced its old SKY NET air defense network with a new network called STRONG NET to provide a comprehensive picture of the surrounding airspace.

Ground-Based Air Defense

The Improved HAWK (I-HAWK) SAM system remains the mainstay of Taiwan's air defense. It is a medium-range, low- to medium-altitude system, designed to defend fixed and mobile assets from high speed aircraft. The standard I-HAWK site consists of a pulse acquisition radar, a continuous wave acquisition radar, a high power illuminating target tracking radar, a range-only radar, and six three-missile launchers. Taipei also has deployed an indigenously-produced SAM – the *Tien Kung* or *Sky Bow* – designed to replace the recently retired NIKE-HERCULES system. The *Tien Kung* is a medium-to-long range system, reportedly based on early versions of the US PATRIOT. The *Tien Kung-I* is a single-stage, solid-propellant missile. It is deployed in two configurations: as a mobile, containerized system employing a quad-box launcher similar in appearance to the M901 PATRIOT missile launcher and as a fixed, silo-launched SAM. A follow-on variant, the *Tien Kung-II*, is configured as a fixed, two-stage, single-rail or silo-launched system. For target acquisition, tracking, and mid-course missile guidance requirements, the *Tien Kung* employs a multifunction, phased-array radar with associated fire-control computer system and a continuous wave dish antenna illuminator which are tied into the radar in order to allow multiple target engagement. As noted previously, Taiwan also has purchased the MADS, a variant of the PATRIOT SAM system, primarily to serve in an antiballistic missile role.

Short-range air defense coverage is provided primarily by the CHAPARRAL and the SKYGUARD systems. The CHAPARRAL consists of four modified AIM-9C SIDEWINDER missiles mounted on a tracked vehicle. The SKYGUARD is an integrated air defense system consisting of a modified AIM-7M/SPARROW AAM and a 35 mm AAA gun. Taiwan is expected to procure the STINGER/AVENGER SAM system. It is a pedestal mounted system with two pods – each with four STINGER missiles – mounted on the back of a High Mobility Multi-Purpose Wheeled Vehicle (HMMWV). Taiwan's Chung Shan Institute of Science and Technology (CSIST) has developed and publicly displayed a new tactical air defense which it has dubbed the ANTELOPE. According to promotional brochures, work on the ANTELOPE began in July 1995 as a direct by-product of the *Tien Chien-I* IR AAM. According to CSIST, the ANTELOPE consists of a target acquisition system, communication components, an operational control system, a carrier, and four 18-km maximum range *Tien Chien-I* missiles. It can be used to intercept low-flying helicopters, fighter aircraft, attack aircraft, and bombers and can be installed on a midsize truck or HMMWV.

PLA Navy

The People's Liberation Army Navy (PLAN) currently numbers approximately 260,000 personnel, with over 50 destroyers and frigates, about 60 diesel and six Han- and Xia-class submarines, and nearly 50 landing ships. This force is complemented by several hundred auxiliary and smaller patrol vessels, as well as a naval air arm of over 500, mostly obsolescent, fixed-winged aircraft and some 30 helicopters. Over the last decade, the PLAN has streamlined and modernized its forces by eliminating large numbers of older ships and replacing them with fewer, more modern units. The number of submarines has declined by about one-half. The size of the major surface combatant fleet has been relatively stable, with older ships slowly being replaced by newer Chinese-built destroyers and frigates. Nearly all of the PLAN's inventory of US-built, World War II-vintage landing ships have been replaced by similar numbers of domestically-produced vessels. Nevertheless, the PLAN continues to lag behind other regional navies, including that of Taiwan, in most technological areas, especially air defense, surveillance, and C4I.

Submarines
China maintains the overwhelming advantage in submarines over Taiwan and this quantitative advantage will continue through 2005. Moreover, while the number of boats in service in China is expected to decrease, their overall qualitative capabilities will increase. China is producing more modern submarines and is using submarine-related technology from Russia. Although the force is oriented principally toward interdicting surface ships using torpedoes and mines, China shortly will begin arming some of its submarines with a submerged-launch cruise missile. The capability of Chinese submarines to conduct ASW operations is expected to improve through 2005, in light of the acquisition of Russian-built KILO-class submarines and the greater emphasis being placed on ASW training. As a result, China's submarine fleet will constitute a substantial force capable of controlling sea lanes and mining approaches around Taiwan, as well as a growing threat to submarines in the East and South China Seas.

Surface Combatants
China's fleet of major surface combatants includes about 40 frigates and 20 destroyers. All carry ASCMs, ranging from the antiquated, first-generation CSS-N-1/SCRUBBRUSH to the more advanced C-801/

SARDINE and C-802/SACCADE. Two Russian-built SOVREMENNYY-class destroyers, which China is expected to acquire in the next several years, likely will be equipped with the SS-N-22/SUNBURN ASCM. The PLAN's surface fleet will continue to strive to enhance both its readiness and endurance for extended operations within the region and around Taiwan. It likely will conduct more realistic training exercises and deploy more advanced anti-ship and air defense missiles and electronic counter-measures.

Amphibious Forces

The PLAN's amphibious fleet provides sealift sufficient to transport approximately one infantry division. The PLAN also has hundreds of smaller landing craft, barges, and troop transports, all of which could be used together with fishing boats, trawlers, and civilian merchant ships to augment the naval amphibious fleet. Shortcomings in long-range lift, logistics, and air support, however, hinders China's ability to project amphibious forces.

People's Liberation Army Naval Air Force (PLANAF)

The missions of the PLANAF include protecting China's coastal airspace, providing air support for naval forces at sea, and conducting maritime search and rescue operations. The PLANAF has only a limited maritime strike capability with some 150 non-standoff B-6/BADGERs, A-5/FANTANs, and B-5/BEAGLEs. However, these aircraft would be only marginally effective against most modern navies. Some of the approximately 30 B-6Ds provide the PLANAF with a cruise missile ship interdiction strike capability utilizing the C-601/KRAKEN ASCM. The standoff-capable FB-7 fighter-bomber, equipped with the C-801/ASCM, will not become operational for another two to three years. It likely will augment the B-6 and eventually replace some of the B-5s and A-5s in the PLANAF's inventory.

Taiwan Navy

The Taiwan Navy has about 68,000 personnel and some 40 major surface combatants. In addition there are four submarines, about 100 patrol boats, 30 mine warfare ships, and 25 amphibious vessels. Despite the Navy's ability to refurbish and extend the service life of its vessels and equipment well beyond expectation, a large portion of the fleet consists of obsolescent World War II-era ships. The Navy's primary mission is to defend the island against a Chinese blockade and to protect Taiwan's sea lines of communication (SLOCs). The Navy's modernization program is intended to replace its aging fleet of surface combatants with newer ships like the French-built Lafayette-class frigate and a domestically-produced variant of the US Perry-class frigate. Taiwan is acquiring advanced anti-submarine warfare technology which will likely improve their ability to counter PLA submarines operating off the coast of Taiwan.

Submarines

Taiwan has four submarines: two relatively modern Dutch-built ZVAARDVIS Design boats (*Hai Lung*-class) acquired in the late 1980s and two obsolete, World War II-era GUPPY II boats provided by the United States in 1973 for ASW training. The two Dutch submarines reportedly are armed with wire-guided torpedoes. The US boats are used primarily as training platforms with a secondary mission to lay mines. Acquisition of additional submarines remains one of Taiwan's most important priorities.

Surface Combatants

Taiwan's naval modernization program – dubbed 'Kuang Hua' or 'Glorious China' – includes the licensed-production of eight Perry-class (*Cheng Kung*-class) frigates; the purchase of six Lafayette-class (*Kang Ting*-class) frigates from France; and, the lease of eight Knox-class frigates from the United States. Both the Perry-class and Lafayette-class frigates are armed with indigenously-produced *Hsiung Feng II* ASCMs, while the Knox-class frigates are equipped with the US-made Harpoon ASCM. Air defense weapons systems include the Standard air defense missile on board the Perry-class frigates and the Sea Chaparral on board the Lafayettes. The primary mission of these newer frigates is sea control, particularly the capability to protect the sea lanes beyond the range of coastal aircraft. The Navy also has more than a dozen older, World War II-era Gearing-class destroyers and numerous smaller combatants and auxiliaries in its operational inventory. The 'Kuang Hua' program also includes the future acquisition of three types of smaller surface combatants: 12 *Jin Chiang*-class 580-ton guided missile patrol combatants; 10–14 1,500–2,000 ton corvettes; and 50 fast attack missile boats (150–250 ton) to replace the aging fleet of *Hai Ou*-class boats currently in the inventory.

Taiwan Naval Air Force

Taiwan's small naval air force consists of 10 Hughes MD 500 short-range ASW helicopters, usually deployed aboard Taiwan's Gearing-class destroyers, and nine Sikorsky S-70C(M) ASW Thunderhawk helicopters, used with Taiwan's Perry- and Lafayette-class frigates. The 30 or so S-2T Tracker ASW/Maritime Patrol aircraft currently belonging to the TAF may be turned over to the Taiwan Navy in the future.

PLA Ground Forces

China's ground forces are comprised of approximately 75 army maneuver divisions. Approximately 20 percent of these divisions are designated 'rapid reaction' units: combined arms units capable of deploying by road or rail within China without significant train-up or reserve augmentation. China is continuing the process of reducing the size of its army. The 500,000-man force reduction currently underway will streamline the force and facilitate funding to equip its 'core' infantry, airborne, mechanized and aviation units with more advanced weapons. The army is supported by a large reserve-militia force numbering more than 1.5 million personnel and a one million man armed police force. Particularly since the 1991 Persian Gulf conflict, the PLA has devoted considerable resources to the development of special operation forces (SOFs). These units likely have been assigned specific missions and tasks in a variety of Taiwan contingencies, to include locating or destroying C4I assets, transportation nodes, and logistics depots; capturing or destroying airfields; destroying air defense assets; and conducting reconnaissance operations.

Traditionally, China's ground forces have been highly cohesive, patriotic, physically fit, and well trained in basic skills. In addition, they are generally strong in operational and communications security, as well as in the use of camouflage, concealment, and deception. Major weaknesses are lack of transport and logistic support. Ground force leadership, training in combined operations, and morale are poor. The PLA is still a party army with nepotism and political/family connections continuing to predominate in officer appointment and advancement. The soldiers, for the most part, are semi-literate rural peasants; there is no professional NCO corps, per se. Military service, with its low remuneration and family disruption, is increasingly seen as a poor alternative to work in the private sector. China's leadership is aware of these weaknesses and is trying to address them in its overall modernization program. Thus, increasingly in the future, officers likely will be promoted on merit as opposed to connections, and the ratio of higher educated volunteer servicemen to conscripts likely will increase.

Taiwan Ground Forces

Taipei's approximate 220,000-member Army is organized and trained to defend Taiwan and the offshore islands against an invasion. About 80 percent of the Army's combat strength is on Taiwan proper, under the control of three field armies. The three offshore island commands – Chinmen, Matsu, and Penghu – have a total of more than 50,000 soldiers. In 1997, the Army began an aggressive restructuring campaign to upgrade its combat effectiveness, emphasizing rapid reaction capabilities, airborne invasion interdiction, and special forces operations. The plan apparently calls for trimming the force to 200,000 personnel. The three existing field armies will remain intact; however, the Army will eliminate divisions as operational units in peacetime. Existing infantry and mechanized divisions will be reorganized into specialized combined arms brigades. The Taiwan Army's equipment modernization effort has focused on improving mobility and fire power, primarily through the acquisition of tanks, helicopters, and short-range air defense missiles. Taiwan is acquiring over 450 M-60A3 medium tanks; they will join an already large tank force consisting of some 450 M-48H and 300 M-48A5 medium tanks and over 1,000 much older M-41 and M-24 light tanks. Taiwan also has acquired 42 AH-1W Cobra attack and 26 OH-58D Kiowa scout helicopters.

China – Information Operations

Information Warfare
China's information warfare (IW) program is in the early stages of research. It currently focuses on understanding IW as a military threat, developing effective countermeasures, and studying offensive employment of IW against foreign economic, logistics, and C4I systems. Driven by the perception that China's information systems are vulnerable, the highest priority has been assigned to defensive IW programs and indigenous information technology development. Some technologies could provide enhanced defensive or offensive capabilities against Taiwan military and civilian information infrastructure systems. Computer anti-virus solutions, network security, and advanced data communications technologies are a few examples. Chinese open source articles claim that the PLA has incorporated IW-related scenarios into several recent operational exercises. Efforts have focused on increasing the PLA's proficiency in defensive measures, especially against computer viruses.

Computer Warfare
In the area of Computer Network Attack, China appears interested in researching methods to insert computer viruses into foreign networks as part of its overall Information Operations (IO) strategy. Beijing reportedly has adequate hardware and software tools and possesses a strong and growing understanding of the technologies involved. China's strategic IO use of advanced information technologies in the short- to mid-term likely will lack depth and sophistication; however, as it develops more expertise in defending its own networks against enemy attack, it is likely to step up attempts to penetrate adversarial information systems.

Electronic Warfare
The thrust of China's electronic warfare (EW) efforts continues to focus on technology development and design capabilities improvement, accomplished mainly through cooperation with Western companies, through

reverse engineering efforts, and through the procurement of foreign systems. The inventory of Chinese EW equipment includes a combination of 1950s–1980s technologies, with only a few select military units receiving the most modern components. China is procuring state-of-the-art technology to improve its intercept, direction finding, and jamming capabilities. In addition to providing extended imagery reconnaissance and surveillance and ELINT collection, Beijing's unmanned aerial vehicle programs probably will yield platforms for improved radio and radar jammers. Additionally, existing earth stations can be modified to interfere with satellite communications. Finally, the PLA is developing an electronic countermeasures (ECM) doctrine and has performed structured training in an ECM environment.

Antisatellite (ASAT) Programs

China currently can detect and track most satellites with sufficient accuracy for targeting purposes. Beijing's only current means of destroying or disabling a satellite, however, would be to launch a ballistic missile or space launch vehicle armed with a nuclear weapon. Press articles indicate Chinese interest in a laser ASAT. Beijing apparently has research programs involving the relevant technologies, and already may possess the capability to damage, under specific conditions, optical sensors on satellites that are very vulnerable to damage by lasers.

Sensors for Detection and Targeting

China currently is acquiring and developing new systems which will give it a variety of targeting capabilities it currently lacks. Detection and targeting will improve over time, as space-based sensors are launched; long distance reconnaissance drones are produced; and AEW aircraft are put in service. Beijing reportedly is developing several reconnaissance satellites which could provide initial targeting data to long-range reconnaissance aircraft. The acquisition of an AEW platform capable of conducting data relays has held a high priority in the PLAAF's efforts to modernize. Beijing is expected to acquire several PHALCON AEW systems mounted on IL-76 airframes. The Chinese Navy also reportedly is acquiring Skymaster AEW radars. While Chinese officials claim these radars will be used for search and rescue operations, they could be used in AEW and surface surveillance roles. China conceivably could have fully operational AEW platforms by 2005. By 2000, Beijing will have access to commercial remote sensing overhead imagery in the 2.5 meter resolution range. Access to new overhead imagery platforms in the near term will enhance China's ability to map, surveil, and target. The Chinese already have had access to commercial satellite imagery from the French SPOT satellites, Indian IRS-1c satellite, Canadian RADARSAT, and various

Russian satellites. This widely available commercial satellite imagery can be used to develop digital terrain maps for targeting, missile guidance, and mission planning.

Telecommunication Infrastructure

China's telecommunications infrastructure, composed of both civil and military communications networks, currently is being modernized. China's C4I infrastructures, supporting all levels of military and civilian leadership, are receiving specific attention. The PLA communications network supports all branches of the armed forces and uses the same types of communications mediums as the civil network. Multiple transmission systems create a military communication system that is survivable, secure, flexible, mobile and less vulnerable to exploitation, destruction or electronic attack. Thus, while China's command and control networks could be degraded, it is unlikely that they could be denied. Overall, network performance is assessed as adequate. The military's lack of communications satellites could force the PLA to rely on foreign satellite services to meet military needs in wartime or a crisis. In the event of crisis, it is believed the military would preempt the domestic satellite systems for combat operations. Within the operational forces, mobile communications equipment probably will be fielded in greater numbers to maneuver units and increasingly will incorporate features such as encryption and frequency hopping. As a result, the PLA leadership eventually will be able to control its forces in a much more secure and timely manner over a wider and more dynamic range of missions than is currently possible.

Deception

The PLA's modernization program includes improving military denial and deception doctrine and capabilities for use against potential adversaries at the strategic, operational, and tactical level. Recent Chinese military writings affirm that 'high technology warfare' requires developing denial and deception techniques for countering US precision weapons, advanced reconnaissance sensors, and command and control warfare doctrine. A 1993 Chinese National Defense University treatise, *High Technology and Military Camouflage*, suggests that the PLA recognizes the value of conducting deception operations, especially in a crisis involving Taiwan, to create ambiguity about Chinese intentions and force the Taiwan political and military leadership to misallocate resources. According to this study, 'deception is intended to induce the enemy to reach erroneous conclusions about the activities, deployment, and combat objectives of our forces. Camouflage and deception can disperse the enemy's troops, waste their firepower, and disrupt their high technology weapons.'

Psychological Operations

The PLA historically has made extensive use of psychological operations (PSYOP) in all its military campaigns and has integrated PSYOP into its national military strategy. China is believed to have a robust capability to conduct PSYOP against Taiwan. Moreover, prominent articles on PSYOP in the *Liberation Army Daily* over the last few years indicate that the PLA is committed to improving its PSYOP capability. In earlier military campaigns – such as China's prolonged confrontation with Taiwan military forces on the offshore islands in the 1950s and 1960s and China's brief border war with Vietnam in 1979 – the PLA demonstrated that it has a range of techniques for disseminating PSYOP messages to opposing military forces and civilian populations. During these conflicts, PLA PSYOP units employed loudspeakers, leaflets, posters, and radio broadcasts to spread propaganda messages. China also has demonstrated in past conflicts that it is not averse to using 'black' propaganda and disinformation campaigns based on specious assertions and fabricated evidence. Perhaps the best example of this was the 'germ warfare' propaganda campaign that was aggressively pursued by Chinese propagandists during the Korean War. This massive PSYOP campaign attempted to convince an international audience that US forces, in collusion with Japan, were spreading biological toxins in Korea and China.

Taiwan – Information Operations

Information Warfare

As one of the world's largest producers of computer components, Taiwan has all of the basic capabilities needed to carry out offensive and defensive IW related activities, particularly computer network attacks and the introduction of malicious code. While information on formally integrating IW into warfighting doctrine is not available, there are indications that formal doctrine development to guide future employment of these capabilities may be in progress. As new computer systems and technology are developed and as Taiwan increases its role in the manufacture of these systems, its capability to exploit its position for IW activities can be expected to increase substantially.

Computer Warfare

Taiwan has demonstrated a significant knowledge of viruses. A virus known as 'Bloody' or '6/4' protesting the Tiananmen Square crackdown was first discovered in Taiwan in 1990. In 1992, personnel from The Hague – with support from INTERPOL – investigated the dissemination of the 'Michelangelo' virus by a Taiwan firm. In 1996, Taiwan virus writers developed and distributed a computer virus protesting Japanese claims to the Diaoyutai Islands. The following year, opponents of the Taiwan government developed a widely circulated Word-macro virus known as 'Con-Air' which protested social problems on the island. Taiwan also is well known for the efforts by researchers and corporations to combat computer viruses. Trend Micro – formerly known as Trend Micro Devices – is an industry leader in anti-virus software and, to a lesser extent, other network security products. Trend Micro was the first company to develop a response to the 'Michelangelo' virus; it currently dominates the anti-virus software market in Japan. Trend Micro also has led in the area of virus recognition technology. Taiwan's Academia Sinica also has made impacts in the area of anti-virus software development.

Sensors for Detection and Targeting
During the 1980s, Taiwan's reconnaissance capability and 1970s vintage photographic technology was adequate for the limited capabilities and low threat posture of the PLAAF. Taiwan's airborne reconnaissance capability, however, began to decline precipitously in the 1990s. Last year, the TAF retired the last of its RF-104G tactical reconnaissance aircraft and replaced them with reconnaissance-configured RF-5E aircraft. Taipei continues to seek a new imaging system capable of exploiting targets at greater distances from the coast, but without exposing its reconnaissance flights to China's increasingly more sophisticated air defenses. Taiwan conducts technical and human intelligence operations against China and purchases French SPOT and U.S. LANDSAT commercial imagery for exploitation.

Telecommunications Infrastructure
Taiwan's telecommunications infrastructure is composed of a civilian communications system and a separate military communications system. The civilian system consists of a nationwide network of fixed telephone lines (coaxial and fiber optic), microwave, wireless (satellite, cellular, paging), and TV and radio broadcast. The military system reportedly also consists of a nationwide network of fixed telephone lines (coaxial and fiber optic) and microwave, as well as satellite, troposcatter and HF/VHF radio. Taiwan is rapidly developing its telecommunications infrastructure with the goal of becoming an Asia–Pacific telecommunications hub. The Taiwan military could benefit from any improvements to the commercial architecture. In the past, satellite communications have played a relatively minor role in domestic communications; they were used primarily to link Taiwan to its offshore islands. INTELSAT provides this domestic function as well as international connections for Taiwan. Satellite communications using very small aperture terminals (VSAT) were placed into commercial service in 1989. Satellites may begin to play a more prominent role both domestically and internationally with the advent of a number of new satellite systems. Taiwan also is working on building its own satellites

under the ROCSAT program. ROCSAT-1, which will include an experimental communications package, is scheduled to be launched in January 1999.

Psychological Operations

Taiwan reportedly possesses a well-developed PSYOP capability, under the auspices of the General Political Warfare Department (GPWD). During previous periods of tense confrontation across the Taiwan Strait, the GPWD has demonstrated its ability to employ a wide variety of PSYOP techniques, including broadcasting propaganda messages; using balloons, kites, artillery shells, and various flotation devices to deliver propaganda messages; and offering financial inducements to potential defectors. China's leadership reportedly is considered an especially hard target for Taiwan's PSYOP forces. Given the continuous attention the Chinese military leadership has given to the indoctrination of its forces, PLA troops also are not likely to be susceptible to Taiwan PSYOP.

China – Other Factors

Military Leadership

The PLA does not approach leadership in the same way as Western military forces, placing greater emphasis on technical skills than on leadership development. The PLA's leadership culture is also risk averse, favoring the status quo over change. Historical experiences and decades of Communist propaganda have made the majority of Chinese military leaders suspicious of the outside world and its attitudes toward China's increasing power and influence. Relatively few senior officers have traveled abroad, although the military has undertaken a significant military diplomatic effort since the early 1990s that is overcoming this deficiency. The result of this physical and intellectual isolation has been the development of a strongly nationalistic outlook among the officer corps that could color negatively the leadership's approach to international developments seen impacting China's sovereignty or security.

China's military leadership is united on its desire to acquire or improve selected military capabilities in the near term. In the longer term, military leaders want to overhaul significantly the entire armed forces to create a smaller, technically more advanced instrument to fight in the immediate vicinity of China's borders. There also is a corresponding emphasis on military professionalism in China. While the political commissar system still exists and political officers share joint command with their operational brethren, the military now emphasizes operational training over political indoctrination. This trend will create a less politicized officer corps, especially among junior and mid-grade officers. It also will move the military leadership toward forming a more corporate military identity.

Senior Chinese officers are studying modern technological advances and how these can best be incorporated into the current and projected military doctrine and structure. These officers are still generally more familiar and comfortable with an operational level of conflict that relies primarily on ground forces to achieve objectives. Below the most senior level, an increasing number of officers in command positions are conversant in, and somewhat experienced with, modern technological and operational concepts like joint operations. Nevertheless, the military has recently renewed its emphasis on upgrading scientific and technical education in order to overcome perceived deficiencies in the officer corps in this respect.

Training

In recent years, China has shown a growing willingness to experiment with new aspects of training. Training has become more realistic and challenging, with an increased participation by opposition force units and greater emphasis on combined arms. Although intraservice training at the tactical level is improving, joint exercises are still tightly controlled and indicative of the difficulty the PLA likely would have in executing operational-level battle plans. While this past year's summer floods disrupted training for a large percentage of the PLA, certain exercises were not canceled, particularly those emphasizing Beijing's commitment to improve joint training.

Professional Military Education

Professional military education for both officers and NCOs in the PLA is a high priority for Beijing. Institutional structures designed to instill a high degree of professionalism throughout the force were conspicuously absent in China until 1978, when the PLA began to address educational shortfalls. Since that time, Beijing has established a number of educational institutions throughout the military, although the emphasis remains on the officer corps.

The key organization shaping the professional development of the senior PLA officer corps is the National Defense University (NDU). It instructs senior officers in areas such as strategic studies, operational art, organizational command and management, combined arms and joint service operations, foreign military studies, and logistics. The NDU also provides information and advice on military modernization and broad strategic issues to national-level organizations; it also performs research on various strategic and operational military issues. The second tier in the PLA's officer education system consists of military colleges and academies which prepare field grade officers for regimental-level command and address the fundamentals of joint and combined arms operations. The curriculum concentrates on company, battalion, and regimental tactics.

In addition, the schools teach basic joint operations. A small number of schools also trains students in specialty staff duties, such as engineering and communications. The lowest tier of officer education is provided by military colleges and academies for junior officers and mid-rank officers; they provide multiple avenues for undergraduate and general military education. The curriculum consists of three and four year undergraduate programs and a two year vocational program. The majority of the cadets are upper middle school graduates.

The PLA's NCO Corps is in its infancy, having been established only in the late 1980s. Chinese NCOs – former conscripts who are allowed to remain on active duty following their initial enlistment – are classified as either 'master sergeants' or 'technical sergeants.' Newly selected NCOs attend a six month training program at the MR academies. Training is limited to tactics for the master sergeants and technical subjects for the technical sergeants. Beijing has not yet established formal education programs for NCOs beyond their initial training.

Joint/Integrated Operations
The PLA conducts interservice exercises at the tactical level, but the services are not fully integrated into a cohesive combat force. Disparate elements train simultaneously and in proximity, but do not appear to be controlled at the operational level by a joint commander and staff. Ground and air components exercise together with regularity and are improving their interoperability. Integration of ground and naval forces, however, is rarely exercised, particularly at the operational level, where synchronization and command and control are of greatest importance in the conduct of complex operations. The Navy is beginning to conduct more combined operations between ships and naval aircraft. The PLA also is looking into the possibility of instituting a 'joint command' structure at the operational or theater level, similar to that of the US military. Accordingly, a commander would exercise operational control over all military forces assigned to and deployed in a particular area. These 'joint commands' likely would be given specifically assigned missions in response to particular threats or security requirements.

Morale
Morale within the PLA, particularly among enlisted personnel, is assessed as generally low. Problems of desertion, declining relations between officers and troops, reluctance to train with obsolete equipment, high consumption spending by officers, anti-corruption audits which restrict outside earnings, and food shortages have been reported in the Chinese press. Low pay in comparison to other segments of Chinese society is a key factor. The PLA's involvement in business – at least until just recently when it was directed to divest itself of its commercial interests – also

distracted many of its more competent officers from their military duties. Some Chinese military leaders believe that many of the morale problems can be solved by increased pay and allowances, further professionalization of the force, and improved quality of life.

Logistics and Sustainability

The PLA's logistics structure and doctrine still reflect, for the most part, the decades-long focus on fighting a large-scale ground conflict, wherein a MR commander would conduct autonomous combat operations over an extended period. The logistics infrastructure developed to support such regional operations is highly decentralized, based on interior lines of communication, and optimized to depend on local depots and stock-piles for resupply. MR commanders apparently were given broad leeway to develop region-specific logistics management procedures. These practices have inhibited the implementation of PLA-wide standards, since the separate management systems made interregional operations virtually impossible. In recent years, the PLA has devoted attention to improving its logistics support to military operations in a Taiwan scenario – operations which would include a higher tempo of operations and use of high technology weapons and equipment. It reportedly has automated many inventory control processes, streamlined procurement, and improved mechanisms for getting supplies to deployed troops. While these developments appear to offer a modest capability to support some types of military operations in the region, the PLA has made only incremental improvements in its ability to support a large-scale, long-term, high optempo engagement.

Taiwan – Other Factors

Military Leadership

Overall, Taiwan's military leadership is competent and capable. Taiwan officers of all services and ranks exhibit a relatively high degree of professionalism. They generally are well educated, operationally profi-cient, and technically sophisticated – especially when contrasted with their PLA counterparts – and pro-US in their outlook. Balanced against these attributes, the officer corps functions within a culture that values caution over innovation and initiative. Junior officers are familiar with technological improvements but recent modernization efforts will challenge their management skills and may require adjustments to unit training and operational tempos. The Taiwan military will face an ongoing challenge in retaining qualified junior officers as employment oppor-tunities in the civilian sector remain enticing. The increased importance of technology in modern warfare has led to an increased emphasis in Taiwan on modernizing the technology-intensive services, namely the Air

Force and Navy. While Army officers continue to dominate the senior leadership positions within the defense hierarchy – the Army comprises more than 50 percent of the armed forces – the emphasis on the Air Force and Navy may lead to a corresponding rise in the influence of air and naval officers over matters such as defense procurement priorities and employment doctrine. Taiwan President Lee Teng-hui strongly supports the promotion of native Taiwanese officers to senior military positions. Currently, the Chief of General Staff and commanders of the air force and marines are ethnic Taiwanese. This trend will continue and probably will have a positive effect on the morale and cohesion of the lower ranks of the armed forces, who themselves are overwhelmingly native Taiwanese.

Training
Taiwan's large-scale training normally takes place quarterly with the major training centers hosting limited maneuver and live-fire exercises. *HAN KUANG 14*, conducted in mid-May 1998, was one of Taipei's more typical joint exercises to date. Primarily a C4I exercise, the training was of very short duration and the scenario allowed for only limited exercise play. Taipei scheduled another 'joint exercise' on 12 October 1998, but then canceled it as a 'goodwill gesture' toward Beijing in the run-up to the resumption of high level cross-Strait talks on 14 October. A dress rehearsal on 7 October also was canceled, although a 'preliminary dress rehearsal' was held on 2 October. It consisted of a series of live-fire demonstrations showcasing some of Taiwan's most modern military equipment.

Professional Military Education
Professional military education of Taiwan's officer corps is conducted along two developmental lines: the *universal* track for regular career officers and the *professional* track for officers in specialized fields like political affairs, medicine, and engineering. The *universal* track is the general military education for officers provided at the three service academies. Graduates receive a bachelor's degree after completing 130 university-level credit hours. The Naval Academy concentrates on science and engineering, while the Air Force Academy curriculum focuses on aerospace-related courses and includes supervised flight training beginning in the second year. Newly commissioned Army officers go on to branch schools, i.e., infantry, army, and artillery. Education in the *professional* track is conducted at such specialized schools like the Fu Hsing Kang College, the Defense Medical College, the Defense Management College, and the Chung Cheng Institute of Technology. Mid-career and senior career professional military education is conducted at the Armed Forces University (AFU). Tracing its roots back to 1906, AFU is the highest level institution in the Taiwan military education system. It is

responsible for training strategic-level command and staff officers, as well as specialists in defense administration and military intelligence. It also conducts research into the development of war strategies and political warfare. AFU includes four colleges: the War College for senior field grade and general officers, and the Command and Staff Colleges of the Army, Navy, and Air Force for junior field grade officers.

Morale
Morale, especially among the enlisted ranks, is generally assessed as poor, amidst efforts to retain competent, educated service members in the face of stiff private sector competition. The military competes poorly with the civilian economy in attracting Taiwan's youth, especially those who are technically-oriented. Continued personnel shortages stemming from low retention rates – especially among NCOs – will remain a serious problem affecting morale. The military also is hampered by systemic problems of poor, antiquated management and a traditional military culture with very rigid command structures which discourages lower-level risk-taking, decisionmaking, and innovation. The Taiwan Army especially is facing morale problems stemming from the ongoing restructuring and down-sizing. While the operational outlook and overall morale of TAF pilots is significantly better than that of PLAAF pilots – largely due to better training opportunities and exposure to and hands on experience with more modern Western equipment – there exists a disparity between the military and civil aviators in pay and benefits, which inevitably affects morale.

Logistics and Sustainability
Taiwan's logistics capability will support some defensive operations on Taiwan, but its probability of success is highly dependent on the tempo of operations. The military reportedly is trying to make the logistics system more efficient to better support combined or joint force oper-ations. In the interim, logistics support will remain cumbersome – but effective – for localized engagements. Taiwan's defenses rely heavily on air and naval forces, both requiring an extensive maintenance and repair infrastructure to support weapons systems and equipment. The critical requirements are major equipment end items like engines and trans-missions, ammunition, fuel and especially obsolete spare parts which no longer are being manufactured.

IV. The Dynamic Balance

Currently, China's more than 2.5-million-man PLA dwarfs Taiwan's defense force of about 400,000. In most cases, equipment totals also are lopsided. Only a portion of this overall strength, however, could be brought to bear against Taiwan at one time. China has nearly 4,500 combat aircraft, as compared with some 400 on Taiwan. The Chinese Navy has about 65 attack submarines – five of which are nuclear powered – as compared with four diesel attack submarines for Taiwan. China has over 60 major surface combatants while Taiwan has no more than 40. China has nuclear weapons and a ballistic missile force that can deliver nuclear or conventionally-armed warheads against Taiwan. In terms of the quality of their military equipment, however, Taipei possesses an edge over Beijing, as new weapons systems – particularly fighter aircraft and naval frigates – are entering the inventory.

Should China decide to use military force against Taiwan, there are several options or courses of action available to Beijing, including – but not limited to – an interdiction of Taiwan's SLOCs and a blockade of Taiwan's ports, a large-scale missile attack, and an all-out invasion.

Blockade

The primary intent behind a blockade of the island would be to cripple Taiwan economically and isolate it internationally. China's leaders apparently believe that this option would be less likely to provoke outside intervention than others. Beijing probably would choose successively more stringent quarantine-blockade actions, beginning with declaring maritime exercise closure areas and stopping Taiwan-flagged merchant vessels operating in the Taiwan Strait. Operations likely would include mine laying and deploying submarines and surface ships to enforce the blockade. Barring third party intervention, the PLAN's quantitative advantage over Taiwan's Navy in surface and sub-surface assets would probably prove overwhelming over time. Taiwan's military forces probably would not be able keep the island's key ports and SLOCs open in the face of concerted Chinese military action. Taiwan's small surface fleet and four submarines are numerically insufficient to counter China's major surface combatant force and its ASW assets likely would have difficulty defeating a blockade supported by China's large submarine force. The PLANAF's B-6D bombers armed with C-601 ASCMs would place Taipei's merchant ships and combatants at serious risk.

Missile Strikes

Within the next several years, the size of China's SRBM force is expected to grow substantially. An expanded arsenal of conventional SRBMs and LACMs targeted against critical facilities, such as key airfields and C4I nodes, will complicate Taiwan's ability to conduct military operations. By 2005, China will have deployed both the CSS-6 and CSS-7 SRBM. In addition, the PLA could have a first generation, air-launched LACM in its inventory. Should Beijing choose escalation, a rapid transition from relatively low-intensity blockade operations to massive missile strikes would be a likely step, particularly as a pretext to an invasion. These missile attacks most likely would be high-volume, precision strikes against priority military and political targets, including air defense facilities, airfields, Taiwan's C2 infrastructure, and naval facilities. China, however, could encounter problems coordinating missile firings with other concurrent military operations, such as air and maritime engagements. Exclusive Taiwan reliance on active missile defenses and associated BM/C3I, however, will not sufficiently offset the overwhelming advantage in offensive missiles which Beijing is projected to possess in 2005.

Air Superiority

Maintaining air superiority over the Taiwan Strait would be an essential part of any Chinese effort to mount a military operation against Taiwan. China currently has an overwhelming quantitative advantage over Taiwan in military aircraft and will retain that advantage beyond 2005. On the other hand, Taiwan's more modern aircraft will provide it with a qualitative advantage that should be retained at least through that period. PLA electronic warfare operations against air defense radars, disruption of command and control networks, and/or large scale conventional SRBM and LACM strikes against airfields and SAM sites would reduce the effectiveness of Taiwan's air defenses.

The future effectiveness of the TAF will depend on the implementation of sound pilot training, sufficient logistic and maintenance support, and the ability of the TAF to integrate satisfactorily several disparate airframes into a cohesive, operational fighting force.

For its part, Beijing is faced with similar training, maintenance, and logistics challenges, complicated further by a still questionable capability on the part of its aerospace industry to keep pace with rapidly evolving technologies. Nevertheless, while the majority of the mainland's air fleet will still be composed of second and third generation aircraft, the sheer numerical advantage of older platforms augmented by some fourth generation aircraft could attrit Taiwan's air defenses sufficiently over time to achieve air superiority.

Amphibious Invasion

An amphibious invasion of Taiwan by China would be a highly risky and most unlikely option for the PLA, chosen only as a last resort to force the total surrender of the island. It most likely would be preceded by a variety of preparatory operations to include a blockade, conventional missile strikes, and special operations on Taiwan. These operations would play a critical role in determining how China would pursue the *coup de grâce*, with an amphibious assault only one facet of a multi-pronged invasion plan. Beijing's amphibious lift capability is extremely limited at present and there are no indications that China is devoting resources to improve significantly its amphibious assault capability. As a result, success only would be achieved with a massive commitment of military and civilian assets over a long period of time and without third party intervention; furthermore, an invasion would bring almost certain damage to China's economy and its diplomatic interests, especially in the Asia–Pacific region.

The first move in an invasion plan likely would be a SLOC/blockade interdiction operation. The PLAAF and PLANAF would try to establish an air defense umbrella over the Taiwan Strait in preparation for local air superiority operations. Ground-based air defense assets would deploy forward and be integrated into the umbrella. Naval surface actions groups would begin operations near Taiwan's major ports. Announced missile closure areas and port mining by submarines would be designed to canalize traffic and force Taiwan naval vessels into engagement areas. Ground force mobilization likely would begin and PLA combat air patrols over the Taiwan Strait would intensify. Invasion operations would follow sufficiently close on the heels of conventional missile attacks to prevent Taipei from repairing and reconstituting damaged facilities. As the PLA's amphibious lift capacity in 2005 would still be limited, an amphibious over-the-beach assault would be extremely problematic. Rather, airborne, airmobile, and special operations forces likely would conduct simultaneous attacks to the rear of Taiwan's coastal defenses to seize a port, preferably in close proximity to an airfield. Seizing a beach-head likely would constitute a supporting attack. An airborne envelopment would facilitate amphibious operations by cutting off Taiwan's coastal defenders from supply lines and forcing them to fight in two directions.

Beijing's suppression of Taiwan's air defenses would be followed rapidly by a 'second-wave' air attack which would attempt to establish air superiority over an invasion corridor in the Taiwan Strait. Priority for air defense protection and fighter escort operations would shift from bombers carrying ASCMs to fixed- and rotary-wing transports ferrying additional airborne and airmobile assault forces. Both China's amphibious fleet and a large portion of its huge merchant fleet would complete rapid reaction unit upload operations and depart from ports along the central coast. China also likely would saturate the Taiwan Strait with a huge number of noncombatant merchant and fishing vessels, with the aim of confusing and overwhelming Taipei's surveillance and target acquisition systems. The PLA's success in establishing and maintaining a foothold on the island would rest on a variety of intangibles to include personnel and equipment attrition rates on both sides of the Strait; the interoperability of PLA forces; and the ability of China's logistic system to support adequately optempo operations.

In order for an invasion to succeed, in other words, Beijing would have to possess the capability to conduct a multi-faceted campaign, involving air assault, airborne insertion, special operations raids, amphibious landings, maritime area denial operations, air superiority operations and conventional missile strikes. The PLA likely would encounter great difficulty conducting such a sophisticated campaign by 2005. Nevertheless, the campaign likely would succeed – barring third party intervention – if Beijing were willing to accept the almost certain political, economic, diplomatic, and military costs that such a course of action would produce.

Information Dominance

The Chinese currently are focusing on eliminating specific deficiencies they have in both areas of IO/IW technology and training. The PLA is engaged in efforts to improve the staff planning process by applying joint forces concepts learned from studying foreign IO/IW doctrine. Recent IO/IW military exercises claim to have included computer network attack and defend exercises. Public disclosure of these IO/IW exercises serves as an informational tool for the PLA to the future importance of IO/IW in Chinese military doctrine and reaffirms China's intent to continue developing and improving its IO/IW capability. In spite of these activities, the Chinese have many challenges to overcome and Beijing's ability to paralyze Taiwan's command and control appears limited at best.

On the other side of Taiwan Strait, IO may be an attractive – but untested tool – in multiplying the effectiveness of Taiwan's military forces. As one of the world's largest producers of computer components, Taiwan has all of the basic capabilities needed to carry out offensive IO-related activities, particularly computer network attacks and the introduction of malicious code. Formal doctrine development to guide future employment of these capabilities already may be in progress. As Taiwan increases its role in the manufacture of new computer warfighting systems, Taipei's capability to exploit its position for IO activities can be expected to increase substantially.

V. Conclusions

During the twenty-year period from 1979 to 1999, the security situation in the Taiwan Strait has exhibited simultaneously both significant change in some respects and remarkable constancy in others. The greatest change has occurred in the political and diplomatic arenas, a reflection of the political changes which have taken place in both Beijing and Taipei, and between Beijing and Taipei. On the other hand, despite the modest qualitative improvement in the military forces of both China and Taiwan, the dynamic equilibrium of those forces in the Taiwan Strait has not changed dramatically over the last two decades, except in a few niche areas like China's deployment of SRBMs.

Despite anticipated improvements to Taiwan's missile and air defense systems, by 2005, the PLA will possess the capability to attack Taiwan with air and missile strikes which would degrade key military facilities and damage the island's economic infrastructure. China will continue to give priority to long-range precision-strike programs. Similarly, despite improvements in Taiwan's ability to conduct ASW operations, China will retain the capability to interdict Taiwan's SLOCs and blockade the island's principal maritime ports. Should China invade Taiwan, such an operation would require a major commitment of civilian air and maritime transport assets, would be prolonged in duration, and would not be automatically guaranteed to succeed. In the end, any of these options would prove to be costly to Beijing – politically, economically, diplomatically, and militarily.

Beyond 2005, development of a modern military force capable of exerting military influence within the region, achieving deterrence against potential enemies, preserving independence of action in domestic and foreign affairs, protecting the nation's economic resources and maritime areas, and defending the sovereignty of the nation's territory will remain one of China's national priorities. Beijing will strive to create a smaller, more modern, better trained, more professional, and better logistically supported force, with an emphasis on air, naval and missile forces. China will continue to improve its regional force projection capabilities, but will not possess the conventional military capabilities to exert global influence.

The PLA will field large numbers of increasingly accurate SRBMs and introduce LACMs into its inventory. China's naval forces will continue their transition from a large coastal defense force to a smaller, more modern force able to conduct limited sea control operations against regional opponents in the East and South China Seas. China's air force will continue to assimilate greater numbers of fourth generation aircraft into its inventory, upgrade its regional IADS, and expand its airborne refueling and AEW capabilities. China will retain a numerical advantage over Taiwan in terms of both personnel and weapons.

On the other side of the Taiwan Strait, by 2005, Taipei will possess a qualitative edge over Beijing in terms of significant weapons and equipment. The TAF will have over 300 fourth generation fighters. Six French-built Lafayette-class frigates, eight US Knox-class frigates, and eight Perry-class frigates will form the nucleus of Taiwan's naval force. Taiwan will possess an advanced air defense network, comprising an AEW capability, an automated C2 system, and several modern SAM systems, which will provide Taiwan with an enhanced defensive capability against both aircraft and missiles. The mobility and firepower of Taiwan's ground forces will have been improved with the acquisition of additional tanks, armored personnel carriers, self-propelled artillery and attack helicopters.

Taiwan's primary security goal beyond 2005 will be to maintain the status quo, while retaining its long-term objective of eventual peaceful reunification with China on terms favorable to Taipei. Taiwan will seek to advance its international status, maintain a strong economy, modernize its military forces, and further democratize the island's political system. At the same time, Taipei will endeavor to expand political, cultural, and economic ties with Beijing, thereby reducing tensions with China and lessening the prospects of military conflict in the Taiwan Strait. Taiwan's military strategy will remain defensive. Its success in deterring potential Chinese aggression will be dependent on its continued acquisition of modern arms, technology and equipment and its ability to deal with a number of systemic problems – primarily the recruitment and retention of technically-qualified personnel and the maintenance of an effective logistics system – lest Taipei once again risks losing its qualitative edge.

NOTE

1. Source: Defense Link, US Department of Defense website.

Bibliography [1]

Accinelli, Robert. *Crisis and Commitment: United States Policy toward Taiwan, 1950–1955* (Chapel Hill: University of North Carolina Press, 1996).

Aspin, Les. *Report on the Bottom-Up Review* (Washington DC: Department of Defense, October 1993).

Austin, Greg, ed. *Missile Diplomacy and Taiwan's Future: Innovations in Politics and Military Power* (Canberra: Australian National University Press, 1998).

Bader, William B. and Jeffrey T. Bergner, eds. *The Taiwan Relations Act: A Decade of Implementation* (Indianapolis IN: Hudson Institute, 1989).

Baldwin, Robert E. *Political Economy of U.S.–Taiwan Trade* (Ann Arbor: University of Michigan Press, 1995).

Bernstein, Richard and Ross H. Munro. *The Coming Conflict with China* (New York: Knopf, 1997).

Bitzinger, Richard A. and Bates Gill. *Gearing Up for High-Tech Warfare?* (Washington DC: Center for Strategic and Budgetary Assessments, 1996).

Borthwick, Mark. *Pacific Century: The Emergence of Modern Pacific Asia* (Boulder CO: Westview, 1992).

Bullock, Mary Brown and Robert S. Litwak, eds. *The United States and the Pacific Basin: Changing Economic and Security Relationships* (Washington DC: Woodrow Wilson Center, 1991).

Caldwell, John. *China's Conventional Military Capabilities: 1994–2004: An Assessment* (Washington DC: Center for Strategic and International Studies, 1994).

Carter, Ashton B. and William J. Perry. *Preventive Defense: A New Security Strategy for America* (Washington DC: Brookings Institution, 1999).

Carter, Jimmy. *Keeping Faith: Memoirs of a President* (New York: Bantam Books, 1982).

Cha, Victor. *Alignment Despite Antagonism: The United States–Korea–Japan Security Triangle* (Stanford CA: Stanford University Press, 1999).

340

Chang Jaw-Ling, Joanne, ed. *ROC-US Relations, 1979–1989* (Taipei: Academia Sinica, 1991).

Chang, Parris H. and Martin L. Lasater, eds. *If China Crosses the Taiwan Strait: The International Response* (Lanham MD: University Press of America, 1993).

China: U.S. Policy Since 1945 (Washington DC: Congressional Quarterly, 1980).

Chiu, Hungdah. *Koo-Wang Talks and the Prospect of Building Constructive and Stable Relations Across the Taiwan Straits* (Baltimore: University of Maryland School of Law, 1993).

Clough, Ralph N. *Island China* (Cambridge MA: Harvard University Press, 1978).

Clough, Ralph N. *Reaching Across the Taiwan Strait: People-to-People Diplomacy* (Boulder CO: Westview, 1993).

Clough, Ralph N. *Cooperation or Conflict in the Taiwan Strait?* (New York: Rowman & Littlefield, 1999).

Cohen, William S. *Report of the Quadrennial Defense Review* (Washington DC: Department of Defense, May 1997).

Cohen, William S. *1998 Secretary of Defense Annual Report to the President and the Congress* (Washington DC: Office of the Secretary of Defense, 1998).

Copper, John F. *Taiwan: Nation-State or Province?* (Boulder CO: Westview, 1990).

Directory of People's Republic of China Military Personalities (Hong Kong: Defense Liaison Office, US Consulate General, annual).

Downen, Robert L. *The Taiwan Pawn in the China Game: Congress to the Rescue* (Washington DC: Georgetown University Press, 1979).

A Draft Agreement between the Government of the United Kingdom of Great Britain and Northern Ireland and the Government of the People's Republic of China on the Future of Hong Kong (London: HMSO, September 26, 1984).

Garver, John W. *Face off: China, the United States, and Taiwan's Democratization* (Seattle: University of Washington Press, 1997).

Gertz, Bill. *Betrayal: How the Clinton Administration Undermined American Security* (Washington DC: Regnery, 1999).

Gibert, Stephen P. and William M. Carpenter, eds. *America and Island China: A Documentary History* (Lanham MD: University Press of America, 1989).

Glynn, Patrick. *Closing Pandora's Box: Arms Races, Arms Control, and the History of the Cold War* (New York: Basic Books, 1992).

Goncharov, Sergei N., John W. Lewis and Xue Litai. *Uncertain Partners: Stalin, Mao and the Korean War* (Stanford CA: Stanford University Press, 1993).

Green, Marshall, John H. Holdridge and William N. Stokes. *War and*

Peace with China: First-hand Experiences in the Foreign Service of the United States (Bethesda MD: Dacor, 1994).

'Guidelines for National Unification' (Taipei: National Unification Council, 1991).

Harding, Harry. *A Fragile Relationship: The United States and China Since 1972* (Washington DC: Brookings Institution, 1992).

Harding, Harry and Yuan Ming, eds. *Sino-American Relations, 1945–1955: A Joint Reassessment of a Critical Decade* (Wilmington DE: Scholarly Resources, 1989).

Heinrichs, Waldo. *Threshold of War: Franklin D. Roosevelt and American Entry into World War II* (London: Oxford University Press, 1988).

Hickey, Dennis Van Vranken. *United States–Taiwan Security Ties: From Cold War to Beyond Containment* (Westport CT: Praeger, 1994).

Hood, Steven J. *The KMT and the Democratization of Taiwan* (Boulder CO: Westview, 1997).

Institute for National Strategic Studies. *Strategic Assessments 1997: Flashpoints and Force Structure* (Washington DC: National Defense University Press, 1997).

Institute for National Strategic Studies. *1998 Strategic Assessment: Engaging Power for Peace* (Washington DC: National Defense University Press, 1998).

International Institute for Strategic Studies. *The Military Balance* (London: Oxford University Press, annual).

Jackson, Karl D., ed. *Asian Contagion: The Causes and Consequences of a Financial Crisis* (Boulder CO: Westview, 1999).

Kissinger, Henry A. *White House Years* (Boston: Little, Brown, 1979).

Klintworth, Gary, ed. *Taiwan in the Asia–Pacific in the 1990s* (Canberra, Australia: Allen & Unwin, 1994).

Klintworth, Gary. *Asia–Pacific Security: Less Uncertainty, New Opportunities* (New York: St. Martin's, 1996).

Koenig, Louis W., ed. *Congress, the Presidency, and the Taiwan Relations Act* (New York: Praeger, 1985).

Lasater, Martin L. *The Security of Taiwan: Unraveling the Dilemma* (Washington DC: Georgetown University Press, 1982).

Lasater, Martin L. *The Taiwan Issue in Sino-American Strategic Relations* (Boulder CO: Westview, 1984).

Lasater, Martin L. *Taiwan: Facing Mounting Threats* (Washington DC: Heritage Foundation, 1987).

Lasater, Martin L. *Policy in Evolution: The U.S. Role in China's Reunification* (Boulder CO: Westview, 1989).

Lasater, Martin L. *U.S. Interests in the New Taiwan* (Boulder CO: Westview, 1993).

Lasater, Martin L. *The Changing of the Guard: President Clinton and the Security of Taiwan* (Boulder CO: Westview, 1995).

Lasater, Martin L. *The New Pacific Community: U.S. Strategic Options in Asia* (Boulder CO: Westview, 1996).

Lasater, Martin L. *The Taiwan Conundrum in U.S. China Policy* (Boulder CO: Westview, 1999).

Lasater, Martin L., ed. *Beijing's Blockade Threat to Taiwan* (Washington DC: Heritage Foundation, 1985).

Lee Teng-hui. *Taiwan's Viewpoint* (Taipei: Liou Publishing Company, 1999).

Lilley, James R. and Chuck Downs, eds. *Crisis in the Taiwan Strait* (Washington DC: American Enterprise Institute and National Defense University Press, 1997).

Mandelbaum, Michael, ed. *The Strategic Quadrangle: Russia, China, Japan, and the United States in East Asia* (New York: Council on Foreign Relations, 1994).

Mann, James. *About Face: A History of America's Curious Relationship with China, from Nixon to Clinton* (New York: Knopf, 1999).

Metzger, Thomas A. and Ramon H. Myers, eds. *Greater China and U.S. Foreign Policy: The Choice between Confrontation and Mutual Respect* (Stanford: Hoover Institution, 1996).

Mosher, Steven W. *China Misperceived: American Illusions and Chinese Reality* (New York: Basic Books, 1990).

Myers, Ramon H., ed. *A Unique Relationship: The United States and the Republic of China under the Taiwan Relations Act* (Stanford CA: Hoover Institution, 1989).

Nathan, Andrew J. and Robert Ross. *The Great Wall and the Empty Fortress: China's Search for Security* (New York: Norton, 1997).

A National Security Strategy of Engagement and Enlargement (Washington DC: The White House, July 1994).

A National Security Strategy for a New Century (Washington DC: The White House, May 1997).

Nixon, Richard M. *RN: The Memoirs of Richard Nixon* (New York: Grosset & Dunlap, 1978).

Pillsbury, Michael, ed. *Chinese Views of Future Warfare* (Washington DC: National Defense University Press, 1997).

Ross, Robert S., ed. *After the Cold War: Domestic Factors and U.S.–China Relations* (Armonk NY: M. E. Sharpe, 1998).

Shambaugh, David. *Beautiful Imperialist: China Perceives America, 1972–1990* (Princeton: Princeton University Press, 1992).

Snow, Edgar. *Red Star Over China* (New York: Modern Library, 1944).

Solomon, Richard H. *Chinese Political Negotiating Behavior, 1967–1984* (Santa Monica CA: RAND, 1985).

Spence, Jonathan. *To Change China: Western Advisers in China, 1620–1960* (New York: Penguin Books, 1980).

Sutter, Robert G. *Shaping China's Future in World Affairs: The Role of the United States* (Boulder CO: Westview, 1998).

Sutter, Robert G. *U.S. Policy toward China: An Introduction to the Role of Interest Groups* (Lanham MD: Rowman & Littlefield, 1998).

Swaine, Michael D. *The Military and Political Succession in China* (Santa Monica CA: Rand, 1992).

'The Taiwan Question and the Reunification of China' (Beijing: Taiwan Affairs Office and Information Office, State Council, August 1993).

Takayuki, Munakata. *The True Nature and Solution of the Taiwan Problem* (Taipei: Taiwan International Interchange Foundation, 1999).

Tow, William T. *Encountering the Dominant Player: U.S. Extended Deterrence Strategy in the Asia–Pacific* (New York: Columbia University Press, 1991).

Tucker, Nancy Bernkopf. *Taiwan, Hong Kong, and the United States* (New York: Maxwell Macmillan International, 1994).

The Twelfth National Congress of the CPC (Beijing: Foreign Languages Press, 1982).

US Congress, House of Representatives. *House Report 105-851: Report of the Select Committee on U.S. National Security and Military/ Commercial Concerns with the People's Republic of China* (Washington DC: GPO, 1999).

US Congress, House of Representatives, Committee on Foreign Affairs. *China–Taiwan: United States Policy* (Washington DC: GPO, 1982).

US Congress, Senate, Committee on Foreign Relations. *Taiwan: Hearings on S. 245* (Washington DC: GPO, 1979).

US Department of Defense. *A Strategic Framework for the Asian Pacific Rim: Looking Toward the 21st Century* (Washington DC: Department of Defense, April 1990).

US Department of Defense. *A Strategic Framework for the Asian Pacific Rim: Looking Toward the 21st Century: A Report to Congress* (Washington DC: Department of Defense, February 28, 1991).

US Department of Defense. *A Strategic Framework for the Asian Pacific Rim: Report to Congress 1992* (Washington DC: Department of Defense, 1992).

US Department of Defense. *1992 Joint Military Net Assessment* (Washington DC: Joint Chiefs of Staff, August 1992).

US Department of Defense. *Worldwide Threat to U.S. Navy and Marines Forces: China* (Washington DC: Office of Naval Intelligence, 1993).

US Department of Defense. *United States Security Strategy for the East Asia–Pacific Region* (Washington DC: Department of Defense, February 1995).

US Department of Defense. *Proliferation: Threat and Response* (Washington DC: Office of the Secretary of Defense, November 1997).

US Department of Defense. *United States Security Strategy for the East Asia–Pacific Region* (Washington DC: Department of Defense, November 1998).

US Department of Defense. 'The Security Situation in the Taiwan Strait: Report to Congress Pursuant to the FY99 Appropriations Bill' (Washington DC: Department of Defense, March 1999).

US Department of Defense. 'Report to Congress on Theater Missile Defense Architecture Options for the Asia–Pacific Region' (Washington DC: Department of Defense, 1999).

Welfield, John. *An Empire in Eclipse: Japan in the Postwar American Alliance System* (London: Athlone Press, 1988).

White, Lynn T. 'Taiwan's China Problem: After a Decade or Two, Can There Be a Solution?' (Washington DC: SAIS Policy Forum Series, December 1998).

Wilhelm, Alfred D., Jr. *The Chinese at the Negotiating Table* (Washington DC: National Defense University Press, 1994).

Wolff, Lester L. and David L. Simon. *Legislative History of the Taiwan Relations Act: An Analytic Compilation with Documents on Subsequent Developments* (Jamaica NY: American Association for Chinese Studies, 1982).

Yang, Maysing H., ed. *Taiwan's Expanding Role in the International Arena* (Armonk NY: M. E. Sharpe, 1997).

Yang, Richard, ed. *China's Military: The CPLA in 1992/1993* (Taipei: Chinese Council of Advanced Policy Studies, 1993).

Yu, Peter Kien-hong. '"Taiwanization" Programme in the ROC's Forces.' *Jane's Defence Weekly*, December 9, 1989, pp. 1288–9.

Yu, Peter Kien-hong, ed. *The Chinese PLA's Perception of an Invasion of Taiwan* (New York: Contemporary U.S.–Asia Research Institute, 1996).

Yu, Peter Kien-hong. *Bicoastal China: A Dialectical, Paradigmatic Analysis* (New York: Nova Science Publishers, 1999).

Yu, Peter Kien-hong. 'The Choppy Taiwan Strait.' *Korean Journal of Defense Analysis*, XI, 1 (Summer 1999): 39–66.

NOTE

1. For sources in Chinese, please refer to the endnotes in Chapters 4–6.

Index

348